A HUNGER FOR HOME

Frontispiece. Louisa May Alcott, formal portrait photograph. Courtesy of the Concord Free Public Library.

Sarah Elbert

A HUNGER FOR HOME

Louisa May Alcott's Place in American Culture

RUTGERS UNIVERSITY PRESS
New Brunswick and London

Elbert, Sarah.
A hunger for home.

Includes index.
1. Alcott, Louisa May, 1832–1888. 2. Domestic
fiction, American—History and criticism.
3. Women in literature. 4. Sex role in literature.
5. Home in literature. 6. Feminism and literature—
United States. 7. Novelists, American—19th
century—Biography. I. Title.
PS1018.E4 1987 813'.4 [B] 86-31313
ISBN 0-8135-1199-2

British Cataloguing-in-Publication information available

It is not always want, insanity, or sin that drives women to desperate deaths; often it is a dreadful loneliness of heart, a hunger for home and friends, worse than starvation, a bitter sense of wrong in being denied the tender ties, the pleasant duties, the sweet rewards that can make the humblest life happy; a rebellious protest against God, who, when they cry for bread, seems to offer them a stone . . .

Louisa May Alcott, *Work*

Contents

List of Illustrations

Frontispiece. Louisa May Alcott, formal portrait photograph. Courtesy of the Concord Free Public Library.

(following p. 142)

1. Union Hotel Hospital, Georgetown, Washington, D.C., scene of Louisa May Alcott's service as a Civil War nurse. Courtesy of Brown Brothers Photo Service.

2. Nurse Periwinkle and baby Africa from Alcott's autobiographical *Hospital Sketches*. Courtesy of the Concord Free Public Library.

3 and 4. Two illustrations from the 1880 edition of *Little Women*—done by Frank T. Merrill, a young Concord artist—show Beth mourning her dead canary after the sisters' holiday from housekeeping and Jo sacrificing her "one beauty," her mane of chestnut hair. Courtesy of the Concord Free Public Library.

5. Louisa May Alcott created popular juveniles and earned five hundred dollars a year as editor of *Merry's Museum*. This issue dates from 1869, the year after she wrote *Little Women*. Courtesy of the Concord Free Public Library.

6. Bronson Alcott, an impoverished eccentric during Louisa Alcott's younger days, eventually enjoyed respectable status as resident muse of the Concord School of Philosophy. Lectures by William Torrey Harris and Julia Ward Howe drew adult students to this refurbished barn of Orchard House in the 1880s. Courtesy of the Concord Free Public Library.

7. Abba May Alcott, in her last years, seated in the parlor of Orchard House. Courtesy of the Concord Free Public Library.

8 and 9. May Alcott Nieriker's sketch of Thoreau's hut on Walden Pond and her detail of a staircase in Emerson's summerhouse, which was designed and built by Bronson Alcott with the help of Thoreau. Courtesy of the Concord Free Public Library.

10. Louisa May Alcott is shown here at her cottage by the sea with her niece and namesake, Louisa May Nieriker. Courtesy of the Concord Free Public Library.

ix

Acknowledgments

History, Jacob Burckhardt sensibly remarked, is the only field of study in which one cannot begin at the beginning. David Brion Davis initially encouraged me in the study of intellectual and cultural history. In Cornell seminars Michael Colacurcio, Cushing Strout, and Jonathan Bishop communicated their sensitivities to American literature and culture. Mary Beth Norton directed my dissertation, "Louisa May Alcott and the Woman Problem," giving generously of her time and wisdom.

So many friends shared skills and knowledge in ways that became invaluable that I can only appreciate rather than enumerate them all. A few people must be thanked for special gifts, however. William Riley Leach stimulated my research and generously edited early drafts. Other scholars helped me to trace Alcott's concerns as central themes in women's history. I am grateful to Alice Kessler Harris, Heidi Hartmann, Linda Gordon, Ellen DuBois, Kitty Sklar, Mary Ryan, Laurie Nisonoff, Sue Armitage, Corky Bush, Joan Jensen, Ann Douglas, Joan Smith, Gerda Lerner, Jean Fagan Yellin, Allison Lurie, and, Bonnie Smith.

Anna Davin, Sally Alexander, Lee Davidoff, and Barbara Taylor in England, and Kirsten Mellor, Kirsten Drotner, and Hanne Grodahl in Aarhus, Denmark, shared international perspectives on women's history and literature. Students at SUNY Binghamton, Cornell University, and Cal Poly challenged my theories and shared their appreciation of Alcott's life and works.

The Alcott scholars' circle is graced by Madeleine B. Stern and Leona Rostenberg. Their work has made the current "new wave" of scholarship and appreciation of Louisa May Alcott possible. Charles Strickland shared his work with me at an early stage of my research.

xi

ACKNOWLEDGMENTS

Madelon Bedell's wisdom and generosity are greatly missed from the circle; her work remains to inspire readers and reformers.

This edition of *A Hunger for Home* is enriched by lively exchanges with a new generation of Alcott scholars: Angela Estes, Peggy Lant, Janice Alberghine, and Elizabeth Keyser.

The late William Bond and Mrs. F. Wolsey Pratt kindly gave me access to Alcott materials and permission to quote from them. Marcia Moss, curator of Concord Free Public Library, has helped in innumerable ways and does Alcott scholars the honor of keeping our studies in the glass bookcase housing Alcott's own volumes.

Ken Arnold, Marilyn Campbell, Christina Blake, and Leslie Mitchner of Rutgers Press shared enthusiasm and determination with me. I am grateful to Jane Dieckmann for peerless editing, sensitivity, and patience through this revised edition.

Without Sander Kelman, and Adam and Carrie Kartman, this work would have been neither necessary nor possible. I look forward to hearing Susan Holman Kartman read *Little Women* to Kate and Martina.

SARAH ELBERT

San Luis Obispo, California
March 1987

Introduction

Louisa May Alcott's lifelong heroine was her father's friend and contemporary, Margaret Fuller. In the early 1840s, like many Romantic reformers of her generation, Fuller celebrated the "tides of life" flowing within herself and every unique individual being. She also rebelled against current social and literary conventions. Her growing pains had a sexually specific ache: nineteenth-century society insisted that "one should be either private or public."[1] Fuller, however, refused to choose between a private life and a career. Using her powerful intellect to carve out a brilliant, public role at the center of the American Renaissance, she also longed for love and ordinary domestic warmth, crying out, "The life, the life! O, my God! shall the life never be sweet?"[2]

Louisa May Alcott, a feminist of the following generation, helped make those two demands inseparable. Women should, she argued, have significant public roles in a democratic society, and they could also share with men or other women in creating warm egalitarian homes. Alcott's great gift lay in reaching ordinary women with the broad-ranging program of nineteenth-century feminists. She wrote out of her own experiences, struggling to make her stories "true;" combining women's fiction and Romantic children's literature, she created a new genre.

Margaret Fuller once called Louisa May Alcott and her sisters "model children," prototypes of a new generation of Americans who might shape a more democratic Eden.[3] Born into New England's reform movement, Louisa May Alcott chose to remain at its center all her life—the famous author of *Little Women* commonly signed her letters "Yours for reform of all kinds, L.M.A."[4] Readers found it natural that Bronson Alcott's daughter should write with exceptional empathy for juvenile audiences. Her father, after all, had canonized childhood in meticulous observations of his daughters' early development.[5] In fact, he and Abigail May Alcott were at the forefront of Romantic efforts to reform family life and thereby transform society at large, and they achieved immortality as the model parents in *Little Women*. Yet Alcott herself understood that universal reform also depended upon changing larger social relationships and institutions. Contemporary reviewers judged her a "benefactor of households" partly because she seemed to "enter into the lives and feelings of children," but also because she made explicit connections among domestic equality, woman's work, and woman's rights.[6] Not only Sarah J. Hale, the influential editor of *Godey's Lady's Book*, but also woman's rights leaders such as Lucy Stone, Susan B. Anthony, and Julia Ward Howe valued Alcott's works.

Between the publication of *Little Women* in 1868 and her death in 1888, through several novels and dozens of short stories, Louisa Alcott chronicled an entire history of nineteenth-century woman's life and work. The March family trilogy of *Little Women*, *Little Men* (1871), and *Jo's Boys* (1886), which has never been out of print, has been translated into twenty-seven languages. In addition, Alcott wrote four popular adult novels—*Moods* (1865, rev. ed. 1882), *Work* (1872), *A Modern Mephistopheles* (1877), and *A Whisper in the Dark* (1888)—and a series of pseudonymous romantic thrillers as well as reviews, poems, and articles for such major periodicals as *Atlantic Monthly*, *Putnam's Magazine*, *Harper's New Monthly*, *Commonwealth*, and *The Independent*.[7]

Alcott's heroic spinsters and her "lurid but true" fallen women belong to the secret garden newly opened by feminist scholars. Jo March, the rebel girl of *Little Women*, must now be understood amid a large sisterhood, one Louisa May Alcott herself claimed in writing both domestic fiction and tales of passionate romance and intrigue. She rattled the bars of woman's gilded cage, inspiring her female readers to claim a freer sexuality, to work and earn the means of independence, and to settle for no less than egalitarian, convivial domestic lives. At the same time, her pseudonymous thrillers in particular presented the dark demonic potential in the caged woman. Hungry, fierce, and vengeful, like Bertha Mason, the imprisoned Creole wife in *Jane Eyre*, Alcott's own Jean Muir, heroine of *Behind a*

xiv

Mask, refuses to remain a fallen woman. An actress and mistress of disguises, she reveals herself finally as both victim and avenger. Muir threatens to bring down an entire genteel household if she is denied access to its domestic warmth and security on her own terms. Those terms include acceptance and understanding of the disguises and confidence games she has played to survive and remain free. Unlike Bertha Mason, Jean Muir, in the end, wins the right to her own individuality and her own home.

As Nina Auerbach argues, about Victorian heroines and their relation to real women, "a cultural myth of a slain and self-restoring heroine merges imperceptibly with the lives of those who believe in it and thereby into the history they make."[8] Alcott's archetypal American Girl is a self-transforming heroine, and in all her guises— confidence woman, rebel slave, and restless tomboy—she has become part of many readers' identities and their shaping of history. Like many other nineteenth-century women, Louisa Alcott regarded sentiment as a powerful impulse toward social change. Sentiment was an acknowledged woman's right. While the modern reader thinks of "women's rights," in nineteenth-century culture the individual woman struggles toward her own transformation by acting upon her deepest feelings and she is then empowered to fight for all humanity. Women's rights emerges from woman's rights.

Louisa May Alcott's name remains a household charm invoked by writers as diverse as Betty Smith (*A Tree Grows in Brooklyn*) and Gertrude Stein (*Everybody's Autobiography*). Within a generation after Alcott's death, however, Ednah Dow Cheney, a family friend and her first biographer, felt it necessary to remind young readers that "Miss Alcott was very much interested in the question of woman's suffrage." Although a shy woman, "Miss Alcott" spoke publicly in behalf of woman's rights when the subject was "very unpopular."[9] The author of *Little Women* even attended an 1875 meeting of the Woman's Congress in Syracuse, New York, proudly counting herself a delegate from Massachusetts.

In 1926 Thomas Beer amused a new generation of twentieth-century readers with the Alcott family's nineteenth-century eccentricities. Although he expressed sympathy for Miss Alcott's hard life as a working woman, he nevertheless denounced her as the first "titaness." The Romantic adventures of such nineteenth-century

American men as Bronson Alcott, it seems, had aroused the ire of petticoat tyrants. According to Beer, the mothers of America preferred a cloying diet of domestic tranquillity gleaned from the pages of *Little Women*. They were turning their husbands, brothers, and sons into "Miss Alcott's boys," thereby castrating all that was vital and masculine in American society.[10] Beer's diatribe, *The Mauve Decade*, represents a long wave of antifeminism which tended to equate woman's rights with repression and sentimentality.[11] Deaf to Alcott's plea for an abundant and adventurous life, Beer, like many succeeding critics, saw her domestic realism as a challenge to the natural world presented in *Huckleberry Finn*. He never knew that Louisa May Alcott had created Jean Muir.

Female readers in particular have always been attracted to Jo March, the heroine of *Little Women*. Over the years a new feminist contingent gathered. Suspicious of the sentimental appeal in Alcott's fiction, younger feminists feared that their susceptibilities were false consciousness; after all, Jo, a warmhearted tomboy, seems doomed to wander forever in the secret garden of female adolescence, never becoming an adult. Yet Alcott's works appeal to generations of female readers precisely because women always face an involuntary choice between domestic life and individual identity. This social choice remains a personal, painful part of growing up, much as Jo March felt it. Jo, like Margaret Fuller, and like Alcott herself, wanted both domesticity and individuality—her predicament was part of the "woman problem"—and her refusal to yield either part of herself lies at the heart of the woman's rights struggle. In this sense, all Alcott's writings are feminist polemics that insist on woman's right to both home life and individuality.

Domesticity and feminism have veered apart and come together many times since the first woman's rights movement. Perhaps this uncertain linkage explains why readers have all but forgotten that a generation of liberal feminists, including Alcott, linked their demand for democratic households of various sorts to demands for woman's suffrage and a democratic society. A reading of Alcott's life and works in their contemporary context will enable us to see the nineteenth-century woman problem as Alcott presented it to her popular audience. She was a most autobiographical writer, and her contemporary readers knew about her Romantic inheritance and her woman's rights sympathies. This study of her fiction and feminism therefore is structured within the narrative chronology of her life. Alcott tested the limits of Romantic individualism in both her life and her early fiction. Increasingly she doubted the universality of Emerson's prescriptive pathways to self-reliance, love, and individual identity. Women, she found, simply could not maintain unique relationships to nature, prescribed and bound as they were to private households. She painfully concluded further that the communal experiments of her childhood years had not altered the sexual division of labor.

Her family's desperate poverty and her father's belief in individual perfectability as a model for society led him to found Fruitlands, a short-lived communal farm near Harvard, Massachusetts. He attempted to reaffirm agrarian patriarchy as a way to escape the new industrial capitalist order. Domestic tragedy resulted, but the Alcotts emerged from it a more democratic household.

Determining the right relationship among woman, labor, property, and the family is most strikingly evident in the working out of dietary restrictions at Fruitlands and at most other nineteenth century intentional communities. Alcott satirized men's fearful retreat from female abundance in "Transcendental Wild Oats," and she emphasized bountiful harvest tables laid out by women in much of her fiction.[12] By the 1850s Louisa Alcott's generation of reformers, unlike Bronson Alcott's cohorts, confidently expected American society to conquer the ancient problem of scarcity. Abundance, moreover, no longer seemed to be a serpent in the garden of Eden.

The Civil War played an enormous part in moving Alcott and her generation from Romantic perfectionism to rational realism. Her involvement in local and then national organizations espousing antislavery, Sanitary Commission work, woman's rights, and temperance were representative of many liberal reformers' activities. Setting national standards and expanding organizational bureaucracies seemed to go hand-in-hand with a concerted national reform effort. Alcott's *Hospital Sketches*, the record of her own brief Civil War nursing experience, was her earliest popular success.[13]

After the Civil War, Alcott's fiction reflected this changing reform perspective. Using home life as a metaphor for social order, she argued for a corporate rational world. Postwar woman's rights advocates valued true love over romantic passion, and household democracy over patriarchy; they viewed coeducation as a model for institutional change. Romantic individualism seemed painfully impossible in a world of huge social problems. Significantly Alcott revised her romantic first-published novel, *Moods*, giving her heroine a happier if less melodramatic fate; she also edited and commented upon her early diaries. The issues she addressed remained the same in her own mind: individual rights and cooperative community, the search for democratic access to American abundance, and woman's right to be an individual and to have a home. Her revisions, however, tended to soften the hardships she and her family endured in their struggle for individual security. She had, of course, achieved security for all the Alcotts with the publication of *Little Women*. Her personal success, however, was not the only reason for softening her literary perspective.

Alcott never felt comfortable outside her native-born, genteel circle of liberal reformers. Asserting the absolute sanctity of the individual soul, she nevertheless promoted a strategy of indoctrination and assimilation for the urban working classes, embattled farmers, blacks, and immigrants. She generally overlooked contradictions between individuality and social control, assuming that everyone wanted to be just like the people she knew and loved. Equality of opportunity, she argued, meant enabling the less privileged to gain the values, tastes, habits, and skills of Louisa May Alcott's "regular set." With a little institutional help, the less fortunate would be free to sell their labor power and rise to the middle class, where there was room for all, she reasoned.

Alcott eventually wrote about a home for poor newsboys in New York City. The working boys paid a small sum for dormitory space and a hot meal, but Alcott was particularly interested in the boys' opportunity to save their pennies. In the dormitory stood a great table "full of slits, each one leading to a little place below and numbered outside, so each boy knew his own. Once a month the bank is opened, and the lads take out what they like, or have it invested in a big bank for them to have when they find homes out West, as many do," she wrote, and "they make good farmers." The overseer told her how "that very day," a young man came in to report that he was a newsboy who had gone west and now owned "eighty acres of land

and a good house." He had come back to New York to find his sister and "take her away to live with him."[4]

Alcott and her circle imagined a new Garden of Eden in America, one in which sexual relationships were purged of conflict and betrayal. They had faith in America's ever-expanding economy; progress came from unimpeded growth. Alcott presented positive portraits of abundance; feminists' social influence would resolve social conflicts through coeducation and helpful sheltering institutions. In *Jo's Boys*, her last novel, she presented a model university community presided over by the heroines of *Little Women*. She did not live long enough to develop the careers of the social housekeepers she was educating at Laurence University. We do not know if the new generation would have joined Edward Bellamy's nationalist clubs or the Fabian socialists, as did Elizabeth Cady Stanton's daughter, Harriet Stanton Blatch, and Frances Willard, president of the Women's Christian Temperance Union. Certainly Alcott's heroines did not withdraw from the world; they went forth to clean it up.

Alcott's life and her works demonstrate the full range of feminist concerns in the nineteenth century. Above all, she cared about woman's "hunger for home" and "the cry for bread," central facts of any ordinary woman's life.[5] She moved from Romanticism to rationalism, from a near mystical union with nature to faith in social science. And her allegiance to a liberal woman's rights program never wavered, and her fiction made an important contribution to popular acceptance of liberal reform institutions. The woman problem remains, of course. Perhaps we may gauge the success of feminism by the appearance of a future generation of "little women" who will not recognize Jo March's dilemma as their own.

ONE

Something to Love and Live For

It is too true that love is a mere episode in the life of a man. It is a whole history in the life of a woman.

Abigail May to Amos Bronson Alcott, *June 10, 1829*

In the twilight of a snowy Christmas Eve during the Civil War, four sisters sit before a crackling fire, knitting quietly. Their poverty is softened by the "comfortable old room," graced with books, pictures, and Christmas roses blooming in the window. But Jo March, the heroine of *Little Women*, rebels:

It's bad enough to be a girl anyway, when I like boys' games and work and manners! I can't get over my disappointment in not being a boy; and it's worse than ever now, for I'm dying to go and fight with papa, and I can only stay at home and knit like a poky old woman.[1]

Contemporary female readers of *Little Women* understood Jo's rebellion. One hundred years later, however, the relationship between Alcott's fiction and what her friends called the "woman problem" still elicits deeper analyses. Her biographers sympathetically identified many of the real people and incidents that Alcott fictionalized, thus opening the way to understanding her life and work within a larger body of fiction and historical reality.

To grow into manhood in Alcott's time meant the distinct possibility of individual achievement, accompanied by the chance of failure. It was harder for women. Like most of her readers, Alcott accepted woman's traditional commitment to family and home life; yet she also demanded individuality as her "natural right." She brilliantly

I

communicated the tension between woman's traditional household cares and her new right to individual achievement. To resolve the conflict she presented an inviting range of domestic arrangements and income-producing work in alternative communities. Her ability to communicate the tension between old responsibilities and new rights while simultaneously offering viable alternatives to patriarchy partially explains her enduring popularity as a writer for women.

THE CONNECTICUT YANKEE

Louisa May Alcott's perspective on womanhood in American society was grounded in a notable family legacy. She was both a May and an Alcott. Her mother, Abigail May, descended from distinguished colonial gentry. Her contemporary relations were members of Boston's elite: prosperous and influential ministers, bankers, lawyers, and merchant capitalists.[2] Had Abigail May married within her class, Louisa's literary talents might have remained a graceful avocation. But she chose Bronson Alcott, the son of an impoverished farmer.[3] In the four generations following the American Revolution, the substantial family lands dwindled to bare subsistence acreage and the family name changed from Alcocke to Alcox and finally to Alcott. Captain John Alcocke, a Revolutionary soldier, settled in Wolcott, Connecticut, and accumulated nearly one thousand acres of Spindle Hill before he died. His son, Joseph Alcox, married Anna Bronson and their son Amos Bronson Alcox was the eldest of eight surviving children. He grew up in an unpainted, three-room frame house, cobbled together from two older cabins on eighty acres of stony land. Although his mother was barely literate herself, the money she earned from spinning and weaving had helped send her brother Tillotson Bronson to Yale.

Amos Bronson Alcock, however, never attended college. At the age of thirteen he left a small common school in Wolcott, ending his formal education. His experience was not isolated. Horace Mann, another Massachusetts school reformer, labored in his father's fields while spending less than ten weeks at school per year; he too left school at thirteen. Raised on his family's own meat, corn, grain, and milk, Bronson wore homemade clothes that were spun, woven, and sewn by his mother. His father supplemented the family's income by making baskets and plow handles in the evening, using the light supplied by their own molded tallow candles.

Theirs was a hard, meager life without the good pictures or books that later softened Alcott's fictional portraits of genteel poverty. Bronson's Uncle Tillotson, on the other hand, became the headmaster of Cheshire Academy and owned a home filled with books that entranced his nephew. Bronson spent a month with his uncle as a charity student at the academy, but being a poor, rural bumpkin at an elite Episcopalian boys' school proved humiliating. He returned to Spindle Hill and began his own lifelong experiment in self-education. With his cousin, William, he gathered a small store of books from neighbors and friends. The most influential and comforting was *The Pilgrim's Progress*.

Bronson's youth was certainly impoverished materially but it was rich in emotional, religious opportunities. Connecticut revivals in the first decade of the nineteenth century reached Wolcott in the person of Lyman Beecher himself. Bronson's Episcopalian parents allowed him to choose his own denomination and, after hearing Beecher, their eldest son understood the connection between evangelical Congregationalism and moral reform. Human beings could be active in their own regeneration. *The Pilgrim's Progress* was even more satisfying to the young seeker because it valorized the emotional, mystical experience central to Puritanism. Bronson traveled fast and far emotionally; at seventeen he was ready to reject both Calvinism and Episcopalian ritual. He chose his own personal, antisectarian religion, eventually finding his spiritual community among Transcendental believers who shared his blend of inner light and direct personal experience with nature.

Bronson's journals record many readings of Bunyan's nonconformist text, and later he re-created its adventures for his daughters, encouraging them to playact the odyssey. Alcott prefaced *Little Women* with her own adaptation of the second half of the book, in which the pilgrim's wife, Christiana, accompanied by her children and her friend, Mercy, finds her own way to Heaven. Emphasizing that girls take up women's burdens early, she wrote:

3

Tell them of Mercy: she is one who early hath her pilgrimage
begun. Yea, let young damsels learn of her to prize the world
which is to come, and so be wise; for little tripping maids may
follow God along the ways which saintly feet have trod.[4]

His brothers and sisters found work in local factories, but Bronson, ambitious and adventurous, joined the new throng of Yankee
peddlers traveling the South to sell American manufactures stimulated by the War of 1812. His stock—three hundred dollars' worth of
combs, jewelry, thimbles, spectacles, sewing silks and cottons, nee-
dles, purses, playing cards, and puzzles for children—was taken on
consignment from a Norfolk dealer. His biographer, Odell Shepard,
calculated that the young peddler walked a hundred miles, tin trunks
in hand.[5]

Bronson quickly found himself a commercial and social success.
He talked to gentry, brought them news of the road, visited their
libraries, and slept in their outbuildings. He had begun just after
New Year in 1819; by April he made one hundred dollars, enough to
travel to New York, buy himself a new suit, and still give his father
eighty dollars with which to frame a new house.

On a second peddling trip, accompanied by his cousin William, he
walked twenty miles a day in the company of Dutch drivers who
drank rum and swore a great deal. Hoping to gain temporary teaching jobs in South Carolina, both men walked another six hundred
miles through swamps and forests to Norfolk, Virginia. There Bronson caught "typhus fever" and William nursed him through it. The
experience cured sober William of itinerancy and may have inspired
him to take the medical course at Yale, thence to become a well-
known physician and author of one hundred and eight popular advice pamphlets. But Bronson, fond of cider and good company,
forged on with another cousin, experiencing what he called a jolly,
easygoing time. This hopeful start at recouping the family's fortunes, however, ended bleakly when his father had to sell a portion
of the small homestead to pay debts accumulated by unsold and
consigned goods from Bronson's later trips.

At this time, the cousins changed their name from Alcock to
Alcott. Amos Bronson Alcock became A. Bronson Alcott and his
cousin became William Andrus Alcott; their genteel new names,

4

however, brought no commensurate prosperity. In 1819 a severe depression struck the East. Bronson disregarded the hard times and his debt to his father and merchant suppliers, and spent the small cash reserves from his third trip in a flourish of vanity. He bought a "black coat, and a white cravat of daintiest tie, crimped ruffles, gleaming amethystine pin."[6] This mild extravagance quickly became a token of immoral material ambitions to the young man and to his family.

Bronson was determined to earn enough cash to free the family from debt before he was twenty-one. Yet by twenty-three he had merely reinforced his family's indigence. Nevertheless, he had set out on a path consistent with the contemporary belief that entrepreneurial drive benefited both the individual and society as a whole. This secular belief, aided by the older Protestant faith in individual responsibility and freedom of will, added fuel to Bronson's sense of failure. He might have joined the swelling urban migration and become an industrial wage earner, but did not chose to do so.

For a brief time, however precariously, he had escaped his childhood in a rural backwater. He learned to enjoy convivial visits with men of property and taste. Yet his relatively small commercial failure effected a larger, subjective impoverishment; much that was spontaneous and vivid in his personality was repressed. The self-conscious capacity for charming others remained with Bronson, enlarged and refined, but he was henceforth reserved, even calculating. Father Isaac Hecker, who shared Bronson's desire for spiritual community many years later, recalled his personality in a kindly but skeptical fashion: "Alcott was not a man of great intellectual gifts or acquirements. His knowledge came chiefly from experience and instinct. He had an insinuating and persuasive way with him."[7]

What Alcott made of her father's youth is instructive. In her early works, including both juvenile and adult fiction, itinerants appear as impoverished and homeless male orphans or disappointed lovers. Taken in by warmhearted surrogate mothers, their dangerous habits are changed by the love and security of proper family life. Once grown, they require careful monitoring and must prove themselves by stable useful employment. Later, Louisa Alcott colored her father's youthful experience and reflected his gentle reputation in the father of the "Little Women." "Eli's Education," which she pub-

5

lished in the popular children's magazine *St. Nicholas*, features a young man, Eli, who spends his small peddling profits on a fancy broadcloth suit and ruffled shirt, hoping to attract the attentions of a pretty girl. As a result his father is forced to mortgage part of the family farm. Properly ashamed and repentant, Eli works hard as a peddler and endures many hardships to repay his father and recover his sense of modesty and decorum. Eli learns wisdom and virtue, and later, like Bronson Alcott, becomes a famous teacher, "diffusing good thoughts now as he had peddled small wares when a boy." This gentle tale locates a young man's minor vanity and selfishness in puppy love; it also was a sympathetic tribute to Bronson from his daughter. "This is a true tale," she wrote, "of a man becoming famous for his wisdom, as well as much loved and honored for his virtue and interest in all good things."[8]

Missing from this story, however, and perhaps from Bronson's awareness as well, was his fierce, youthful vanity and ambition, his need to be the center of attention. Instead, he turned his feelings of rejection and his quest for gentility into a moral imperative to self-sacrifice and goodness.

Bronson's mother, Anna Bronson Alcox, undoubtedly admired her oldest son; she marveled at his intellectual attainment in light of her own meager education: "If he is my son, his mind is great; it goes up and spreads far and broad."[9] She conveys in a terse but vivid way that his aspirations and struggles were a fulfillment of her own dreams. Bronson treasured her encouragement and memorialized their relationship:

> I was diffident,—you never mortified me; I was quiet,—you never excited me; I loved my books—you encouraged me to read, and stored my mind with knowledge. You helped me when I needed help, were glad at any success of mine, never frowned upon me when I failed. You knew my love for neatness of appearance, my sense of the beautiful,—and you cherished it. These things I have not forgotten.[10]

A grateful tribute to be sure, but one written to a mother whose approval, as he recalled it, was for an ideal son whose successes and failures replicated those of Bunyan's pilgrim. She loved him as he loved to be good. His desire to preen a bit, to escape from farm drudgery and homemade clothes into a larger society that valued drawing-room conversation and elegant attire was translated into "a love of neatness" and innate aesthetic sensibility. She knew, or Bronson felt she knew, that he meant to be good, altruistic, saintly.

But was Bronson a saint? His wife and children were never wholly sure whether they lived with a saint or merely with an unusually unrealistic man. One family friend recalled that he knew of only two occasions in which Bronson's wife, Abigail May, manifested impatience with Bronson's "saintly" behavior. On one of these she exclaimed, "I do wish people who carry their heads in the clouds would occasionally take their bodies with them."[1] This rare critique points to the larger truth about Bronson's "saintliness": he refused to accept his own weaknesses as a human being, preferring to assume the mask of idealized goodness. Bronson never felt that his own commercial failure or dandyism were ordinary lapses to be accepted and forgiven; his need to achieve and his commitment to an ideal self could be sustained only by constant affirmation from his parents and friends, and later from his children. Alcott, though often confused about her feelings toward her father, sensed his need for that affirmation and confirmed much of his idealized self in her fiction.

In Alcott's short story, Eli turns to teaching to repay his debts, with the help of his Uncle Tillotson. Bronson took the same path, and for the same reason. With his uncle's help he gained a position as master of the Center District School in Cheshire, Connecticut. It was a new start, a new way to prove his goodness, and an auspicious moment to win respectability, even influence in the community. The state's schools were in sorry shape by the time Bronson began teaching. Despite the legacy of public generosity—Connecticut appropriated over one million dollars as a permanent education fund in 1795—the school population had outgrown the state budget. The number of children in public schools had doubled in thirty years and funds were inadequate to equip schools or pay teachers a living wage. Male schoolmasters earned twelve dollars a month; and female teachers, who taught only in the summer, made six. Pupils sat on backless benches in twenty-foot schoolrooms that might house fifty or sixty students, as Bronson's schoolroom did. They had few books or slates, and little motivation to learn under the traditional recitation method.[12]

Bronson and his cousin William, who also taught school, joined once again in a new venture. They read, talked, and felt themselves part of a new educational reform movement upon which the fate of the republic seemed to rest. A new view of childhood and education was sweeping America in the aftermath of eighteenth-century philosophical and republican reform. Enlightenment science provided grounds for optimism about progress and order in human society. All matter shared certain observable properties, making possible the discovery and application of physical laws. The heavens and the earth were not only ordered but comprehensible to educated people. Scientific laws properly applied contributed to a technological and industrial revolution. It seemed to many eager witnesses of these changes that human beings themselves could be scientifically educated to perfect human consciousness and behavior.

Bronson Alcott forged his own educational ideas in this new intellectual context. Just as he chose to nourish his own "goodness," so too he thought that proper family nurture and enlightened education would produce a virtuous and harmonious society of "good" individuals. He read the *American Journal of Education*, which spread the gospel that supervised recitation or even the rational presentation of instructional materials was not enough. Rather, proper education depended upon the arts of emotional persuasion. These new methods, pioneered in Bronson's time by the Swiss educator, Johann Heinrich Pestalozzi, among others, stressed what are often called "modernizing principles": the mastery over one's own passions, a belief in objective order, the value of work as an end in itself, and the ability to postpone gratification. Bronson also read and reread John Locke, finding further confirmation for a progressive reform of education. Locke's notion that the mind itself is a "tabula rasa," a blank slate that simply receives impressions about the material world through sensory organs, ran counter to older ideas of children's inborn depravity. Old New England primers, such as those Bronson had read as a child, taught that the most children could hope for, if they died in infancy, was "the easiest room in hell." Puritan theology assumed that even a newborn babe was doomed by the original sin of Adam and Eve in the Garden of Eden; only stern adult discipline

8

and the suppression of children's naturally craven tastes could overcome innate depravity.

Along with many other reforming schoolmen, Bronson rejected these beliefs, arguing instead that childhood was an innocent state and that children might delight in learning if gently led by loving parents and teachers. He also drew his ideas from Robert Owen's *New View of Society*. Human beings, Owen maintained, were not nasty, brutish, and competitive, but naturally cooperative if they could escape the constraining institutions of private property and individualism. While Locke supported a society of enlightened individualists, Owen supported an enlightened society of socialists. For the time being, Bronson was content to follow Locke in the schoolroom.

He had notable success in wooing pupils to think for themselves and to develop their capacities to learn, inducing the *Boston Recorder* to commend his school.[13] Bronson himself helped pay for these improvements, putting backs on the benches, buying one hundred and sixty-five books as a lending library for the whole community, and hanging inspiring pictures. He encouraged singing and dancing at a time when playgrounds were unknown. Bronson was able to express all the warmth and physical affection for his small pupils that his own childhood lacked. He was gratified by their admiration. But he did not, perhaps could not, save enough to pay back his six-hundred-dollar debt to his father.

Some parents resented Bronson's charismatic influence over their children, despite his election to the new Connecticut Society for the Improvement of Common Schools. To add to his troubles, a second public school opened, and with renewed competition from a nearby academy, he found himself back on the road to his parents' home. This time, however, he was not a tired poverty-stricken pilgrim, but the Pied Piper of a new generation of children who he intended to lead to the Promised Land. His success still lay before him.

THE MAY CHARACTER

In March 1826, Reverend Samuel May, a young Unitarian minister, member of the local school board, and the brother of Bronson's future wife, organized a series of common school reform conventions

9

in Brooklyn, Connecticut. In response to an invitation circulated the following year, William Alcott sent in a report of his cousin's school, accompanied by Bronson's descriptions of children, the "idea books" he encouraged them to keep, and his innovative practice of democratic self-government in the schoolroom. Reverend May was impressed, generously hospitable, and full of energy for the great task of reform. He invited Bronson Alcott to visit him in Brooklyn.

A gentleman with strong democratic leanings, May welcomed his poor country colleague as one of the reform brethren. He and Bronson shared an important belief—that education was an inalienable right. As May declared, "No one shall be compelled by the poverty of his parents to live in darkness and sin."[14] Although their backgrounds could hardly have been more different, theirs was more than a chance meeting of minds. It was the curious historical conjunction of diverse social reformers dedicated, for very different reasons, to changing as well as conserving the relationship between American society and culture. For both of them the intellectual and moral culture of the whole people was the key to individual success and to the harmonious well-being of the republic.[15]

In July 1827, Bronson called upon the Reverend May and his wife at the May home. By chance the minister was out; his wife was resting upstairs, recovering from the birth of their first child. Bronson was greeted by Abigail May, the Reverend's sister, visiting from Boston. She was a twenty-seven-year-old spinster, tall, amply proportioned, with heavy features and dark complexion. Though scarcely pretty, Abba May possessed a force of personality and a vivacity that animated her face and lightened her stately figure.[16] She loved music and dancing, and moved with a graceful assurance that Bronson had rarely seen in the rural girls of his own class. He recorded his initial impression of Abigail May in his journal: "An interesting woman we had often portrayed in our imagination. In her we thought we saw its reality." Abigail May also described this first meeting, but in a manner more shrewd and less inhibited: "I found . . . an intelligent, philosophic modest man," she said, "whose reserved deportment authorized my showing many attentions."[17]

Bronson was only a year older than his hostess; and by all accounts unusually tall, blond, and handsome. As a friend observed, Bronson's "glance was bright and eager, though not deep, which sparkled upon you."[18] Abigail was a gently reared, well-educated young woman, unprepared for the dislocation that followed her mother's death and the remarriage of her father, Colonel Joseph May, a year later. As the youngest in her family, with sisters already married and established in their households, she had expected to assume her place as hostess of her father's gracious Federal Street home. But her stepmother, Mary Ann Clary May, was not inclined to share those pleasant responsibilities. Still, Abigail found much to do in her brother's parsonage, helping his wife, Lucretia Coffin May, with the duties of a parson's wife and the care of a one-month-old infant. She also helped maintain the genteel tone of the household with a tact that appealed to Bronson. Indeed, on his first visit to the family, he stayed for almost a week.

It may be true, as Madelon Bedell argues in her rich history of the Alcott family, that "for both it was clearly love at first sight." But it is more certain that Bronson was powerfully drawn to the genteel, comfortable atmosphere of the May household. He found the "May character" lovable, and spoke of the whole family enthusiastically as "distinguished for their urbanity, benevolence—their native manners—and nobleness of soul—moral purity and general beneficences."[19]

The Mays possessed considerable means to "influence public opinion," as Bronson put it.[20] They were also untouched by the rigors of deprivation. Neither brother nor sister had ever attended a public school nor faced the hard facts of rural poverty. In fact, Sam's recollections of their education were of "my generous father, who thought the best patrimony he could give his children was a good education—so we were sent to the private schools in Boston that enjoyed the highest reputation."[21]

Sam May was properly grateful for the education appropriate to gentlemen. After attending what he called "ma'am school," run by respectable ladies for small gentry, he left his sisters with their schoolmistresses to attend a series of private preparatory schools for boys. At thirteen, when Bronson left formal schooling forever, Sam was being readied for Harvard by Master Elisha Clapp. Sam, along with sons from other distinguished Boston families—the Otises, Eliots, and Parkers—received instruction in Latin, Greek rhetoric, and mathematics at a cost of one hundred dollars per pupil. He entered the Harvard class of 1817, along with his cousin, Samuel Sewall, and his friend George Emerson, brother of Ralph Waldo Emerson. Classwork was mostly recitation, even at the university. At that time the library owned fewer than 20,000 books, though an infusion of European-trained scholars and an expanded program of library acquisitions lay in the near future.[22]

At twenty, Sam May entered Harvard Divinity School and studied the philosophy of John Locke, along with Biblical criticism and theology. When he completed his training in 1820, he possessed, as his father put it, "an education that will enable you to go anywhere, stand up among your fellow men and by serving them in one department of usefulness or another, make yourself worthy of a comfortable livelihood, if no more."[23] Bronson Alcott could scarcely have disagreed with the pronouncement, but he knew that such an education was far more likely for young men with family connections and substantial material resources.

"Usefulness" for the Mays meant reform activity in a broad range of social institutions; these included antislavery, education, prisons, charity relief, and politics. Bronson had slept in slave quarters and sold goods to slave owners on his peddling trips. Like many early nineteenth-century citizens of enlightenment, he hoped and expected that slavery would die a natural death. Having observed what he took to be cordial, even friendly relationships between masters and slaves, the actual deprivations of slave life went unremarked in his journals. But Sam May's first glimpse of the "peculiar institution" was quite different. In his memoirs he recalled a trip south to celebrate his approbation as a minister by the Boston Association of Unitarians.

We saw, standing by the roadside, a row of Negro men, 20 or 30 in number, and soon perceived that they were all handcuffed, and that the irons about their wrists were fastened around a very heavy chain that was passed between them attached to the tail of a large wagon in which were bundles, apparently of clothes, and some young children lying upon straw, 4 or 5 black women were passing along the line and giving to each man a thick slice of coarse bread. . . . We had heard of the abomination of slavery and the internal slave trade, but had not seen it before . . . . I never before felt so grateful, as I do now, that I was not born where human beings can be bought and sold, and treated like cattle . . . . I am ashamed of my country and my race.[24]

By the time Bronson Alcott and Abigail May were married, Sam was an antislavery agent. He had defended Prudence Crandall, a Quaker schoolteacher in Connecticut who accepted black pupils only to be arrested by the local sheriff. Sam May's ideals were no less admirable than his courage in carrying them out. And although she lacked the formal education and civic opportunities afforded a male citizen of her class, his sister was of one mind and heart with him.

Abigail May's coming of age did not include a graduation ceremony releasing her into a world rich with possibility. Even as children, only Sam was free to explore Boston's wharves, engage in snowball fights on the Commons, and race his sled with playmates down Beacon Hill. His sisters' domestic roles were shaped by their mother's lessons in baking, scrubbing, and washing. Like other notable housewives, Mrs. May thought that the mistress of a proper household should possess the skills to supervise her staff's daily chores. She also had Abigail trained in the customary French, music, and dancing. Beyond the practice of these skills, Abigail's life was circumscribed. She traveled only in the company of family or close friends. At home she learned what she could of the outside world from Sam, who brought Harvard friends home to visit.

Her education was "finished off" by a year of study with one Miss Allyn of Duxbury, an educated spinster who undertook such work for the daughters of family friends. Abba Alcott later told her daughter Louisa that as a young girl she studied "French, Latin, and botany, had read history extensively, and made notes of many books such as David Hume, Edward Gibbon, Hallam's *Middle Ages* and Robertson's *Charles V.*"[25] Her reading followed the pattern later recommended by her close girlhood friend, Lydia Maria Child, in *The Mother's Book* (1831). Child advised girls to read history, biography, and even current novels, providing that they respected woman's ability to reason. One of Child's favorite novelists was Catharine Maria Sedgwick, whose books Abigail read as a young woman. Sedgwick allowed her female heroines an innovative independence and a strong desire for education. She pioneered a new fiction that Abigail's daughter would later develop and deepen in her own books for girls.

By the time Abigail May met Bronson Alcott she was a well-educated, active woman by the standards of her generation. After Bronson returned to Cheshire following his visit with the Mays, Abba toured Boston schools, talked with teachers, and even read a biography of Pestalozzi. She and Sam not only urged Bronson to move to Boston, Abigail declared herself ready to become his assistant. She found a school on Salem Street which would welcome Bronson as master and herself as his assistant. Sam, taken aback by this unexpected assertiveness, strenuously objected to the impropriety of his unmarried sister teaching with a single man for whom she felt such obvious attraction. He wrote to her:

> I will frankly say that I see no other objection than the remarks and opinions of the world. A man may bid defiance to these, a woman cannot, without incurring the greatest danger. The circumstances of our acquaintance with Mr. Alcott, and his having gone to Boston at my suggestion and with my recommendation, would lead a censorious world to ascribe selfish views both to myself and you if you were to unite with him in his school. For this reason, and for this alone, I decidedly advise you to relinquish the plan altogether.[26]

Acceding to Sam's wishes, Abba chose merely to introduce Bronson to the May circle of influence. Bronson accepted the position of master at the Salem Street primary school. He left there barely a year later to found his own school on Common Street with Abba's friendship but without her presence as his assistant.

"WE LOVE HER . . . SHE LOVES US"

The Boston so familiar to Abigail May was still a small city of no more than 58,000 residents in 1828. But even the critical English visitor, Harriet Martineau, found it unique in young America, a place, she believed, that compared only to London in the richness of its population. The Commons provided constant entertainment and recreations, including July 4 fairs and open stalls for outdoor refreshments. Children could sail their boats on the frog pond in fine weather and sled down the snowy slopes in winter. Nearby, two walks served such citizens as Colonel May, Ralph Waldo Emerson, and now, Abigail May and Bronson Alcott.

Bronson thoroughly savored his move to Boston, grateful for the introductions provided by Sam and Abigail May to the city's most influential citizens and its most edifying cultural activities. He heard Emerson preach and approved mildly of the liberal Unitarian. He also listened to Lyman Beecher, whom he found too intent on building one particular faith. His reading of Robert Owen's socialist, freethinking philosophy had already moved him into an idealistic frame of mind beyond both rational Unitarianism and enthusiastic evangelism. He and his friend Miss May were more drawn to circles of universal reform that included the abolitionist William Lloyd Garrison and Frances Wright, an Owenite speaker and champion of free love (though that doctrine proved too advanced for the young couple). They also met William Russell, editor of the *American Journal of Education*, and Elizabeth Peabody, a disciple of William Ellery Channing who had opened an infant school in Roxbury.

In this stimulating world, Bronson and Abigail's friendship blossomed into romance. Yet it was romance plagued by serious problems, ranging from Bronson's poverty and fears of commitment to Abigail's understanding that love is a "whole history in the life of a woman."[27] Her recognition of how much depended upon this momentous event in a woman's life reflected her personal experience of the social realities in antebellum America.

By her own account, Abigail May was "much indulged—allowed to read a great deal—fed nice food and had many indulgences not given my brothers and sisters. I was a good child—but willful."[28] While she certainly had little direct knowledge of her father's public responsibilities, his departure and return each day were major events in her domestic world. She watched for him at the front window and at seventeen wrote him that he was her "morning song and evening lullaby." But by her late twenties the privileges and pleasant intimacies a favored girl enjoyed with her father were supposed to be transferred to her husband. In early nineteenth-century America the guardians of public welfare agreed with the prescriptions of William Alcott's popular books on marriage and family life. In *The Young Wife* Alcott wrote that only modern times have revealed the "silent" power

> which woman has in governing the world. She is to wield the sceptre, first over her husband, and next over the children whom God may give her. . . . It is vain, or almost in vain, to hope for any single amelioration of our race, through family influence, til this point is secured—til woman's life, amid her household, is one uninterrupted series of kind actions, words, tones and gestures, and til she has overcome and transformed her husband.[29]

With a characteristic bustle of energy and enthusiasm, Abigail May hurried to fulfill her mission. Feeling unworthy, however, Bronson drew back, perhaps remembering his days as a peddler and his unsuccessful efforts to support his family. In his eyes theirs was an "ambiguous relationship." After spending much time with Abigail, he shared his journal with her, but he mystified her by praising her "character" without mentioning his very real emotional and physical attraction to her.[30] It was Abigail who finally spoke up. "I told him my feelings," she wrote. "They were innocent and only needed explanation to be cherished or rejected by him."[31]

Bronson chose to cherish Abigail, and she wrote delightedly to her brother Sam of her engagement:

> I am engaged to Mr. Alcott not in a school, but in the momentous capacity of friend and wife. . . . I do think him in every respect qualified to make me happy. He is moderate, I am impetuous—He is prudent and humble—I am forward and arbitrary. He is poor— but we are both industrious—why may we not be happy? . . . I never felt so happy in my life—I feel already an increase of moral energy—I have something to love—to live for—I have felt a loneliness in this world that was making a misanthrope of me in spite of everything I could do to overcome it.

She signed her letter to "the most affectionate and tender of brothers," as "your sister Abba."[32]

Their engagement lasted for two and a half years. Bronson now felt relaxed enough to use the family's names for his betrothed, calling her Abba or Abby. Initially, Colonel May was not pleased at the match and even more displeased at his daughter's engagement without "asking my permission or advice." But he wanted peace in the family, and above all peace in his old age when "the shadows of evening are advancing." He invited Mr. Alcott to visit and took the trouble to "draw him out."[33] Bronson expressed his deepening feelings in his journal, which bore more than a little resemblance to the sentiments in Abigail's favorite romances: "I do love this good woman," he wrote, "and I love her because she is good—I love her because she loves me. She has done and continues to do much for me. How can I reciprocate her goodness?"[34]

A quick succession of family tragedies contributed to the delay of the marriage. In November 1829 Abba was crushed by the death of her sister, Louisa Greele, and a month later by the death of little Joseph, the son of Sam and Lucretia. Bronson, emotionally and physically distant, failed to express his sympathies. The distraught Abba needed comfort and material help, but he was able only to intellectualize the meaning of "sorrow." Abba was left with the care of her sister's two small children; she took them to Sam's parsonage, where her brother and sister-in-law shared in the anguish and consequent responsibilities. Bereaved and more than a little shaken by Bronson's behavior, Abba struggled to understand a man whose life seemed so different from her own. In an earlier time, she would have become engaged to someone of her own class and background, possibly to a man of more suitable temperament. In 1829, Abba's engagement to Bronson led her to think seriously about her future. She could not take for granted the status and role enjoyed by her mother's generation of privileged ladies.

Slowly she began to assert her needs and convictions, communicating to Bronson her own romantic vision of companionate marriage. She argued that women were no longer the servants of men. As a daughter of the American Revolution she further claimed that woman's place was at man's side and in his heart, refining and civilizing him, "compelling him by the irresistible force of merit to accept her as an intelligent companion." Inchoately, Abba was working out the beginnings of her own domestic feminism, trying to forge a union between an older and a newer perspective. On the one hand, she believed that woman's first priority was the care of her home and family; on the other, she argued that sexual equality in marriage and outside it would rescue "one half the world laboring under conscious and almost contented inferiority."[35]

What she meant by equality was something quite different from her daughter's understanding of that word a generation later. Abba wanted to become Bronson's companion in a deeply romantic sense— "in his heart." She tenderly—almost sentimentally, at this point in her life—placed being rather than doing at the center of loving marriage. Abba was also inclined to believe that a union of true hearts could not admit impediments to happiness; she invited and expected Bronson's correction of her faults. But she wanted to be loved as much for herself as for her possibilities. Bronson, on the other hand, loved her because she loved him.

If, upon occasion, Bronson seemed distant, Abba never really accepted emotional distance in her suitor. His cool, lofty presentation of himself was certainly softened by an almost homely simplicity in his personal tastes. The American reverence for the founding fathers, at that time, found more to admire in Franklin-like simplicity than in upper-class elegance. Bronson, for example, loved New England apples and cider, cold spring water, and cottage bread. Above all, his dignified reserve, which quite possibly concealed fears of rejection and humiliation, seemed familiar to Abba. His serenity, his air of moral rectitude, his acceptance of her unstinting love, all reminded her of her father. It never occurred to Abba that her husband would be less than an adequate provider, though he lacked Colonel May's position in the world. Nor did she suspect that Bronson could and would reject the role of provider altogether. He was her Connecticut Knight. His emotional armor had protected him in the many battles she saw him waging on his way from Spindle Hill to Boston, and Abba assumed that he would battle even more bravely for the honor of his lady.

Abba's halting efforts to understand Bronson and to prepare herself for an unconventional marriage reflected the uncertainty and confusion that many Americans felt over the relations between the sexes in the 1820s. Traditional grounds for marriage—similarity of birth, class, social status, the subordination of women, and the obligation of men to support their wives and children—were increasingly challenged by a new generation.

Thanks largely to circumstances that neither controlled, Abba and Bronson were among those who labored to create a new basis for marriage; unlike many of their contemporaries, they chose the most romantic of grounds. Ideally, they would marry to perfect their individual lives and to produce children who would contribute to the perfection of the human race. In the forefront of Romantic reform, Abba and Bronson agreed to fashion a perfect society through perfect domesticity.

This approach to marriage seemed unrealistic, even foolish, to Abba's relatives in particular. Still wedded to older patriarchal principles, and concerned with the couple's "housekeeping" and financial prospects, Colonel May viewed Bronson as a possibly dangerous marital choice. He believed that men and women from different backgrounds should not marry. Moreover, men should possess sufficient material resources to support their wives and children. Romantics premised a unique spiritual and creative force present in every individual human being at birth. A growing recognition of woman's spiritual equality concurrently led some prescriptors to accept the notion of household democracy as promoting domestic harmony. Serious doubts and misgivings over the virtues of such courtships as Abba's and Bronson's nevertheless resonated throughout the remainder of the nineteenth century. People remained troubled because romantic relationships so clearly failed to create a firm foundation for the relations between the sexes. Women, above all, were disturbed by the dangers of romantic love, even as they were drawn to its liberating potential.

Insistence upon the ultimate integrity of the individual soul, in the absence of the older corporate community, commonly led to conflict with social conventions and prescriptive norms. One might transcend ordinary economic and social barriers to personal achievement, to be sure; for this reason romanticism had a strong attraction for laissez-faire Jacksonians. Romantic love might also join two people of more than usual enterprise and adventure, helping them to overleap the barriers of their social system. Wedded in defiance of family and custom, a couple could deepen and enrich their courageous union. On the other hand, when individuals listen only to an inner voice, ordinary human selfishness could bloom into domestic tyranny. Furthermore, a denial of the outside world's constraints could result in spiritual anarchism.

A cooperative awareness of domestic problems, Louisa Alcott observed, was more likely to lead to democratic solutions. Individuality might otherwise be lost in an orgy of possessive individualism. She argued that true love, not romantic passion, guaranteed mutual concern for the needs of everyday life, and she offered a liberal, rational alternative to romantic relationships through the fictional courtships and marriages portrayed in her novels.

Alcott believed that romantic marriages also undercut possibilities for genuine female self-reliance. In all her fiction she challenged the Romantic belief that differences of temperament, class, and culture constitute the essence of constructive challenge and growth within domestic unions. Yet she was all too conscious of the thrill, the passionate attraction of such differences. In fact, her underlying admiration for her parents' romance kept that passionate impulse alive in her fiction, and made the rational alternative she demanded more difficult for her readers to accept.

On May 22, 1830, at King's Chapel, a reform Unitarian church that Colonel May helped establish, Abba and Bronson declared their bonds. Neither reported the attendance of any Alcott relatives, but Colonel and Mrs. May, faithful to the gentility that so marked their circle, gave the young couple a gracious reception. Soon thereafter, the Alcotts took up residence in one room of a nearby boarding house. This living arrangement, a product of the couple's penury, was not unusual for many young couples. It was, however, a harbinger of Abigail May Alcott's precarious future.

TWO
Model Children

Our birth is but a sleep and a forgetting:
The Soul that rises with us, our life's Star,
Hath had elsewhere its setting,
And cometh from afar:
Not in entire forgetfulness,
And not in utter nakedness,
But trailing clouds of glory do we come
From God, who is our home:
Heaven lies about us in our infancy!
William Wordsworth, "Ode: Intimations of Immortality"

To the delight of both herself and Bronson, who looked upon children with a nearly mystical respect, Abba became pregnant within a month after their wedding. Being parents and educating a new generation of nineteenth-century Americans seemed a political responsibility to them, as it did to many of their reformist generation. The "rights of children,"as they were newly perceived, seemed to follow logically upon the acceptance of the rights of man. If, as Wordsworth wrote, "Heaven lies about us in our infancy," a divinely democratic promise awaited the children of rich and poor alike; every child was born with a unique, creative perception of the world.

CHILDHOOD HATH SAVED ME

Romantic premises overturned traditional Calvinist orthodoxy, but they were not the principal causes of nineteenth-century anxiety over child raising. Children's feelings and lives were of concern because structural changes in family life and work resulted in the separation and removal of middle-class children from the adult world. By 1830, particularly in such cities as Boston, fathers spent little time with their children in domestic activities. Mothers, on the other hand, enlarged their sphere to form maternal associations and infant school societies, including the one whose female board of managers hired Bronson Alcott. As one contemporary observer put it, "The sphere of duty assigned to woman considered singly is limited to one family and one circle of society: but the fulfillment or neglect of those duties are [sic] extended almost beyond belief."[1] Accordingly, as households ideally became refuges from the competitive, public world of men, women's identities were redefined. They became associated with goodness, but a goodness that needed cultivation and supervision.

In the 1830s and 1840s a spate of new books, pamphlets, and especially magazines featuring advice and family-oriented fiction and poetry supplanted older domestic authorities.[2] Horace Bushnell, Theodore Dwight, and William Alcott all wrote for *The Mother's Assistant* and *Young Lady's Friend,* and their articles appeared with pieces by such new female experts as Lydia Maria Child, Catharine Sedgwick, and Catharine Beecher. Bronson Alcott contributed as an educator while awaiting his first child. By tapping a market for advice materials, in fact, he hoped to guarantee a comfortable living for his family. He published a pamphlet, *Observations on the Principles and Methods of Infant Instruction,* in the fall of 1830.[3] While *Observations* did not win the competition sponsored by Philadelphia's public school system for a proposal on infant education, the work interested two Quaker philanthropists, Robert Vaux and Reuben Haines. Haines offered Bronson Alcott and his friend and colleague William Russell the opportunity to implement their ideas at a new school in Germantown, Pennsylvania.

Alcott's educational principles and methodology have often been viewed as "too advanced and experimental . . . for use in a common school."[4] Alcott's ingenuous estimation of himself as an "original" has reinforced this view. Social historians, however, who have analyzed the enormous body of nineteenth-century prescriptive literature, place Bronson Alcott in the mainstream of liberal reformers. Bronson's dogged application of current liberal educational theory to raising the Alcott girls is impressive partly because he recorded the experience so thoroughly.[5] Sam May, Henry Barnard, and Horace

Mann, as well as Bronson Alcott and Lydia Maria Child, read the same Pestalozzian works, which espoused a system of parenting and education in harmony with the development of each child's instincts and abilities.[6] In particular, Pestalozzi stressed what later became dogma for progressive educators: children were to learn by doing and to experiment with real objects. Louisa May Alcott's fiction for children was also directed at their parents; she too preached the Pestalozzian method.

Bronson Alcott presented himself as a devoted American disciple in his essay, "Pestalozzi's Principles and Methods of Instruction," published in the *American Journal of Education* in 1829.[7] In that piece he emphasized the most contradictory aspect of Pestalozzi's philosophy and method without observing the contradiction. Developed from Locke's dictum that all knowledge proceeds through sensory perception, the proper nurture and education of children depended upon the cultivation of three faculties: reason, emotion, and will. But Locke's premise depended upon the tabula rasa, the mind's originally blank slate. Bronson Alcott, however, like so many other educational reformers, presumed the existence of neoplatonic ideal forms. The infant was born not merely innocent, but emerged "trailing clouds of glory"; he possessed an innate moral sense that required only a balanced environment to grow up "naturally."

Wordsworth's American devotees managed to combine an appreciation of innate goodness with a fervent trust in environmentalism. They wanted to perfect socialization through the senses and the emotions, ultimately evoking the power of the will to do good—even more, to be good.

In a discussion of Romantic theory M. H. Abrams notes that "in any period, the theory of mind and the theory of art tend to be integrally related and to turn upon similar analogues, explicit and submerged."[8] Bronson Alcott was determined to shape his environment in the deepest sense: he repeatedly invoked Wordsworth's metaphors of the soul as "our life's star," "trailing clouds of glory." Romantics saw an observing mind as one that projected the soul's light upon material reality and then received back something greater than mere reflections of nature. Bronson intended his "Journals" and "Observations" to be both monuments to his own mind and works of art.

He trusted Wordsworth's reassurance that, although our sensibilities fade with age "into the light of common day," the mind still retained its supple recollections, the "fountain light of all our day."

Though dedicated to infant education, Bronson was more concerned to validate his own mind as a projecting, original force. Both his childlike persona, admired by many of his friends, and his devotion to childhood itself were entirely consistent with a Romantic faith that human nature was everywhere the same and that feeling was the great common denominator. Before social institutions spoiled them, children were the closest to their natural sensibilities—the wellspring of creativity. By preserving his childhood innocence, Bronson felt he possessed reliable aesthetics and politics. He was all but oblivious to social struggles for the control of childhood going on around him.

A larger battle was nevertheless raging in the public school movement. Sam May was hotly engaged in this battle throughout his long life. By the 1830s and 1840s people throughout New England— including workers, newly arrived immigrants, and middle class reformers—were debating such questions as state versus local control, school standards and curriculum, and the place of the normal (teacher training) schools in the educational system. Class conflict, for example, underlay a controversy concerning the establishment of normal schools, a reform championed by Sam May, Henry Barnard, and Horace Mann. The very citizens who were supposed to benefit from professionally trained teachers often suspected that taxpayer's money merely educated the daughters of the rich and provided them extra income while they awaited marriage.[9] Other matters shaped the debate. Some people charged that normal schools would drive up the cost of hiring teachers, while others objected that professional training for teachers was undemocratic. One might have expected Bronson Alcott, a self-taught teacher, to join the fray; he did not.

His deep commitment to education, nonetheless, was reflected in the singular intensity he brought to being parent to his first two children. Anna Bronson Alcott, the first of four Alcott daughters, was born in Germantown on March 15, 1831. Her father immediately began recording his "Observations on the Phenomena of Life as Developed in the Progressive History of an Infant during the First Year of Its Existence."[10] His final manuscript of some 2,500 pages, which records both Anna's and Louisa's earliest years, has been duly appreciated as one of the first American diaries of child development. Inspired by similar diaries kept by Europeans and also eager to recapture the romantic innocence of his own childhood, Bronson was determined to test the limits of individual perfectability in himself and his daughters. "Childhood Hath Saved Me," he wrote, thereby revealing his own needs.[11]

Both Bronson and his intellectual mentor, Pestalozzi, believed that children's innate morality was constantly challenged by inherent weakness, depravity and "wildness." The best child-rearing method was, consequently, one that gently awakened and reinforced a child's own moral instincts. Cruelty toward a child or excessive discipline would only harden a delicate nature, confirming the worst instead of the best in each small pupil.

Bronson's methods, if not their underlying emotional pathology, were shared by a number of prescriptive writers. Lydia Maria Child, for instance, accepted "evil propensities" as perhaps hereditary, but she counted upon gentle nursery influences to keep those propensities from being aroused.[12] Alcott and Child agreed that the development of enlightened understanding and the capacity to act from principle rather than passion was at the heart of primary education.

Bronson's recurrent striving for perfectability distinguishes him from the more moderate reformers. "We do not yet know," he wrote, "what favorable influences from birth will do for the infant, from the beginning, and paying due respect to his whole nature, we shall cooperate with it, in due accordance and harmony with the laws of its constitution, and suggest to the world, both by success and failure, what the human being may become."[13] This tendency to indulge in abstractions, expressed in such phrases as "his whole nature," set him apart from his wife who had a concrete interest in her first baby. More preoccupied with the work of mothering, than with the usual preference for a son, Abba Alcott enjoyed holding and nursing Anna. She wrote to her brother Sam and his wife:

> Lucretia, I suppose, is ready with her condolence that it is a girl. I don't need it. My happiness in its existence and the perfection of its person is quite as much as I can well bear. Indeed, I cannot conceive that its being a boy should add there to.[14]

25

MOTHER LOVE: INFANT PERFECTION

Bronson's salary was sufficient to hire a housekeeper and nurse for Anna's first few days. But even at the beginning Abba was determined to care for the child by herself, a determination vigorously encouraged by both Bronson and contemporary attitudes. In Jacksonian America motherhood was the primary holy responsibility of women, precluding all other duties and interests. Bronson, who accepted this general outlook, observed mother and infant at a dispassionate distance; this suited him temperamentally, and he rationalized that emotional distance helped in the task of recording and testing. By July the record of Anna's progress was one hundred pages long, the beginning of a history that Bronson hoped would become a history of human nature.

During Anna's first year, Abba so arranged her life around the infant's needs that "the occasions for tears were few," as her father put it.[15] Such "management" of very young babies was not at all unusual. In fact, Anna's first few months, and to a certain extent Louisa's, followed standard, prescriptive advice. What was unusual, perhaps, was the complete commitment of both parents to following the prescriptions.[16]

Supported by the views of her friend, Lydia Maria Child, who believed that children should rarely cry if a mother is wholly attentive and caring, Abba nursed her child frequently, on demand. Both parents hoped to maintain the child's "naturally" happy disposition, even at the expense of neglecting to wash or dress her, which might bring on tears. Anna thrived, and by six months she had a small swing for her amusement and a cart for daily outings. The child-centered household granted Anna the right to sleep in her parents' bedroom, and more often than not Abba went to sleep with Anna at the infant's bedtime.

While recording Anna's "animal activity," Bronson also reported the presence of a "conscious and intelligent soul" in her at two months.[17] He was sure she had smiled at a vase of violets, a response to beauty clearly indicating a divine soul. Rocking cradles, sudden noises or movements were all shunned, as the manuals suggested, to avoid intrusions on infant peace. Bronson, however, occasionally violated these prescriptions by making scary faces that made Anna cry. He wished to prove that she possessed an imagination, could conjure up a vision of what had frightened her, and thus repeat the fear and the tearful response.

Bronson's observations in Anna's early months reflect a blend of earlier Protestantism and the beginnings of "modern" emotional manipulation. They extol the virtues of freedom while insisting upon the internalization of parental ideals:

> The child must be treated as a free, self-guiding, self-controlling being. He must be allowed to feel that he is under his own guidance and that all external guidance is an injustice which is done to his nature unless his own will is intelligently submissive to it. . . . He must be free that he may be truly virtuous, for without freedom there is no such thing as virtue.[18]

Alcott rejected the idea that external rewards or punishments should shape the moral life of children. Instead, children should be encouraged to choose freely the moral life that most pleased their father. Clearly, he thought that children possessed freedom of the will and that freedom could be a choice made only for morality. The contrast with Abba is striking, for she had no inclination whatever to test her daughter's moral sense at this early stage.

The following incident is typical. Anna, accustomed to falling asleep in her mother's presence, resisted being put to bed alone. Bronson concluded that she missed the light in the parlor. Her father went into the room and spoke kindly but firmly, indicating that he wanted her to go to sleep in the darkened room. She stopped crying and fell asleep, whereupon her father assumed that she had yielded to the tone of his instructions. Anna was seven months old at this time. Bronson was undoubtedly correct in surmising that she did not understand his words, but other explanations of her behavior did not occur to him: she might have missed her mother's company, not the light, and her father's voice may have provided reassurance in Abba's absence.[19]

As on many occasions, Alcott made use of her family history in her fiction. In *Little Women*, for example, she presents a similar situation, though the small son is already several years old. Used to his mother's company until he falls asleep, he also resists going to bed alone. The father goes to the child's room, speaks firmly about going to sleep without his mother's company, and then insists that the mother remain in the parlor while the child cries himself to sleep:

> The minute he was put into bed on one side, he rolled out on the other, and made for the door, only to be ignominiously caught up by the tail of his little toga and put back again, which lively performance was kept up till the young man's strength gave out, when he devoted himself to roaring at the top of his voice. The vocal exercise usually conquered Meg; but John sat as unmoved as the post which is popularly believed to be deaf. No coaxing, no sugar, no lullaby, no story, even the light was put out, and only the red glow of the fire enlivened the "big dark" which Demi regarded with curiosity rather than fear. This new order of things disgusted him and he howled dismally for "Marmar" as his angry passions subsided and recollections of his tender bondwoman returned to the captive autocrat.

His "Marmar" tries to yield to her darling, bravely announcing, "He's my child, and I can't have his spirit broken by harshness." But the father insists that the child not be spoiled by indulgence. Father wins out, and assuming that the quieted child is asleep, covers him up. But the child is not asleep, and asks with a penitent hiccough, "Me's dood, now?" The end of the incident finds "Marmar" tenderly watching both husband and son asleep together, the child cuddling "close in the circle of his father's arm and holding his father's finger, as if he felt that justice was tempered with mercy."[20]

Overindulgent mothers and firm but merciful fathers balance one another in the ideal homes Alcott created, but she also identified a thornier problem that surely existed in her own childhood. A good mother might be so wrapped up in maternal duties that she forgot to be a good wife. Such domestic reformers as Bronson and Abba Alcott placed equal emphasis on companionate marriage and parental devotion. Nursemaids, like cooks and housemaids, might free up a matron's time so that she could please her husband with attention to details of dress, housewifery, and culture. Too great a reliance on such "help," however, conflicted with domestic democracy and with perfectionist values.

LOUISA MAY: THE FIRST YEAR

In the summer of 1832 Bronson's observations were interrupted by Abba's second pregnancy, a development which tired and occasionally depressed her. Moreover, their living situation was altered by the death in October of the Alcotts' patron, Reuben Haines. Bronson's subsidy vanished and the Alcott-Russell school was closed. Bronson opened another school in Philadelphia, with Vaux's help, but it lasted less than a term. Still, Bronson found time to observe Anna, and somehow had the leisure to read. Abigail had to endure increasing domestic chores and diminishing income.

In Germantown, at yet another boarding house, their second daughter was born on November 29, 1832. "Abby May inclines to call the babe Louisa May," Bronson wrote Colonel May, "a name to her full of every association connected with amiable benevolence and exalted worth."²¹ It was the name of her deceased sister, Louisa May Greele. Bronson assured his father-in-law that Abba was comfortable and would soon be able to take charge of her domestic and maternal duties. Of her earlier depression and longing for the company of friends, he said nothing, assuring the family that his wife was "formed for domestic sentiment rather than the gaze and heartlessness of what is falsely called society." During her second pregnancy Abba had done most of the housework herself, while at the same time caring for their five small boarders, Bronson's pupils, whose room and board money were necessary to the family income. Abigail found it a "thankless employment to take care of other people's children."²² The whole situation meant that Louisa May Alcott's first few months were considerably less fortunate than Anna's. Even so, Bronson began a new record of Louisa's progress.

Louisa was a sturdier, more assertive infant than Anna. "A fair complexion, dark bright eyes, long dark hair, a high forehead, and altogether a countenance of more than usual intelligence," was one friend's description of this second daughter at two months. She held her own even when Anna showed her jealousy by biting or scratching her little sister. She learned very early to make her needs and dissatisfactions loudly known, whereas Anna had been privileged to have her mother anticipate them. Bronson, who again maintained a scientific detachment, commented on a lack of maternal attention to Anna, who accompanied Bronson to his schoolroom because he could no longer afford a housekeeper. Abigail Alcott interpreted the problem somewhat differently: "Mr. A. aids me in general principles, but nobody can aid me in detail."[23]

Overworked, living in a crowded apartment but still convinced of her obligation to achieve maternal perfection, Abigail blamed herself for the children's suffering. Bronson prescribed a summer vacation, which meant that he left Abigail and the girls with his mother at Spindle Hill while he went to Boston to meet with publishers and seek the means for a new school.

In the fall they returned to another Philadelphia boarding house. In these unsatisfactory, depressing, even monotonous quarters, Bronson found "free uninterrupted thought" almost impossible. The situation was equally oppressive to Abigail, but it was Bronson who in the spring of 1834 took a room of his own across the street from the Philadelphia library in order to read and continue his writing. This solution led to a more intensified and isolated domesticity for Abigail, however. She and the girls moved to a cottage in Germantown. Louisa, less than two years old, had to make do with her mother's distracted care, her sister's resentment, and her father's weekend visits. Bronson was not earning any money and his ascetic furnishings in Philadelphia—a bed, clothes trunk, washstand, two chairs, and books—seemed proof to him of his own self-sacrifice. Dwelling on the hardships of his own childhood and adolescence, he demanded compensations now. "Thrown into the world and left to seek my intellectual pittance for myself, how have I been vainly striving to feed on husks."[24] He congratulated himself on his own "generous heart" and "innate tendency to pure ideality," which had produced a man of high purpose despite deprivations. The thought both pleased and pained him, for he was aware of Abba's burdens and the children's dissatisfactions. "I cling too closely to the ideal to take necessary advantage of the practical and my wife and children suffered from this neglect."[25]

They unquestionably suffered. On May 20, Abba nearly died from a miscarriage, saved only because her landlady quickly summoned a physician to the cottage.[26] This incident probably confirmed Abba's fears about her own health and the survival of the babies. Her eldest sister, Catherine, died at twenty-nine, leaving a small son; her sister Louisa died at the age of thirty-six while Bronson and Abigail were engaged; and a brother, Edward, had died when Abigail herself was scarcely two years old. Samuel May was the third son of her parents to receive that name, the only one to survive infancy. Fever, dysentery, and whooping cough were only a few of the contagious diseases that carried off about 35 percent of the children born to every mother of Abba's generation.[27]

After Abba's recovery the family reunited and moved back to Boston, where Bronson resumed writing his diary on child development. Friends of the Mays and fellow school reformers such as Elizabeth Peabody helped recruit pupils for Alcott's new Temple School. The families of his students included Chief Justice Lemuel Shaw (the father-in-law of Herman Melville), Josiah Phillips Quincy (cousin to John Quincy Adams), and George Emerson. Elizabeth Peabody and her sisters, Sophia (later Mrs. Nathaniel Hawthorne) and Mary (later Mrs. Horace Mann), became part-time teachers and close friends of the Alcotts. Margaret Fuller, the brilliant author of *Women in the 19th Century*, also joined the Temple school's small staff.

Bronson emphasized philosophical studies in this new school. He abandoned his older faith in Lockean ideas, turning instead to such works as Coleridge's *Aids to Reflection*, which synthesized Platonic ideas with Christian precepts. He invented a new motto, "Plato for Thought, Christ for Action," and determined that the "historical" Jesus was no more or less divine than he was himself.[28] Moreover, he interpreted the life of Christ more radically than the religious liberals of his times. For Bronson, Jesus existed as the ideal spirit within each child, and he was determined to commune with that divine spark in his pupils. If children's minds could be turned in-

31

ward, if they could become conscious of their own divine spark of truth, then they might become truly good.

Alcott's conversion from Locke's materialism to Plato's idealism was shared by many supporters of the Temple School; it reflected, if radically so, the paradox of Emersonian individualism. Transcendentalism, the philosophic movement that united Bronson Alcott, Emerson, Elizabeth Peabody, and Margaret Fuller, was both a challenge to the competitive materialist spirit of the Jacksonian age and a reinforcement of its belief in individual enterprise. Locating true virtue within the individual soul, it fostered self-reliance and also made every citizen his own policeman. Transcendentalism provided a new basis for order in an expansionist age by replacing external, community controls with internalized, individual ones. There was, of course, a strain of antinomian heresy in Transcendental assertions that every person possessed a private pipeline to the Universal Will. But Bronson's education of his own children proved that the bonds of affection and emotional dependency could be strengthened to check selfish individualism. His own "model children" were the vanguard of a new generation whom Bronson hoped to educate.

THE TERRIBLE TWOS

Creating the models for citizenship within his own family occupied Bronson intensely. He found Anna at three and a half docile, shy, and fearful. Louisa, he thought, was a dangerously independent infant, too stubborn, assertive, and even rude. Bronson reasserted control, imposing a discipline he thought Abba too gentle to supply.

A strict schedule was set up for the girls, and they were separated to maximize parental supervision and reduce quarrels. Both arose at 6:00 A.M., were dressed and washed by their father, and played until breakfast at 7:00. At 8:00 Louisa was given over to her mother's care, while Anna went to the Temple School with her father. After Louisa's nap, the two girls would lunch with the family and take a walk with Bronson or a servant. Then came playtime in the apartment, a light meal at 6:00, and conversations with their father before a bedtime ritual at 7:30.[29]

Alcott encouraged this firm, structured schedule in her prescriptive stories for children, but she emphasized intimate bedtime chats with mother rather than father. In fact, in *Little Men* Aunt Jo keeps the same kind of careful records and observations of all twelve Plumfield students that her father pioneered. In Alcott's version of the system, however, Jo records the development of each child as a special private interchange between herself and the pupil. She tells one, "I dont show my records to any but the one to whom each belongs. I call this my conscience book: and only you and I will ever know what is to be written."[30]

Bronson's schedules allowed a generous amount of bodily freedom. At evening time the girls would romp unclothed in the privacy of their rooms. They were never restrained from exercise, a conditioning that Alcott continued as an adult. She found rugged walks and even scrubbing floors a means of venting frustrations and soothing her temper. In *Little Men* she depicts weekly pillow fights that release the children's pent-up energies at bedtime. The naughtiest pupils are encouraged to run out their passions or dig and hoe in the school's garden.

As the Alcott sisters grew, Louisa became a dominant and frequently aggressive playmate; Bronson observed how Anna's earlier hostility toward her sister slowly abated. He analyzed the situation, and concluded that at two years Louisa was still the prisoner of instinct, undisciplined, "pursuing her purposes by any means that will lead to her attainment." He suspected that eating meat was part of her problem, and that she had also inherited her mother's volatile temperament. "The will is the predominating power," he believed, in both Louisa and Abba, and it must be "broken" by both physical discipline and spiritual encouragement. Louisa preferred to sit in her mother's lap at the table; Bronson insisted that she stay in her own chair. Refusing to "mind father," she shouted, "No, No," a rather ordinary display of behavior we now associate with the "terrible twos." Bronson spanked her, and repeated the spanking until she sat "on the little chair by the side of her mother."[31] He disliked such discipline because it contradicted his belief in the divinely granted individuality of each human being. But it was necessitated, he thought, by her mother's previous indulgence. Today we might judge Louisa's "No" merely a natural assertion of precisely the individuality her father cherished.

33

PASSIONATE BABY, STUBBORN GIRL

Louisa competed with her sister for nurturance and attention from the moment of birth, and this fact, no less than her parents' genuinely loving encouragement, provoked her initiative and independence. By the age of three she was a frequent visitor to Temple School. She developed a large vocabulary for her age, supplementing her speech with all sorts of pantomine, and she even played the heroines in impromptu family dramas. Both Bronson and Elizabeth Peabody used literature to develop analytic powers in the children at school, and Bronson found that his smallest pupil, Louisa, appreciated "all the relations of expression, using every part of speech."[32]

Bronson read Wordsworth ("Our birth is but a sleep and a forgetting") to Louisa and to his other pupils. He wanted to instill in them, even at so young an age, the ideas he had gleaned from his reading of Wordsworth and Jesus. The children also learned *The Pilgrim's Progress* by diagraming it and acting it out in little plays. Louisa and her sisters acted out Pilgrim's journey at home with Abba's help. The storytelling and the conversations gave the girls great pleasure, confirming Elizabeth Peabody's view that Bronson had a way with children beyond any teacher she knew.[33]

Discipline at school was consistent with that at home: self-examination led to all-important development of self-sacrifice. Since one child's behavior might result in group punishment, the Temple School pupils monitored one another. Peer pressure, as we call it today, frequently checked disobedience. The principle of self-sacrifice was even more intensely instilled at home. When Anna's sprained ankle won her the rocking chair that Louisa coveted, Bronson asked the older girl to give it up to her sister. He reminded her that "very good little girls give up their own wants to the wants of their little sisters, whom they love. Love makes us want to give up our own wants. If you love your little sister, you will give up the chair to her." Anna, almost four years old, insisted that she loved her sister but also wanted to sit in the chair. Finally, Bronson had to reward her with a very material object, an apple, in order to elicit the required sacrifice. When he asked if Anna gave up the chair for love or apple, Anna admitted, "because I wanted the apple . . . and I like sister too."[34]

Apples apparently served both as treat and temptation in the girls' training. Bronson later left an apple on a wardrobe as a temptation to little girls who should not take things without permission. When he left the room, both girls climbed to get it, but Louisa grabbed first and then shared the prize with her sister. Anna confessed first, admitting that her conscience troubled her and would restrain her in the future. Louisa grinned and said, "I wanted it," tardily admitting that she was naughty. The experiment was repeated, and Louisa instructed herself, "No, No, Father's. Me not take Father's apple, Naughty, Naughty." Her own appetite triumphed, however; she ate the apple and then told her mother, "Me could not help it. Me *must* have it."[35]

Years later Alcott recalled a more public demonstration of her education in self-denial. On her fourth birthday, which was also her father's thirty-seventh, a party was held at Temple School. She remembered that she wore a crown of flowers and

> stood upon the tale to dispense cakes to each child as the procession marched past. By some oversight, the cakes fell short, and I saw that if I gave away the last one I should have none. As I was queen of the revel, I felt that I ought to have it and held on to it tightly til my mother said, 'It is always better to give away than to keep the nice things; so I know my Louy will not let the little friend go without.' The little friend received the dear plummy cake, and I a kiss and my first lesson in the sweetness of self denial, a lesson which my dear mother beautifully illustrated all her long and noble life.[36]

Alcott's written reminiscence did not include a recognition that she shared her birthday with her father, or that the party had been chiefly in his honor. What she still felt was sharp regret at publicly having to sacrifice the "dear plummy cake."

She remembered a good deal more from this time, much of which found its way into her fiction in only slightly altered form, including the fact that "running away was one of the chief delights of my early days."[37] On one occasion, she joined some Irish children in the ash heaps and wastelands of Boston, sharing their cold potatoes and salt fish. Together they trooped to the Commons and had a fine time until nightfall brought them back to Bedford Street; then, to Louisa's astonishment, she heard a towncrier announcing the loss of "a little girl, six years old, in a pink frock, white hat and new green shoes." Her parents had sent the crier, and when Louisa arrived home they disciplined her by tying her to a sofa.[38] This method of punishment was one Louisa's mother may have learned from Lydia Maria Child, who recommended it in her advice books. Alcott clearly approved of it in retrospect, and used it to punish her favorite tomboy, Nan Harding, for straying off in *Little Men*.

THE GOSPEL LESSON

At about the time Louisa began discovering the world on her own, Bronson Alcott was encountering diverse difficulties maintaining the Temple School. They led to its collapse in a cloud of heresy and scandal. In the mid-1830s Bronson expanded his conversations with children to include both Sunday School dialogues with adults and Wednesday morning sessions on the New Testament with interested ministers and lay people. These spirited discussions clearly expounded heretical doctrines. Human beings, Alcott argued, were directly in touch with the Divine Spirit—in touch, moreover, without benefit of institutionalized religion. And Christ, whom Bronson always referred to as Jesus, was a perfect man, but possessed of no more immaculate origins than any other man. Influential clergy of less liberal persuasions, including the powerful William Ellery Channing, disapproved of these views, and attendance at the Wednesday morning sessions gradually fell off. The most vociferous protest, however, came over Alcott's publications.

In 1837 he published *Conversations with Children on the Gospels*, a relatively inoffensive discussion of human birth which explained that a mother gives her body up to God, who with her aid "brings forth the Child's Spirit in a little body of its own."[39] It created a furor. Never mind that Sophia Peabody, a notably genteel censor, felt elevated by Bronson's "Conversations." Nor did it matter that Dr. William Alcott, who did not associate himself with heresy of any sort, commended his cousin's work. Dr. Alcott's own *The Physiology of Marriage* delicately presented the issue of sex to readers with the express purpose of restraining sexual passions, which led to ill health and madness.[40]

The controversy raged throughout 1836 in the *Courier*, the *Boston Daily Advertiser*, and the *Christian Register*. Friends rallied to Bronson's defense, and even Judge Lemuel Shaw offered advice to save the school. Most of these friends approved of Bronson's influence upon their children, but urged caution and a less public espousal of unpopular notions. Bronson neither yielded nor concealed his views.

The Panic of 1837 further affected his diminishing enrollments and financial credit. A second depression indicated that it was no time for gentry to entrust their children's education to unpopular critics.

The radical agitation that marked Boston politics reinforced Alcott's image as a dangerous figure. As early as 1829 he joined William Lloyd Garrison and Sam May in organizing the Massachusetts Anti-Slavery Society. Abigail May Alcott was already a charter member of the Massachusetts Female Anti-Slavery Society, as were Lydia Maria Child and Elizabeth Peabody. In 1833 Garrison founded the American Anti-Slavery Society, using his abolitionist newspaper, *The Liberator*, to stir up support. A Boston mob attacked Garrison, and during the ensuing riot Abba Alcott hid Garrison's portrait of George Thompson, the English abolitionist. Afterward she visited and comforted Garrison, "the poor man who had been good to the slaves."[41] In those years, abolitionism, Transcendentalism, communitarianism, and woman's rights seemed all of a piece and equally dangerous to many people.

The withdrawal of pupils forced Bronson to sell his school equipment. Even then he was several thousand dollars in debt. He tried to open a smaller school, then a still smaller one on Beach Street. He had plowed his small profits back into his schools, continually purchasing the newest and best books and equipment. In the final year of his last, tiny school (1839), he accepted a black girl as one of his students. Abba and Sam May, who remembered the heroism of Prudence Crandall in Connecticut, supported him in this action. Yet it served as final proof to his few remaining patrons that Alcott was beyond the limits of good sense and caution. By June only a few children, including Anna, Louisa, and Elizabeth Alcott, along with their black classmate, Susan Robinson, remained as Bronson's students.[42]

The girls' education in self-sacrifice continued in the context of this long cycle of poverty and hard times for the Alcott family. While the recurring business cycles of prosperity and depression certainly contributed to the instability of small experiments like Temple School, it was also clear that Bronson Alcott lacked practical shrewdness. More opportunistic schoolmasters prospered in the expanded public market for education during that period. Bronson's devotion to democratic opportunities for learning, especially the extension of equal schooling for blacks, was cheered by the expanding reformist circle, but it infuriated potential patrons.

Bronson's pedagogy and his parental practices in general were designed to control even while they appeared to liberate the spontaneity of children. Anna, for example, was encouraged in every way to exhibit only what was expected of her, and she fused completely with Bronson's expectations. The confirmation he sought was found in Anna, but it made her deeply dependent upon him. Louisa was less satisfying to her father in many respects, a failure that may have saved her from the conformity that dominated Anna. Bronson's emotional interrogations, however, evoked a self-consciousness that made Louisa feel greedy, selfish, impulsive, jealous, and aggressive.

Alcott's personal "success" notwithstanding, the self-sacrifice and repression driven into her was taught not only by such parents as Bronson, but by society at large. Unselfishness can be explained as a simple Christian virtue, but for women of Alcott's era its meaning was more complex. In mid-nineteenth century New England, women's unpaid work lowered the cost of labor and helped provide emotional and financial "capital" for the "take-off" period of industrial development. To be sure, the cult of domesticity made the home a refuge in a cruel and heartless world, but it also reinforced the notion that women should be family housekeepers for love, not money. Female labor in the home could not be reimbursed because such payment would deplete the capital that went to build canals, railroads, mills, and factories. Furthermore, many thought that a man's individual responsibility promoted optimism and entrepreneurial drive. When the fortunes of the marketplace contracted, however, casting working men out, that proud individualism created feelings of personal worthlessness. A good woman was supposed to help her man bear failures. She should and often did keep the family going by a variety of means—sewing for others, taking in boarders, doing laundry, or earning meager wages that were viewed as "pin money" by employers.[43] Certainly Bronson was less than pragmatic about his entrepreneurial ventures, but Abba suffered the social circumstances attending his personal failures. She could do little after the closing of Temple School to support her family, however. They had borrowed again and again from Colonel May, and relations between Abba and her father were continually strained.

In 1838 Bronson Alcott's misfortunes were exacerbated by family calamity. Abba suffered another miscarriage, and a year later bore a stillborn son. Reform-minded friends came to the Alcotts' aid once again, confirming Louisa's lifelong conviction that her personal relationships were more reliable than any institutions. Among those who helped, none was more important than Ralph Waldo Emerson, who had befriended Bronson during the Temple School days. The two men had first met to discuss publishing one of Bronson's manuscripts, *Psyche: The Breath of Childhood*, a record of Elizabeth Alcott's infancy. Emerson was kind but firm. The manuscript, he believed, was pedantic, mannered, and overblown. Still, he felt that Bronson Alcott "unerringly takes the highest moral ground and commands the other's position, and cannot be outgeneralled." He saw courage and nobility in Bronson's emotional distance from the opinion of others. On March 31, 1840, the Alcott family left Boston for a small house in Concord, about a mile from the Emersons.

THREE

Armies of Reform

It is said to be the age of the first person singular.
Ralph Waldo Emerson, *1827*

One of Louisa May Alcott's biographers observes that the young Louisa never knew anyone who was less than a general in the armies of reform.[1] She grew up in the company of triumphant individualists, some of whom believed in competitive enterprise, while others, like Emerson, proclaimed the natural moral order complete in each individual soul. "Trust thyself," Emerson wrote, "every heart vibrates to that iron string."[2] Louisa's parents believed, along with most of their reformist generation, that Americans stood on the edge of a new Eden even as the spirit of laissez-faire laid waste to the very wilderness that promised them prosperity, liberty, and happiness.

The spiritual equality guaranteed by new beliefs conflicted with a deepening social stratification both in Eastern cities and in the more sparsely settled West. Working men demanded an end to the "aristocracy of talent and place" and a political guarantee of their free enterprise through reforms providing "equal education, equal property and equal privileges." Antislavery advocates challenged slaves' bondage as a barrier to all liberty. The welfare of the blind was championed by Dr. Howe, and the care of the insane by Dorothea Dix. The rights of children were championed by Bronson Alcott himself.[3] The moral equality (some said superiority) of women did not in itself change their subordinate status in society. But Mary Wollstonecraft's *Vindication of the Rights of Women*, which Abba and then Louisa read, resonated to Emerson's "iron string": "If woman be allowed to have an immortal soul, she must have, as the employment of life, an understanding to improve."[4]

Spiritual self-improvement as the means to a perfect society gradually created a terrible contradiction in the Alcotts' family life. Wollstonecraft had quoted Lord Bacon in a passage that defines Bronson's growing conflict with his wife and daughters: "He that hath a wife and children hath given hostages to fortune; for they are impediments to great enterprises, either of virtue or mischief." Private property was the basis of family life for the Alcotts as for most Americans; yet, as the reformers said, the drive to gain property led men to sell their souls.

If private property was the barrier to family harmony and spiritual perfection, perhaps (Bronson was coming to believe) communality was a proper basis for society. In the meantime, the children found much to enjoy in Concord. The Hosmer cottage stood near the Old South Bridge of the town. Only a few open fields separated it from the Concord River where willow and cattails sheltered children and small wildlife; its banks became a playground for the Alcott girls. The house itself was large compared to the rented rooms and cottages of Louisa's earlier years. At seven and a half, she now had the run of a cottage that offered a maze of small rooms available for hide-and-seek and playacting of all sorts. Outside there were barns, sheds, and almost two acres of land on which Bronson planned to cultivate vegetables and fruits.

Behind them eighteen miles away in Boston, were six thousand dollars in debts and memories of failure and despair. In the midst of anxieties over the closing of Temple School, mounting debts and reduced income, Lydia Maria Child became a friend in need. She took care of Abba daily for five weeks after the stillbirth in 1838. In the following autumn forty-year-old Abba became pregnant again, and this time the outcome was a tragedy she continually mourned in later years. A son was born in April 1839; he survived only a few minutes and was buried in the May family vault.[5]

The move to Concord temporarily revived Abba's spirits and physical energies. Bronson repaired the house and barns, plowed and planted a large garden. Anna attended a Concord private school run by Henry and John Thoreau—her father was content with their progressive educational practices—and Elizabeth and Louisa enjoyed an infant school in Emerson's home, taught by Mary Russell. It was a bustling but hopeful time again. Yet the Alcott household allowed little privacy. Contemporary reformers called for the separa-

41

tion of innocents from the marketplace, but Louisa enjoyed no such tranquillity. The years between her sixth and tenth birthdays were precarious and insecure, and she matured beyond the innocent trustfulness encouraged by prescriptive literature.

The children in Alcott's fiction share their families' privations, if any, and even very young boys and girls are conscious of their material and emotional environment. Over many years she came to divide her literary children into three categories: the naive, gentle-hearted dependents of secure homes, often somewhat selfish in their removal from the larger society; the self-sacrificing and self-conscious offspring of fallen gentry; and the tough skeptical urchins who survived in the streets by a premature self-sufficiency. In many ways her parents were the privileged innocents of the Transcendental period, while she herself developed the perspective of an urchin. Her awareness of her family's fragility and the contradictions between self-reliant individualism and woman's dependency made her a very practical little girl. Anxious, responsible, and increasingly self-critical, she felt protective even as a child of the parents who could not protect her or themselves from the insecurities of the larger world.

The move from the center of Boston's commercial disarray to the reform activities in Concord represented far more than a journey of eighteen miles. To appreciate the enormous social distance the Alcotts traveled in Louisa's childhood, we should understand the peculiarly American flowering of Romantic reform that called itself Transcendentalism.[6] The Transcendentalists criticized the dominant materialist ideology, but remained optimistic about human perfectability. They believed that the transformation of human consciousness marked a first step toward creating an earthly paradise. Often less interested in the struggles of democratic politics than in the creation of a social community supporting "instinctive selfhood," they envisaged a free society made up of self-reliant, natural men and women. In a sense the Alcotts saw themselves and their country outside of history and politics, born again into a unique relationship with their environment and each other.

The Transcendentalist Club met for the first time in September 1836 and included such men as George Ripley, Ralph Waldo Emerson, James Freeman Clarke, Orestes Brownson, and Bronson Alcott. With the exception of Alcott all were ministers or former ministers, and graduates of Harvard College. Emerson urged his friend Bronson's admittance to the group on the grounds that he was a "God-made Priest." The group grew to include Cyrus Bartol, Theodore Parker, Jones Ripley, and Margaret Fuller.[7] Although an impressive sampling of what historians have called the "American Renaissance,"[8] it did not encompass the entire spectrum of those concerned with America's "manifest destiny."[9]

UNIVERSAL BEING

Nevertheless, Louisa experienced the full range of the Age of Reform. Her childhood reverberated with conflicts between the social pillars of established order and the various outcasts who struggled to shape a new order. Yet reform and material success were not wholly incompatible. Horace Mann and Sam May for example both prospered, confident that the expansion of business and educational opportunities would benefit workers as well as owners. Bronson Alcott, however, was an outcast. The failure of Temple School put him outside the circle of genteel reformers. The whole family shared Bronson's feelings of despair and alienation. Abba tried to defend him to her father, who had always thought Bronson irresponsible. Why had Alcott failed? Because he refused to "cut his suit to fit the cloth," as Colonel May had advised.

In his own mind, Bronson had no choice but to join those who "came out" of sin to fashion a community to fit their intentions. As Bronson filled his journal with nostalgic evocations of Spindle Hill, he began to imagine an ideal, organic community of simple values. He even planned to become a peddler again, this time distributing ideas instead of Yankee goods. He was not alone in dreaming of a utopian alternative, nor in looking both backward and forward at the same time. One could "come out" from the sins of materialist avarice and join the growing band of universal reformers in such communities as Brook Farm, Hopedale, and Oneida, where one could build an environment conducive to spiritual perfection.

Bronson took heart from his friendship with Ralph Waldo Emerson and set about exploring opportunities to engage "a band of valiant souls gathering for conflict with the hosts of ancient and honor-

43

able errors and sins."[10] After settling on the Hosmer estate, Bronson's friendship with Emerson deepened through prolonged visits and conversations.

Emerson's friendship opened doors to Bronson in nearby Watertown and Newton as well as Concord, where he once again delivered his "Conversations." For her part, Louisa delighted in the friendship of both the Emerson children and their father, whose hospitality included a distinguished library open to the Alcotts. Throughout her life she acknowledged the friendship and influence of Emerson on her life and work.

Indeed, during her childhood, Emerson's esteem and affection for the Alcotts filled an emotional vacuum left by Colonel May's withdrawal. Still a faithful ally of his sister, Sam had strong reservations about Bronson's growing dissociation from liberal institutional reforms. Emerson's social status, however, more than matched that of the lofty Mays and Sewalls. Moreover, Emerson viewed the Alcotts' "family straits" as part of a general affliction visited upon the purest, most enlightened souls of his generation. Their trials were ultimate proof of the corruption infesting an American society that failed to appreciate its noblest hearts.

Like Bronson, Emerson proclaimed a new age in which "a nation of men will for the first time exist, because each believes himself inspired by the Divine Soul which also inspires all men."[11]

Echoing the fervor of the Puritan Jeremiad, Emerson implored Americans to withdraw from corrupt social institutions. In August 1837, he stated that the existing society was such that it alienated man from himself and nature. "The tradesman," he declared, "scarcely ever gives an ideal worth to his work, but is hidden by the routine of his craft, and the soul is subject to dollars."[12]

In "Nature," Emerson expressed the heart of Transcendentalism. "There is a property in the horizon," he asserted, "which no man has, but he whose eye can integrate all the parts, that is, the poet. This is the best part of these men's farms, yet to this their warranty-deeds give not title."[13] The philosopher and the poet were one in experiencing nature as the emblem of the spirit, in seeing natural law as the twin to moral law, divinely given and intuitively felt by all free men.

"Nature always wears the color of the spirit," Emerson said, dis-

carding the older Lockean notion that the material shapes our perceptions. The incandescent spirit within man shines forth and illuminates the world. Indeed, the spirit alone sees and constructs the
world. "I become a transparent Eye Ball. I am nothing. I see all. The
currents of Universal Being circulate through me: I am part or parti-
cle of God."[4]

In both Europe and America this kind of antinomian belief inspired a transformation of literature and art. Nature became an emblem of the spirit and the human viewer a creative artist through his
perception alone. Wordsworth and Coleridge exemplified the Romantic revolution in England, and they inspired Hawthorne, Whitman, Thoreau, and Emerson. A whole reform generation matured at
the feet of these Romantics, among them Bronson and Abba Alcott.
Louisa Alcott also drew on this legacy, as did many women who saw
a progressive potential in romanticism. They believed that women
no less than men shaped the world about them through their perception of it. Like the Christian perfectionists and evangelicals they
resembled, Romantic idealists cherished each human being's original, unmediated relationship to the universe.

Louisa May Alcott explored these views in her life and in her
fiction. Though a girl, she imagined herself to be the son in
her family. Her temper and her active body made her feel alien to
the gentle, submissive character her father and even the most radical
male reformers thought natural for little girls. At eight she wrote her
first poem, "The Robin," and her mother was convinced that she
would "grow up a Shakespeare."[5] Poems, impromptu plays with
her sisters, and storytelling became acceptable outlets for her independent fantasies. In these she could be anybody, an adventurous
boy or a daring, romantic heroine. Her mother's warm encouragement, however, was balanced by her father's constant admonitions.
Both parents left notes on the children's pillows. In one, Bronson
gave Louisa two pictures, one of a child playing the harp and the
second of an arrow. He wrote, "Two passions strong divide our
life—meek, gentle love, or boisterous strife." Below the harp he
printed, "Love, Music, Concord," and beneath the arrow, "Anger,
Sorrow, Discord." Years later Alcott wrote above his note, "Louisa
began early, it seems, to wrestle with her conscience."[6] Bronson's
prescribed struggles for self-effacement were matched by her own

45

stubborn demand for experience in the world. She accepted Emerson's essays as if their titles were signposts on a woman's pilgrimage; later she preached the importance of friendship as a preface to love in the lives of women, thereby integrating the best Romantic dicta with woman's rights.

To Bronson Alcott and his friends, then, Emerson's essays seemed to light a path to a better world. But unlike Emerson, who had wealth at his disposal, Alcott suffered from poverty that prevented him from pursuing his utopian dreams. He hired out as a day laborer, mowing fields and chopping wood for his neighbors at one dollar a day. He found some employment in his precious "Conversations"; there was more demand for them as the Lyceum movement swept the nation. More successful lecturers, like Emerson, were booked into towns, cities, and villages to provide cultural stimulation for a nation hungry for specifically American genius. Growing more leery of any commercialization of his efforts, however, Bronson charged no fixed fees, depending instead upon the generosity of his hosts and their guests. He might give two or three talks in series on "Self Culture" or "Human Life," walking to his sponsors' homes and relying upon their hospitality if the distance required an overnight stay. There might be twenty or thirty persons, old New England citizens, of cultivated minds interested in hearing this prophet of "newness."[17]

The difference between reformers who confronted political and religious institutions directly and those who withdrew from society to seek personal salvation were great. But both groups often shared general principles and goals. For example, Garrison communicated with John Humphrey Noyes, the founder of the Christian perfectionist community at Oneida; the two agreed in their criticism of the relationship between private property and the state. Both men, along with Bronson and his closest friends, increasingly saw slavery as the incarnation of sinful private property which they viewed as the most important obstacle to achieving Christian perfection in America.

Emerson and Alcott were supportive of George Ripley, who lost the pulpit of Boston's Purchase Street Church in 1841 by declaring that the "purpose of Christianity is to redeem society, as well as the individual."[18] Bronson sat in Emerson's house and listened to Ripley's plans for a new society. The result was Brook Farm, and the new model community was soon joined by Margaret Fuller and Nathaniel Hawthorne. The Alcotts were invited to participate, but the group was not spiritually minded enough to suit Bronson. The Brook Farm members were to receive ten cents an hour for their work, physical and mental; also, they ate meat and sold their produce for butter and other animal products.[19] As Bronson attended more discussions about intentional communities, his particular needs assumed specific dimensions. There must be no money involved in the community's sustenance, no meat, no stimulants of any kind, and the spiritual enlightenment of members must be paramount. Bronson could not subsume his personality, or what he saw as his unique principles, to Brook Farm's leadership.

He agreed with Emerson that the ways of trade had become theft, and commerce so abused that it was unfit for any man's livelihood. The cotton worn by New Englanders was drenched in the blood of slaves; one man in ten died every year in Cuba so that Americans might have their sugar. As long as some men lacked property, Emerson thundered, the title of those who owned their own land was tainted. Emerson's solution was an end to the division of labor. Only when men refused to engage in trade and rejected wages could social institutions be reformed and all men be "equally restored to selecting the fittest employment of their individual talents."[20]

Bronson, Abba, and their daughters were moving farther from the moderate stance taken by Colonel May. Partly to effect a reconciliation, Louisa was sent to visit her grandfather in Boston. Her father soon forwarded her a short note with a sketch of the Hosmer cottage and an admonition to "step lightly and speak softly about the house. Grandpa loves quiet, as well as your sober father and other grown people."[21] If the Colonel was impressed by a quiet granddaughter, her behavior did not compensate for the reports he heard of her father's activities. Joseph May was an antislavery man, and his son was a passionate spokesman for the abolitionist cause, but Bronson's friends were now disrupting public order with their demonstrations, and they were increasingly met with violent opposition.

The political situation was growing more heated. Some of the Alcotts' friends set up small alternative stores where customers could be sure of purchasing goods made only by free labor. William Lloyd Garrison was refused a platform in every Boston church when he preached not only boycotts of slave-produced goods, but civil disobedience to prevent the return of fugitive slaves. After an angry mob threatened Garrison, he was put in the Leverett Street Jail, ostensibly for his own safety. Bronson was his first visitor, and he also went regularly to the office of Garrison's paper, *The Liberator*. In those pages Garrison had declared, "I am in earnest, I will not equivocate; I will not excuse; I will not retreat a single inch, and I will be heard."[22]

While Garrison agitated and courted imprisonment, and Emerson preached and wrote, Bronson Alcott seemed determined to live the ideals he shared with his friends. He neither owned land nor engaged in trade, and by January 1841 the Alcotts' financial situation was hopeless. The Temple School creditors were still unpaid, and by now the family owed money to Concord tradesmen as well.

In February Colonel Joseph May died, attended by Sam and his only surviving daughter, Abba. Colonel May left a total of $17,627 by the executors' first reckoning, and a substantial amount of household goods.[23] He divided his money in equal shares, not only to Abba and to her two surviving brothers, Sam and Charles, but also to his adopted daughter, Louisa Caroline Greenwood, and to his dead daughters' surviving children in trust with their legal guardians.

The residual legacies finally amounted to only $1,150 each, scarcely enough to meet the Alcotts' debts in any event. And Colonel May had treated Abba, in her view, like her orphaned, dependent nephews and nieces, who were unable to administer their own affairs. Certainly the Colonel was tough-minded and specific in his will, giving "to my daughter Mrs. Abigail Alcott, one hundred dollars and her share of the estate." Sam received one hundred dollars, all his father's books, and his "wardrobe," and Louisa Caroline Greenwood was given one hundred dollars, the Colonel's gold watch, and his "pew no. 20 in King's Chapel." On the face of it this seemed fair, but Abba was crushed by a further restriction he placed upon her share of the cash monies. "I direct that the share of my daughter Abigail, " he declared, "as well as the hundred dollars before given to her be secured by my executors to her sole and separate use, without the control of her husband or liability for his debts in such manner as they judge best."

48

LOVE AND PROPERTY

The inventory of Joseph May's estate revealed that Bronson owed his father-in-law $1,729. Joseph May had kept careful track of the money he lent his children, and entered the sums (with interest) in his books along with business credits and debts. But he forgave his son, Charles May, "all whatever sums of money which may be found charged against him in my books, amounting to more than two thousand dollars besides interests." And he also left him, in addition to his share in the residual estate, "fifty dollars and also my silver watch." Bronson's debts were not forgiven. When the will went into Probate Court, the executors "prayed Allowance" for certain charges made against the estate, including a payment to William Minot for the costs of defending suit against Amos Bronson Alcott for $2,400, April 29, 1841. Another $75 went to W. Minot "for defence of suit of blank assignee of A. B. Alcott vs. Executors."[24]

In the fall of 1841 the final accounting by the executors still listed $1,729.02 due from Bronson Alcott to his father-in-law's estate. By the time the will was out of probate, all debts having been collected and proper disbursements made to those with claims upon Colonel May's property, there was about $15,000 left. No record indicates that Bronson ever paid off his debt. But Bronson's creditors sued May's estate, and the legal fees for defending the properties had to be subtracted from the residue, paid by heirs.[25] It was just as the prudent Colonel May had feared.

Certainly Abigail's father had given ample warning to Bronson of his concern for his daughter's financial security. In 1834 he had written to her expressing his concern, and bluntly stated her indebtedness:

You have made several mistakes since you began to manage for yourself, and without or against the advice of your friends—marrying without possessing the needful to keep a house—and without having tried the success of your Friend's pursuits to obtain a support—changing your places of residence—removing to Germantown—furnishing a large house there to accommodate boarding scholars—selling your furniture at auction—removing to

49

Philadelphia—all which have consumed four and a half years of the best part of your life—nearly all your property—and left you burdened with a debt of $1,000 or more.[26]

Abba replied that her husband was not a "spendthrift" and that neither of them was self-indulgent. She ended with a blow to the family status: "Would you have me take in washing?" she asked. By the time her father made his will, his lack of faith in her had indeed forced Abba to dismiss her laundress and take in sewing, if not washing.

The careful terms of Colonel May's will in fact reflected Abba's social and legal status as a married woman in 1841. Before the reformed married women's property act was passed in Massachusetts in 1845, a wife's inheritance from a benefactor, as well as her wages and any property not guaranteed to her use by a premarital agreement or trusteeship, belonged to her husband. She was not a legal person in her own right; her husband had legal right to her body, her property, even the custody of her children should she seek a separation or divorce. As a Suffolk County trustee of poor widows and orphans, Colonel May knew their fate well. He was determined to protect his bequest to his daughter from Bronson's creditors, Bronson's idealism, and from Abba herself. She did not appreciate his stewardship. "I had supposed," she wrote with some sadness, "that time was mellowing his severe judgment of my motives, and that my husband and children were becoming objects of care and regard to him . . . he did not love me."[28]

The predicament of a nineteenth-century married woman who could not shape the laws of the democratic society that governed her, nor use her resources in a way that suited herself, was doubly tragic. Obliged by honor, and in her case with ties of love, to follow her husband's fortunes, Abba was also "protected" from lifting the financial burdens she legally shared. Louisa May Alcott did not overlook the pressing grievances endured by married women. Nor did other women, who campaigned successfully in state after state to reform the property laws governing the rights of married women. It was a radical reform enlisting many conservative men who opposed granting wider political rights to women. Elizabeth Cady Stanton, however, claimed that legislative victories for married womens' property rights really reflected the needs of middle-class businessmen who sought to secure portions of their property from creditors (like Bronson's) by passing property over to their wives for safekeeping.[29] In any case, the redress of this particular inequality came too late to help the Alcotts, though they participated in the petition drive for legislative reform.

The year of 1841 passed leaving their debts unsettled and the inheritance still entangled in inventories, property management, and sales. In the following winter, Bronson's despair and stalemated efforts to earn a living by itinerant "Conversations" frightened Abba enough to write her brother that she feared for her husband's sanity. "If his body don't fail his mind will—he experiences at time the most dreadful nervous excitation—his mind distorting every act however simple into the most complicated and adverse form—I am terror-stricken at this."[30] There was other bad news. Emerson's son, Waldo, died early in 1842. One of the Alcott girls, inquiring after her playmate, brought the news home to Abba.

Emerson bore his pain stoically, however, and two weeks after his own tragedy he offered such a generous gift to Bronson that it promised to transform his future. Emerson would raise the money for Bronson's passage to England, where Alcott at least might be cheered and restored to health by congenial society. Bronson had a small reputation in England and even some friends, including an English disciple of Pestalozzi named James Pierrepont Greaves, who had corresponded with Alcott. Harriet Martineau had also taken news of Bronson's Temple School to England, though she had serious reservations about the romanticization of childhood. Alcott had forwarded signed copies of *Conversations with Children on the Gospels* and *Record of a School* to Greaves. By 1842, in company with the like-minded reformers Henry Wright and Charles Lane, Greaves established a communitarian experiment at Ham Common near Richmond, England. They named it Alcott House and invited their American preceptor to visit and even preside over the experiment.[31]

After persuading his brother Junius to take "my place in the family during my absence," Alcott sailed for England on May 8, 1842, with ten sovereigns and a bill of exchange for twenty pounds in his pocket, courtesy of Emerson's fund-raising efforts. Although mildly worried about Bronson's journey alone, Abba accepted it without complaint. She wrote Sam that marital affections were still warm, but that "our diversity of opinion has at times led us far and wide of a quiet and contented frame of mind—I have been looking for rest—he for principle and salvation—I have been striving for justice and peace—he for truth and righteousness."[32]

Cottage life during the months of Bronson's English visit was peaceful, if impoverished. The executors released small sums for Abba's subsistence, Emerson was quietly generous as usual, and the reduced family managed with visits from friends who rarely came without contributions of food, clothing, or tiny comforts for all. Abba and the girls sent warm, affectionate messages of local news to Bronson, intermixed with reassurances of their own fidelity and longing for him. It was an interlude of harmony and self-sufficiency for the female family, although Louisa felt the burdens keenly. Her lifetime of service in behalf of Marmee and her sisters begins at this period.

On Louisa's tenth birthday Abba gave her a pencil case accompanied by a tender note. She had observed that Louisa was "fond of writing" and wished to encourage the habit. A year later Louisa received a picture of a mother and daughter with the words, "I imagined that you might be just such an industrious daughter and I such a feeble but loving mother, looking to your labor for my daily bread." Louisa was not yet eleven years old, but she put the picture in her journal and wrote a poem to her mother under it:

To Mother

I hope that soon, dear mother,
  You and I may be
In the quiet room my fancy
  Has so often made for thee,

The pleasant, sunny chamber,
  The cushioned easy-chair,
The book laid for your reading,
  The vase of flowers fair;

The desk beside the window
  Where the sun shines warm and bright

And there in ease and quiet
The promised book you write;

While I sit close beside you,
Content at last to see
That you can rest, dear mother,
And I can cherish thee.[33]

Meanwhile, Bronson was enjoying a stimulating trip. He went to the Anti-Corn Law Conference at Westminster, where he heard fiery denunciations of the burdens of taxation, low wages, and disenfranchisement. He predicted an imminent revolution in England to his correspondents at home. He tried to tell George Thompson, the abolitionist and radical political reformer whose portrait Abba had saved, that "it was not bread or wages . . . but property, gain and the list of gain—these are parents of the ills they suffer." "Thompson," according to Alcott, was "too busy to hear, and the people too hungry to believe."[34] Nor would Robert Owen hear Alcott's arguments, especially his Transcendental message of individual withdrawal, self-denial, and purification. Owen, like Thompson, was appealing to Parliament in behalf of reform legislation that would shape a new response to English working people's demands. Bronson concluded that the Transcendental Club was wiser by far than these English radicals, who welcomed him as an American reformer and a bearer of Garrison's letter of introduction, but rejected his favorite philosophical formulas. Even Carlyle, Emerson's preeminent man of genius, seemed uncongenial to Bronson. The two found each other impossible after Bronson, invited to breakfast, innocently mixed the strawberries and potatoes on his plate until the juices ran together.[35] Carlyle was convinced that Alcott was eccentric beyond hope.

But Bronson did find sympathetic souls, especially Charles Lane and Henry Wright, men who would play a great and troubling role in Alcott's life. Greaves had died suddenly, just before Bronson's visit, but his library and his principles were intact at Alcott House in the care of Lane and Wright. The "friends of human progress" met there, some twenty of them, to hear Alcott and his two new comrades argue that the laws of man, which "inculcate and command slaughter," were not to be obeyed. They propounded "no government" theories, and proposed a New Eden in New England, where temptations might be avoided. For his part, Bronson exhorted his listeners to adopt Emersonian "politics." Quoting the Concord Sage, he declared that "character is the true theocracy," and that natural law must be based on the simple ground of man's innately moral nature. Flushed with a new excitement, Bronson appeared to his audience as a man capable of transforming Emerson's abstract principles into concrete reality.

In the autumn of 1842 Charles Lane, his son William, and Henry G. Wright returned with Bronson to Concord, where they intended to "plant Paradise." They brought with them Greaves's library of 1,000 books as well as several hundred additional volumes on philosophy, mysticism, vegetarianism, health reforms, and astrology which they purchased with cash gifts from English admirers. Lane had $1,888, savings accrued from his former career in business as the editor of the *London Mercantile Price Current*.[36]

Abba and the girls were delighted to have Bronson home and they welcomed his new friends. Walking together after their arrival, Louisa asked Abba, "Mother why am I so happy?" to which her mother replied, "Kind friends, Dear Husband."[37] The model family was reunited and enlarged with Bronson's friends. They were happily unaware that their pleasure would be shortlived, for Bronson brought back from England a set of utopian ideas that would throw his domestic life into turmoil. His English experiences made him suspect that his miseries were largely due to the contradictions inherent in a family's simultaneous pursuit of spiritual perfection and genteel domesticity. It was not the first time he had considered this problem, but he had always cast aside his doubts and tried harder to combine the two goals. His English friends led him to question anew the meaning of "husband," "father," and "friend." A New Eden must have an innocent family life, they argued, one that removed "selfish" maternal and paternal obstacles to perfect union. To transcend those obstacles, Bronson might have to construct an association free of special, biological bonds.

Ralph Waldo Emerson would never have gone this far. In his introductory lecture on "The Times," he warmed against those "perfectionists and come-outers," who possessed only a portion of the truth and who proposed utopian social improvements that would violate the sanctity of private life.[38] In a sense, Emerson was describing Alcott, a man he valued as a companion, but whom he also found intellectually unreliable and narrow. "He is not careful to understand you," Emerson said of the "reformer." "If he gets half a meaning that serves his purpose, it is enough. He hardly needs an antagonist, he needs only an intelligent ear." Emerson did not know it, but Bronson had found willing ears and allies in Charles Lane and Henry Wright.[39] Abba Alcott innocently confided her bewilderment about Bronson's new reformist friends to her diary. Newly aware of her own abilities to manage the household and maintain a peaceful nursery, she wrote,

What a union of these dear English friends will effect, is an interesting problem now before us to solve—can Mr. Wright do what this dear Father can do? At present the children are doing very well furnished with few simple and harmless materials, they manufacture their own employment and recreation, and seem to derive more satisfaction and pleasure, than they have ever done by suggestion.[40]

FOUR

Transcendental Wild Oats

Give me one day of practical philosophy.
It is worth a century of speculation.
                    Abigail May Alcott, Journals, *1842*

Daily rehearsal for the New Eden began at Hosmer cottage in the
fall of 1842. The household's diet grew still more spartan: breakfast
plates became unnecessary as each resident put a portion of cottage
bread, apples, and potatoes on a napkin, washing the food down
with a mug of water. Presumably the absence of plates meant less
work for the women, although Abba and her daughters continued to
do the general cleaning, laundry, and sewing for the household.[1]
The sexual division of labor, in fact, became more rigid, as did the
educational regime established for the children.

At the heart of these changes was Charles Lane, benign but unre-
lenting. He helped carve out the sphere of public activity as the
proper domain for men's work. While the women worked at home,
Lane, Bronson, and Wright visited other New England radicals and
wrote articles for *The Dial*, *The Liberator*, and various other reform
periodicals. The men, not the women, cast about for a new location
for their experiment.

The children were involved in the "newness" not only through
their curtailed diet, but also because parental authority was now
shared equally with Charles Lane, who undermined the authority
Abba exercised in her own sphere. He became the children's primary teacher in morning and afternoon lessons; diary keeping, spell-
ing, conversations, grammar, and arithmetic followed the old Temple School model with even stricter emphasis on self-criticism. After
lunch there were more lessons with Lane in geography, drawing,
geometry, French, and Latin. It was only after four o'clock that the
children were turned out to sew with Abba or play. Then came a

frugal supper, similar to breakfast, followed by spiritually uplifting conversations with all the residents. The entire household was asleep by nine.[2]

The Alcotts sought to transcend the problems of the larger society by intentionally shaping a community where relationships could be uncontaminated, spiritually committed, and free from selfish power struggles. Yet an enormous power struggle ensued within the new household itself. For the first ten years of her life, Louisa's father had been the undisputed "head of the house." His right to exercise that role remained unquestioned so long as Abba and her daughters felt themselves part of a natural domestic order. Certainly there was volatile conflict in the household; Abba's complaints were common knowledge, but they centered around financial difficulties and loss of status. Believing her marriage to be ideal, Abba attributed her privations to external forces buffeting the family. The business world was both unprincipled and unpredictable, which meant that doing good and doing well were often contradictory. Perhaps Bronson was too good for that world. On the other hand, she knew that her brother Sam and others who practiced what they preached were able to support their families.

Bronson's decision to challenge the traditional structure of the conjugal family put great pressure on Abba, pressure she was ill equipped to handle and less disposed to accept. Poverty, diminished social status, even the disapproval of her father and stepmother, were hard enough to bear. This revolution in family life, however, Abba found intolerable. Lane and her husband had struck at her influence in the home, which according to contemporary norms provided compensation for the exclusion of women from public decision making. Louisa understood her mother's unhappiness at the loss of her domestic influence, and she supported Abba's search for power within the consociate family.

Bronson had invaded the female domains of nursery and kitchen many times before, but his assaults had been sporadic. This time he and Lane proposed to dissolve the privileged bonds joining a married couple and their children, and to forge a larger union of perfect love with no privileged, special relations. Any number of like-minded people might join, and all, according to Lane, would have to adjust their habits to the new "industrious order." Lane perceived that Abba was not adjusting well, however. He wrote to a friend, "Her pride is not yet eradicated and her peculiar maternal love blinds her to all else."[3]

Abba had welcomed friends and kin into her home before. Elizabeth Peabody boarded with the Alcotts in the Temple School period, and William Alcott and his wife had shared the Alcott home at Cottage Place in the last months of Temple School and helped meet the rent. But on each occasion Abba viewed herself as a generous matron, extending temporary hospitality to help others and make ends meet. This time, worn out and oppressed by the new changes, she fled Hosmer cottage on Christmas Eve of 1842. "Circumstances," she wrote in her journal,

> most cruelly drive me from the enjoyment of my domestic life. I am prone to indulge in occasional hilarity but I seem frowned down into stiff quiet and peace-less order. I am almost suffocated in this atmosphere of restriction and form . . . a desire to stop short and rest, recognizing no care by myself seems to be my duty.
>
> I hope the experiment will not bereave me of my mind. The enduring powers of the body have been well tried. The mind yields, falters and falls. . . . They all seem most stupidly obtuse on the causes of this occasional protraction of my judgment and faculties. I hope the solution of the problem will not be revealed to them too late for my recovery or their atonement of this invasion of my rights as a woman and a mother. Give me one day of practical philosophy. It is worth a century of speculation.[4]

Like many other women of her day, Abba accepted the sexual division of labor. Her voluntary assumption of the burden of domestic work and responsibility, she felt, should command man's respect for woman's rights in her own sphere. Thus she was willing to be her own mistress and maid, but would not be maid to Master Lane. Nor could she accept a token equality as one among others to be consulted by Lane and Bronson on domestic arrangements. To Abba, democratic domestic management meant that household workers controlled household affairs; she and her daughters were the principal domestic workers.

Unsure of a way to deal with this usurpation of power, Abba fled to her May and Sewall relations, and took Louisa and William Lane along to enjoy a traditional Boston Christmas of good food, social visits, church services, and even a public lighting of the Christmas tree at Amory Hall. She came back to Concord soothed and refreshed, but hardly more amenable. Again, Lane tried to convert her with a vision of the exalted and expanded domestic role she might enjoy as mother of all humanity. He referred to himself as "thy brother, Charles," and said that he had not overlooked her "excellences." Her approval of "any important step was highly desirable." He offered her the opportunity to be a "warming, shining light . . . in which you may rise above all annoyances and crosses whatever, and shed a benign lustre on husband, children, friends, and the world."[5] Some writers have concluded that Abba was briefly pacified, but there is substantial evidence to the contrary. Indeed, there is evidence that each member of the new consociate family viewed this utopian experiment differently; each hoped to realize very individual, disparate goals in the venture.

CONFUSION OF HOPES

Deep but hidden differences about sexual mores and property rights surfaced almost immediately. Henry Wright deserted the consociates. He had married in England and fathered a child (not in that order) without the approval of his celibate brethren. Having left his wife at home, he fell in love in the New World with Mary Sargeant Gove, who, after eleven years with a brutal husband, had run away with her young daughter. Their brief love affair ended sadly when Wright died in Mary Gove's arms, penniless and outcast. She eventually remarried another reformer and published her recollections of the consociates as part of her novel, *Mary Lyndon*.[6] In this work, both Alcott and Lane are charged with abandoning Wright. Lane, moreover, is depicted as cheating Wright out of his share of a valuable cargo of English books. Whatever the true circumstances,

Wright's sexual behavior obviously lay outside the limits of the consociates' admittedly confused sexual plans. Scholars disagree, in fact, on whether the Alcott House group in England was celibate, homosexual, or merely intent on regulating and controlling sexuality in the same intense way they organized their social lives. Certainly the Alcott House and Fruitlands had distinctive, even eccentric practices, but their emphasis on socially controlled and proscribed sexual relations, subject to spiritual justification, is typical of many intentional communities in the 1840–1870 period.

The defection of Wright unsettled everyone, distracting them from the necessity of finding a permanent place for their community. Emerson noted that Bronson had a genuine revulsion for hiring out his labor, and an equally sincere belief that beautiful, rich farmland "should be purchased and given" to him. Emerson refused to raise the money for Bronson's one-hundred-acre farm, but there were other potential benefactors. Isaac Hecker, partner with his brothers in a New York grain mill and bakery, was living at Brook Farm. Like many other communitarians, he visited various settlements, weighed and compared their merits, and even lived in several communities. Bronson invited Hecker to join the consociates and in a letter outlined rather abstract plans for the proposed venture. Hecker was too cautious to invest his money in such an indeterminate scheme, but he did live with the group once the "free use of a spot of land" was obtained. Later he recalled that Alcott received him at Fruitlands "very kindly but from mixed and selfish motives, I suspect he wanted me because he thought I would bring money to the community. Lane was entirely unselfish."[7]

Charles Lane's unselfishness was genuine in that he welcomed like-minded communitarians regardless of their ability to invest money. Confident of his own capacity to earn a living, he did not feel a need for wealthy benefactors. In fact, he believed that abundant and relatively cheap American land removed the major material obstacle to living out perfectionist ideals. Furthermore, there is no evidence that he ever shared Bronson's confusion about dependency and spirituality. It was never clear, for instance, whether Bronson was unable to make money or simply refused to do so (perhaps feeling that charity bestowed by more worldly friends was evidence of his own saintliness). But if Lane was comfortable about sharing his capital, he was also possessive of Bronson's friendship, at least from Abba Alcott's point of view. Nor, as mentioned before, did he accept the priority of a married couple's bonds.

Bronson never grasped the deep conflict between Abba's priorities and Lane's dogmatic vision. Odell Shepard comes closest to explaining why. He observes that Bronson did not like England because "he did not see it."[8] The landscape was of no interest to him; consequently he failed to realize what underlay English reformist demands: a large population long since thrown off the land, a rigid class system, and virtually no possibilities for small freeholds. While Bronson could not earn money to buy land for either his own family or a consociate community, Lane saw earning the necessary capital as an ignoble means to a noble end; he impatiently took up the burden of financing their venture. "I do not see," he said, "any one to act the money part but myself."[9] He wrote to Junius Alcott, as part of his new family, and asked his advice. "I hope the little cash I have collected will suffice to redeem a small spot of the planet. . . . Please put your best worldly thought to the subject and favor me with your view as to how and where we could best lay out $1,800 or $2,000 in land, with orchard, wood and house."[10] Lane was bent on escaping the historical burdens of old England in New England.

Emerson suggested they locate at The Cliffs, near Walden Pond. Alcott was receptive, but Lane "came home first" bringing news of a farm at Harvard, fourteen miles from Concord. The next morning Lane and Bronson walked there, talked with the owner, Wyman, and viewed the "90 acres, 14 of them wood, a few apple and other fruit trees, plenty of nuts and berries, much of the land very good, the highest part very sublime. The house and barn were very poor, but the water excellent and plentiful." Wyman wanted $2,700, but agreed to sell the land for $1,800 and to lease the buildings rent free for a year. They had found Fruitlands.

AN AMERICAN KITCHEN GARDEN

In forming "basis for something really progressive, call it family or community or what you will," Lane was not only sowing "Transcendental Wild Oats," but hungrily planning an English kitchen garden in the wilderness. This garden had "90 acres much of it first rate; some worth 100 dollars per acre, the whole 20 dollars per acre; would that some of the English half starved were on it."[11] As he wrote an English friend, "This I think you will admit, looks like an attempt at something which will entitle transcendentalism to some respect for its practicality."[12]

Sam May was also involved in financing Fruitlands, although in a somewhat confused fashion that augured badly for the future. He and Abba apparently shared one view of the May contribution toward ownership and property rights, Lane quite another, while Bronson felt himself above such petty issues. To Bronson, Fruitlands was "universally owned," but he could not leave Concord without paying his family's debts. Lane wryly noted, "I need not tell you on whom that falls."[13] He paid the debts, leaving himself five hundred dollar poorer. Bronson, however, also asked Sam May to sign a promisory note for three hundred dollars needed to complete the purchase price of the farm. This sum was payable to Wyman's agent over two years in biannual installments of seventy-five dollars each, the first payment due in November of 1843.[14]

The confusion over who was responsible for those payments is further indication of the serious disagreements among the settlers. Abba saw Lane's payment of the Alcotts' Concord debts as reimbursement for her housekeeping chores. In other words, she saw her family as conventional householders who had taken Lane in as a paying boarder. Lane's understanding was that Sam May was lending money from the May estate to reimburse him for settling Bronson's debts. Hence it seemed proper that May money would go toward the November payment for a communal homestead. Sam's version indicates some contradictions in his own views of communitarian versus conventional family life:

> When Mr. Lane purchased the farm in Harvard, without consulting me, he had the Deed made to me as his agent, and came to me with it, ready to be delivered into my hands, so soon as I would sign with him a joint promissory note to Mr. Wyman for three hundred dollars. After some hesitancy, I consented to sign the note, and to accept the trust. I did this hoping, as I told him, by doing so to secure to my sister a house for herself and family.[15]

If Sam May really assumed he was merely acting as his sister's trustee in the purchase of her home, one wonders why he took up a similar trusteeship on November 1, 1843, for a communal experiment in Skaneateles, New York. Along with seven other individuals, he agreed to hold that property deed ("to be enjoyed in common henceforth and forever") for seventeen residents and nineteen others who would work the land. His signature generously guaranteed conveyance to "all other persons upon the globe who might wish to join." These signatories also agreed that exclusive and individual property holding was wrong, that governments based on force were destructive, and that "all buying and selling is wrong."[16]

Such an avowal put May in close agreement with Charles Lane, who said about the Fruitlands deed: "Let my privation be ever so great, I will never make any property claim on this effort. It is an offering to the Eternal Spirit, and I consider that I have not more right than any other person; and I have arranged the title deeds, as well as I could to meet that end."[17] Lane was clear in his mind on the issue of property, but May remained uncertainly committed to both entrepreneurship and Christian socialism. He was for "newness."

In any case, with the help of Sam May, Bronson and Lane finally had their property. In early June they arrived at Fruitlands to greet their new recruits; they settled on the floor for the night, "having no time to put up bedsteads."[18] Within a short time newcomers joined the group, including two from Brook Farm: Samuel Larned, aged twenty, described by Lane as "a counting house man and . . . what the world calls genteel,"[19] and Isaac Hecker. The others included Abraham Everett, known as the "Plain Man," a forty-two-year-old cooper whose "rather deep experience" entailed being shut up in an insane asylum by some relatives who hoped to get his money. Wood Abram (or, as he was originally called, Abram Wood) was a friend of Thoreau's and led the children on nature walks. Samuel Bower, a nudist, came from Alcott House in England. Besides Bronson, only one member of the group, Joseph Palmer, possessed any real knowledge of farming. He was known as the "man with the beard," or the "Old Jew," as a full beard such as his was unusual in those parts before the Civil War.[20] Heckled, persecuted, even fined and imprisoned when he refused to shave, Palmer stuck to his principles. He was an abolitionist, a temperance man, and fully subscribed to

63

Fruitland's goals. Yet he never accepted its impractical agricultural notions. Although hired laborers and beasts of burden were outlawed as being inharmonious with natural freedom, Joseph Palmer brought his plow and team to supplement the spade work. He never actually lived at Fruitlands during the consociate experience, but he had property nearby and was a daily source of support.

Finally, there was one venturesome woman, Ann Page, who arrived from Providence, Rhode Island. She shared in the domestic chores and child care as her contribution to spiritual perfectionism. A spinster of about forty years, she left after a stormy scene with Abba, the specifics of which were never made clear.[21]

The June migration to Fruitlands began a golden summer. The consociates' simple crop of vegetables and grains flourished while Anna conducted school for her sisters and William Lane. They sang, did their sums, wrote in diaries, walked, and played in the woods. Their diary entries that summer make Fruitlands seem simply another family home, one delightfully situated in the country.

The older girls helped their mother bake, cook, sew, and wash dishes, while the men "planted corn, and cut wood, and fixed round about the house out of doors."[22] Less isolated from friends and playmates for the children than the lack of a public road might have indicated, Abba at first had outside help with the laundry and sewing. Anna recorded that she and Louisa walked home with a "Mrs. Willard," who came to help their mother with the washing and took home some sewing for the Alcotts. The sisters visited with Mrs. Willard's daughter and were invited to come again.

Even lessons, when they centered on simple reading, writing, arithmetic, or singing, were pleasant. Anna did "some sums with fractions with Mr. Lane" and seemed more self-confident than usual. "I think," she said happily, "I have learned more lately than I ever did before. I think I understand what I learn too." She also wrote out a French fable in "very good French."[23] By September, however, a slight chill fell on Anna's faithful journals. Shutting out the "ugly" things, arming herself with books, placating dissenters in the community with small gifts of flowers and with her own poems, Anna tried to make everything appear "beautiful." "Beautiful is my favorite word," she said. "If I like anything I always say it is beautiful. It is a beautiful word. I can't tell the color of it, . . . I wrote down all the beautiful names we could think of, and in the evening wrote the colors of them."²⁴ Anna made other, sad entries, but Bronson's notations show that he had read them and chose to remove them. Louisa felt less inclined to stress the "beautiful" in their life together. Her favorite pastimes included roaming the woods and fields and playing at being a horse.²⁵ She also noted a number of times that she "felt sad because I have been cross today." Crying made her feel better, as did reciting poetry, which also put her to sleep. She faithfully recorded visits from grownups, who included Parker Pillsbury (who "came and talked about the poor slaves"), Emerson, Thoreau, William Russell, and Lydia Maria Child.²⁶ Louisa continued to love acting, but she hated music lessons with Miss Page.

When her father and Mr. Lane went "preaching" in such far-off cities as Boston or New York, Louisa was happiest. Then, she said, with striking honesty, "it was very lovely." She hated to be without her mother and sister Lizzie. When Abba and Lizzie visited Boston without her, she mournfully declared, "Nobody is as good to me as dear Marmee." Often feeling cross, she made promises to herself and Mother to be better. "If only I kept all I make," she sighed, "I should be the best girl in the world, but I don't, and so am very bad." Forty years later she reread the smudged lines and appended: "Poor little sinner! She says the same at fifty."²⁷

A BARREN HARVEST

It is hard to imagine how much better she might have been at age ten—with ironing, husking corn well into the night, cooking, minding baby Abba (Abigail May, the youngest daughter), and still finding time to read Plutarch, as well as Byron, Dickens, Maria Edgeworth, and Goldsmith's *Vicar of Wakefield*.²⁸ She eventually bestowed the same feelings and the same literary tastes on Jo March, her alter ego in *Little Women*.

After reading a story about "Contentment," Louisa wrote, "I wish we were all rich, I was good, and we were all a happy family this day."²⁹ Clearly she wavered between feeling that the family's miseries were due to poverty and the suspicion that her own failings made her parents unhappy. She also wrote poetry and in a four-stanza rhyme entitled "Despondency" expressed her fears about the future, hoping that God, who fed the birds and flowers, would also take care of the Alcotts.[30] Anna thought her sister's poems were fine, but Louisa "didn't like them so well."[31] She was much less sure than Anna of her ability to please critics, a feeling Lane reinforced by pressing both girls to work harder. He exhausted them with long, demanding, often unrewarding lessons which they soon learned to resent. Convinced, like Bronson, of the great profundity lying dormant in a child's mind, Lane was apt to ask the girls such questions as, "What is man?" After much Socratic coaching, they learned to reply (by rote), "A human being is an animal with a mind, a creature; a body; a soul and a mind."[32]

Most recruits to Fruitlands came and went after brief encounters with the rigid life. Isaac Hecker left Brook Farm partly because he wanted even more spartan simplicity in daily life, but also because he had seen directly into the heart of Fruitlands' dissonance. He had brought "three pairs of coarse pants and a coat,"[33] the better to begin hard work for his simple diet at once. A humble man, he doubted whether "the light is light." Hardly lacking the "will to follow or light to see,"[34] Hecker merely wondered if the "perfect" life could be achieved at all on an earth beset by worldly temptations. Nevertheless, he thought the Fruitlands people had much to recommend them. "I desire Mr. Alcott's strength of self-denial and the unselfishness of Mr. Lane in money matters."[35] He was certain that he could not go back to his own family, much as he loved them, because he could not engage in the family business or indulge himself in their luxuries. Alcott and Lane encouraged Hecker to stay, but he was candid about his reservations, which he communicated directly to Bronson. He observed Bronson's "want of frankness, his disposition to separateness rather than a disposition to win cooperation with the aims in his own mind; his family who prevent his immediate plans of reformation; the fact that his place has very little fruit on it, when it was and is their desire that fruit should be the principal part of their diet; my feeling that they have too decided a tendency towards literature and writing for the prosperity and success of their enterprise."[36]

Isaac Hecker was as close to understanding Fruitlands' rapid deterioration as any participant observer could be, although he failed at that time to include the most important reason. Later he put his finger on it. "Somebody once described Fruitlands," he declared, "as a place where Mr. Alcott looked benign and talked philosophy while Mrs. Alcott and the children did the work."[37] Indeed, as Lane and Alcott grew increasingly averse to the daily imperatives of subsistence farming, more of the work fell to Abba and the children. A visitor to the farm inquired if they had any beasts of burden, and Abba bitterly replied, "Yes, one woman."[38] In the late fall, while Bronson and Lane were preaching the consociate gospel in the salons of Boston and New York, Abba and the girls were forced to harvest a substantial barley crop by themselves. Dashing about in a rising windstorm, they filled laundry baskets and sheets with cut barley, and dragged them to the barn in hopes of salvaging this staple of their diet. They were utterly exhausted when the men returned. Moreover, an early winter brought unusually cold weather. The house was drafty, the woodpile insufficient to keep the main fireplaces going, and everyone suffered from colds and fever.

At about this time Bronson and Lane began to discuss new communal arrangements in earnest. They considered alternative communities that might offer them shelter, and most important, broached the feasibility of separating Abba and the girls from Bronson. Bronson had taken Anna on a summer trip to the Oneida Community in upstate New York. But he quickly concluded that "complex marriage," another means of avoiding exclusivity in love and providing for children's support, was no more acceptable to Abba than the Shakers' celibacy. Moreover, Oneida already had one securely dominant patriarch, John Humphrey Noyes. Louisa wrote tersely in her diary, "Father and Mr. Lane had a talk, and father asked us if we saw any reason for us to separate. Mother wanted to, she is so tired, I like it, but not the school part with Mr. Lane."[39]

Abba had been writing pathetic letters to her brother describing her plight and entreating his aid in saving her family. Sam was outraged at her description of their situation, once confirmed by Lydia Maria Child, who entertained Bronson and Lane on one of their trips to New York and wondered if they were quite sane.[40] Sam refused to make the November payment on the money owed to the Wyman creditors. In a letter written in January, he justified his wish to be "exonerated from the liability to pay the 300 hundred dollar note," because "Mr. Lane and Mr. Alcott have separated and my sister and her family have left the place."⁴¹ In fact, Sam had already given notice to Lane in November (when the consociate family was still together) that he would not meet the note.

Mrs. Alcott informed the others that she would heed the advice of her brother and friends. As Lane reported to an English friend, Abba's plan was to

> withdraw to a house which they will provide for herself and her four children. As she will take all the furniture with her, the proceeding necessarily leaves me alone and naked in a new world. Of course Mr. A. and I could not remain together without her. To be 'that devil comes from Old England to separate husband and wife,' I will not be, though it might gratify New England to be able to say it. So that you will perceive a separation is possible. Indeed I believe that under the circumstances it is now inevitable.⁴²

So Abba fled Fruitlands once again, this time for good. Her rebellion brought the experiment to an abrupt end.

Although the reasons for Abba's rebellion and for the crisis at Fruitlands are already clear, the various explanations offered by the major participants are worth exploring. They not only illuminate the conflicts between the sexes in the nineteenth century, but go far to explain the emergence of a feminist movement. They show, in part, why Louisa Alcott's novels have been so appealing to so many women for so long a time.

CELIBACY AND THE SEXUAL DIVISION OF LABOR

In a long letter written at Concord shortly before the move to Fruitlands and published in *The Herald of Freedom*, Lane and Alcott laid out their plans for a purer family as the means to spiritual perfection.⁴³ Significantly, Abba did not sign it, although she was not averse to putting her name on numerous public statements and reform petitions. Several key motifs in that long letter reveal the sources of communal conflict as well as the issues that led many mid-nineteenth-century Americans to try alternatives to traditional arrangements of sexuality, family, labor, property, and community. Lane wrote, "The Holy Family, in its highest, divinest sense is our true position, our sacred earthly destiny. It comprehends every divine, every human relation consistent with universal good, and all others it rejects, as it disdains all animal sensualities."[44] He comes dangerously close here to embracing the virtues of celibacy and eliminating traditional family relations, as did the Shakers. He claimed he "did not wholly agree with the Shakers," but saw them as entitled to "deeper consideration." Such serious attention was warranted in part because

> we witness in this people the bringing together of the two sexes in a new relation, or rather with a new idea of the old relation. This had led to results more harmonic than anyone seriously believes attainable for the human race, either in isolation or association, so long as divided, conflicted family arrangements are permitted. The great secular success of the Shakers; their order, cleanliness, intelligence and serenity are so eminent, that it is worthy of enquiry how far these are attributable to an adherence to their peculiar doctrine.[45]

Certainly the Shaker model had much to recommend it for many women. Its female members found relief from the burdens of pregnancy, and those already with children were made welcome. Shaker work patterns reflected less of a sexual division of labor than found in the larger society, and all work was equally valued. Further, women had an equal vote in the common government. The Shakers understood that the traditional family relations, which rendered women dependents of the men who "owned" them, was an obstacle to the salvation of both sexes.[46]

Lane as well as Bronson wanted to impose on Abba something approaching this Shaker model. Even more than Alcott, Lane insisted (in principle) that Abba should be consulted about consociate life, that her support of every aspect of the venture was vital to its success. At the same time he fully understood that "Mrs. Alcott has no spontaneous inclination towards a larger family than her natural one; of spiritual ties she knows nothing though keep all together she does and would go through a great deal of exterior and interior toil."[47] Yet Lane, ordinarily so sensitive, wanted his own way. He saw no hypocrisy in men imposing celibacy, dietary regulations, household schedules, and a host of other restrictions on Abigail May Alcott.

Both men assumed that domestic activities were natural to women. Neither dreamed that there was anything artificial about the sexual division of labor at Fruitlands; nor did they see anything wrong with telling Abba and the girls how to manage their work. Lane sympathized with Abba's burdens as the only woman resident, but he thought her work could be lightened by recruiting more women for domestic chores.

Bronson, of course, had his own special perspective on the Fruitlands' experience. For years he had wanted to escape the burdens of supporting a large family; he wanted "spiritual," not material, responsibilities. He wanted to free the body and human relationships from all imperfections, everything that constrained the "free" pure spirit.[48] The consociate family gave him a temporary solution to his problems—unsatisfactory to be sure, from Abba's point of view—for it freed him from his duty to support the family while ironically strengthening the sexual division of labor.

THE TROUBLE WAS WOMEN

In the end both men blamed the women for the crisis at Fruitlands. The obstacles to harmony and community were females, who seemed irrationally committed to the exclusive love of their own biological family. Lane went further in pointing to the "maternal instinct" itself as the source of the difficulty. Both the maternal instinct and the family, he wrote Emerson, "are selfish and oppose the establishment of the community which stands for universal love."[49]

After the breakup, Lane authorized Sam May to transfer the deed to the property to Emerson. Both Abba and Sam later claimed, rather incorrectly, that Lane had turned Abba, Bronson, and the children into the cold, that he retained ownership of the land, and that he tried to break up the Alcott family. Lane was deeply committed to avoiding the ownership of private property, however. Emerson accepted the trust and eventually the property was bought by Joseph Palmer in installments. Lane returned to England with his son, began another school, and married an English matron whose commitment to communal life had been tested by previous residence in another intentional community. He continued writing in a friendly way to Joseph Palmer, expressing his "hope that you will have prosperity enough in the culture to release yourself gradually from my encumbrance whereby I may be enabled just to pay the rent on an acre or two to cultivate with my own hands."[50] The mortgage was finally paid off in 1851.

Dedicated and persevering, unshaken in his beliefs, sure that his personal perspective was universal, Lane cherished the best of his American experience. "I am differently employed now," he wrote, "but I still desire the field and the garden. If I had such a spot here as Fruitlands I should not quit it, but enjoy a life fruitful in all good."[51]

Bronson responded differently to the troubles at Fruitlands. Not only did the outcome of the venture leave him seriously ill for a time (a sign, perhaps, of his temperamental dislike of conflict), but he also learned to temper his view of the family and sexual relations. As he wrote many years later,

I have long since questioned the fitness of any considerable number of persons for community life. A school is a possibility. Yet any separation from parents for any long time, seems undesirable unless in the case of their unfitness to have charge of their children. The family is *the unit* around which all social endeavors should organize if we would succeed in educating men for the true ends of existence. And the cooperation of women in the practical working out is indispensable.[52]

Bronson also relented a little in regard to food consumption, although he would always feel ambivalence toward matters of the flesh and self-indulgence. He dined often with Emerson, who had refused to invite Charles Lane to dinner for fear that Lane's lectures on the evils of meat, yeast breads, and wine would "destroy the appetite of his guests." On one occasion, when Emerson was carving up an expensive roast, and discussing the horrors of cannibalism at the same time, Alcott remarked, "If we are to eat meat at all, why should we not eat the best?"[53]

Bronson Alcott changed his views about the family in large measure because Abba had declared her independence. Abba's conception of Fruitlands diverged sharply from that of the men. She felt they neither understood nor acknowledged the value of female self-sacrifice. Women's domestic duties, she said, were simply taken for granted:

> A woman may perform the most disinterested duties. She may 'die daily' in the cause of truth and righteousness. She lives neglected, dies forgotten. But a man who never performed in his whole life one self-denying act, but who has accidental gifts of genius, is celebrated by his contemporaries, while his name and his works live on from age to age. A man passes a few years in self denial and simple life, and he says, "Behold A God."[54]

Visiting the Shaker community with the men, Abba observed on the spot that the model was not for her. "There is servitude somewhere," she declared, "I have no doubt. There is a fat, sleek, comfortable look about the men and among the women there is a stiff, awkward reserve that belongs to neither sublime resignation nor divine love."[55]

More important, Abigail resisted the larger consociate unit planned by the men because she believed it threatened her legitimate power in the family and therefore her personal identity. The roles she found thrust upon her were those of "universal mother" and maid of all work, both of which appeared to her as a mockery. Almost immediately she was thrown into an overt struggle with Bronson to save the family she cherished. And in trying to preserve domesticity, Abba painfully asserted her equal right to make decisions affecting herself and her daughters. In so doing she radicalized a female perspective she had been developing since her courtship.

Empowered by the money left to her exclusive use by her father (which Bronson and his creditors vainly tried to get), Abba removed herself from the consociates, thereby forcing her husband to choose between his family and his experiment. She acted with exhilarating independence, and arranged to rent four rooms in a nearby Still

River farmhouse. She was joined by the children and later by Bronson, and the family lived cheaply and practically there.

DOMESTICITY AND WOMAN'S RIGHTS

Abba realized that she, Louisa, and Anna would have to earn a living for the family if they expected to determine their domestic life. Ironically, Abba's desire to preserve the forms of the past led her to develop a stronger version of domestic feminism. Abba's chief ally was Louisa, who refined and passed on that legacy to all women and men who read her books. Her fiction gives us perhaps the fullest picture of the struggles over sexual relations and domestic life at Fruitlands—and for that matter, at other intentional communities in which reformist, middle-class men tried to impress their values upon community life as a whole.

In her amusing short story, "Transcendental Wild Oats." Alcott depicts practically everyone who lived at Fruitlands. The story is often sarcastic at the expense of the "brethren." For instance, she describes the garden at Fruitlands as a riot of confusion because each of the brethren has sown his chosen grain in the common field; barley, rye, and oats wave companionably together in the summer sun. The members also plant an orchard in the expectation of autumn harvest, though the trees need at least three years to mature and bear edible fruits.

The humor of the story, however, often yields to grim reflection, particularly in Louisa's version of the conflict between Charles Lane (Dictator Lion) and her mother (Sister Hope). She casts her father as Abel Lamb, a docile, sweet, and passive man, who accedes to the wishes of Dictator Lion but who later accepts the wise management of his wife. By making Bronson the innocent victim of Lane's alleged plot against women and the family (when Bronson was hardly innocent at all), Alcott preserves the image of a benign father while elevating her practical mother to a dominant position in domestic life.

In the story the struggle between Lane and Abba takes place over every important aspect of the domestic and communal economy. Dictator Lion seeks to control women by making them subservient

73

drones in the new order. At the very moment he is preaching about the "truth" that "lies at the bottom of the well," Sister Hope is slaving in the kitchen to prepare meals for eleven people. Later, after the Dictator decides to retire to a Shaker community, Sister Hope is left to starve in the old house, bereft of money and friends. "You talk to me about justice," she declares, "let us have a little since there is nothing else left."[56]

Alcott's portrait of Lane's attitude toward women is darkened by her contention that he intended to found a colony of Mormons, who "under his patriarchal sway, could regenerate the world and glorify his name forever." Why did she make such a sensational claim when she must have known that Fruitlands, whatever its faults, had little in common with the Mormon's tightly organized capitalism and patriarchal polygamy? She probably chose this analogy because she wanted to show how far Fruitlands diverged from a feminist democracy. Fruitlands was not only far from a gender democracy, it was a community where male values substituted for male property holding as the patriarchal basis for control.

In her other fiction, and particularly in *Work*, Alcott refined her view of women's domestic labor, implicitly arguing against the position stated by Lane and her father: "Of all the traffic in which civilized society is involved, that of human labor is perhaps the most detrimental, from the state of serfdom to the receipt of wages may be a step in human progress, but it is certainly full time for taking a new step out of the hiring system."[57] In Louisa's view, the male boarders at Fruitlands wanted to build a community around household production and "humble exchange . . . without the interval of money."[58] They also wanted to withdraw from the existing industrial capitalist order, which led them to reaffirm agrarian patriarchy as "newness."

Alcott had little sympathy with these notions. Wage earning for women, she believed, made escape possible from the tyranny of patriarchal families and equally patriarchal communal ventures. Of course, wages were often exploitative; cooperative, small endeavors were better, but essentially women needed wages to command respect from others in the nineteenth century. For Alcott, the new order offered genuine possibilities for freeing women from house-

hold drudgery, not by bread and apple picnics, but through coeducational public schooling and through remunerative work for women
outside and inside their homes.

In "Transcendental Wild Oats" as well as other works, Alcott
shows the way that food and diet and also domestic labor become
concrete vehicles for the expression of sexual conflict. In their broad-
side announcing Fruitlands, Bronson and Lane said this about animal foods:

> It is calculated that if no animal food were consumed, one fourth
> of the land now used would suffice for human sustenance. . . .
> The sty and the stable too often secure more of the farmer's regard
> than he bestows on the garden and the children. No hope is there
> for humanity while Woman is withdrawn from the tender
> assiduities which adorn her and her household to the servitudes of
> the family and the flesh pots.

They went further. They equated the spread of manure on the fields
with the infusion of diseases into the human body. The diseases
resulting from consumption of meat and vegetables grown in ma-
nured fields required cure by "stimulants and medicines . . . which
ended in a precipitation of the original evil to more distances and
depth."[59] Ominously, they suggested that the body's befoulment,
its excrement and dirt, might infect the soul. This perfectionist, anti-
sensual approach to food and diet did not sit well with Alcott. Scattered through the thirty-five pages of "Transcendental Wild Oats"
are eleven paragraphs devoted to the sexes and their attitudes toward
food. The men are portrayed as ascetic and self-denying; they forbid
the consumption of "sugar, molasses, milk, butter, cheese and
flesh."[60] The women, however, offer abundance and comfort, "the
bread and wine of a new communion."

Alcott, like her mother, was not persuaded by Lane's contention
that a kitchen without animal food and pastries would be a better,
freer place for women. On the contrary, she realized that the men
were, in their desire to purify their behavior and master their own
drives, attempting to invade and eliminate women's right to dispense
the abundance they themselves created. Alcott even suggests that the

men were seeking refuge from the sensual lives of women. Certainly she felt deprived as a child of the small treats that mothers try to dispense from the leanest larders. Years later in her fiction she presented kind nursies dispensing "warm sweet stuff" to soothe children's throats, and mothers cheerfully providing gingerbread and milk to little women and men.[61]

Louisa was a thoughtful, self-critical girl at Fruitlands. Openly partisan, she became intensely conscious of the life-sustaining character of women's domestic work. In addition, she accepted the work as inescapable; men would not or could not do it. But having grasped the meaning of her mother's experience, she began to realize that women who lacked a voice in community government were powerless to extend their spheres of activity beyond the household.

Louisa was awakened to a new link between domestic reform and woman's rights. She grasped the personal necessity of feminism. While opponents cried out that feminists destroyed sacred family bonds, she learned at Fruitlands that feminism could provide a new basis for family survival even as it challenged the traditional structure of households and society.

Alcott did not mention sex directly in "Transcendental Wild Oats," but she quoted her father and Lane: "Pledged to the spirit alone, the founders anticipate no hasty or numerous addition to their numbers. The kingdom of peace is entered only through the gates of self-denial; and felicity is the test and the reward of loyalty to the unswerving law of Love."[62] Lane and Bronson might have meant that the colony should not become a refuge for the poor and homeless, at least not in its initial stages. On the other hand, Bronson believed that future parents must be free of all selfish lust if the spiritual seed with which God himself impregnates human beings was to reach fulfillment. There should be no unplanned babies and no sexual intercourse between parents who were not perfected to nurture the divine seed.

Abba was forty-two years old at Fruitlands, and she had survived eight pregnancies in ten years. She was scarcely hoping for another pregnancy, but she found involuntary celibacy dictated by the beliefs of strangers distasteful. Perhaps more threatening, Bronson clearly intended family ties to be no stronger than the generalized spiritual bonds that connected him to Lane and other kindred spirits.

Throughout her writing career Alcott insisted that women's domestic work was important and that women's voices be heard in the larger world. She learned at Fruitlands that these demands were inseparable. Her experiences there shaped her fierce loyalty to the natural family and also her perception that the burdens of motherhood were inescapable.

FIVE

The Trials of Life Begin

The trials of life began about this time, and happy childhood
ended. One of the most memorable days of my life is a certain
gloomy November afternoon, when we had been holding a
family council as to ways and means.
Louisa May Alcott, Journals, *1847*

"The bright days of summer" came once more to Louisa and her
sisters in Still River, where the Alcotts moved after a bleak winter in
rented rooms at the Lovejoy farm in Harvard village. Their playmate, Annie Clark, recalled the "happiness of the little people" on
rides and picnics with Mrs. Alcott and Miss Chase, the village schoolteacher.[1] It was the summer of 1844. "Hay carts would be provided
with seats and trimmed with evergreen and carefully stowing away
our luncheon baskets, we one by one would take our seats in the
rustic omnibuses, and start away, singing and laughing for a long
day's pleasure." Louisa's Still River schoolmates remembered those
months thirty years later as seeming "very much like a chapter from
one of Miss Alcott's stories."[2]

At twelve years, Louisa's most serious crime was speaking disre-
spectfully to her mother and then escaping punishment by sneaking
out with her best friend Sophie Gardner. The two friends ran into
the pasture, past Bronson serenely hoeing in the garden, to visit the
grave of a spider Louisa had accidentally crushed the day before.[3]

In a short while the Alcotts found themselves on the road to a new
home in Concord. And it was Abigail Alcott, having asserted her
authority at Fruitlands, who continued to initiate plans that would
determine the future life of the family. In May she filed a request
with the Suffolk County Probate Court for appointment of her
cousin, Samuel E. Sewall, and her brother, Samuel J. May, as "trustees for my benefit under the will of my father."[4] William Minot and
the elder Samuel May reliquished their trusteeship, and in August

Abba's new guardians received "one thousand and fifty dollars, being Mrs. Alcott's share of the residue and remainder" of her father's estate, "to be held in trust for her separate use according to said will."[5]

While Abba secured her inheritance, Sam May and Bronson talked seriously about ways to provide for May's conception of conventional material security and Alcott's spiritual needs. Sam wrote to Emerson in December that he had "spent time with Mr. and Mrs. Alcott in consultation upon their plans for the future." He noted, delicately, that "Mr. A. must have something to do." "For a while," however, "it seemed difficult to so arrange the proposed purchase of a place-house and land—that my sister and her family might have a shelter secured to them, without implicating him in the sin of living upon soil appropriated to his exclusive use."[6] The plan they devised was that May and Sewall, as Abba's trustees, would expend $1,000 of her legacy in buying the old Coggswell house in Concord and a small amount of its land "to be secured to her and her children." It is not clear that Abba Alcott would have chosen Concord without its particular advantage of congenial society for Bronson. Emerson's presence was the most important, for he would "keep a rational view in sight, and there will be less of ultraism and yet perfect freedom of action," as Sam May saw it.[7]

Emerson in fact donated money to purchase the remainder of the Coggswell estate so that, as Sam May said, "all the children of men, if they could get upon the land, might feel welcome there as to a common inheritance." For emphasis, Sam restated his sister's property rights: "As it respects the rest Mr. Sewall and myself are bound as trustees to see that whatever may be bought with Abba's money is secured to her and her children so far as any legal protection can secure it."[8]

Sam May never doubted his sister's hospitality ("every one who knows her, knows that like her heart her door will be wide open to any of the human race who may need a home"), nor did he doubt Bronson's sincerity. But he treated Bronson as if he were in a prolonged adolescence. May assured his partner in benevolence, Emerson, that he would, if possible, "give to Mr. Alcott as large a portion of the earth as he might need, to gather about him as many as he could draw to him. Not that I fully apprehend his thought—nor think the plan practicable so far as I do understand it. But he is so sincere, so devout, so full of faith that I long to have him try his experiment to his own entire satisfaction."[9]

The Alcotts moved back to Concord under those arrangements. Secure for the moment in her property rights, Abba was hospitable to all who needed a home, as her brother predicted. She even invited Charles Lane to live with them in Concord. He visited for a time and helped with the children's lessons, much to Louisa's chagrin. But he did not remain long, because he perceived Emerson's gift as one made in individual friendship, not in genuine commitment to a communal dream.

Bronson also invited a young teacher, Sophia Ford, to share their home, hoping to secure a school for himself in Concord, and an assistant in Miss Ford. Louisa took her lessons with Miss Ford, and for a while with Mr. Lane. But she yearned for the fun of Still River, writing a friend that she did not "have half so good a time as I did at Miss Chase's school, the summer I went there was the happiest summer I have ever spent in the country, there was such a lot of jolly girls to play and blab with."[10] Sensitive about the donated baskets of clothing and food that everyone knew had sustained her family in the Still River months, she now referred to Sophia Ford as "my governess" and talked about wading through ponds and climbing apple trees "tearing our clothes off our backs, luckily they were old and breaking our bones (!); playing tag and all sorts of strange things. We are dreadful wild people here in Concord, we do all the sinful things you can think of."[11] Louisa had learned to portray Alcott eccentricities as if they were normal high jinks, and she softened them into a kind of genial respectability. Her friends tenderly noted the contradiction. "To one who knows the destitute circumstances of the Alcott family in this period," wrote Annie Clark, in retrospect, "the little Louisa's somewhat airy references to summers in the country and 'my governess' may afford innocent mirth."[12]

Louisa entered a new phase of her life in Concord. She was no longer simply an observer of woman's troubles (her mother's) for she had embarked upon her adolescence—although in those days no one thought "little women" went through such a stage. Protected from worldly experience, their innocence preserved, little women presumably experienced nothing of the turmoil and stress that we now associate with female adolescence. Destined for marriage and mother-hood, young women supposedly knew only a chaste, confined do-mesticity between girlhood and womanhood.

On the other hand, male adolescence was viewed as frightening and dangerous. Men such as Bronson and William Alcott, Sylvester Graham, and Samuel Fowler, who feared the demands of their own bodies, were among those who warned against the dangers of male adolescence. These reformers "chose the body as the focus of their reform effort," and the male adolescent body in particular.[13] Cut off from an older moral system with clear lines of authority and subordi-nation, young men in Jacksonian America constituted threats to the established order. Their behavior could be controlled through indi-vidual restraint and through permanent, domesticating relationships with women. "Boys," wrote William Alcott,

in their fancied wisdom and strength, grow impatient of parental restraints and are more or less ungovernable. The passions become strong, or at least active; and so do the appetites. . . . At this very period—this stormy period—this Tierra Del Fuego of human life, the young in the usual course of things are to be scattered abroad. . . . This separation of the sexes, occurring at the time when it does what shall prevent a most inevitable and fatal ship-wreck? At this critical period . . . it is wisely ordered that a new passion spring up. . . . It is love of the opposite sex.[14]

Ideally, the May-Alcott marriage should have calmed Bronson's fears. American girls were still pure, and their civilizing influence was supposed to save men. The problem, as Carroll Smith-Rosenberg describes it, was that

in return for this grant of sexual power, a woman was to limit her own sexual desires even more stringently than she did her hus-band's. She was expected, as well, to remain subservient to him and to her children in all other areas of life; she must narrow her horizons to the hearth and the nursery, be obedient, self effacing and nurturant within that sphere.[15]

Nevertheless, Bronson found Eve's temptations even in rural Fourth of July picnics; holiday food apparently could trigger the destructive power of male sexuality. Nurturant women prepared the "dough-nuts, cold meat, pickles, cakes and pies" that Bronson brusquely declined at Still River. "Vanity," he said, "and worse than vanity." Yet his daughters were not "averse from sharing more varied foods" at outings and at the tables of their friends. They had been raised on the blandest of vegetarian menus, but even this proved no protection against their sexual maturation.

The contradictions between female restraint and female abun-dance were nowhere more apparent than in contemporary assess-ments of youth. Male adolescent passions were supposedly domesti-cated by youthful love matches with innocent girls, but this reassur-ing view ignored the fact that girls, even when fiercely constrained by social conventions, did pass through an adolescent stage marked by sexual and emotional turmoil. Louisa May Alcott has given us ample evidence of this volatility in both her domestic fiction and in her life. She was aware of her own superabundant energies, and equally conscious of the need for self-restraint.

It is commonly assumed that Louisa May Alcott's most popular novels, like most nineteenth-century domestic works by women, evaded the problem of adolescent female sexuality by separating it from the safer subject of domesticity. A number of explanations have been offered for this evasion: first, that sexual awakening in young women was inappropriate material for genteel, young female read-ers. A more probing explanation is that female writers were reinforc-ing attitudes already established in the lives of their female readers, who at that time were asserting increasing control over their fertility. This explanation receives support from other analyses that focus on a growing separation of the sexual spheres in a dynamic, capitalist marketplace; this separation encouraged a female distaste for male sexuality and a male fear of individual excess.

Madeleine Stern's rediscovery and publication of Louisa's "tales of passion" suggest a third explanation for Alcott's supposed failure to deal with adolescent and adult female sexuality.[16] That Louisa pro-duced many of these stories under a pseudonym seems to suggest a dichotomy in her mind (and possibly in the minds of her readers) between a fiction that is genteel and sanitized and one that is Gothic and passionate. In these pseudonymous tales Alcott writes of fallen women who express sexual desire, but only with disastrous consequences. Yet this theory ignores a central theme in all of Alcott's fiction: the problem of presenting domesticity and female adolescent sexuality at the same time. As Madelon Bedell points out, Alcott's writings repeatedly portray a

> romance between a child-woman and an older man; the latter often a guardian, an uncle, or an older male friend; in short, a displaced father. The theme is constant. It runs like a thread through her works, from the early sentimental short stories she published in her twenties, to the pseudonymous thrillers she wrote in her thirties, the children's novels of her mature period, and the later melodramatic works she began to revive as she grew old.[17]

In the domestic novels Alcott proposes safe marriages to kind, protective fatherlike figures who will channel the energies of their young wives to good works. In the Gothic tales and the fully Romantic novels, heroines reject "fathers" as too powerful and threatening, precisely because they awaken women's sexual passions. Preoccupied with the motif of the father-lover, Alcott had clearly linked the volatile relationship between the domestic and sexual elements of a young woman's life. But she was doing more. As Bedell remarks of the Romantic and Gothic stories, Alcott was warning women against marriages based on a love that would destroy their "independence and power."[18]

THE MOST BEAUTIFUL GIRL RUNNER

It is not necessary, however, to turn to Alcott's fiction for evidence of a passionate adolescence. Her life is proof enough. As a young woman, Louisa enjoyed sexual role playing and romping with boys, however briefly or circumscribed from our point of view. In that short, golden summer at Still River, she "married" a boy in a mock gypsy ceremony attended by family and friends in the woodshed. The bride and groom even jumped over a broomstick. But bliss was shortlived. The couple had a tiff, the bride slapped the groom, and the marriage was "annulled." Against her mother's strong objections Louisa later participated in "kissing games." On one occasion, out of sight of Abba, she "commandeered a neighbor's horse and sleigh and took a friend, Clara Gowing, for a short drive, returning the team to where she found it. Remembering the incident years later, she wrote to her old friend, with enjoyment, that "Bart kissed me when I got out." Gowing annotated this confidence with the reminder that "promiscuous kissing was under a ban in their family."[19]

Her awakening at first took physical forms conventionally permitted only to boys in the 1840s. She ran and played with fierce energy. Her journal entries reveal an unusual freedom to run outdoors, to enjoy nature, and to express herself fully. One entry in particular survived the cautious editing and deletions of later years:

> I had an early run in the wood before the dew was off the grass. The moss was like velvet, and as I ran under the arches of yellow and red leaves, I sang for joy, my heart was so bright and the world so beautiful. I stopped at the end of the walk and saw the sunshine out over the wide "virginia meadows." It seemed like going through a dark life or grave into heaven beyond. A very strange and solemn feeling came over me as I stood there, with no sound but the rustle of the pines, no one near me, and the sun so glorious, as for me alone. It seemed as if I *felt* God as I never did before, and I prayed in my heart that I might keep that happy sense of nearness all my life.[20]

Alcott left this entry intact (after reading it in 1885) because it marked the day "that little girl got religion . . . in the wood when dear Mother Nature led her to God."[21] Just as other women gained a sense of power from evangelical religion, Louisa found hers in a romantic union with Nature. These experiences laid the groundwork for her feminism. "Dear Mother Nature" presided over a reassuring personal conversion; the sun shone "as for me alone," and she experienced a solemn feeling of female autonomy that she had acquired outside conventional paternal religious structures.

Louisa's friends observed the emergence of her adolescent passions and energies. Llewellyn Willis described her in that period as a girl with

a clear, olive brown complexion, and brown hair and eyes, she answered perfectly to the ideal of "the nut brown maid." She was full of spirit and life, impulsive and moody and at times irritable and nervous. She could run like a gazelle. She was the most beautiful girl runner I ever saw. She could leap a fence or climb a tree as well as any boy and clearly loved a good romp. She was passionately fond of nature, loved the fields and forests, and was in special harmony with animal life. Her brief description of herself in the opening chapter of *Little Women* is most accurately true.[22]

Willis gave similarly detailed and romantic portraits of Louisa's sisters. Anna was an "ox-eyed Juno," amiable, quiet, and possessed of a dignified sense of humor. Beth looked very like her counterpart in *Little Women*; sweet and sunny, she played the piano "with something of a real appreciation, and behaved like Cinderella in the kitchen." Abba May, who decided early to call herself May, was "the baby of the family and much petted. . . . Inclined to be childishly tyrannical at times," she had the clear blue eyes and golden curls of her counterpart Amy in her sister's fiction.[23]

STRANGE FEELINGS

In September of 1845 the two oldest girls acknowledged "strange feelings, a longing after something. I don't know what it is" (as Anna put it for both of them).[24] They talked about "how we should like to live and dress." Louisa dreamed of becoming a writer as a way to escape poverty. Her mother encouraged this dream because she saw it as a refuge for her daughter's "troubled spirit," while Anna announced that Louisa would "write something great one of these days." Both girls took the Romantic devotion to creativity seriously. Anna, however, regretted her lack of special talent. "As for me," she said,

I am perfect in nothing. I have no genius, I know a little music, a little of French, German, and Drawing, but none of them well. I have a foolish wish to be something great and I shall probably spend my life in a kitchen and die in the poor house. I want to be Jenny Lind or Mrs. Seguin and I can't and so I cry.[25]

The girls' longing represented a dramatic change in female expectations from those of Abba's youth. Being a model wife and mother in behalf of a model Republic meant little to them. Abba knew this, and hoped to help them sort out their feelings. In particular, she urged Louisa to continue expressing herself in notes and journal entries.

Abba was busy desperately trying to make ends meet in Concord. Bronson had not gotten his school after all, but he reconstructed their house and cultivated and harvested most of their food. Finally, in March of 1846 his carpentry allowed Louisa the privacy of her own room, which she had wanted for a long time. She confessed that "it does me good to be alone, and Mother had made it pretty and neat for me. My work basket and desk are by the window, and my closet is full of dried herbs that smell very nice. The door that opens into the garden will be very pretty in summer, and I can run off to the woods when I like."[26]

This early phase of Louisa's Romantic adolescence corresponded with the rise of feminism in America. Abba, herself commited to this new movement, aimed at giving her girls comfortable dress, healthy diet, exercise, and intellectual stimulation; these goals were gaining ground among educators and homeopathic physicians, and by 1890 the most popular ladies' magazines agreed with the reformers. Important family friends, above all Harriot K. Hunt, set new models for female advancement, stirring the imagination of such young girls as Louisa.

Harriot K. Hunt demanded that "every girl see to it that she has the means of her own support," a demand already abundantly clear to the Alcott women. "When labor becomes honorable and elevating," Hunt continued, "then will every woman prepare herself for useful occupation and follow it. Then will man see that industrial avenues are open to women—that they can follow any business or profession to which they are qualified without being exposed to

contemptible insults which are heaped upon those who have independence enough to step out ot the beaten track."[27]

When Louisa was fifteen years old, "fretted by the restraints and
restrictions which were deemed essential to the proper girls," Harriot Hunt was applying to Dr. Oliver Wendell Holmes for permission to attend medical lectures at Massachusetts Medical College,
who with the President and Fellows of Harvard found it "inexpedi-
ent" that she should receive the "scientific light" she requested from
her male colleagues at the Medical College.[28] Unshaken, she continued practicing medicine and preaching women's rights. Eventually
she received an honorary M.D. from the Female Medical College of
Philadelphia in 1853.

In her autobiography, *Glances and Glimpses*, Hunt cast off the wide-
spread notion that the treatment of adolescent girls and boys should
be different. Like her Romantic contemporary, Margaret Fuller, she
argued for a more fluid, even androgynous educational regimen, in
which "boys should be taught every pleasant kind of handwork that
girls are," and girls freed to "run, and walk, and play with hoop and
ball." "Parents," she said spiritedly, "in the development of your
children it is for you to beautify all uses, not to sexualize them:
giving it to a feminine boy, manhood; and to a masculine girl,
womanhood."[29]

Louisa's youthful journals mirrored Hunt's prescriptions:

I have made a plan for my life, as I am in my teens, and no more a
child. I am old for my age, and dont care much for girls things.
People think I'm wild and queer; but Mother understands and
helps me. I have not told anyone about my plan; but I'm going to
be good. I've made so many resolutions and written sad notes, and
cried over my sins, and it doesnt seem to do any good! Now I'm
going to *work really*, for I feel a true desire to improve, and be a
help and comfort, not a care and sorrow, to my dear mother.[30]

If her resolutions to "work really" deepened, so did her inclination
toward romantic attachments. In fact, her fifteenth year marked the
beginning of "my romantic period . . . when I fell to writing poetry,
keeping a heart journal and wandering by moonlight instead of sleeping quietly." She started to read Romantic writers, including Haw-

thorne and Charlotte Brontë. "*The Scarlet Letter*, she wrote, "is my favorite. Mother likes Miss B. [Frederika Bremmer] better, as more wholesome. I fancy 'lurid things' if true and strong also."[31] In both *The Scarlet Letter* and *Jane Eyre*, a young heroine barely out of childhood meets her fate in the person of a much older man. Alcott would later reflect critically on such relationships, but now she was fascinated by their possibilities.

Louisa developed attractions for her own older men during this period, above all for Thoreau and Emerson. They were sage objects for her adolescent fantasies, and later the father-lovers of her fiction. Louisa had already known Thoreau through the Thoreau brothers' school in Concord, a successful enterprise that preceded the Fruitlands experiment. Louisa herself drew close to Thoreau; he soon became her idol and friend.[32] Thoreau's "prejudice for Adamhood," which led him to experiment in rustic semiseclusion at Walden Pond, made him a hero for Louisa. He had briefly courted her distant cousin, Ellen Sewall.

Thoreau eventually boarded with the Emersons on Lexington Street, although he worried about "dangerous prosperity" and "success without identity" in such a comfortable home. He was searching for his own home and perspective within the Transcendental model. In 1842 his brother John accidentally cut his finger, and the injury developed into a painful, fatal case of lockjaw. Thoreau nursed him and held him in his arms as he died. The death of John Thoreau, along with that of Emerson's son, deeply affected everyone in the Concord circle, including Louisa. Thoreau's loss and his struggles for self-realization struck a sympathetic chord in her. In two of her novels, *Moods* and *Work*, fictional replicas of him become fit lovers for her forthright, strong heroines.

The Concord world of Louisa's adolescence was a tight circle, the friendships intertwining. It was Emerson who bought land at Walden Pond, enabling Thoreau to cut his wood (with Bronson's help), and to build a cabin in the spring of 1845. The first draft of *Walden* and *A Week on the Concord and Merrimack Rivers* were written by Thoreau at the cabin and read aloud to Bronson as the two men walked in the woods, Louisa often trailing behind them. The Alcotts brought picnic refreshments to their friend, who regularly emerged from isolation to dine with the Emersons and his mother.[33]

Thoreau took the Alcott girls and Llewellyn Willis in his boat to see the reflections of heaven and earth on the water. He played his flute for them. He told them more about Indian history and legends than anyone Louisa knew, and she found his combination of idealistic philosophy, biology, and culture far more entrancing than the abstract authoritarianism of Charles Lane or the fussy recitation style of Misses Page and Ford. More than anything, his youthful journey down a river (both real and emblematic) sparked Louisa's own determination to find herself and make a living for her family. It was a task deeply complicated by her sex.

To forgo domesticity in favor of individual freedom was unthinkable for a woman unless, like Margaret Fuller, she possessed remarkable genius and strength of character. Even Fuller suffered, of course, perhaps more so because she was so exceptional. She noted sorrowfully that the wives around her—Sophia Peabody Hawthorne, Lidian Emerson, perhaps even Abigail May Alcott—"don't see the whole truth about one like me."[34] By "truth" she meant the social consequence of her powerful bid for individuality. Transcendentalism had crowned her its queen, but she reigned alone, without the domestic hostages or nurturance that usually sustained men's quest for individual realization. Yet if women saw her true circumstances, she wrote,

> they would understand why the brow of Muse or Priestess must wear a shade of sadness. . . . They have so much that I have not, I can't conceive of their wishing for what I have. (Enjoying is not the word: these I know are too generous for that.) But when Waldo's wife, and the mother of that child that is gone thinks me the most privileged of women, and that Elizabeth Hoar was happy because her love was snatched away . . . and thus she can know none but ideal love: it does seem a little too insulting at first blush. And yet they are not altogether wrong.[35]

Fuller was not an everyday presence in Louisa's life. Her regular visits were nevertheless impressive, and would bear fruit in Alcott's first Romantic novel, *Moods*. By 1845 Fuller lived in New York City, and Alcott's closest connection to her was through Ellen Fuller Channing. Margaret's sister, married to Ellery Channing and living in

Concord, was unable to take her older sister's dispassionate distance from married men's romantic friendships. Henry Thoreau, like Emerson and Margaret Fuller, sympathized with poor Ellen, but also validated Ellery's right to "freedom" despite his marital ties.[36] Transcendentalism found the domination of one human spirit by another to be the greatest sin. Alcott felt the effects of such dominance, fought it in the next few years, and later described the experience in stories.

Alcott's early writings give little hint of the strong challenge she would mount against the conventional ideal of genteel womanhood. She wrote poems and fairy tales for her family and Ellen Emerson in a style considered appropriate to her sex: the language of flowers, which was both a Romantic convention and a sentimentalized means of joining prescriptive homilies with appealing fantasies. But she also tapped her passionate imagination by writing blood-and-thunder melodramas for amateur theatricals in the barn. Later her family and friends encouraged this "safe" outlet for passionate fantasy. One of her characters, Rudolpho, was often played by Louisa herself in magnificent boots, which Jo March was to wear in *Little Women*'s home theatricals. "The Mysterious Page" and "Norma or the Witches Curse" thrilled the Emerson family, the Ellery Channings, and the Hosmers as much as did Louisa's subsequent "Captive of Castile," "The Unloved Wife," and the "Prince and the Peasant."[37]

The Alcott girls and Willis formed their own Pickwick Club and acted out Dickens. During this time Emerson, the most available candidate for Louisa's adolescent affections, gave her books by Goethe, Shakespeare, and Dickens. After reading a translation of Goethe's romantic correspondence with fifteen-year-old Bettina Von Armin, Louisa played Bettina to Emerson's Goethe in her fantasies. She was fourteen. The Transcendentalists had sanctioned the relationship of Goethe and Bettina as "pure and poetic," so Louisa felt free to substitute the forty-three-year-old Emerson for Goethe. She wrote him poems, dropped wildflowers at his door, and sighed melodramatically "in a tall cherry tree at midnight, singing to the moon till the owls scared to bed." Emerson remained happily ignorant of Bettina's mooning, but he later heard of the unrequited romance from Alcott herself. He was "much amused," she said, "and begged for his letters, kindly saying he felt honored to be so worshipped."

She admitted to having burned the evidence, but she never lost affection for her "master who did a great deal for this admirer by the simple beauty of his life, and the truth and wisdom of his books, the example of a great, good man, untempted and unspoiled by the world which he made better while in it and left richer and nobler when he went."[38]

As Louisa developed safe infatuations for Thoreau and Emerson, she moved away from her father. When Abba replaced Bronson as the dominant figure in the Alcott household, Louisa began treating her father as a harmless eccentric. At a party during her early twenties Alcott met a young Massachusetts artist named C. W. Reed. She invited him to sketch their second Concord home, Orchard House, which he began to do the very next morning. "When Louisa spied him," a friend later remembered, "she bound down the path across the road and at a hand vault cleared the bars of the gateway and entered the field where he drew." Looking over his shoulder, she inquired about the details of his drawing technique; Reed replied that he simply drew the lines as he saw them.[39]

Alcott watched the completion of the work, then asked Reed in to meet her father. Bronson looked at Reed's sketch, placed his hand on the young man's head and remarked, "Young man, you are a child of light, a child of God." Reed did not understand, so Bronson elaborated while taking him round the flower garden. Before Reed could venture any comment, Louisa "gave him a poke with her toe as a hint for him to keep silent and let her father ramble on in his own deep faraway manner, which he did for a time . . . then Mr. Alcott retired to his study and the young people chatted after their own manner."[40] When she went over the journals in later years, Louisa was likely to add references to her father as Plato. Her manner, not quite disrespectful, suggests a fond mother, tolerant of an adolescent son's vagaries and pretensions.

CITY LIGHTS

At the very time Alcott's Romantic period was reaching full flower, she was drawn away through the influence of her mother. During the 1840s Alcott was still grappling with Romantic "self-culture," the reform of self through introspection, self-discipline, and moral self-improvement. But increasing ties with northeastern feminists and their male reformist allies were leading her to question the capacity of Transcendental individualism to liberate women. It had failed for the Alcotts in Fruitlands and Concord. Now personal solutions seemed ever less adequate in the face of newly emerging industrial and urban conditions—conditions which Abba had come to understand better than Bronson Alcott ever would.

In 1847 the Alcotts were still in financial trouble. That year they earned or received less than five hundred dollars, and when that was gone they were still two hundred dollars in debt to local merchants. That fall a water-cure hotel in Waterford, Maine, offered employment to Abba and Bronson; Abba would serve as its matron and Bronson could assume a vague appointment as resident "preacher and teacher."[41] Bronson would not accept the move, but Abba broke loose. She left Concord with her youngest daughter, Abigail May, and Eliza Stearns, a young girl whose parents had boarded her out with the Alcotts in hopes of curing her mental and emotional retardation. Since Anna was teaching in Walpole, New Hampshire, only Bronson, Elizabeth, and Louisa remained home in Concord.

Abba was a thorough success at organizing institutional structures. In a whirlwind of activity she supervised the housekeeping at Waterford, consulted on "the best methods of diet," tried out the baths and wet packs, and took vigorous walks to cure Eliza.[42] Above all, she earned a living. She also enjoyed the fact that the guests at Waterford were New England gentry, including artists, writers, and such reformers as Elizabeth Peabody.

But successful employment away from her husband and family evoked intense anxieties. She returned to Concord that summer after suffering a series of nightmares, including one in which Lizzie needed her mother's help in practicing the piano (she could not find the right note), and Louisa, "running in the lane," screamed out for her mother. Dominating her dreams was the struggle with Bronson over domestic responsibilities. One night she dreamt of a conversation in Concord between herself and Bronson. Bronson declared he was "planning an observatory," while she replied that she "had other purposes." "Don't do anything to make this place more attractive," she said to her husband, "I want to find a different home for the girls." Bronson replied, very cheerily, "don't be anxious, young people are very apt to find homes for themselves."[43] Abba clearly felt that her adolescent girls still needed a mother's guidance, and that Bronson, assuming his usual idealistic distance from their real needs, was merely anticipating his own freedom when his children disappeared to find homes of their own. Young women, she believed, needed to move gradually toward full independence; the home provided for by mothers (and increasingly, by maternal networks) offered the best protection en route to self-reliance.

In the fall of 1848, Mrs. James Savage, wife of a prominent Boston merchant and a longtime friend of the Mays, urged Abba to move to Boston, where a circle of wealthy female philanthropists planned to privately subsidize a "missionary to the poor." Emerson's personal charity to the Alcotts, even supplemented by the income from the residue of Abba's inheritance, had already proved insufficient; both Anna and Bronson needed more remunerative work. Bronson happily imagined possibilities for a school, "a reading room, a Journal, a press, a Club," in Boston.[44] Louisa would supervise the household while her younger sisters attended school; Anna would work as a governess to Louisa Greenwood Bond's children; and Abba would become a missionary. This opportunity pleased Abba immensely because it meant she could watch over her children. It also meant she could combine domestic reform, which emphasized the role of mothers in ameliorating the lives of poor girls and boys, with earning a living.

Abba's participation in Boston's voluntary associations marked her entrance into public life. Louisa eagerly approved. Like many of her friends, including Emerson, she had become engaged with the pressing social changes occurring around her. Perfectionist aspirations of the Transcendentalist period were left behind. By then Margaret Fuller herself was traveling in Europe meeting with Parisian workers. In England she found Giuseppe Mazzini, who helped her to cast off the individualistic ethic of which she had been the high priestess. He offered instead a collective social movement led by himself and Saint-Simon. Fuller also met George Sand and discovered, as Bell Gale Chevigny puts it, "her own androgynous ideal."[45] In one blazing historical moment Margaret Fuller realized the possibilities of combining feminism, political change, and personal growth.

While Fuller was becoming a citizen of the world, Louisa May Alcott was becoming one of Boston's 161,400 residents in 1850. The country had grown. The American population had increased from thirteen million inhabitants in the year of her birth to twenty-three million by the Civil War (at age thirty). But population growth was only one of many changes. In Abba's childhood farmers outnumbered city dwellers by fifteen to one, but by Louisa's girlhood the ratio was five to one. Moreover, the Bostonians of Louisa's generation were twice as mobile residentially as Americans today, with one household out of three moving each year. Although their constant uprootings in search of a livelihood were representative, the Alcotts felt their mobility was exceptional. Like other contemporary native-born Americans, they cherished domestic stability and blamed hard luck for their constant moving.

During Louisa's Temple School years, Boston's residents were 95 percent native-born Americans. When the Alcotts took up residence there in the 1850s the foreign-born inhabitants constituted half the city's population. In particular, the large Irish immigration of the 1840s strained the institutions designed to contain and assimilate the laboring classes. Middle-class residents, including reformers of all persuasions, were alarmed by the immigrants' observable ethnic differences from "American Victorianism as a culture."[46] Progressive, "modern" values, such as "rationality, specialization, efficiency, cosmopolitanism and an interest in a future that can be better than the present in material and social terms,"[47] seemed threatened by "the dangerous classes," as they were increasingly called.[48] Acculturating this European rabble to middle-class values and behavior was precisely the "missionary work" that Abba Alcott embarked on.

Abba's initial backers numbered only twenty-one well-to-do liberal philanthropists who believed that their city's problems should be handled through traditional voluntary relief work. Later, a sewing circle of church ladies subsidized other work for her. She distributed Bibles and baskets of clothing and food. She gave lectures on the dangers of unchecked fertility, the advantages of cleanliness, frugality, and sexual continence, as well as advice on domestic economy. In addition, she took in homeless children and adolescent girls, in order to protect them "from the sharks and lusts that wait." With the help of Louisa and Anna, she struggled against racism in Boston by teaching literacy classes to black adults. Like her fellow missionaries, who belonged to the countless private and independent charity endeavors of the antebellum period, Abba tried to place young and mature women as domestic servants and to find farm work for men.[49]

Historian Eric Schneider estimates that by 1860, the Boston Employment Society found jobs for "21,839 females, 1,859 of them 15 or younger, and for 2,540 males; of the 24,379 persons involved, 55% (13,460) had been placed in the country." He concludes that "instead of organizing the charities, the Society organized an employment service for its sponsors."[50] That was exactly the conclusion drawn by Alcott when she fictionalized her own and her mother's experience with such agencies. Abba found work for her clients in middle-class homes; at one point she even found a job for Louisa as a domestic servant. Her daughter bitterly described the details of such "service" in *Work: A Story of Experience* and in a short story, "How I Went out to Service."[51]

Since the exploitation and degradation of children was a major concern to the public at large and to charity workers in particular, Abba visited poor families, "investigating their wants and merits."[52] She also surveyed the pattern of welfare dispensation and solicitation of funds in the city. In her thorough, practical way she sought out the causes of the misery she encountered daily among the poor. Her conclusions brought her into direct conflict with the guardians of public welfare, including her distant cousin, Joseph Tuckerman. As a founder of the Society for the Prevention of Pauperism, he represented mainstream liberal Brahmin reformers as well as any individual could. In his published report of 1874, the summary of many years' work as "minister at large in Boston," Tuckerman warned against the reproduction of the "dangerous classes" through the infection of children with the lewdness, dishonesty, and profanity of their parents.[53] He argued that poor children did not really have a family life as the middle classes knew it. Poor children lived their lives alone or in bands on the streets where "every child who is a beggar, almost without exception, will become a vagrant and probably a thief."[54] For Tuckerman, the expansion of the public schools, the employment of truant officers, and the establishment of reform schools and other institutions were the only solution to the problem.

Louisa's uncle, Sam May, thought he faced a microcosm of the same situation in Syracuse, New York, and he vigorously championed the same school of thought as Joseph Tuckerman. The building of the Erie Canal in the 1820s had stimulated rapid commercial growth and brought the first influx of Irish immigrants to the city. There were 1,600 children in Syracuse by 1855, 600 of whom had never attended school at all. Middle-class distress may be further gauged by one common school in the 1850s being in the basement of a tavern, with its pupils subject to "the brawl and confusion of dram drinking, arrival and departure of noisy travelers and their lumbering vehicles."[55] Syracuse was still small enough for May to think reform possible through a vigorous common school association and the leadership of his own Unitarian congregation. May's record was impressive. He led the expansion of the public schools, campaigned for "idiot asylums," and demanded that the New York State legislature provide a "house of refuge" designed as a reform school for "canal boys" and other juvenile delinquents. He introduced to Syracuse the work of Eduard Seguin, a pioneer educator in training inmates of "idiot asylums."[56]

May argued for woman's rights as another necessary step toward a sane society. He urged Andrew Dickson White, later president of Cornell University, to "have both sexes educated equally."[57] May made clear his position that education was the cure for social ills, and that women were the best pupils and eventually the best teachers of the unenlightened masses.

Margaret Fuller's belief that the Old World's social problems required radical solutions (perhaps even wars of national liberation that generated social revolution) reached her American friends through her letters and newspaper articles. The sons and daughters of the American Revolution, her compatriots and the mainstay of nineteenth-century American reform movements, however, saw few parallels between downtrodden masses of Europe and the "dangerous classes" of New York or Boston. After all, this was the New World, the land of social mobility for all hard-working folk. Some American novels of the 1840s and 1850s argued that well-intentioned but misplaced philanthropy actually encouraged beggary, pauperism, and vagrancy. The root cause of pauperism, in this analysis, was a lack of proper entrepreneurial spirit. Generally the heroes of these novels—

plucky, native-born, country-bred young Americans—proved themselves superior to the lowly immigrants.

Abba and her contemporaries were convinced of the propriety of their own civic virtues, and deeply concerned with acculturation and reform. At what age, they asked, could social deviants be most effectively integrated into society? Did that age differ for males and females? At what point should reformers try to separate, contain, and punish miscreants, rather than reform them? Conventionally, boys of the "dangerous classes" were treated differently than were girls. Although they might commit the most heinous offenses, society still believe that boys were amenable to reform, that their characters might be restored by hard work, education, and the faith of their middle-class saviors. On the other hand, girls' crimes were a threat to moral order. Primarily defined by their sexual nature, these crimes threatened the family, that institution most responsible for preserving and reproducing social order and harmony.

A SINGLE STANDARD

Abba at last broke ranks with many of the male reformers because of the double sexual standard. With other feminist reformers, she came to reject the conventional wisdom; the real solution to the problem was a society based on sexual equality, with high standards for morality, companionship, education, and industry. Institutional and individual efforts at charity and reform, however, lagged behind an ideal. The best that conventional reform could achieve was to avoid financing "schools for scandal," which meant ignoring sexually active girls and concentrating reform efforts, eventually, on institutions for boys. In the 1870s "girls over thirteen and colored girls" were still considered unplaceable and unsupervisable by the Boston Children's Aid Society.[58]

Exhausted, Abba gave up her job as a paid social worker in 1850. The experience had taught her a great deal. Her contact with Boston's growing poverty, and above all with the exploitation of poor girls and women, set her own struggles in perspective. She no longer viewed the Alcott family's distress as unique; nor did Louisa Alcott. Their sympathies expanded as they identified with the people they tried to help. Abba also developed a deeper understanding of the social and economic causes of poverty. She could no longer blame the victims, nor hope that broader education and stricter supervision would solve the problems. After handling two hundred cases a month, working after hours and bringing some of the most desperate cases home to the Alcott apartment, she had become exasperated with her employers, who she claimed addressed the symptons rather than the real causes of poverty. "My position among them," she wrote, "has been uncomfortable from the simple reason that while they are sympathizing in the detail of wretchedness and want, I am busy with the *causes* of so much poverty and crime. Why it is so is a better question than what shall we do. The former implies prevention, the latter signified the need of cure."[59]

Abba went even further: her radical assessment of the causes of poverty joined her maturing feminism. Unlike her last employers, the ladies of the South Friendly Society, she knew at first hand the poor women who earned $1.50 a day sewing for their betters, and she understood the cause of their exploitation:

Incompetent wages for labor performed, is the cruel tyranny of capitalist power over the laborers' necessities. The capitalist speculates on their bones and sinews. Will not this cause Poverty— Crime—Despair? Employment is needed but just compensation is more needed. Is it not inhuman to tax a man's strength to the uttermost by all sorts of competition that a certain result may be accomplished in a given time. Alas! for the laborer too often proved an Infernal machine, so he finds himself bankrupt in health and energy, and woman too, how often I am told as an apology for exquisite and extra stitches, that it furnishes employment, for the poor: this hackneyed reply can no longer shield the miserable vanity that can only find gratification in the servitude of numerous fellow beings.[60]

Abba had stretched her own domestic feminism to include the lives of other oppressed women. Her need for a broader interpretation of woman's condition drew her increasingly into the most advanced feminist ranks.

Just as Abba changed in this new environment, so too did Louisa.

Except for a brief sojourn at her great-uncle Samuel May's house, she had lost a room of her own. She had also lost the privilege of running freely in the woods and acting out amateur theatricals with family and friends. She had even lost the full-time companionship of Anna and Abba, both of whom were working. Louisa herself had begun to work, teaching with Anna in a small primary school a block away from their cramped South End rooms. The family's hard times were intensified by Bronson's emotional fragility. Hardly recovered from his miseries at Fruitlands and his transitional period in Concord, Bronson found the women's survival skills both comforting and threatening. Yet Boston did supply congenial listeners for his conversations. Perhaps the most rewarding member of this group was Ednah Littlehale. A young, brunette devotee, Ednah apparently sparked anew Bronson's capacity for romantic friendship; he was almost fifty years old when they met in 1848. According to Madelon Bedell, however, Ednah's name never appears in Bronson's journals after her marriage to Seth Cheney in 1853.[61]

Whether or not Abba and the girls knew of Bronson's flirtation, they included Ednah Cheney in their circle of friends for many years. Ednah, like Louisa, adored Margaret Fuller and grieved deeply when Fuller died in a shipwreck off Fire Island in 1850. Returning to America with her Italian husband and young son, Fuller was about to face the mixed reactions of Americans who admired her courage and feared her influence. Her New England friends were moving from Romantic idealism to positivist social science as they tried to keep their faith in both individualism and democracy. She had chosen a more radical path in the Old World, and perhaps she might have brought it to the New World had she landed safely in New York.

At eighteen, Alcott stood between two worlds. Aware of the active woman's movement, though too busy to attend the first woman's rights conventions in Seneca Falls, New York, and then at Syracuse, she avidly sought news of them. She heard reports of the meetings directly from her Uncle Sam, who was a member of a central committee for the conventions which also included Harriot Hunt, Lucretia Mott, and Elizabeth Cady Stanton. He sent her copies of the *Proceedings* of the Syracuse Convention.[62] Meanwhile, under her mother's influence, she taught literacy and Sunday School classes in Boston's South End. What she learned in this period—the need for a single sexual standard, the conflict between heredity and environment, between city and country, familial versus institutional responsibiltity for oneself—she would later integrate into her novels.

For the moment her own passage from adolescence to young adulthood was her most pressing problem; it took place within a broader, intellectual transition from Romantic beliefs in individual salvation to positivist faith in social environmentalism. Like many of her contemporaries, she did not give up the old Romantic faith easily, but she went beyond nostalgia to explore causality. In what ways did a young person's inherent strengths and weaknesses "harden" into character? How much of human society was the result of inherited personal and social history, and how much could be changed in the character of one person? In one lifetime could both the individual and society be redeemed? Alcott began to explore these questions in *Moods*, the book which marked the end of her "Romantic period." Years later Abba wrote that women should assert their right "to think, feel, and live individually . . . be something in yourself."[63] Testing the Emersonian path to individuality on behalf of her sex, Alcott would try to find the relationship between womanhood and human identity. She would pit the heroes and heroines of her girlhood against one another in her first novel, testing their analyses and their solutions to her dilemma. Margaret Fuller had named the problem Alcott tried to explore fully:

> Ye cannot believe it, men; but the only reason why women ever assume what is more appropriate to you, is because you prevent them from finding out what is fit for themselves. Were they free, were they wise fully to develop the strength and beauty of woman, they would never wish to be men.[64]

SIX
Outward Bound

Seventeen years have I lived, and yet so little do I know, and so
much remains to be done before I begin to be what I desire—a
truly good and useful woman.

Louisa May Alcott, Journals, *May 1850*

Alcott found every day a battle against Boston's bustle and dirt.
Moreover, the city mocked her pride as it tempted her youthful
vanity, daring her to do the things she longed to do and could not,
because she was both an Alcott and a young woman. She felt that
family portraits of Hancock, Quincy, and the Sewalls, ghosts of the
city fathers, looked askance upon her. It was seven years after her
arrival, when she wore her first new silk dress (the gift of a kind aunt)
on New Year's Eve in 1857, before she felt the family portraits
smiled approvingly on her.[1] The "wilfull, moody" girl believed herself at last to be a "truly good and useful woman."[2]

CARE AND WOE

In the years between poverty-stricken anonymity and the first
evidence of literary talent, Louisa's self-doubts and unwelcome passions often seemed to tire her to death. The mother who had so often
comforted her was very busy, preoccupied with earning a living for
them all. Louisa was all alone in a crowded city. It was not in her
character to sit passively at home, waiting for adulthood. She triumphed over her own self-doubts and the restrictions of poverty and
sex by going into "service." Her experiences as a working woman
during the 1850s permanently shaped the way she thought and
wrote about the world. Although working would not resolve her
own delicate, inner battle, it gradually prepared her for an active role
in the social ferment around her.

Still, inner turmoil at the age of seventeen seemed more threatening to Louisa than the "exile, danger, and trouble" her family faced during Boston's smallpox epidemic that summer. Moving twice in one year (first from Dedham Street to Temple Place) provided no relief from the "bustle and dirt" that Louisa hated in Boston's South End. After going from Dedham Street to Temple Place, the Alcotts moved that spring to Samuel May's house in Atkinson Street; there Louisa hoped for some leisure, privacy, and a few small comforts to lift the "care and woe" she felt.[3] Her hopes were not realized. Sensitive and proud like her mother, she cherished the "romantic tastes" which her cousins thought presumptuous in poor relations. She had asserted the importance of her need for "solitude and out-of-door life," and she resented the loss of both when she had to sew, launder, and clean for well-to-do families at two dollars a week. The contrast between Atkinson Street and scrubbing for a living only exacerbated Louisa's "moodiness."

Abba had her own troubles, importuning her relatives for funds while resisting their advice to separate from Bronson. The whole family caught smallpox, possibly from an immigrant family whom Abba had taken into the garden and fed.[4] Poverty felt doubly humiliating, even terrifying, as the Alcotts endured illness in Boston while their wealthier friends and relatives fled the city's heat and contagion. Bronson was ill enough to frighten them all but he finally recovered with the help of their homeopathic treatment of rest, plain food, and isolation. In August Abba started her own "Intelligence Service" on High Street. Birth and education, she felt, should have made her a philanthropic employer of domestic workers in her own house. Instead, she was the proprietor of an employment agency which daughter Louisa later described as the "purgatory of the poor."[5] For the next three years, the Alcott women balanced, wavered between providing "cooks, good parlor and chamber maids, seamstresses, toilette women and dressmakers" for the rich, and taking such job themselves.[6]

Yet Abba still found time to write encouraging notes in Louisa's journal. Louisa, in turn, fantasized about a time when she could provide "a lovely quiet home" for her mother with "no debts or troubles to burden her." Stretching her imaginary bounty further, Louisa also installed Anna, who was away working as a nursemaid, in a "nice little home of her own."[7] Having established everyone else in comfortable domesticity, she also hoped to find her own inner peace, "a happy kingdom in myself," as she put it.[8] But such a poor young woman scarcely had the time or energy for voyages of self-discovery. And still she blamed her own restless mind for some of her troubles. It was a sort of "confused and dusty room that needed sweeping out," and she found herself lacking a housewifely temperament to do it.[9]

She also thought about being an actress with "plenty of money and a very gay life."[10] Instead she entered into domestic service when James Richardson called at the Intelligence Service to find a light housekeeping companion for his elderly father and spinster sister.[11] Richardson lived in nearby Dedham; he was not unfamiliar to the Alcotts, having attended Bronson's "Conversations." Abba sent him her second daughter. May family pride was partly salvaged by remembering that an earlier generation of honest rural folk sent daughters into service in their neighbors' households. So far Louisa and Anna had earned their keep among friends and relatives. These were humbling circumstances to be sure, but hardly comparable to the exploitation endured by Irish girls, and certainly light years away from the involuntary servitude being attacked more and more frequently by the Alcotts and other abolitionists in meetings all over New England.

Aware of the existing exploitation, Alcott viewed her prospective employment in the James Richardson household as a harmless adventure. She was wrong. She spent a total of six weeks as maid-of-all-work in this home. She found herself cooking, cleaning, making fires, and running errands; as if these chores were not enough, she was called upon to serve as a one-woman audience for Richardson's philosophical discourses. She described the experience twenty years later in "How I Went out to Service." After all those years she still was furious with an employer who thought he had bought her selfhood when he had only hired her labor.[12] "I was not to read, but to be read to . . . to be a passive bucket into which he was to pour all manner of philosophic metaphysical and sentimental rubbish. I was to serve his needs, soothe his sufferings and sympathize with all his sorrow . . . to be a galley slave in fact.[13] When she refused to perform according to Richardson's ideal of female companionship, he treated her like a man-of-all-work. She shoveled snow, hauled wood and water, and generally exhausted herself. When she finally quit she discovered that the purse containing her six weeks' wages held only four dollars. However empty their larder, the Alcotts kept their pride. Louisa sent back the insulting sum.[14]

Ednah Cheney recommended Alcott's "How I Went out to Service" to those "who condemn severely the young girls who prefer the more independent life of the factory or shop to what is considered the safety and comfort of service in families."[15] She meant that domestic service in her time was often considered safe, even privileged work for young women. Well-to-do employers felt that their "girls" were elevated by the discreet gentility of the homes they served. Even reformers argued that young maids in their service were learning domestic economy. Ideally the young women would serve their time, give their employers proper notice, and then marry enterprising young workmen or farmers, their improved habits and skills serving as a sort of dowry. Cheney felt that Louisa's experience of exploitation, the denial of her privacy and her identity as well, exploded this myth. Her story explained why most girls preferred factory work, which at least allowed them to struggle for more of their own "free" time.[16]

One year later, in 1859, Nathaniel and Sophia Peabody Hawthorne bought Hillside, the Alcott home in Concord. The payment was carefully divided to reimburse Emerson for his initial gift of five hundred dollars and to return one thousand dollars to Abba. Emerson promptly established a small trust fund for Bronson, and Sam Sewall secured Abba's portion in the same discreet manner. Once again the Alcotts moved, this time to Pinckney Street in Beacon Hill, where the rent was three hundred and fifty dollars—as much as Abba, Louisa, and Anna had earned the entire previous year.[17]

In the spring of 1859, Alcott sold a "romantic" story she had written at sixteen to *Olive Branch*, a popular weekly that the Alcott girls read avidly.[18] (Years later, when she made the incident a part of *Little Women*, she described reading her "great rubbish," as she called it, to her family.) In the same year Harriet Beecher Stowe's *Uncle Tom's Cabin* became the publishing success of the nation, selling 300,000 copies. Alcott listed it as one of her favorite "best novels," and one she hoped to emulate.[19] By this time Abba was fifty-one and exhausted, no longer with enough strength to be the family's chief breadwinner. Alcott began to teach herself to write in order to support the family. Encouraged by her modest start and by the success of other women's fiction, she felt it could be done and must be done.

Ever since the failure of Fruitlands, the Alcotts had lived from day to day, unable to make long-range plans and implement them. Alcott, "grubbing away as usual," combined teaching in the family parlor with sewing at night and writing stories whenever she could snatch the precious solitude.[20] Abba took in boarders and sewing to help make ends meet. Anna was in Syracuse during 1854, where Sam May had found her a job teaching school, and May was a pupil in a Boston school. Elizabeth was the family housekeeper. She vaguely considered attending normal school to become a certified teacher, and also had a suitor at this time. Aside from indefinite references in family correspondence, however, there is no real mention of Elizabeth's marital plans. Bronson had engaged on a financially unremunerative series of "Conversations" in the West. Arriving home in February, he opened his purse and showed his wife and daughters one dollar. "Only that!" he said. "My overcoat was stolen, and I had to buy a shawl." "Real love," Alcott decided, was her mother's forbearance and gratitude that her husband was safely home, and her father's comfort in his faithful wife and children.[21]

For Alcott at twenty-two, love was not enough, and she frantically devised schemes to increase her earnings. She considered her progress: "I have eleven dollars, all my own earnings—five for a story and four for the pile of sewing I did for the ladies of Dr. Gray's society, to give him as a present." She decided that this sounded funny, but begged Anna in her letter not to "laugh at my plans; I'll carry them out, if I go to service to do it. Seeing so much money flying about, I long to honestly get a little and make my dear family more comfortable, I feel weak-minded when I think of all they need and the little I can do." Having confessed a moment of frailty, she returned to her increasingly boyish tone; she called Anna "my good little lass," but also admitted that she had privately shed her "quart" of tears over their lot.[22] In public she showed greater strength. When a cousin delivered her story to an editor and brought her the five-dollar payment, she seemed to relish his treatment of her as a tough breadwinner. "Now, Lu," he said, "the door is open, go in and win." "So I shall try to do it," she replied.[23]

Practical plans were important to Alcott because they signaled her ability to control the circumstances of her life. She began by plotting out the stories she would write for popular magazines. By exploiting the issues enunciated by woman's rights advocates, which were also the everyday problems of her own life, she created stories for women like herself and her mother. There was now a large reading audience of women who wanted to see their own experiences described in the fiction they read.

PENS AND NEEDLES

Still a literary novice, Alcott had to supplement her writing income with needlework for several more years. But she was fortunate in having literary connections, and she was able to justify her own need for independence because it coincided with efforts to support her family. Slowly her fiction entered the stream of contemporary passionate thrillers, children's stories, and domestic novels. Undiscouraged by her long apprenticeship, family pride, and fierce determination to "live and have no time for sentimental musings" kept her planning and writing.[24] In 1855 at the age of twenty-three she finally saw the publication of a complete volume under her own name, Flower Fables, a revised version of the fairy tales she had created in Concord for such younger friends as Ellen Emerson.[25]

Alcott felt she had learned a good deal about publishers, financing, and marketing, and she put an advance copy of Flower Fables into Abba's Christmas stocking. She called it her "first born," but hoped to "pass in time from fairies and fables to men and realities."[26] George Briggs and Co. planned to market the book as a Christmas gift selection. They had little to lose, since the first run was subsidized by Miss Wealthy Stevens, an Alcott family friend. The dedication of the book to Ellen Emerson by "her friend the author" should have added to its marketability. It did not make its author rich, however; Louisa received only thirty-two dollars from the sales.[27] Nevertheless, looking back in 1886 at her carefully saved "notices" she commented that she was "prouder over the thirty-two dollars than the eight-thousand dollars" she received for six months of receipts thirty-one years later.[28]

The opening fable, "The Frost King, or the Power of Love," seems only a sentimental reminder to children of the necessity of self-sacrifice and faithful work.[29] If these stories had any pretensions to emblematic meaning in the Romantic convention of nineteenth-century flower language, no critic noticed it. But there is one striking theme in "The Frost King": the complete separation of sexual spheres. The warm, sun-filled abundant kingdom of the Fairy Queen is engaged in a life-and-death struggle with the cold, windy, frigid domain of the Frost King.

The Frost King, slowly expanding his territory, seeks to kill the tender blossoms in other lands with his cold wind. Violet, "the weakest fairy" in the Queen's band, offers herself as a messenger to the Frost King, hoping to warm his heart. She flies off, brings a garland of fresh flowers for him, and sheds her own golden light upon his "cold dark gardens." He tries to send her back, but Violet, even though she has seen her garland freeze and die around his neck, insists on staying. She shares her warmth and sunshine with the creatures there and grows moss, flowers, and vines. At length the Frost King, slightly thawed by Violet's unselfish gardening, promises not to harm flowers in the Fairy Queen's own realm; he will kill only those outside her domain.

Nearly dead from her labors to save all the flowers, Violet accepts the king's final challenge to build him a palace fairer than his own icy castle. If she can do this, he will never freeze another flower. Violet manages to create a New Eden in the Frost King's sterile, icy land with the help of all her loving friends. In the end, the Frost King's own spirits, "casting off their dark mantles," kneel "before him and beseech him not to send them forth to blight the things the gentle Fairies love so much." The Frost King chooses a flower crown, pays homage to Violet, and watches his icy castle melt away.

This tale is remarkable, given the Fruitlands experience. Unable to produce life, the Frost King is bent upon destroying it. The Fairy Queen does not battle him directly, but allows her "weakest" fairy to tame the enemy through love. The king's own male spirits desert him, won over to the warmth and abundance of domesticity by busy spinster spiders, breadcrumb-sharing fairies, and monastic cells trans-

formed into country kitchens. It was Alcott's first effort in fiction to
save the people she loved by blending domesticity and feminism.

In the summer of 1855 Anna's and Louisa's various earnings,
together with the small income from trust funds, sufficed to send all
the Alcotts to Walpole, New Hampshire. Eliza Wells, the married
daughter of Abba's dead sister, Catherine, provided a house rent
free. To the Alcott's anxious relatives, the move seemed sensible.
Walpole's quiet hills invoked memories of Spindle Hill, and a diet of
vegetables and fruit from the garden Bronson immediately planted
would conserve money. Abba and the girls made tallow candles,
soap, and lye from ashes, and rendered sheep fat.

Walpole was not just a sleepy village but was also a fashionable
summer encampment for artistic, unconventional visitors. Besides
gardening, fresh air, and rest, Louisa and Anna enjoyed "plays,
picnics, and pleasant people," such as "Fanny Kemble, Mrs. Kirkland, and Dr. Bellows," all of whom joined in creating impromptu
theatricals, including one of Alcott's blood-and-thunder plays.[30]

Alcott found time to write as well as to act. She finished a second
book of fairy tales, *Christmas Elves*, enlisting May's talents as illustra-
tor. In October she set out for Boston to sell her book. By
November, her birth month, which she called "the dullest month of
the year," she found out it was much too late to publish a book for
Christmas shoppers. Nevertheless, having earned twenty dollars
with stories for the *Saturday Evening Gazette*, and with two book-
length manuscripts to her credit, she was ready to seek her fortune
through writing.[31]

Alcott frequently mentioned acting as a career possibility in her
journal, and friends and family years later remembered the Alcotts'
semiprofessional performances. Perhaps she could comfortably admit to being "stage struck" because she shared its delights with
Anna, who appears to have been the truly gifted actress in the family. More than likely the theater also interested her as a vehicle for
her own plays and as an outlet for her fiercely personal sense of
comedy and tragedy. She was particularly fond of improvising eccentric old ladies, Dickensian widows and spinsters, and even, on occasion, Mrs. Malaprop. Among her most popular parlor sketches were

satirical imitations of reformers and their critics, including both woman's rights advocates and antifeminists.

Madeleine Stern correctly points out "it was impossible for the historian of the March family to write a story without theatricals, for when she produced her best work she took her materials from her own life, and that life had included a more-than-common interest in the drama."[32] Her "moody," passionate feelings found an acceptable outlet in melodramas, and comedies provided a means of expressing the outrage she often struggled to suppress in snobbish social situations. Alcott, often an outsider, turned her snubs into powerful critiques of polite hypocrisy when she played "character" parts. Significantly her acting experiences were also part of a wave of parlor theatricals accompanying the cultural transformation of America's middle class in the late 1840s, 1850s, and 1860s.[33] A more confident, secure class was just beginning to laugh at itself and perfect its rituals in the form of amateur parlor theatricals. The Alcotts and their friends created original and memorable neighborhood entertainments, and their performances were often substantial fund raisers for charity. These activities were not at all unusual, however; parlor dramas were the most popular form of middle-class entertainment.

Alcott used the dramatic devices, methods, and techniques of the stage to fashion a distinctive writing style. Her most interesting work included forms of tableaux, charade, pantomime, as well as brilliant use of cosmetics, costumes, and grand "unmaskings." Louisa and Anna found lively and talented dramatic players in Walpole and then in the Concord Stock Company in 1857 and 1858. The sisters developed a wide repertoire including a "Grand Dickens Cosmorama."[34]

Despite longings for professional success as an actress, Louisa Alcott's true calling was finally literary. It may be that she simply did not get the "breaks" every actress knows represent an important factor in success. In any case, she had recorded a passionate determination to succeed as an author as many times over the years as she noted having "stage struck fits." In 1860, which she called "A Year of Good Luck," she finally admitted that she had been working on her first serious novel, *Moods*. She belittled her efforts: "Daresay nothing will ever come of it." Yet she added, "But it *had* to be done, and I'm richer for the experience." The feeling that she had been "possessed" by her work made it easier to justify her writing, and *Moods* is full of playacting, costume changes, and melodramatic expressions of emotion. She half jokingly used the expression, "genius burned," in the belief that all artists acted as instruments in the expression of inspiration.[35]

THE YEAR OF GOOD LUCK

Like so many gifted women of her day, Alcott's ambitions to become an independent artist conflicted with conventional stereotypes of feminine behavior. As early as October 1856 she confided, "I was born with a boy's spirit under my bib and tucker, I can't wait when I can work so I took my little talent in my hand and forced the world again, braver than before and wiser for my failures."[36] Born with a boy's spirit, she was also clearly a young woman at the age of twenty-four. The conflict made her vacillate between two paths: she could combine marriage with writing, or remain single. Married women might take to writing in order to support their loved ones. Harriet Beecher Stowe and Lydia Maria Child had done so, but they also accepted domesticity as a woman's primary role—insofar as fictional heroines can be trusted to reflect their authors' values.

The second path, a common topic in Alcott's journal and fiction, was a single life. Though she had several "adorers," she disparaged them all as "queer."[37] She clung to the privileges of boyhood as long as she could, salvaging the best memories of childhood for her fairy tales. She continued to describe herself and her sisters as the Alcott "girls," a verbal tactic that excused their work as nonthreatening girlish fancies and emphasized their sisterhood. Yet the events in her life dispelled the illusion of perpetual childhood. Soon Alcott would follow her chosen path of a single life with a clearer sense of herself.

The changing character of her sisters' lives had much to do with this transformation. Anna found her future husband, John, and increasingly spent her leisure time with him. May, "fortune's favored child," traveled back and forth between Walpole and Boston seeking the best art training available for women at that time. Louisa found small sums from her own earnings to give her, while May and Sewall relations also enjoyed helping the bright, outgoing May. But it was Beth, the homebody, who gave her family the most concern.

Elizabeth, whose family pet names were Lizzie and Beth, never moved beyond the pious passivity prescribed for girls in mid-nineteenth century. She was seriously ill, partly as a result of scarlet fever thought to have been contracted from one of Abba's charity visits to a poor family. She declined rapidly. Even a visit to the seashore failed to restore her wasted body, which weighed less than ninety pounds. Her case was critical, though the actual physical malady remained unknown. The Sewalls offered land in Walden to build a suburban house for Bronson, Abba, and the invalid. But both Bronson and his dearest girl wanted to move back to Concord.

He found a farmhouse with over ten acres of land and an orchard of apple trees for nine hundred and fifty dollars. Emerson once more contributed the largest share of the capital, and other friends put up the difference. Abba's income from the sale of Hillside remained safely invested. Yet Bronson too had become more pragmatic. This time he found no fault with property ownership, and when Beth seemed a bit better he set off on another western tour to earn money. But Beth did not live to enjoy Orchard House.[38] Waiting in another rented cottage for renovations of Orchard House to be completed, she faded into fitful unconsciousness, dosed against pain with opium, ether, and finally morphine.

The entire family hovered anxiously about her. Abba, the competent nurse of so many other invalids, wrote, "I watched her with jealous care—and I think the cold and perhaps want of more cheerful society—as well as the absence of certain nutritive diet may have caused this sad wrench of her frame."[39] By Christmas Beth would allow only Louisa to carry her downstairs. Soon she could not leave her room at all or sew the little comforts she loved to give as gifts to family and friends. Torn between guilt and misery at her sister's cruel reward for being so selfless and submissive, Alcott would use Beth's death as the model for the most moving episode in *Little Women*.

Bronson was called back home in January because Beth was dying. Louisa wrote that it was "a hard thing to bear, but if she is only to suffer, I pray she may go soon." When Bronson arrived he asked Beth if she knew how serious her condition was, that she might not get well? She replied that she could "best be spared of the four," and that her family would have her still in death as in life. Finally she asked to sit in her father's lap and kissed her mother and sisters. Her last audible words were, "Well now mother, I go, I go. How beautiful everything is tonight."⁴⁰ She was only twenty-three. Her emaciated body was like a small child's but her hair had entirely fallen out as if she were a very old woman. Emerson, Henry Thoreau, Frank Sanborn (Bronson's disciple and biographer), and John Pratt (Anna's fiancé) bore her coffin to Sleepy Hollow Cemetary in Concord.

Still in mourning, the Alcotts moved to Orchard House that spring. In April Anna told the family she wanted to marry John Pratt. His father, Minot Pratt, had been a director of Brook Farm, and like the Alcotts the family moved to Concord after their communal experiment ended. John and Anna shared a love of home drama productions and a reverence for Bronson's character and philosophy. John worked in an insurance company and he offered his fiancée a loving, secure home. It was too soon after Beth's death however for the Alcotts to contemplate another daughter's leaving the house, even for such an acceptable union. The young couple agreed to wait for a while.

Louisa was deeply distressed by Anna's love affair. In the midst of Elizabeth's final sufferings, she wrote that "I'll keep my lamentations over Nan's affairs till this duty is over."⁴¹ In May she admitted that John Pratt was a "true man," but still likened Anna's engagement to Beth's death. "So another sister is gone," Louisa said. She had only one sister left and vowed to "turn to little May for comfort."⁴² The two did indeed draw closer, but it was more than obvious, even to Louisa, that May was the prettiest Alcott daughter, the liveliest, most sociable, and surest to follow Anna's example. Being a daughter and a sister were no longer enough. Louisa increasingly felt forced to be herself.

In the fall she was back in Boston. "The only bread winner just now," more alone and depressed than ever, she walked the familiar streets thinking about her sister's death and her own relentless struggle to earn a living. She came to Mill Dam. The Great Bay of the Charles River was on one side, alive with commerce, and the stagnant waters of Back Bay spilled out from the other. Impulsively she thought of suicide, but drew back. "There is work for me and I'll have it," she wrote afterward about her despair and recovery.[43]

Reverend Theodore Parker helped her regain faith and energy when he preached on "Laborious Young Women": "Trust your fellow beings and let them help you. Don't be too proud to ask, and accept the humblest work till you can find the task you want." Alcott said it was what she needed to hear. "A test of character and courage," she called the alternate periods of employment and distress she had endured.[44] At twenty-six she looked back and felt that "the past year has brought us the first death and the first betrothal, two events that change my life. I can see that these experiences have taken a deep hold and changed or developed me."[45] Once before, on an early morning run in Concord's woods and meadows, she had felt God's grace imminent in her life. Now she felt God's presence even when no one else cared about her. "If this is experiencing religion, I have done it."[46] She defended Parker's radical theology and his agreement with George Ripley that Christianity must change society as well as individuals. Although some considered Parker no Christian, Alcott countered, "He is my sort; for though he may lack reverence for other people's God, he works bravely for his own and turns his back on no one who needs help as some other pious do."[47]

What Alcott called "practical Christianity" bridged the gap between her adventurous tomboy self and her role as cranky, overburdened "Aunt Lu." Parker provided safe transport from childhood to young womanhood by recognizing Louisa May Alcott's membership in a large class of young working women. He not only publicly accepted the need of many young women to work, he honored their labor. Inspiring Alcott to call him Reverend Power in her novel *Work*, he strengthened the young author at a crucial moment in her life, helping her learn the difference between eccentricity and Romantic heroism. Indeed, Alcott was not ready for a permanent decision to remain single. Marriage was still the most important event of a woman's life in America.

Alcott assumed that temperament was inherited, as did most of her contemporaries. Nevertheless, she comforted herself with Emerson's promise that balance and serenity could be won through experience, careful introspection, and self-discipline. The effort was worthwhile, not only as a means to personal growth, but also because social progress was still thought to be the aggregate of individual perfections. The difficulty for such American women as Alcott was that only young men enjoyed the worldly experience that encouraged much personal and social growth. In the eyes of conventional society, women remained fixed in the private domestic world, the lifelong dependents of men. Parker countered that it was not so, validating Alcott's feminist experience—an experience that increasingly found its way into her short stories and novels.

YOUNG WOMEN AND YOUNG LADIES

The same culture that prescribed childlike innocence and isolation from the real world as ideals of young womanhood expected a miraculous transformation on a girl's wedding day. As soon as a woman became a matron, she was expected to keep household accounts, discipline her children, counsel her husband, and in short, mother the Republic. Alcott seized upon this contradiction in women's lives for *Moods*. She elaborated the critical shortcomings of a young girl's conventional upbringing, claiming she had a right to an adolescent period of experience and self-reliance. Only this transitional period in women's lives could give them the mature individuality that both Emerson and the feminist movement claimed for all Americans.

Alcott had already aired this new dimension of the woman problem in her stories for the *Gazette*. At first she created patient Griseldas, only a trifle more realistic than Violet, the self-sacrificing little fairy in "The Frost King." Little Genevieve, for instance, the heroine of one *Gazette* story, flees into the snow, victim of her heartless father who had deserted Genevieve's mother and taken their baby with him. Years later, little Genevieve seeks and finds her mother, now a fallen woman. Patiently waiting for her mother outside her apartment in the bitter cold night, Genevieve freezes to death and the heartbroken mother enters a convent.[48]

Alcott's storytelling gradually matured beyond such sentimentality. Slowly she integrated her own experience into her fiction. In "The Sisters' Trial" four young women fulfill a promise to their dead mother by finding happiness in doing their duty. They bravely attempt a year of independent work to earn their living, and in so doing find their true vocations for both useful labor and marriage.[49] In another story Louisa examined differences between independent and dependent women. Written in the fall of 1856, "The Lady and the Woman" defends the virtues of the kind of wife sought by true men.[50]

At this time Alcott was happily attending Theodore Parker's Sunday evening discussions, reporting that they "did her good."[51] Emboldened to present young women closer to herself, she wrote about two female friends in their early twenties who take a rural holiday accompanied by a young bachelor both admire. A sudden fierce storm sends one friend into fainting fits. While the man stays behind to tend the unconscious girl, the other friend, Kate, sets out to bring help in the face of an impending flood. Strong and self-reliant, Kate is a "true woman," seasoned by years of supporting her orphaned brothers. The doctor she brings back observes that she must be single because no husband would allow her out in such a storm. The young bachelor is not at first attracted by Kate's courage. The author tells us that he dislikes "strong minded women" and idolizes "beautiful, tender creatures, submissive to the will." Kate informs him, however, that "an affectionate or accomplished idiot is not my ideal of a woman." She sets forth her own ideal, really a portrait of herself:

> I would have her strong enough to stand alone and give, not ask, support, brave enough to think and act, as well as feel. Keen-eyed enough to see her own and other's faults and wise enough to find a cure for them. I would have her humble, self-reliant; gentle though strong; man's companion, not his plaything; able and willing to face storm as well as sunshine and share life's burdens as they come.[52]

Ultimately she wins the affection and respect of the doubtful bachelor.

These short stories form the basis of a narrative formula Alcott refined throughout her writing career. Her heroines demand a period of independence or even modest adventure, not as an alternative to domesticity, but as a necessary precondition to its success. If special talents, family responsibilities, or "moods" bar a companionate, equal marriage, the alternative is honorable spinsterhood. According to Alcott, society must grant women a measure of the same experiences that test men in order that they too can be prepared for important roles in the family and in society.

From February 2 to 25, 1861, Alcott wrote and revised *Moods*, a book that explores the Romantic path to female individuality. She paused only for a run at dusk. Otherwise, she remained sitting, cuddled in a green and red "glory cloak" with a matching silk cap that Abba sewed for her. Surrounded by groves of manuscripts, living for immortality, as May observed, she was also the center of her family's devoted attention. Abba wandered in and out with cups of tea, and Bronson brought cider and apples to "Pegasus." Louisa found it "very pleasant and queer while it lasted." She read the book aloud to the family. Abba and Anna, both bursting with pride, thought it was wonderful, while Bronson thought "Emerson must see this." Alcott admitted, "I planned it some time ago, and have had it in my mind for ever so long; but now it begins to take shape."[53]

In April President Lincoln declared war against the South. Alcott longed to be a man and fight, but had to content herself with "working for those who can." From her war experiences came the writing of *Hospital Sketches*.[54] A notable popular success, its publication in 1862 led A. K. Loring to accept *Moods*. After badgering Alcott for months to change the lesson of the book, so that the readers might find themselves purified and ennobled by it, he finally published the first edition of *Moods* in 1865. Loring knew the public would be shocked that Alcott allowed her heroine to decide that youth and inexperience had led her to marry the wrong man. Even worse, the heroine seriously considers leaving her husband for her romantic lover. Loring urged Alcott to preach a different moral:

> When the sad awakening comes to either party each should straitway confess to the living and before God resolve that with His aid the vows shall be kept, the marriage sanctified and together, forever they will live out the noble life a sanctified marriage renders possible to all.[55]

Alcott agreed to have her heroine die at the end, unable to remain married to the wrong man. The revision of *Moods* to the author's satisfaction, allowing the heroine to survive her mental adultery, did not come until 1881, when Alcott bought the copyright back from her publisher for one dollar.[56] By that time her international reputation as the author of *Little Women* assured a devoted audience convinced that Miss Alcott would not suggest an immoral course of action. The two versions of *Moods* measure what had changed—and what had remained the same—in Alcott's life and in the world during seventeen crucial years of American history. By 1882 Alcott had long passed out of her Romantic peroid, and Transcendentalism had all but faded from American culture. The woman's movement she formally joined had altered some social conventions and a great many state laws, especially those governing divorce and married women's property rights.

Alcott's experiences as a single young woman, however, remained embedded in both editions of *Moods*, testimony that some obstacles facing young women had not changed much, she thought, by the end of the nineteenth century. Having begun her outward journey, she did not retreat, except to retrace the paths and adventures she had taken for her readers.

SEVEN

Moods

Life is a train of moods like a string of beads, and as we pass
through them they prove to be so many coloured lenses, which
paint the world their own hue and each shows us only what lies
in its own focus.

Ralph Waldo Emerson, "Experience," *1844–1845*

In 1865 the young Henry James dismissed the first edition of
Moods as an unconvincing version of "the old story of the husband,
the wife, and the lover." Since James assumed that a thirty-year-old
spinster author could scarcely possess original insight into the eternal
triangle, he found her attempt to deal with any deeper problem
laughable. "Has Miss Alcott proposed to give her story a philosophical bearing? We can hardly suppose it," James wrote acidly.[1] In her
preface to the revised edition of the novel in 1882, Louisa Alcott
replied, maintaining that the first work was so altered for the publisher that "marriage appeared to be the theme instead of an attempt
to show the mistakes of a moody nature, guided by impulse, not
principle."[2] The sincere selfhood so admired by mid-Victorians required a steady education toward principled behavior. Alcott revised
Moods to suit her own mature self and the appreciative audience who
firmly identified her with *Little Women* by the time *Moods* was reissued. *Little Women*, of course, is distinguished by its heroines' steady
progress toward principled, sincere, selfhood.

The first edition of *Moods* bears careful reading nonetheless; written at the close of what Alcott called her sentimental period, the
1850s, her first novel is part of the phenomenon that feminist scholar
Jane Tompkins calls "the other American Renaissance."[3] The popular explosion of sentimental literature usually dealt with domestic
relations, and Tompkins cogently argues that it was all the more
"realist" because it dealt with commonplace actualities that women
could not escape by running away to sea. Her argument reminds us

that Henry James was neither the first nor the last critic to find domestic realities less significant in American life and fiction than hunting whales.

For seventeen years, however, between the first and second *Moods,* Alcott remained touchy about her novel's reception, convinced that its themes did indeed offer important "philosophical bearing" on the relations between the sexes. Henry James notwithstanding, critical reviews in *Harper's Weekly* and the *Reader* of 1865 praised the novel as "Transcendental Fiction," and even applauded the attempt to deal with problems of marriage and divorce, issues central to the woman's rights movement and to Victorian Americans generally.[4] Unquestionably, *Moods,* first written within the context of domestic issues being forwarded in woman's rights conventions, proposed in sentimental novels, and debated in every newspaper and popular magazine, enlarges the parameters of the other American Renaissance. Like many other mid-nineteenth-century writers such as Margaret Fuller, Rebecca Harding Davis, Caroline Dall, and Caroline Stansbury Kirkland, Alcott struggled to portray her heroine's self-transforming powers without betraying woman's rights.[5]

The evangelical writers, most notably Susan Warner and Harriet Beecher Stowe, rewrote the mythology of American womanhood, presenting self-sacrificing heroines who redeemed themselves and often their fallen sisters and brothers as well. Paradoxically, of course, they gained a greater spiritual power over the Simon Legrees of the world by exercising such pure moral influence.[6] *Moods* also claimed a special role for woman's moral influence, but in a Transcendental mode. Its author insisted upon woman's right to selfhood; without it, she could not develop and exercise her natural spiritual powers. Alcott, in other words, argued that women had to possess themselves in order to behave effectively as selfless missionaries.

A few months after the September meetings of the 1852 National Woman's Rights Convention adjourned, she had the *Proceedings* at hand.[7] Sam May had forwarded them, and they included the resolutions of Lydia E. Fowler, secretary of the convention. Fowler resolved

That as it is universally acknowledged, that when a truly great work is performed, it proves the right of the performer to do it;

119

therefore, let each woman here assembled, determine that during the coming year, she will labor to accomplish some great and useful end, either in the bosom of her own family, in perfecting her own "God-inspired self-hood," in living out the full tide of her emotions and aspirations, or fulfilling the instincts of her genius, whether as a poet, artist, physician or minister.[8]

The limitations on women's "God-inspired self-hood," were graphically described by Horace Greeley in a letter to the delegates and by Ernestine Rose, an immigrant and a labor organizer, present as a delegate. Greeley found the "bread problem" at the root of women's unequal status. Women needed education, franchise, and above all work—the development of manufacturing industry, he thought, would ultimately benefit both women and society.

Ernestine Rose insisted that marriage was at the heart of the woman problem: "What an inconsistency, that from the moment she enters that compact (marriage), in which she assumes the high responsibility of wife and mother, she ceases legally to exist and becomes a purely submissive being. Blind submission in woman is considered a virtue, while submission to wrong is itself wrong, and resistance to wrong is virtue alike in woman as in man."[9] Several delegates, in practical terms, described their direct observations that ordinary women went far beyond their spheres and that legal reforms should merely confirm reality as they knew it. Mrs. C.I.H. Nichols, for instance, spoke of farm women in her home state of Vermont. Women's rights, she argued, were nothing more than the means of carrying out their responsibilities.

Sarah Fish of Rochester sent a letter in which she made women's responsibilities also the duties of men. She also envisioned a future in which "there will be mutual responsibility . . . father and mother, brother and sister, will feel alike inspired by all the old affections, conjugal, parental, fraternal, and filial, to make home beautiful, attractive and happy."[10]

Moods is part of the expanding Victorian mythology of womanhood that Nina Auerbach unveils, forming, as she says, a "subversive paradigm." The angel and the demon, the spinster and the fallen woman—all these are many faces of a single image—"the demonic angel rises from within the angel in the house."[11] Recalling her own conflicted, stormy youth, Alcott brilliantly portrays a vital, sensitive "little woman," Sylvia Yule, struggling with her angelic demon.

THE STORY

With the original drafts of *Moods* lost to us, we can never know exactly how much of Louisa May Alcott's compelling instinct and imagination were deleted from the published first edition.[12] With all its flaws, the 1865 *Moods* still evokes profound sympathy for its heroine. Sylvia Yule is just eighteen, poised between childhood and young womanhood. She lives with her widowed father and an older brother and sister in a luxurious home opening onto a fine garden. Lonely, sensitive, and intelligent, she yearns for companionship and experience in the world; above all she searches for a more purposeful life. Her character is unformed, but her potential is clear—evident in her "moody" yearnings to be more than an accomplished household ornament. Sylvia has honesty, talent close to genius, and a face that just misses beauty for its "want of harmony." A motherless childhood, however, has left her undisciplined, starved for love. Prue, her sister, can offer only boring fashionable distractions, and Sylvia, flitting from girlish petulance to tomboyish spading in the garden, is ripe for trouble.

It is her hunger for love, which she confuses with an equally genuine need for friendship and experience, that brings tragedy. As a birthday gift she is allowed to join her older brother, Max, an artist, and his friends Geoffrey Moor and Adam Warwick, on a two-day excursion down the river. The trip proves pivotal in Alcott's tale. Both Warwick and Moor immediately fall in love with Sylvia, thus "spoiling" the period of experience, friendship, and self-reliance she needs for growth into true womanhood, before finding true love.

Both men press the confused "little woman," as her brother calls her, to marry and she sees no alternative means to gaining companionship or wider experience. In fact her interactions with the men take place, as it were, on stage sets, the scenes shifting from parlor to garden and back to parlor again. Even the river journey is a series of outdoor sets changing as their "kelpie" boat touches various shores. Sylvia is quite sure that what she feels for gentle Geoffrey Moor, the

sentimental ideal of a husband, is friendship. In brief indoor courtship scenes she shyly tells him that he may hope for nothing more.
On the other hand she also suspects that the passionate stirrings she
feels for Adam Warwick, a Romantic hero, "the manliest man" she
has ever met, may well be "true love."

Certainly Adam Warwick's adventurous life tempts her; she can
imagine herself as his companion in a thrilling, noble life. Their
scenes together are often outdoors and active, offering a taste of more
daring travels to come. But Adam, unbeknown to Sylvia, must first
extricate himself from a half-promise to the Creole beauty, Ottila.
He leaves to free himself from Ottila, determining to return and
court Sylvia openly. While he is gone Sylvia waits faithfully for
some months, trusting correctly that her unexpressed feelings are
returned. Then she meets the touring Ottila and hears that the
gorgeous creature is Warwick's fiancée. Her deepest sensibilities having been aroused and then, as she thinks, betrayed, Sylvia impulsively turns to Moor, accepting his proposal of marriage. She does
not tell him that she loves Warwick and Geoffrey, knowing that she
still feels only friendship for him, confidently assures Sylvia that she
will learn to love him as she grows up under her husband's tender
tutelage.

Moor and Sylvia Yule marry, in a double ceremony with Sylvia's
brother Max and his fiancée. In the mountains, on her honeymoon,
Sylvia once again meets Adam Warwick, returning to court her. The
unlucky lovers can only part immediately, hoping that time will heal
their pain. Instead, Sylvia grows pale and thin while Adam wanders
away in search of work to distract him, all in vain. Returning again,
by chance in the company of Moor's cousin, the spinster Faith Dane,
Warwick confronts Sylvia with their still powerful attraction for one
another. Uncertain, Sylvia turns to Faith Dane, who counsels her to
wait patiently and do all she can to save her marriage. If a wife's
earnest efforts to make an empty marriage into a meaningful union
fail, then she may choose separation. Despite Sylvia's self-sacrificing
intentions, the situation deteriorates still further and Moor urges his
wife to tell him what stands between them. "Adam Warwick," she
finally answers.

Crushed and angry, Moor leaves and, again with Faith Dane's

counsel, a waiting period ensues. Moor and Adam Warwick, their friendship still miraculously intact, leave together to fight in Italy with Garibaldi. Sylvia is left to care for her aging father and her brother's young family. Predictably, she grows up. Faith tells her that a union with Warwick would be doomed in any event; he is an "eagle" and Sylvia is a "wood dove." Unequal partnerships inevitably lead to the domination of the weaker spirit by the more powerful. Sylvia cannot, in other words, have herself and Warwick; he will, unavoidably, crush her fragile selfhood. On the other hand, separation and time to grow on her own may make Sylvia a fit, contented companion to Moor. Either alone or in a "friendship" marriage, Sylvia can keep her integrity and Moor will have, at least, his self-respect. At the end of the separation period, having learned that she has a fatal illness, Sylvia sends for Moor. Warwick and Moor embark for home, but their ship is wrecked and Warwick dies, just off-shore, helping Moor into a boatload of survivors. Sylvia and Moor are reunited, just briefly enough for Sylvia to relate her dream of a great scarlet word, "Amen," in the sky as a universal "sigh of hope from human hearts goes up." As a great wave rolls up before Sylvia, she sees her mother's face and knows she will rejoin her in Heaven. Sylvia dies before spring and her death, in the first edition, relieved her of a "long bewilderment of life and love."

THROUGH FLOOD AND FIELD AND FIRE

Alcott uses Sylvia Yule's life to illustrate what can happen to a young girl with little or no experience in the world. Her own youth had prepared her to present Sylvia's plight, and such novelists as Hawthorne and Brontë supplied fictional models. In both *The Scarlet Letter* (1850) and *Jane Eyre* (1847), women suffer from love partly because they know little of life.[13] Hester Prynne leaves her parental home without any preparation for worldly experiences, and Jane Eyre has only a charity school education and a cold outcast life to prepare her for romantic ventures.

Despite her deprivations, or perhaps because of them, Jane speaks in defense of women's human feelings and aspirations:

Nobody knows how many rebellions besides political rebellions ferment in the masses of life which people the earth. Women are supposed to be very calm generally: but women feel just as men feel; they need exercise for their faculties, and a field for their efforts as much as their brothers do; they suffer from too rigid a constraint, too absolute a stagnation, precisely as men would suffer; and it is narrow-minded in their more privileged fellow-creatures to say that they ought to confine themselves to making puddings and knitting stockings, to playing on the piano and embroidering bags. It is thoughtless to condemn them, or laugh at them, if they seek to do more or learn more than custom has pronounced necessary for their sex.[14]

Alcott tried to show that Sylvia, like Jane, needed "exercise," and at eighteen she was ignorant of the choices available to her. Untried in the world outside her garden, a prisoner of childhood, Sylvia could only boyishly rebel and demand experiences reserved to young men. Throughout the novel Alcott contrasts Sylvia's struggle with the easy, unobstructed male acquisition of experience. Thus her brother Max explores the world without restraint while Sylvia sits at home, trying to sew placidly, but thinking about forbidden pleasures: "I don't see why I must sit here and hem nightcap strings when the world is full of pleasant places and delightful people," she sighs. "If I could only be allowed to go and find them. . . . I wish I were a boy, or could be contented with what other girls like."[15]

The disparities in male and female experiences become even more apparent in the holiday journey Sylvia takes with Max, Warwick, and Moor. For source material Alcott drew on expeditions in her own youth and on Thoreau's trip down the Concord and Merrimack rivers. Although this voyage lasts only two days, it is crucial both to the Transcendental union with nature and the concomitant realization of unique individuality; these rites of passage are familiar in all classical literature.[16] Both rites, however, are forbidden to women, as Henry James made clear in his review. Caring not a whit for the female pilgrim's progress, he described the incident purely in terms of the heroine's indiscretion. Sylvia goes off on a camping out expedition of a week's duration, in company with three gentlemen, no superfluous luggage, as far as we can ascertain, "cockle shell stuck pilgrim wise in her hat." It is hard to say whether the impropriety of this proceeding is greater or less from the fact of her extreme youth, the fact is at any rate kindly overlooked by two of her companions who become desperately enamored of her before the week is out.[17]

James overlooked the fact that Sylvia was indeed undertaking a form of pilgrimage. His insensitivity to the heroine's aims, of course, was not unusual for the time.

The domestic novels of the nineteenth century make little note of what Harriet Martineau calls the "substantial, heartfelt interests for women of all ages and under ordinary circumstances, quite apart from love."[18] The quest to satisfy these interests was reserved to men, with the exception of certain discreet travel books designed for ladies' vicarious education. For Alcott such limitations prevented more than picnics. They prevented any true religious experience, for instance; without it, women were fundamentally cut off from the divine order and left to languish in disquieting moods.

Warwick and Moor indulge Sylvia's wish for romance, but remain ignorant of what the journey really means to her. In the 1882 edition of *Moods* Alcott inserted an outdoor theatricals incident to give her readers a clear hint of what Sylvia needed to become a true woman. In humble gratitude for companionship, Sylvia performs a series of dramatic sketches with a rug, shawl, and cloak from her wardrobe. She creates a full evening of illusion for her admirers on their first evening of camping. Moor considers her performance only the result of a lady's education in parlor arts. Warwick, however, understands that a woman may have natural genius and declares she "has it all in her and needs no master." He approves of her playacting, because for women "pent up emotions can find a safer vent in this way than in melancholy dreams of daring action," although he denies Sylvia's need for the journey as anything but "romance." He advises the others to "let her alone, give her plenty of liberty, and I think time and experience will make a noble woman of her."[19] Here Warwick, in the second edition, strikes at the moral center of the novel.

Through him Alcott argues that self-expression, although perilous in an undisciplined child-woman, can be a treasured possession in a mature woman, the very soul of her capacity for creativity. Yet Warwick, who momentarily supports Sylvia's independence, is still more intent on creating a fit playmate for his own romantic needs. The mature Alcott rejects him for her heroine.

In the first version of *Moods*, a berry hunt with Warwick reveals an important disparity in their attitudes. Sylvia bets Warwick that she can gather more berries, and when the two compare their harvest, Warwick is touched by her efforts: "You are a true woman, Miss Sylvia, for though your palm is purple there's not a stain upon your lips, and you have neither worked nor suffered for yourself it seems."[20] Her companion remains positive that her fair face is an index to her womanly heart; she is "pleased, yet somehow abashed." Warwick sees her as exemplifying womanly self-sacrifice; he fails to perceive she wants to be his equal. The difference between the narrative perspective in the two editions is one of emphasis only. Romantic heroes want a woman's self-sacrificing "moral sentiment"; they do not want competition, even in fun.

A GOLDEN WEDDING

True womanhood, Alcott admits, cannot develop through competitive berry picking. Instead, Sylvia next seeks her identity in the past world of domestic self-sufficiency. A summer storm drenches the campers and they seek shelter in a "red farm-house standing under venerable elms, with a patriarchal air which promised hospitable treatment and good cheer." Three generations of farm folk are celebrating Grandma and Grandpa's golden wedding anniversary and the travelers are welcomed into the family circle. The golden wedding couple are a priest and priestess of an older faith, their authority tangible and unquestioned; their values and skills are happily reproduced in the loving progeny gathered to celebrate family ties. This fictional farm couple had identical interests and therefore coalescing spheres.

Sylvia feels the difference between this home and her own troubled family. Not only motherless, but fatherless too in a sense, she suffers the emotional conflicts created by a weak father who provides material comforts but little else. Even his wealth is suspect, because he married Sylvia's mother for her money and social position, not for love.[21]

Sylvia's brief contact with this lost world of corporate domesticity is filled with nostalgia and regret, a nostalgia only heightened by her own fragmentary, vulnerable existence. A central scene in *Moods* evokes the homely details of kitchen abundance Alcott ultimately made famous. During the family banquet, she summons up lessons "not learned from books": the fragrance of coffee and "babies borne away to simmer between blankets until called for." "The women unpacked baskets, brooded over teapots and kept up a harmonious clack as the table was spread with pyramids of cake, regiments of pies, quagmires of jelly, snowbanks of bread, and gold mines of butter; every possible article of food, from baked beans to wedding cake, finding a place on that sacrificial altar."[22]

This scene is partly based on Alcott's reading of the biography of the German novelist, Jean Paul Richter. A writer popular with the Concord circle, Richter delighted in all "these humble, simple religious ceremonies."[31] In one of his novels, *Jubelsnoir*, he depicted "the beautiful and simple celebration of an aged minister and his equally aged wife, celebrating the anniversary of their marriage festival."[3] Alcott uses the golden wedding as a foil to establish the tragic character of Sylvia's journey. She plainly views Sylvia as a member of a newer generation of women no longer supported by a patriarchal tradition. According to Alcott, that tradition, although limiting and provincial, did allow women clear domestic authority. It guaranteed them an honorable old age, surrounded by progeny who would respect them. Above all, woman's abundance is honored and the patriarch, surrounded by his children and grandchildren, stands in stark contrast to Adam Warwick and Geoffrey Moor. Adam, like Bronson Alcott, sees persons as "but animated facts or ideas." As Faith Dane says, "he seizes, searches, uses them and when they have no more for him, drops them like the husk, whose kernel he has secured."[4] Geoffrey Moor possesses Bronson's delicate sensibilities, his veneration of holy family life. Like Bronson, he also fears the earthly family and the consequences of passionate involvement with a grown woman. Sylvia is distracted by the incompleteness of each suitor, momentarily turning back, with longing, to a rural self-sufficiency where Grandpa and Grandma acknowledge their interdependency.

Her distraction is brief, and it is conscious playacting, much like the amateur and semiprofessional acting that Alcott herself enjoyed. The golden wedding chapter remains the same in both editions of *Moods*. It is a pageant, directed by "the lively old woman." Sylvia, wearing a farm girl's second best gown, discovers that all the company were "en costume." Moor wears, but cannot fill out, the oldest son's clothes. Max dons an old uniform from the War of 1812, and Warwick puts on Grandpa's sober suit "which became him." The costumes and the "festival" enable the travelers to play parts which they cannot possibly assume as everyday roles. Two of the heroes are anachronistic and Moor isn't substantial enough to inherit the patriarch's domain. Sylvia can be a child among the children. Alcott reiterates the point: "a detachment of half-grown girls was drawn up behind grandma, as waiters: Sylvia insisted on being one of them." She then leans against her brother while the assembled cast sings "Home." The grandfather's prayer closes the scene.

Theatricals, as historian Karen Halttunen reminds us, were enormously popular and very similar to polite parlor conduct in mid-nineteenth-century America. "The stylized and controlled emotional self-expression demanded of parlor players strongly resembled the demonstration of right feeling demanded by sentimentalism."[25] The transparent, sincere "little woman" exemplified by Sylvia Yule in the early *Moods* posed the most serious problem in Victorian America for such young middle-class women as Louisa May Alcott. Alcott's journal reveals her frustration at genteel hypocrisy in her own late adolescence. She loved playing Dickensian characters in particular because she could caricature genteel performances that seemingly valued sincerity while using its forms only as a mask for self-interest. Women were supposed to be sincere and, indeed, their dress, deportment, even their hairstyles were designed to enhance sincerity as opposed to earlier coquetry or romantic artifice. Simultaneously the time, skill, and expense involved in appearing sincere was in itself a betrayal of sincere simplicity. By the late 1880s Alcott, like her contemporaries, had adopted an easier stance about role playing and sentimental culture. Sylvia Yule learns to hide her feelings for her own protection, and her creator presents this matter-of-factly in the later edition of *Moods*. Between the two versions of her first novel, Alcott developed a brilliant treatment of sentimental society's theatricals and unmasking. In her pseudononymous thrillers the importance of what Halttunen calls "Confidence Men and Painted Women" is fully revealed.

That men as well as women play parts is further emphasized in the next chapter of *Moods* entitled "Sermons." It remains almost identical in both editions. Alcott moved the voyagers to a church in the woods. Here New World nature offers another alternative for a girl in search of original relationships and experience. Moor preaches a Thoreau-like sermon promising nature's sweet solace to the weary pilgrims, while Warwick, as Theodore Parker, expounds the new social gospel to his friends. Golden wedding rituals are forgotten as new choices appear for Sylvia's consideration. Warwick is particularly compelling because Alcott has named him after Warwick Castle in England. In an *Atlantic Monthly* essay, Hawthorne told readers that Warwick was "founded by King Cymbeline in the twilight ages." The English, he points out, have based their "new things" on sturdy old foundations.[26]

Adam Warwick in *Moods* is a confusing if attractive New World product constructed out of Old World materials. He appears conversant with European philosophies and politics, but needs the freedom of the American wilderness to maintain his unique distance from ordinary domesticity. He journeys from England to New England, and speaks out against the sins of his companions while concealing his own. He points out that Max is indolent, while Geoffrey Moor is too self-sacrificing, and Sylvia's character is flawed by uninformed self-interest. Warwick advises Moor to be more manly. "For years you have lived for others," Warwick says. "Now learn to live a little for yourself, heartily and happily else the feminine in you get the uppermost."[27] But while Moor must remember himself, Sylvia is counseled to efface herself and work for others, which will bring her a "happy soul in a healthy body" and make her "what God intended . . . a brave and noble woman."[28]

But sermons do not a saved soul make in the second edition of

Moods. In that version Sylvia lies awake half that night, the experience of the voyage offering her a glimpse of the promised land.

> . . . like the fairy Lady of Shallott, she had
>
> Left the web and left the loom,
> Had seen the water-lilies bloom
> Had seen the helmet and the plume,
> And had looked down to Camelot.[29]

Equating Sylvia with the Lady of Shallott in the second version of *Moods*, Alcott reveals a great deal about her own gradual disenchantment with Romantic heroes. As Nina Auerbach perceptively argues, Tennyson's Guinevere is in the background of both Arthur's rectitude and Lancelot's "doomed lust for honor."[30] But Elaine's pure passion for Lancelot "exposes his essential dishonesty, making of her a death's head portending the fall of the kingdom." Sylvia's small kingdom falls too—but she plays both Guinevere and the Lady of Shallott. Having been forbidden to leave her household spinning, dying in fact in the first *Moods*, Sylvia in the second version then triumphantly rises by her own transforming power, with the advice and consent of a good wife, Hope, and a spinster, Faith. It is Lancelot-Warwick who dies and Arthur-Moor, humbled, who lives on as Sylvia's consort.

THE CHILD BRIDE

That Warwick and Moor become desperately enamored of Sylvia is a two-fold tragedy. First, Sylvia is seeking a friend, not a lover; raised as a motherless child she is "heir to ceaseless craving for affection" and therefore vulnerable to any proposal that promises security, warmth, and love.[31] As Alcott argues, Sylvia's attempt to gain both friendship and love in marriage was made improbable by her failure to gain experience and independence in life. Sylvia's plight was hardly unique in the transatlantic fiction of the time. Like Sylvia, Brontë's Jane Eyre cannot resist the offer of love, and marries before her heart is mature enough to join principle to love. Such women, Alcott argues, will yield to impulsive moods and romantic dreams.

A few years before she began *Moods,* Alcott read Mrs. Gaskell's *Life of Charlotte Brontë* in which Harriet Martineau's review of *Jane Eyre* is paraphrased. "All female characters," wrote Martineau,

> in all their thoughts and lives, are full of one thing, or are regarded by the reader in the light of that one thought—love. It begins with the child of six years old, at the opening—a charming picture— and it closes with it at the last page; and so dominant is this idea— so incessant is the writer's tendency to describe the need of being loved—that the heroine, who tells her own story, leaves the reader at last under the uncomfortable impression of having entertained either a double love, or allowed one to supercede another without notification of the transition. It is not thus in real life. There are substantial, heartfelt interests for women of all ages, and under ordinary circumstances, quite apart from love; there is an absence of introspection, an unconsciousness, a repose in women's lives— unless under peculiarly unfortunate circumstances—of which we find no admission in this book.[32]

As Alcott must have surely noted, Martineau understood the central theme of *Jane Eyre,* which is also that of *Moods.* Most women were largely unrecognized as individuals guided by principle precisely because men loved them best as capricious little girls. The "peculiarly unfortunate circumstances" were more the rule than the exception, as indicated by Alcott's census of the "sad sisterhood, a larger class than many of us deem it to be."[33]

The heroine of Alcott's next adult novel, *Work,* discusses *Jane Eyre* at length and condemns Jane's marriage to Rochester as "an unequal bargain." In *Jane Eyre,* as in *Moods,* the union between the main characters is rendered dangerous by disparities in age, education, and experience.

Moor, confident that he can teach Sylvia to love him, has married a child who plays at being a dutiful housewife. Her condition worsens when Warwick appears in the company of Moor's cousin Faith Dane and crushes Sylvia's hand in his passionate grip, breaking the guard and leaving the wedding band rather loosely encircling her finger.

Hoping to avoid choosing again between Geoffrey Moor and

Adam Warwick, Sylvia tries to believe that Faith is Adam's new lover. But Faith's ideal is too high for more than friendship. She tells Sylvia that she "never met the man who would satisfy me." "Not even Adam," says Sylvia, "surely he is heroic enough for any woman's ideal." "No, not even Adam," is the reply.[34]

Faith has given up looking for a man who will accept her as an equal and share the comfortable domesticity she has already created for herself. In her study of *Moods*, literary historian Hannah Bewick has pointed out that "the enraging quality of Moor's love is heightened by its persistence and possessiveness."[35] Faith offers her home to Sylvia as a sanctuary from Moor, who almost deliberately ignores his wife's unhappiness. He hopes she will magically move from the "gay innocence of childhood to the mature devotion of adult womanhood," skipping over a passionate adolescent stage. When she pines away, he puts his dead sister's signet ring on her finger to keep the wedding band from slipping off. Sylvia draws back "because his touch was more firm than tender, and his face wore a masterful expression seldom seen there."[36]

Before her marriage, Sylvia used to enjoy playing with a servant's child, Tilly. Moor brings Tilly home for the evening and presents her to Sylvia "so you can dress your dolly to suit yourself or leave her as she is." This is her final playacting role in the novel—Sylvia parts her hair and puts on her short, "pedestrian" skirt, but finally concludes, "No, I cannot be a child again."[37]

THE SISTERHOODS

In an interesting discussion of nineteenth-century sororal relationships in New England, historians Christopher Lasch and William Taylor observe a connection between female friendships and the limitations of genteel womanhood. Simply put, they claim that women affirmed their purity and established important relationships with one another as a defense against the insensitive, materialist world of their men.[38] Louisa May Alcott offered a different explanation for what she called the sad sisterhood. She argued that the basis for such friendships was not a denial of male sensitivity, nor even an affirmation of female purity, as Lasch and Taylor suggest, but a positive commonality of status as women. Commonality meant at least two things to Alcott—first, most women were denied direct experience that would fit them for independence; second, they were dependent upon men whose status in the world was materially based on an unstable, competitive foundation. These women were sad because they were denied freedom and independence, and they recognized one another because their experiences enabled them to see through the stereotyped masks that women were expected to wear. They did not band together as a sisterhood of crippled, helpless victims, however. Instead, they reached out to nurture and protect one another, and to struggle for reform. Disappointed, abandoned by those who should have protected them, they learned self-reliance through sad experience.

Female friendships were also forged in response to patriarchal relations, which preserved the sexual division of labor but destroyed the recognition and compensation of women's work. Faith and Sylvia developed such a sororal relationship, and so did many women in real life. As Alcott shows in her novels, they did so often at the risk of incurring shame upon themselves and abuse from society.

The theme of sisterhood between ordinary women who have departed in either thought or action from conventional social roles begins in *Moods* and continues throughout all of Alcott's novels. Hester Prynne is the grande dame of this sisterhood. Her scarlet letter illuminates the sins in other bosoms. Alcott likens Sylvia to Hester Prynne; "living in the shadow of a household grief," she

had joined that sad sisterhood called disappointed women, a larger class than many deem it to be, though there are few of us who have not seen members of it. Unhappy wives, mistaken or forsaken lovers; meek souls, who make life a long penance for the sins of others; gifted creatures kindled into fitful brillance by some inward fire that consumes but cannot warm. These are women who fly to convents, write bitter books, sing songs full of heartbreak, act splendidly the passion they have lost or never won; who smile, and try to lead brave uncomplaining lives, but whose tragic eyes betray them, whose voices, however sweet or

grand, contain an undertone of hopelessness, whose faces sometimes startle one with an expression which haunts the observer
long after it is gone.[39]

In Alcott's version of Emerson's command, "Trust thyself, every
heart vibrates to that iron string," Faith Dane says to Sylvia, "You
shall be a law unto yourself, my brave Sylvia."[40] In fact, Sylvia's
conversion by Faith is the moral heart of *Moods*. Yet Sylvia's decision
to take her friend's advice does not make her an outcast the like of
Hester Prynne or Jane Eyre. Unlike Jane, Sylvia need not flee her
comfortable home; nor does she suffer poverty, isolation, and ill-
paying teaching jobs. And unlike Hester, Sylvia suffers no banish-
ment to a cottage at the end of the village, nor is she forced to wear a
badge of shame.

Alcott has given us two sides of female potential: gently reared,
childlike Sylvia, and adversity hardened, womanly Faith. Sylvia,
unlike Jane or Hester, fortunately has a "sister." Faith is described as
"shapely and tall, with much native dignity of carriage, and a face
singularly attractive from its mild and earnest beauty. Looking at her
one felt assured that here was a right womanly woman, gentle, just
and true; possessed of a well-balanced mind, a self-reliant soul . . .
her presence was comfortable, her voice had a motherly tone in it,
her eyes a helpful look."[41] Nothing could be more unlike Sylvia,
with her want of harmony and tendency to willful moodiness. Yet
Sylvia and Faith represent two sides of woman, and of Alcott. Sylvia
has passionate impulses that may only be romantic fancies; she also
leans toward hero worship. Faith is another part; fervent abolitionist
and self-reliant daughter of a contentious home, she chooses direct
experience with life. She also knows that romantic heroes do not
make very good husbands.

The reader half suspects that Faith will ultimately become the
heroine of *Moods*, but she never fully emerges from her mountain
cottage. Faith Dane is the heroine of another Alcott story, however;
Faith's enormous capacity for nurturing, expressed in her care of
Sylvia, appears in "My Contraband" (also called "The Brothers"), a
story Alcott published in *Atlantic Monthly* two years before the publication of *Moods*.[42] In "My Contraband," Faith leaves home to nurse

at a Union hospital; her assistant is a convalescent freedman named Robert. It turns out that Robert and a rebel officer she tends are half brothers. Robert tries to kill his brother because the white man has forcibly raped Robert's wife after selling Robert off the plantation. Although Faith persuades Robert to go North, thereby saving the rebel, she admits, "God forgive me! Just then I hated him as only a woman thinking of a sister woman's wrong could hate."[43]

In the end, Robert joins a black regiment and changes his name to Robert Dane. He kills his brother on the battlefield and receives a mortal wound himself. Faith, having gone to nurse at Port Royal, is with him at the last moment, murmuring that in the next life "my contraband" will find "wife and home, eternal liberty and God."[44] Faith's treatment of Sylvia also displays her experienced nursing of a convalescent bondslave. She has learned her craft well in the abolitionist struggle and expanded her sympathies to those women she recognizes as her equals through sad sisterhood.

Faith Dane represents one of Alcott's important alternatives to the challenge (in *Moods*) of combining domesticity and self-reliance. Her cottage, a refuge for Sylvia, offers a wholesome home life, and Faith has painfully forged an individual identity.[45] "Trust thyself," she says. Although not ready to present a nonconformist heroine as the main character in *Moods*, Alcott shows different ways available to women in this period through the characters of Faith, Sylvia, her older sister Prue, and Max's pretty, conventional wife.

Alcott felt herself part of a transitional generation of women who sacrificed, organized, and placed great faith in the future generation. In fact, the postwar period brought enormous changes for womanhood. She explored the possibilities in her later novels, and incorporated some in the later version of *Moods*.

MOODS REVISED WITH EXPERIENCE

The most interesting change in the 1882 edition of *Moods* concerns Sylvia's ultimate fate. In the first edition, Sylvia dies still loving Warwick, and makes everyone else feel guilty (as James points out). In the revised edition, Sylvia not only survives but realizes that her love for Warwick was a passing "mood." Mature women want equality in marriage.

Alcott reinforces Sylvia's centrality in the second version of *Moods* by removing the opening chapters about Adam and Ottila. Moreover, the youthful Sylvia appears in the opening of the second version dressed in sensible girl's clothing rather than being disguised in a boy's smock as in the first version. The author thus corrects two of Henry James's earlier objections. Adam Warwick, who James dismissed simply as a cad, is now a failed heroic model of romantic individualism. Sylvia demands a freedom of the will not unlike Adam's; neither of them can be accused of seeking license for adventurous impulses in the second rendering of *Moods*.

Something is lost nonetheless in removing Ottila and in presenting a narrower pilgrim's progress toward redemption for Sylvia. The most thrilling scene in both versions of *Moods* remains Adam's second confrontation with Sylvia as a married woman, after she has earnestly tried to be a "child-wife," suppressing her Ottila-like passions. The first *Moods*, in fact, opens with a confrontation between Adam and Ottila, the gorgeous Latin temptress whose race is a mixture of "Spain and Alabama." Ottila is Alcott's embodiment of the demonic angel.[46] Jean Rhys in an early twentieth-century novel, *Wide Saragosso Sea*, speculated upon the childhood and adolescence of Bertha Mason, the mad Creole wife in *Jane Eyre*. Alcott may also be speculating on Bertha's history, wondering about what drove her insane, presenting Ottila as a version of Bertha. Sylvia eyes Ottila at a party with full cognizance of her attraction to Warwick. Sylvia herself certainly has the "moral sentiment" that Adam finds lacking in Ottila.[47] But Adam then selfishly uses Sylvia's sincere morality, tricking her into declaring her true feelings.

Adam asks her to leave her husband in the name of her sincerity. He dares her to continue playing child wife in light of what has happened: "It is impossible to go back to the blind tranquility you once enjoyed. Now a single duty lies before you; delay is weak, deceit is wicked; utter sincerity alone can help us. Tell Geoffrey all; then, whether you live your life alone, or one day come to me, there is no false dealing to repent of, and looking the hard fact in the face robs it of one half its terrors."[48]

Warwick loses Sylvia in part because she sincerely believes in

Moor's self-pitying assertion that he "loves but few and those few are my world."[49] Sentimental convention demands that she choose the less self-reliant man because he needs her more; Sylvia tries to sacrifice herself to preserve Moor's self-respect. Alcott proves her wrong in both editions; in the first *Moods* Sylvia loses both happiness and self-respect by her false generosity. In the second edition she gets both back; Alcott insists that thirty years more of life convinced Sylvia that one could find happiness after disappointment, and she changed the ending so that, "making love and duty go hand in hand, my heroine meets a wiser if less romantic fate than in the former edition."[50]

In a certain sense the second Sylvia loses some of her mythic power as a "fallen woman." Nina Auerbach reminds us that fallen women, in particular, lose their power as outcasts when they are described as victims.[51] Sylvia does become simply a victim of a too early marriage in the second edition, but she also claims the right to return to the sacred hearth, having repented, gained experience, and become a true woman. That is no small accomplishment in one generation.

Alcott, in both versions, emphatically insists upon the convergence of the angel-demon, the wife, and the old maid.[52] Both spinsters and fallen women are beyond conventional identities as wives, mothers, and daughters. Faith Dane and Sylvia Yule, like Adam Warwick, are liminal figures in the first *Moods*. Such figures are powerful, threatening, even subversive in conventional society. Louisa May Alcott and her mother befriended many such outcasts, sisters in poverty, when they lived and worked in Boston. Certainly Louisa saw herself as an "outcast," moody girl. As a successful author, much later in life, she dimmed Warwick's power and made him a flawed hero, perfected only after death by the divine Sculptor, as she put it. He just wasn't worth Sylvia's death. Living on she no longer desires him—her momentary lapse has shaken Geoffrey Moor enough to make him realize that Sylvia is not a child, she is a woman and a worthy equal partner.

While Geoffrey Moor remains partly attracted to Sylvia as a "dear child," even after marriage, Sylvia is unmistakably a woman in 1882. Her coming of age is not accomplished by marriage but rather by her discovery that she and her husband both possess secret, inner lives, "private experiences." Her discovery, even though prompted by her own adulterous impulse, is nevertheless maintained in the second version of the story as an important challenge to the conventional perspective of a wife as simply part of her husband. The narrator announces, "Sylvia the girl was dead, but Sylvia the woman had begun to live."[53]

Alcott's friends were somewhat perturbed by the changes. Ednah Cheney, for one, complained that Sylvia's year of quiet living and mild charity was an inadequate penance for being allowed to live *and* keep her husband.[54] It did not matter that Alcott had told Cheney of a real-life "double relation" in Concord, similar to the one portrayed in *Moods*. Faith Dane, an "inexperienced" spinster like Alcott herself, still shrewdly observed the "old story."[55]

Alcott in fact never wrote a full-length novel with an unmarried heroine. In *Jo's Boys*, written in the late 1880s, the surrogate daughter of a heroine chooses spinsterhood, lives happily and usefully, but we learn this fact only at the end of the book.[56] The small but significant rise in spinsterhood during the last decades of the nineteent!· century probably came too late for Alcott to portray such women in fiction. She herself prefigured those single, creative, "useful" women who founded settlement houses, wrote books, and helped organize successful suffrage campaigns.

Faith Dane's life is presented as an honorable alternative to unhappy marriage. Nevertheless, it is not true, as Cheney intimates, that Louisa May Alcott knew nothing about marriage and disdained fictional analyses of wedded life. After all, she observed her parents for years and used them as models for her fictional characters. Alcott is seriously concerned with two aspects of marriage in *Moods:* the personality each marital partner brings to the relationship and the dynamic interaction between married people. Sylvia Yule brings some of Abba's social and personal problems to her marriage. Sylvia is also the pampered youngest daughter of comfortable gentry, and like Abba remains motherless during her "romantic period." Abba, of course, did mature through great hardships, and her daughter greatly valued her comforting "maternal" air. Faith Dane consequently bears a resemblance to Abba Alcott in her generally nurturant, competent demeanor.

Alcott's perceptions of her father and her struggles with him also found subtle expression in *Moods*. Warwick, Moor, and Mr. Yule, in both editions of the novel, have something of Bronson Alcott in them. Sylvia learns to love her father after Moor and Warwick go off to Europe. In the first *Moods*, Sylvia dies, and a grieving Mr. Yule survives her. In the second version, Mr. Yule dies, after which Sylvia is reunited with Moor and lives happily ever after. In 1861 perhaps even a father's belated love was insufficient to save a sinful daughter from death. In 1882, however, Sylvia in a sense outgrows the need for her father's loving approval. Having matured, she need not fear Moor's persistent patriarchy either. Now her father's equal, she can establish a "household democracy" of her own. In both editions Alcott wrote:

How many roofs cover families or friends who live years together, yet never truly know each other, who love and long, and try to meet, yet fail to do so till some unexpected emotion or event performs the work? In the year that followed the departure of the friends, Sylvia discovered this and learned to know her father. No one was so much to her as he; no one so fully entered into her thoughts and feelings; for sympathy drew them tenderly together and sorrow made them equals. As man and woman they talked, as father and daughter they loved; and the beautiful relation became their truest solace and support.[57]

The older Louisa May Alcott of the 1880s evidently witnessed a reformed domestic scene, graced by more experienced and politically sophisticated women. In 1881, when she sent the revised *Moods* to her publisher, she also recommended that he publish Mrs. Robinson's *History of the Suffrage Movement:* "Do you scorn the whole thing? Better not, for we are going to win in time, and the friend of literary ladies ought to be also the friend of women generally." And the next month she added, "I can remember when antislavery was in just the same state that suffrage is now, and take more pride in the very small help we Alcotts could give it than in all the books I ever wrote or ever shall write."[58]

She was secure enough to state that "the observation and experience of the woman have confirmed much that the instinct and imagination of the girl felt and tried to describe."[59] She was certain, for instance, that inequality destroys marriages but also that marriages in her lifetime invited inequality. So long as women's lives outside the family were subject to political and social constraints, the choice of a husband loomed as an escape or refuge from exploitation and misery. At the same time, men also looked to domestic life as a refuge, and expected wives to play a subordinate, self-sacrificing role in the home. *Moods* begins Alcott's lengthy exploration of this theme, *Modern Mephistopheles* deals with it as Faustian melodrama,[60] and *Little Women* treats it as domestic tragicomedy.

One easily perceives that the pattern of Alcott's own life underlies this theme of domination and subordination in marriage, but that perspective explains only partially the theme's persistence and her own lifelong spinsterhood. Much of the answer lies in Transcendentalism, which had elevated the search for individual identity to a holy cause. Alcott's fear of domination was personal and psychological, of course, but it also reflected a specifically female concern for the problems of breadwinning and marriage. The limits of romanticism in solving them were evident in both Alcott's life and fiction.

Adam Warwick, like Bronson Alcott, believed that proper education and spiritual development create stable marriages and happy families. He expresses this view in a remarkable drawing-room conversation about adultery and divorce initiated by Sylvia's older sister, Prue. In both versions of the novel, Prue tells the assembled guests that a woman in the neighborhood, Helen Chesterfield, "has run away from her husband in the most disgraceful manner." All the guests present have a say about the matter. Warwick argues in favor of preventive education. If he had his way he would "begin at the beginning and teach young people that marriage is not the only aim and end of life yet would fit them for it, as for a sacrament too high and holy to be profaned by a light word or thought. Show them how to be worthy of it and how to wait for it." The practical Prue responds, "That is all excellent and charming, but what are poor souls to do who haven't been educated in this fine way?"

Faith Dane then offers the pragmatic woman's rights answer. Modestly declining to speak at first, because she is a spinster with no right to talk about marriage, Faith then counsels the hypothetical wife to "leave no effort unmade" to save her marriage. Failing that, she has "the right to dissolve the tie that has become a sin, because where no love lives inevitable suffering and sorrow enter in, falling not only upon guilty parents, but upon the innocent children who may be given them."[61]

Through Faith Dane Alcott makes a familiar woman's rights demand for the reform of marriage and divorce.[62] By the 1880s, certainly, divorce laws had become more liberal and Faith's arguments seem standard for progressive circles.[63] They were less so in 1861. Alcott herself, so familiar with the demands of woman's rights congresses from the 1850s on, may not have fully realized how unacceptable these domestic reforms seemed to such people as A. K. Loring, who first published *Moods*.[64] In context of the novel, it is significant that Faith, knowing of the secret romance between Warwick and Sylvia, gave her approval to divorce in parlor conversation. She sympathizes with Sylvia, whispering in her ear, "Dear child, if you ever need any help that Geoffrey cannot give, remember Cousin Faith."[65] Faith offers both an assertion of woman's rights and a personal promise of continued support for Sylvia, her distressed sister.

The reform of nineteenth-century society, many felt, demanded the efforts of mature women who had taken the journey begun by Sylvia Yule, and who resisted "that ceaseless craving for affection" in order to develop their principles and live by them. That Alcott chose to reissue *Moods* when she was a fully established author and an active figure in the woman's rights movement is of some importance. Her later novel, *Little Women*, deals more successfully with the reality of domestic life and reforms of it. *Work* relates the experience of single women in the world, but *Moods* dealt with the prelude to those experiences.

Alcott's first important heroine struggles to resist an untimely marriage and loses. Her fate in the first edition of *Moods* is death, by which, as Henry James insisted, "she puts her husband and everyone else in the wrong by dying the death of the righteous." But thirty years later the heroine comes to life, strengthened by her experience, and Sylvia's dream at the end of the second version of *Moods* certainly heralds the full rise of the fallen woman.

Despite Sylvia Yule's protesting domestic confinement and her enlarging woman's power of self-transformation to gain a better world on *this earth*, she is no less womanly than her evangelical counterparts, such angels as Evangeline St. Clare and Ellen Montgomery.[66] Alcott's heroines often appear as boys but they never want to be men. Both evangelical and liberal women's fiction recognized new sororal relationships that might help women to win the struggle against older patriarchal arrangements. There were, according to Alcott, both "happy women" and the "sad sisterhood." *Moods* radically argues in the two versions that women may, by their own self-transforming power, move from being members of the sad sisterhood to being happy women.

Having once been victims themselves, the successful women warriors in both editions fight against the enslavement of others. The first step in their fight is gaining recognition for adolescence as an important stage for girls bent on becoming self-reliant women. The second battle is a redefinition of true womanhood involving what today's feminist critics term "the rise of the fallen woman." Women, like men, can conquer their baser passions (though not erase them), repent their past mistakes, and achieve self-respect. Above all in Alcott's novels, adult womanhood is a universal sorority. The true woman is distinguished by "moral sentiment" and having it she befriends all other women. She befriends them all partly because she may be any one of them herself in the course of her lifetime— environment alone distinguishes between those who fall and those who, by their own power, struggle to ascend.

Louisa May Alcott never fully rejected her Romantic inheritance, although she moved far beyond the limits it imposed on her life and craft. The Transcendental impetus to find one's unique selfhood through a union with nature sanctified the woman's rights cause for her, as it did for many reformers of her generation. Rational, balanced community was Alcott's next demand for American women. The union of the nation as well as the union in the home required reform and reconstruction when *Moods* was first published in 1865. Despite Alcott's resounding new ending to the novel, the process was still incomplete in 1882.

1. *Union Hotel Hospital, Georgetown, Washington, D.C., scene of Louisa May Alcott's service as a Civil War nurse. Courtesy of Brown Brothers Photo Service.*

2. *Nurse Periwinkle and baby Africa from Alcott's autobiographical* Hospital Sketches. *Courtesy of the Concord Free Public Library.*

3 and 4. Two illustrations from the 1880 edition of Little Women—*done by Frank T. Merrill, a young Concord artist—show Beth mourning her dead canary after the sisters' holiday from housekeeping and Jo sacrificing her "one beauty," her mane of chestnut hair. Courtesy of the Concord Free Public Library.*

5. *Louisa May Alcott created popular juveniles and earned five hundred dollars a year as editor of* Merry's Museum. *This issue dates from 1869, the year after she wrote* Little Women. *Courtesy of the Concord Free Public Library.*

7. *Abba May Alcott, in her last years, seated in the parlor of Orchard House. Courtesy of the Concord Free Public Library.*

6. *Opposite. Bronson Alcott, an impoverished eccentric during Louisa Alcott's younger days, eventually enjoyed respectable status as resident muse of the Concord School of Philosophy. Lectures by William Torrey Harris and Julia Ward Howe drew adult students to this refurbished barn of Orchard House in the 1880s. Courtesy of the Concord Free Public Library.*

*8 and 9. May Alcott
Nieriker's sketch of Tho-
reau's hut on Walden
Pond and her detail of
a staircase in Emerson's
summerhouse, which
was designed and built
by Bronson Alcott with
the help of Thoreau.
Courtesy of the Concord
Free Public Library.*

10. Louisa May Alcott is shown here at her cottage by the sea with her niece and namesake, Louisa May Nieriker. Courtesy of the Concord Free Public Library.

11. *Louisa May Alcott and James Edward Murdoch are seated on the porch of a rented summer cottage at Mount Watchusett. Murdoch, a noted actor and lecturer, had acted as a juvenile with Fanny Kemble and had visited Union Army camps during the Civil War to declaim patriotic poems to the troops. Courtesy of the Concord Free Public Library.*

EIGHT

The Battle Cry of Freedom

I set forth in the December twilight, with May and Julian
Hawthorne as escort, feeling as if I was the son of the house
going to War.

Louisa May Alcott, Journals, *December 1862*

Louisa May Alcott enlisted in a Civil War being fought, as one
observer put it, "in the housewife's front yard."[1] Going to war was
usually reserved to the son of the house, but in this war the traditional boundaries of sex, race and class were blown apart.[2] For a
time, the careful distinction between public and private spheres of
activity was destroyed. Alcott's deepest needs, to find herself and
her work, emerged in the disorder of the 1860s.

She seized the opportunity for direct action and out of her experiences fashioned an unusually diverse body of writing that included a
record of her wartime nursing service, *Hospital Sketches*, three antislavery stories, manuscripts of *Moods* and *Work*, and, as we now know,
several sensational "thrillers," written under pseudonyms, dealing
with men and women who fall prey to the full range of human
passions. Having been told by publisher James T. Fields to "Stick to
your teaching; you can't write," Alcott, "being wilful," as she said,
determined not to teach.[3] She could write, she *would* write and
proceeded to prove it in the Civil War period. Nothing Louisa May
Alcott ever did came easily—though she found her work more surely
than she ever found herself—as the demands and rejections of the
literary marketplace, the brief period spent nursing, and the long
recovery she endured combined to discipline her talents and focus
her energies. A connection grew, developed in Alcott's mind between the needs of men dying in drafty, makeshift hospitals and the
rights of women and slaves.

After the war, a generation of Romantic reformers committed
their energies to reconstructing a rational order. For many of them,
like Alcott, personal and national needs merged. They were sure

that the breakdown of family life, like the war between the states, was due to inequalities between men and women, black and white, rich and poor. Universal laws of balance and harmony must replace selfish, unrestrained individualism. Just before the war, fashionable Boston took up the cause of antislavery and considered the merits of "free religion" and "universal laws" of progress and democracy— much as it had relished "Conversations" on the "newness" a generation earlier.[4] The Alcotts and their well-known causes were almost fashionable in certain parlors as the war clouds gathered and then burst.

THE ANTISLAVERY SET

Family links to what she called the regular antislavery set were especially crucial to Alcott's own feelings of self-respect and authenticity in her year of "good luck." She distinguished between these people and the wider circle of Boston gentry she reluctantly depended upon to widen her literary contacts. When she did have to teach, her small school of twelve pupils, even with Field's donation of forty dollars "to fit up with," did not bring in enough to pay Louisa's board. She consequently "visited around," taking meals with charitable friends. Chafing still further under the slights of "show people," she discovered "what insolent things a hostess can do" and "what false positions poverty can push one into."[5] While critiques of phony gentility and snobbish gossips marked sentimental fiction generally in this period, Alcott's trenchant denunciations of parlor politics burn from her own painful scars.

There were certainly true reformers, newly augmented by young Hegelians and disciples of Auguste Comte, who valued the Alcotts for more than their ability to amuse guests. Among them was Franklin Sanborn, first introduced to the Alcotts by Ednah Littlehale (Cheney) in 1853; he became the family's loyal intimate friend, and the actor-manager of the Concord Stock Company that featured as troupers Louisa and Anna Alcott, John Pratt, and Alfred Whitman, one of the models for Laurie in *Little Women*.[6]

In 1859 Captain John Brown spoke in Concord at a meeting organized by Sanborn, among others. The New England Emigrant Aid

Society had been formed to help fugitive slaves and stop the spread of slavery into the territories.[7] The Alcotts, Sanborn, and most of the antislavery group raised funds for Captain Brown, and they rejoiced when his small force moved against the Federal Arsenal at Harper's Ferry, Virginia, in hope of sparking a slaves' rebellion. Alcott wished to do her part in the effort, but Brown was caught and imprisoned. Sanborn and Bronson discussed the possibility of Bronson's slipping into Virginia and leading a small party to assault the jail and free Brown. Finally, they agreed to ask Thomas Wentworth Higginson, abolitionist leader and soon commander of the first free black troops, to lead a rescue.[8] Every member of the reform circle tried to stay the execution, free Brown, or at least bring comfort and medical supplies to the jail. Elizabeth Peabody traveled to Virginia to beg the governor for clemency. It was no use; John Brown was hanged on December 2, 1859. Concord went into mourning for the liberator whose name became a legend in the battle hymns of the Union army.

Thoreau, Bronson, and Emerson participated in a public memorial service for Brown. Alcott wrote a poem, "With a Rose That Bloomed on the Day of John Brown's Martyrdom," humbly observing that "No monument of quarried stone, no eloquence of speech, / Can grave the lessons on the land his martyrdom will teach." Frank Sanborn helped her publish the poem in *The Liberator* one month later.[9]

The following spring Sanborn received a federal subpoena to testify about his part in the conspiracy to free the slaves. In the middle of the night a party of proslavery men dragged him out of bed in Concord and tried to take him away without a warrant. He fought them off, still in his bare feet, while his sister tried to stampede the carriage and horses to prevent his kidnapping. Both Sanborns yelled loudly for help and succeeded in rousing a crowd of angry Concord residents, including Emerson. They chased the would-be captors out of town and then formed a committee of vigilantes to protect Sanborn, with Alcott a proud member of the defense force.[10]

A schoolmaster as well as an amateur actor and the same age as Louisa, Sanborn offered May Alcott a job teaching drawing in his Concord school in 1860. Committed to abolitionism and woman's rights, he moreover promoted Bronson's lectures and solicited Alcott's work for antislavery publications while reading and praising all her serious fiction. He was a member of the younger generation of reformers which included Moncure Conway, Sam May's daughter Abigail, Ednah Cheney, William Torrey Harris, and Sally Holley, all of whom turned toward "positive" rationalism without losing their faith in "idealism."[11] Eventually, after the war, Sanborn became president of the American Social Science Association.[12]

In July 1860 Mrs. John Brown (called Mrs. Captain) stayed with the Alcotts, who invited a group of supporters to meet her. Mrs. Brown was Alcott's ideal of true womanhood that day, "a tall, stout woman, plain, but with a strong good face, and a natural dignity that showed she was something better than a 'lady' though she *did* drink out of her saucer and used the plainest speech."[13] Louisa Alcott carefully distinguished, in meeting the demands for tea and cake, between the "regular antislavery set" and the tourists who came to gawk at the famous visitors.

The confluence of abolitionism and true womanhood was dramatically reenforced when Louisa heard Harriet Tubman describe her many trips to bring fugitives out of the South. If Louisa May Alcott ever found a period of blessed solidarity with her entire family and their old friends it was during their shared abolitionist work. "M. L.," written in the winter of 1860, was the first in a series of antislavery stories Alcott fashioned as a contribution to the cause. The *Atlantic Monthly* rejected the piece in February, prompting her acid comment that "R. L. (Lowell) won't have M. L. as it is anti-slavery and the dear South must not be offended."[14] By 1863 "My Contraband," her second antislavery offering, was published in the midst of the Civil War by the *Atlantic Monthly*.[15] "M. L." then appeared as a serial in January and February issues of the *Commonwealth* while "Hospital Sketches" and "An Hour" followed quickly, establishing Alcott as one of the *Commonwealth*'s important Civil War writers.[16]

Her literary contributions were part of what has been called the second period of militant abolitionism. Edward Channing correctly understood that the most important effect of the Fugitive Slave Act of 1850 was that it moved Northern and Western Americans from indifference or hostility toward the abolitionists to anger toward the slave power.[17] Even Ralph Waldo Emerson, usually aloof from direct political associations, argued that any attempt to enforce the

Fugitive Slave Act removed his sacred freedom of the will, thereby making him an unwilling party to the degradation of the entire human race.[18] The most common and effective arguments against slavery in American literary works between 1850 and 1861 were moral, religious, and sentimental.[19] Certainly the most famous and powerful of these works was Harriet Beecher Stowe's *Uncle Tom's Cabin*, which appeared, serialized, in the *National Era* in 1851 and 1852. Almost as soon as it came out in book form, there were at least six dramatizations produced, the most popular of which was George Aiken's version, a play the Alcotts saw several times.[20] Stowe followed with her own dramatized version, "The Christian Slave" (1855); she then wrote two other antislavery novels, *Dred* (1856) and *The Minister's Wooing* (1859).[21]

Louisa Alcott's abolitionist stories openly owe a great deal to her admiration for Stowe's works. Alcott subscribed to a tenet of "sentimental power" that distinguished Stowe's work and women's antislavery fiction in general. Like Stowe, who wrote "the summa theologica of nineteenth century America's religion of domesticity," Alcott also believed in literature as a profoundly political force.[22] Furthermore, Alcott, Stowe, and their readers shared a common set of beliefs about womanhood, families, feelings, and power. They believed that spiritual conversion of the heart (sentiment) is the real vehicle of historical social change. The redemptive power of women, who were entrusted with the hearts and homes of the nation, was therefore limitless, at least in literature written by women for women readers.

Jane Tompkins brilliantly argues that given American culture's constellation of beliefs, any full-scale analysis of *Uncle Tom's Cabin*, for instance, must be carried out by mapping its spiritual geography— who is saved or canonized in accordance with "the logic of pre-ordained design?"[23] All readers knew the story of the New Testament and followed its working out in sentimental novels, particularly in such a jeremiad as *Uncle Tom's Cabin*, which depended upon readers' understanding the providential view of history which the fictional characters reenacted. Most important, in sentimental novels or stories, the reenactment takes place in the home—heaven on earth: "Christian love fulfills itself not in war, but in daily living." In Stowe's utopias, as in Alcott's domestic tales, "the home is the center of all meaningful activity; women perform the most important tasks; work is carried on in a spirit of mutual cooperation and the whole is guided by a Christian woman who through the influence of her 'loving word,' 'gentle moralities,' and 'motherly kindness,' rules the world from her rocking chair."[24]

There is one crucial difference between Evangelical Stowe and Unitarian Alcott: once Sylvia Yule is killed off by Alcott's publisher in the first version of *Moods*, Alcott's heroines very rarely have to die for humanity's redemption, though they are frequently willing to do so. Ann Douglas once insisted that Louisa May Alcott, unlike her idealist father, was persistently a "radical materialist";[25] she wanted to create the Celestial City here on earth, through a combination of faith and grit. In "M. L." she aims at nothing less than the conversion of the Gentiles through the triumphant union of her hero and heroine, Paul Frere and Claudia.

The story opens in a genteel parlor where the assembled guests are listening to a remarkable performance by Paul Frere, a poor, handsome singer, rumored to be Spanish and of noble family. The most enthralled listener is Claudia, who "stood alone in the world, a woman of strong character and independent will, gifted with beauty, opulence and position, possessing the admiration and esteem of many, the affection of a few whose love was worth desiring." Claudia is an orphan, but, unlike Sylvia in *Moods*, is also mature and patient. Paul courts Claudia through his wonderful singing and the example of his sincere character. It seems at first a simple story of true love brought about through music; essays and fiction of the period abound with musical love stories. Music, as Bettina wrote in her correspondence with Goethe, is "the soul of love, which also answers not for its working; for it is the contact of divine with human."[26]

When Faith Dane in *Moods* said to Sylvia, "You shall be a law unto yourself, brave Sylvia,"[27] she was, of course, echoing the Apostle Paul's radical insistence that when the Gentiles, who do not take part in the covenant, do "by nature the things contained in the law, these having not the law, *are a law unto themselves.*"[28] Claudia is converted by her love for Paul, whose name links him to the Apostle, having ignored the telltale signs of his mutilated hand, seeing only "black locks streaked an ample forehead, black brows arched finely over southern eyes as full of softness as of fire," and closely folded lips tracing "an impetuous nature tamed by suffering and taught by time."[29] On the eve of their wedding she learns from his own lips that he is the son of a Cuban planter and a quadroon, slave mother. He was sold away from his white half sister, a free heiress.[30]

The nineteenth-century reader could half-guess the rest of the tale; it was commonplace in antislavery literary works. Paul's freedom is purchased by his half sister. The importance of the Apostle Paul's mission to the Gentiles would ensure that the contemporary female reader sympathized with the love of Paul and Claudia—all races are one race in Christ—the converted Gentiles are a law unto themselves.

Claudia marries Paul Frere; their fashionable friends desert them but Claudia has found a "religion that welcomed all humanity to its broad church, and made its priest the peasant of Judea who preached the Sermon on the Mount."[31] Paul finds a brotherhood in those who do earnest work, and the couple move through a Celestial City of like-minded people.

Alcott's literary sources for "M. L." are easy to trace; the two most popular plays prompted by the 1842 fugitive slave case involving George Latimer were "The Branded Hand" (1845) by Sophia L. Little and "Warren, A Tragedy" (1850) by David S. Whitney. The branded hand in the tale prompts a slaveholder's guilty vision of the mutilation and he is converted. And Harriet Beecher Stowe's *Dred* features Nina Gordon, the mistress of her dead father's plantation, who allows her mulatto half brother Harry to conduct her affairs.

The possibilities of misogynous love and family ties under slavery were limitless and the fascination of Northern novelists and playwrights with them and with slave mutilations abound. Alcott was no exception and she used the notion of sexual and family bonds between slaves and white masters or mistresses repeatedly. "My Contraband" and "One Hour" explore the same themes, current at the time and noted by historians of antislavery literature. The antislavery stories must be linked, however, also to the acknowledged as well as pseudonymous "thrillers" in Alcott's oeuvre. Not only were the antislavery stories and thrillers written in the same period, the same dramatic techniques and conventions appear in them all. The troubling problem in considering Alcott's antislavery fiction as part of her passionate thrillers lies in shedding our modern biases. Her perspectives unite abolitionist and woman's rights causes for contemporary readers in her own day. In the two later antislavery stories Alcott clearly distinguishes between *passions*, which include the natural birthright impulses of every man and woman for freedom, and *feelings* (moral sentiments), which are childlike or mature depending upon the long-term environmental circumstances of an individual or a race. Her nineteenth-century readers made the same distinctions.

It is rarely clear in Alcott's works how long an individual or a race had to live under civilizing influences in order to cultivate the highest moral sentiments, those which grant the individual a principled, harmonious life and the race a heaven on earth. Paul Frere's noble feelings, for instance, are portrayed as the result of long, patient pilgrim's progress toward physical freedom and safety and ultimately toward social recognition of his unusual talent and discipline.[32] In many ways, he is Alcott's fictive half brother, the child of her passionate, moody mother and her principled, seemingly serene father. Alcott the woman and the writer is not eager to become passionless; she wants, however, to discipline her passions and govern them by cultivating feelings or moral sentiments. Passions can, after all, be self-destructive or heroically self-sacrificing; *Moods* clearly demonstrates that common nineteenth-century belief.

Paul Frere also bears more than a little resemblance to Alcott herself and to Henry David Thoreau. The tale was written as all the Concord circle worried about Thoreau's final illness. Alcott had much to make her unhappy and rebellious as she kept writing in every spare moment while also doing the housework and sewing for the Concord Alcotts. She managed to complete "A Modern Cinderella," with Anna and John Pratt as hero and heroine of the tale. The story also includes Anna's sisters as a cool blonde artist and an inkstained intellectual who reads esoteric German literature, adores Carlyle, and scribbles away at her own great works. Anna's fictional counterpart called Nan does all the housework while her sisters selfishly develop their artistic talents. The *Atlantic Monthly* accepted "Cinderella" and paid Alcott another fifty dollars.[33]

As the "irrepressible conflict" drew nearer, Alcott lost her most admired exemplar of Romantic rebellion. Thoreau was only forty-four when he died on May 6, 1861. In an advanced state of tuberculosis, he had taken a brief trip West for his health with Horace Mann,

Jr., Hawthorne's nephew. His disease was not arrested. He came home to die, and had his bed moved downstairs so that friends could visit him. Emerson gave the funeral oration, and afterward Bronson read from Thoreau's books at a service attended by all Concord. Thoreau had arranged the exercises for John Brown's memorial; now friends arranged them for his. He was buried in Sleepy Hollow Cemetery, near the Alcotts' plot.[34]

Thoreau had said that "the mass of men lead lives of quiet desperation." Like Adam Warwick in Louisa's *Moods*, he wanted men to submit solely to the control of higher principles, to obey no commandment above nature's dictum that each living being be true to itself. Louisa May Alcott never forgot the message Thoreau outlined in his "On the Duty of Civil Disobedience," although she was ambivalent about its effects upon women left to tend the home alone. She frequently felt her own heart marching to the beat of Thoreau's drum.

When the war came, she could not volunteer for war work immediately. Abba's increasing infirmity and Anna's preoccupations with her own family left Louisa with enormous household responsibilities. As Bronson's earnings barely supplemented her own, she furiously wrote short tales for instant cash and to lay away a supply of publishable fiction. May gratefully but unquestioningly accepted her sister's self-sacrifice. Alcott sewed the young artist's summer wardrobe and also took care of John Brown's daughters, who had come to board with the Alcotts for the summer. She put aside her literary work for a time and "fell to work at housekeeping."[35] In the spring she was one of three hundred women sewing Union uniforms in the Town Hall. Alcott, who had been wearing her sisters' cast-off clothing as she stitched for the boys in blue, received a parcel of new clothes from them.

Women joined the war work in both the North and the South. In the North, a network of female benevolent societies and woman's rights groups became part of a vast civilian auxiliary to the War Department's bureau. The official title was the United States Sanitary Commission. In some ways a forerunner of the Red Cross, it had wide responsibilities during the Civil War for hospitals, relief work, and the transport of wounded from the battlefields. Its staff and funds were all voluntary, and its branches and more than 10,000 local relief societies were run largely by women.[36] In such cities as Boston, Chicago, New York, and Philadelphia, women held Sanitary fairs which raised millions of dollars for medical aid and relief. In December 1863 New York City alone contributed $1,000,000.[37] Alcott contributed poems, stories, hand-sewn flags, and clothing for the Boston fair. In many of the larger cities, workers set aside regular portions of their wages for relief work. Theaters gave benefit performances. The Alcotts worked for every war effort, from fairs and benefits to the collection of household silver and jewelry that were sold for the Union cause. Louisa Alcott, without money to contribute, acted in benefit performances.

Thousands of women, including the Mays, Sewalls, and Alcotts, presided over public meetings, drafted the constitutions and by-laws of various medical branches and relief societies, kept the accounts of the Sanitary Commission, and also wrestled with the endless red tape produced by the Quartermaster Corps and the Medical Bureau. Mary Vaughan, who was a friend of Alcott's, observed that "men, who were usually jealous of woman's extending the sphere of her life and labors, welcomed in this case her assistance in a public work."[38]

Dorothea Dix and Clara Barton supervised the processing of applications for hospital nurses. They rejected women they thought too young or romantic, who might "give way under the labors which required a mature strength, a firm will and a skill in all household duties." Housewives, mothers, sisters, and daughters were gradually recruited to serve the Union. Alcott had spent a year impatiently writing, sewing, and teaching. She sent in her name as a candidate for Union nurse. If accepted, she would receive meals and twelve dollars a month from the government.

She was thirty years old when she received an acceptance letter a few weeks before Christmas; it instructed her to report to the Union Hotel Hospital in Washington. Alcott suddenly realized that she "had taken her life in her hand and might never see them all [her family and friends] again." She reassured herself with the familiar mixture of self-denial and determined autonomy. It was necessary to "let out my pent up energy in a new way." Besides, there was the Union cause, and if that were not enough, her service would relieve the family of one more Alcott to "feed, warm and worry over."[39]

HOSPITAL NURSE

Alcott's small trunk was packed by her mother and sisters with the aid of Sophia Hawthorne. The Sewalls gave her a small cash fund for her own expenses and the relief of her patients. She set forth in December 1862, arriving at the Union Hotel in the Georgetown area of Washington, where several Massachusetts women were already at work.[40] It was an overcrowded, rundown, and poorly ventilated building, hastily converted into a hospital. Washington was still thought to be threatened by Confederate capture, and Union troops were garrisoned everywhere. The windows of the hotel were half-boarded against artillery fire, so fresh air was nonexistent or else a permanent cold draft on patients and nurses. Wards were improvised in old ballrooms, reception areas, and vacated suites; every room was heated separately by a small stove, and hot water was carried to each bed for washing wounds and bodies. The hospital used convalescent soldiers as orderlies, and contrabands (escaped slaves) ran errands, acted as waiters for the staff, and did enormous loads of wash each day. Bandages were often made from old clothes and had to be washed for reuse daily.

Alcott and two other nurses shared a small bedroom furnished with one wardrobe closet, their trunks, one chair, and a tin saucepan as a mirror. A small fire was fed with woodchips; oversized logs from the hotel woodpile had to be pushed into the small grate inch by inch. When no one was there to tend it, the fire went out and plunged the room into damp chilliness. The Sewall fund enabled Louisa to buy apples, crackers, and cheese to supplement the barely edible salted beef and pork rations that were accompanied by moldy hard bread and watered-down, boiled coffee. Alcott, "a vegetable product" as she called herself, lost most of her private food supply to an army of mice who lived in the wardrobe.

On her first morning she witnessed a death in her ward, nursed pneumonia cases, and cared for a man shot fatally through the lungs. She tried very hard to be motherly to her patients, succeeding even when her favorite charge was a handsome Virginia blacksmith named John Sulie, who was just her own age. The most gratifying aspect of patient care to Louisa was her observation of "manly" men who could be as sensitive "as any woman to their stricken comrades." Like many advocates of equal rights, she thought the problems between men and women could best be solved by the cultivation of "masculine" virtues in women and "feminine" virtues in men.[41] The war wounded had clearly demonstrated their bravery and strength in battle; that they exhibited tender feelings for one another and wrote loving letters to mothers and sweethearts was fine proof to Alcott that her convictions were correct.

She felt "ignorant, awkward and bashful," but she found comfort in her ability to tend her charges. Writing long letters home about the hospital routine, she described each patient and his progress or decline. The men responded to her care with small, handmade gifts. Many wrote to her for years after the war and followed her accounts of the Union Hotel Hospital as they were published in the *Commonwealth* (and later reprinted as *Hospital Sketches*).[42]

On a typical day she would be "up at six, dress by gaslight, run through my ward, and throw up the windows, though the men grumble and shiver; but the air is bad enough to breed a pestilence." She would tend the fires and provide blankets and emergency aid for men whose wounds ached after a long, cold night. After a quick breakfast with the other nurses, she dished out rations for her wards, brought food for the "helpless boys," washed all the patients and supervised bedmaking and floor sweeping. Then she assisted the physician to dress the more serious wounds and changed minor bandages herself. She found the amputations hardest to bear, but assisted in the painful process of picking out bone fragments from shattered limbs, always wishing that the doctors would be "more gentle with my big babies."[43] Alcott and the other nurses found themselves in charge of the medication trays for their wards; they also scrounged up bandages and linen, which were always in short supply. Home nursing and hospital nursing were very similar.

The afternoon began by serving the standard Union Hospital lunch; "fried beef, salt butter, husky bread and washy coffee." There was never enough to satisfy the men, so Alcott as well as the many other nurses wrote letters to both the soldiers' families and their own, asking for fruit, jams, pickles, and other niceties. Visitors might bring homemade wine or even bunches of grapes, which were especially cherished. The patients napped in the afternoon, but the nurses had no rest. They read to the sleepless, ran errands, and wrote letters for their patients. Supper at 5 o'clock was followed by the doctor's last round and by the nurses' administering medicines and sleeping draughts. Then, Alcott wrote, "night nurses go on duty, and sleep and death have the house to themselves."[44]

Within a few weeks she took night duty herself, thereby gaining a chance to tour Washington during the day. Once she visited the Senate chamber but found herself too late for the session; so she boldly sat in Senator Sumner's chair and imagined herself cudgeling his assailant, Brooks, within an inch of his life. It was an exciting city. Long trains of army wagons rumbled through the capital's streets with supplies for the front lines while pigs rooted in the gutters, all contributing to an air of distracted bustle that entranced Alcott. She watched the passing throngs with interest, and wrote letters for the people back home in which she described officers in their tight, colorful finery and tired "Billy Yanks" with knapsacks and muskets.

Her "colored brothers and sisters," she said, were more interesting than any of the officers and ladies who promenaded the streets. Southern "colored folk" were different from the few blacks she knew in New England. Warned "not to be too rampant on the subject of slavery," she repressed her most radical thoughts, but still felt affronted by men who "would put two g's into negro" and by nurses who "were willing to be served by the colored people, but seldom thanked them, never praised and scarcely recognized them on the streets."[45] One nurse sniffed at Louisa playing with a contraband baby in the kitchen. "Gracious, how can you?" she said. "I've been here six months and never so much as touched the little toad with a poker." Alcott kissed "the toad" in response.[46]

Alcott did not entirely dismiss the common view that blacks were obsequious, lazy, ignorant, and childish "Sambos." Yet she saw these characteristics as the masks of slavery, and noted that they quickly disappeared in the face of respectful treatment by whites. She observed that "Sambo" was a shrewd disguise for slaves who knew how to use it for their own survival. She was nursing at the hospital on New Year's Day in 1863 when Lincoln's Emancipation Proclamation took effect, declaring that slaves in the rebellious states should be "then, thenceforth and forever free." The government would no longer "repress such persons in any efforts they may make for their actual freedom." Outside the Union Hotel the bells rang out at midnight and Alcott "threw up her windows and cheered in answer to the shout of colored men in the street below. All night they tooted and tramped, fired crackers, and sang Glory Hallelujah."[47]

A few days before, the Union Hotel received many of the Fredericksburg casualties. Some 9,600 men had been wounded in General Burnside's unsuccessful frontal attack against the entrenched forces of Stonewall Jackson and Robert E. Lee.[48] The nadir of Northern hopes, it precipitated Lincoln's most serious cabinet crisis, one the Concord Alcotts followed anxiously in the newspapers. That winter the conflict had reached proportions never dreamed of in 1861.

NIGHT AND THE DARK SPANIARD

The war dragged on for two more years, but not for Alcott. By January she was a victim of one of the common diseases that claimed as many deaths in the Civil War as did the rifle fire and cannonades. Scarlet fever, typhus, pneumonia, even measles and chicken pox raged in the wards. Doctors prescribed heroic doses of calomel for such patients as Alcott, fearing that bodies weakened by fever would yield to pneumonia, consumption, and ultimately death. At first disoriented by the early stages of fever, Louisa refused to take her illness seriously, but the matron, without telling her, telegraphed news of her condition to Concord. Bronson came to Washington, and on January 21, following the death of the matron herself from typhoid pneumonia, took Alcott home. Dorothea Dix brought a basket of wines, tea, and a Bible to comfort her on her feverish, semiconscious trip home to Concord.[49]

For three weeks a severe case of typhoid raged throughout Louisa Alcott's tired body. After glimpsing May's shocked face at the railroad depot and her mother's frightened demeanor at home, she sank into delirium, haunted by nightmares powerful enough to linger in her mind after she woke. The fever had broken, but she found herself "queer, thin-faced, big-eyed." The terrifying dreams suggest the conflicts that troubled her and influenced her writing for the next ten years. "Strange fancies" assumed the shapes of familiar people and danced about her.

> The most vivid and enduring was the conviction that I had married a stout, handsome Spaniard, dressed in black velvet, with very soft hands, and a voice that was continually saying, "Lie still, my dear!" This was Mother, I suspect; but with all the comfort I often found in her presence, there was blended an awful fear of the Spanish spouse who was always coming after me, appearing out of closets, in at windows, or threatening me dreadfully all night long. I appealed to the Pope, and really got up and made a touching plea in something meant for Latin, they tell me. Once I went to heaven, and found it a twilight place, with people darting through the air in a queer way, all very busy, and dismal, and ordinary. Miss Dix, W. H. Channing, and other people were there; but I thought it dark and "slow," and wished I hadn't come.
> A mob at Baltimore breaking down the door to get me, being hung for a witch, burned, stoned, and otherwise maltreated, were some of my fancies. Also being tempted to join Dr. W. and two of the nurses in worshipping the Devil. Also tending millions of rich men who never died or got well.[50]

Like Abba, Louisa had an olive complexion, dark eyes and hair, perhaps reflections of the Portuguese ancestry on her mother's side of the family. Certainly Latin figures were stock representatives of passion in the lurid romances of her day, including the ones she wrote, but why should they appear to haunt her dreams just after her work as a Union nurse? Alcott's experience of close, physical contact with male patients, many of them her own age and younger, may have reminded her of her own "Spanish" self. Perhaps she only partly denied the awakening of desire by emphasizing the maternal nature of her role in the wards. Then, too, she had met Dr. Winslow, a friendly Quaker physician who lent her books and took her to dinner. Did these experiences, innocent as they were, evoke specters of herself as a witch?[51] Probably Alcott felt that her spinster status at thirty was deviant. If not safely "on the shelf" in married domesticity, was she then inherently licentious? Was heaven, "dark and slow," a place devoid of passion? Since Alcott destroyed many of her journals, we may never know the extent of her passionate impulses or the true source of her "moods."

Nancy Cott's observation that "a single conception of women's sexuality never prevails" in any one historical period is a useful reminder when considering the complexity of Louisa Alcott's feelings. By mid-nineteenth century, the evangelical Protestant views of womanhood had elevated woman's moral influence to a plane of passionlessness. Since sincerity was the cornerstone of female moral power, it supposedly followed that women's sexually passive behavior was not simply an affectation, but a true reflection of natural purity.[53] Louisa Alcott, however, never denied the existence or the legitimacy of female sexual drives; she argued for self-control not passionlessness. Her opinions were close to those of Elizabeth Cady Stanton and Rebecca Harding Davis, both of whom acknowledged a healthy sexual instinct in women. "In these rough and tumble days," said Davis, "we'd better give women their places in flesh and blood, with exactly the same wants and passions as men."[53] Alcott agreed with Davis's demand for a single sexual standard in order to eliminate the sexual exploitation of women by men. In *Moods*, Faith Dane insists that Sylvia should not yield to her passionate feelings for Adam Warwick because yielding would invite his domination over her untried and consequently weak sense of self. That same intrepid spinster (in "My Contraband") argues that male passion (both sexual and emotional) must also be controlled if a freed slave is to achieve citizenship.[54] Frank acknowledgment of passion and a plea for self-control play important roles in Alcott's abolitionist fiction.

Once again, as Jane Tompkins, writing about *Uncle Tom's Cabin*, reminds us, "we can and should set aside the modernist prejudices which consign this fiction to oblivion, in order to see how and why it worked for its readers, in its time, with such unexampled effect."[55] Alcott wrote "An Hour" in the middle of the Civil War, after her own service and the Emancipation Proclamation. It should occupy a preeminent place in the literature of the "unwritten war," if only because it marks a final turning point in antislavery fiction.[56] "An Hour" combines a love story and the moral, religious fervor of earlier sentimental antislavery pieces with stern economic analysis. It is also an exhortation to Union soldiers to fight on and complete the work of the Emancipation Proclamation. Alcott angrily reminds Northerners, Christians in particular, that they are responsible for the war having been more concerned with peaceful profits than with justice for enslaved blacks. She echoes a common belief that the Civil War was a scene of the Lord's "trampling down the vineyard where the grapes of wrath are stored," words set, after all, to the tune of "John Brown's Body." "An Hour" could have been written only when it was, crowning the last period of antislavery writings with woman's vision of God and history moving toward the millennium.[57]

The story takes place between eleven o'clock and midnight on a Southern rice plantation during the Civil War. The angel-in-the-house in this story is a white man, Gabriel Butler, son of the dying slaveowner by his first wife. Gabriel, raised in the North by his dead mother's wish, has returned to "receive a slave-cursed inheritance." A wicked stepmother and her two shrill daughters are now dependent upon him. His problem, once his father dies, is to reconcile his principled duty to free the slaves with the consequent reduction of "three delicately nurtured women to indigence."[58] He has no question about the proper course of action, which has, unbeknown to Gabriel, already been decided by the slaves themselves who are in the midst of a bold and vengeful insurrection. The plans are revealed by one of the determined rebels, Milly, a beautiful young house slave. Milly loves Gabriel, distinguishing between the master and man. More precisely she hates the fact that slavery makes their racial differences more hopeless than all the romantic obstacles in popular folklore. The crucial scene presents Gabriel begging Milly to save them all, thereby admitting that she is now in power and that he and his family are dependent upon her ability to be more Christian then they have been.

Milly promises to save the Butlers if Gabriel will free all the slaves the next day. She does not easily accept his word until reminded that Gabriel never took sexual advantage of her. More important, Gabriel himself admits that he has committed a terrible wrong in hesitating to free all the slaves at once. Milly then rushes off to get help, sending an old blind slave, Sandra, to delay the rebel slaves.

As soon as Milly leaves, Gabriel, unable to accept the fact that a woman is acting in his behalf while he remains passively waiting, sets out to meet the slaves. He subdues Big Mose, the strongest slave on the place, using a whip and a bloodhound. He then confronts the gathered rebel slaves and declares them all free just as "the tramp of many feet was heard."[59]

"An Hour" presents a powerful indictment as God and history come together to punish both Northern and Southern whites. And the story makes it plain that slave men and women, followed almost too late by the Grand Army of the Republic, are doing God's work.[60] Alcott's narrative voice is one with Milly's. Gabriel has tried to explain away his failure to free the slaves by raising the issue of his white stepmother and his sisters' dependency. He argues that his responsibility toward safeguarding their human property rights is no less than his responsibility toward enslaved men and women. Milly is justly scornful, replying that three white women are more valuable than two hundred slaves in the eyes of a supposedly Christian, Northern gentleman. There are echoes of Herman Melville's *Benito Cereno* in Alcott's story. The most powerful slave, Prince, wears an iron spiked collar, reminiscent of Ataful in Melville's tale. Alcott, like Melville, argues that one needs more than ordinary consciousness to know what is really happening in the midst of a slave revolt. The white family is almost killed because they simply cannot believe that faithful Milly is actually more faithful to her fellow slaves.

Milly gains earthly, material power over her tormentors, and, even more gloriously, she refuses to lose her superior moral power by an act of vengeance.

Modern readers need to know that Louisa May Alcott wanted to go to Port Royal, to help former slaves in what one historian calls "the rehearsal for reconstruction."[61] She was, moreover, writing her fiction to Union soldiers, their families and friends, in the midst of slave revolts, massive movements of contrabands toward the Union Army, and very real fears that slaves could and would exact righteous vengeance. Moreover, Alcott is not squeamish about the deserved fate of both slave owners and Northern Christians who had looked the other way. She is, in fact, hurrying the troops along; should the armies delay an instant in freeing the slaves, Alcott is approvingly certain that the slaves will "seize the time."

In "M. L." and "My Contraband" Alcott portrays white women in love with ex-slave men. Presumably the white women maintain their social status despite miscegenation because the antislavery cause is holy; moreover these women may gain moral superiority, even power, in loving black contrabands. Alcott is also suggesting that black male contrabands are acceptable objects of true woman's desire. Purified versions of the dark Spaniards, ex-slaves have legitimate passions; they are a law unto themselves.

"An Hour" is the more conventional tale of a white man attracted to a beautiful slave woman. She is unquestioningly his moral superior and he must be willing to die to be worthy of her and to save his own soul if he can. It is not hard to see the wider implications: the Civil War is God's judgment upon slaveholding America. Gabriel has a chance to redeem himself because he has not used his ownership of Milly to abuse her sexually. She, however, must also control her passionate feelings for the man; he is a slaveholder and she betrays herself and her fellow slaves if she yields to her passion for him.

Louisa May Alcott's use of the New Testament and *The Pilgrim's Progress* is not a mere device. The differences between Evangelicals and Transcendental-Unitarian-Deists are real and divisive but Alcott and Stowe meet on a common battleground and they speak the same language.[62] They both have "designs on the world."[63] They want to change it. Alcott is a more powerful writer when she marshals her readers' emotions in favor of domesticity and self-sacrifice. Domestic life is where self-sacrifice is most likely and does the most good. Her readers know that it is possible to change the heart of somebody you love (more easily than somebody miles away) and even easier to change the heart of somebody who has benefited from your love and nurturance. Furthermore, nineteenth-century womanly sacrifices are the more obvious because they are not substitute services. If your ultimate beneficience to the loved one lies in risking your life for him—or actually dying—so much the better in effecting a transformation of character.

Eva, in *Uncle Tom's Cabin*, for instance, loves Topsy who has said that Miss Ophelia wouldn't love her even if she were not so famously naughty: "No; she can't bar me, 'cause I'm a nigger!"[64] In *Hospital Sketches*, Alcott has her alter ego, Tribulation Periwinkle, hug and kiss baby Africa, when another white nurse refers to the child as a "toad." Moreover, in the second edition of the stories, the author adds a striking illustration of Nurse Periwinkle hugging the baby as a contraband mother sits in the background, peeling vegetables for the gruel the nurse is stirring (see Fig. 2).[65]

Paul Frere is transformed by Claudia's selfless, steadfast love. Robert, the contraband hero, becomes Robert Dane and forswears vengeful murder, having been loved and nursed by Faith. Milly's self-transformation effects an astonishing act of generosity on her part. Gabriel's final speech may seem silly to modern readers, but his emotion signifies to Alcott's readers that he has been converted, moved by the recognition that he must sacrifice himself. He has become a manlier man by adopting a woman's path to salvation. It is only right, as Alcott and Stowe argue, because woman's self-sacrifice is an imitation of Christ's. Men's economic and political priorities have buttressed slavery long enough; such writers as Stowe and Alcott insist that the heart's priorities are not only higher, they are ultimately more sensible.[66]

Bronson Alcott feared that his rebellious daughter missed the "higher" spiritual unity behind the fractured material world. She was, perhaps in reaction to his maddening self-absorption, a "radical materialist," as Ann Douglas argues.[67] Alcott also knew that the available means to effect material change was spiritual persuasion. She aimed, no less than Stowe, at a conversion in the spirit such that earthly arrangements might be made to mirror the righteous order of Heaven.

Bronson taught his daughter Louisa that lifelong domestication of animal passions began in the innocence of childhood; children loved to be good because it was "natural" for them to be so.[68] Sexual development proceeded through coeducation with plenty of healthy physical exercise, and from there through a long adolescent stage of travel and education for middle-class youths of both sexes. For poorer youths, public education and healthy exercise was followed by the mastering of work skills spiced with experience through "knocking about" a bit—but never far from the watchful eyes of middle-class reformers and benevolent guardians.

Ideally the pattern was not sexually differentiated, a point Alcott emphatically developed in the March family trilogy. If her domestic dramas seem hardly radical to twentieth-century readers, it may be because she wove them in sentimental, literary forms for contemporary readers who understood the message. In her hands equal relationships between the sexes sometimes seem like bygone rural simplicity.[69] In other stories she sensationalizes the wreck of domesticity upon the rocks of unequal treatment of women, separation of spheres, and surrender to unchecked passions. Her critique of Romantic individualism, however, permeates all her literary forms: sentimental novels, Gothic romances, even fairy tales and antislavery fiction.

The reconstruction of order in Alcott's personal life during her convalescence was, as usual, paralleled by the literary order she created through her writing. Her first effort, "with weak wits too tired to read much," was "Thoreau's Flute," a poem composed one night on hospital duty. Sophia Hawthorne admired it and recommended it to James Fields, the new editor of the *Atlantic Monthly*.[70] He printed it, and Alcott was pleased. But she was more pleased to learn that she had become an aunt. Anna Pratt had given birth to a boy on March 28.[71]

Domestic jubilation over Anna's son did not subdue Alcott's dreams, for "the old fancies still lingered." She kept repeating the incidents in her nightmare to family and friends, all of whom prodded her to pick up her old life again. Frank Sanborn and Moncure Conway suggested that Alcott arrange her "war letters" into printable form and publish them in the *Commonwealth*.[72] Like Sanborn, Conway was a friend her own age, committed to stripping away the irrational layers of Romantic illusion, revealing the "real, rational and unambiguous core of human life."[73] A former Methodist preacher and the son of southern slaveholders, Conway was now a Unitarian, a graduate of Harvard Divinity School. He was deeply interested in all cultural manifestations of the irrational and in finding means of exorcising demons through the exercise of the rational will. Conway was precisely the man to encourage Louisa to describe her experiences with war and death.

Unsure of any popular welcome for the letters which Sanborn and Conway found "witty and pathetic," Alcott set about revising them. At the same time, keeping her eye on the surest source of income, she wrote another tale for Frank Leslie's *Illustrated Newspaper*.[74] Under the name of A. M. Barnard, Alcott had just won a one hundred dollar prize from Leslie for "Pauline's Passion and Punishment." Using Cuba as a setting, as she did for the opening scene of *Moods*, Alcott created a new Spanish heroine, Pauline, who unlike Ottila, gains her revenge upon a heartless lover, but then pays a lifelong penance for surrendering to a fatal passion. Alcott spared no gory detail in satisfying both the requirements of Leslie's readers and her own need to play with the perils of passion. The most telling element in "Pauline" is that both couples are married, but domesticity offers no peaceful haven. Beginning with secrecy and sexual deception, all four marital partners descend into bottomless passion from which light and reason are hopelessly barred.

In this story Alcott sought to exorcise the Spaniard, her dream figure-self who enters through windows and closets and threatens her unprotected household. He appears again and again in her Gothic tales over the next ten years, a literary manifestation of Alcott's struggle to protect herself and her household from the unlicensed chaos brought about by willful selfishness.[75] Murder, divorce, child abandonment, nervous disorders degenerating into madness all figure in Alcott's novels, and even creep into the *Little Women* trilogy. Without a rational, sexually egalitarian society, Alcott felt these abuses would invade daylight reality as well as midnight fantasies. They were the potential outcome of her own desires, and visible in the excesses around her.

HOSPITAL SKETCHES

Reworking her letters into *Hospital Sketches* was a literary departure for Alcott, and it created several new problems. Her solutions marked a turning point in her career. She had written fairy tales and thrillers before, but for the first time she was sending a well-bred, single young woman into a life-threatening, intensely masculine environment. The heroine was herself.[76]

The prospect of publishing this book troubled her in two ways. First, she feared revealing herself as the narrator of the sketches, having previously hidden behind pseudonyms (or behind the guise of an eccentric old lady for charity plays). She felt that her strong-mindedness, abolitionism, and critical condemnation of leisured excess were unfashionable. She had already constructed literary devices for presenting her opinions; these preserved her privacy and guaranteed her freedom to write for a variety of audiences. Second,

Alcott was concerned about defying literary and social conventions by placing a young unmarried woman in an army hospital. As Dorothea Dix knew, only respectable married women could safely extend their maternal responsibilities to such places.[77]

As a result of these problems, her narrative voice in *Hospital Sketches* is uncertain at first. In the opening pages, in fact, she tries different narrative tones to disarm the reader and win a sympathetic audience. Nurse Tribulation Periwinkle, Alcott's heroine, is variously described as embarking on a bridal trip, a jolly boyish voyage, and an errand of mercy. The trip to Washington, on the other hand, is shown from the viewpoint of an eccentric railway traveler, encumbered by a "cavernous black bonnet, fuzzy brown coat, a hairbrush, a pair of rubbers, two books, and a bag of ginger-bread distorting the pockets of same."[78]

Eventually Alcott abandoned the eccentric costume and self-deprecating humor; Trib Periwinkle firmly declares herself a "woman's rights woman" and seems to take courage from Theodore Parker's defense of useful, happy spinsters. Parker argued that a woman who had done everything for house and home was entitled to enter the world. Arguing that technology and free enterprise would one day render most domestic tasks superfluous, he envisioned a time when all women would finish their domestic duties before noon and spend the rest of their day in good works. Although he lamented the rise in spinsterhood, which he saw as a national phenomenon, he believed it merely an historical accident brought on by the unrest of the time and by the prevalence of unequal, unhappy marriages. It was natural, even virtuous, he claimed, for some women to choose honorable spinsterhood over unhappy marriage; ultimately, the reform of domesticity and the expansion of women's social and political rights would restore marriage and the family again.[79]

Alcott treated Nurse Periwinkle as a fictional example of Reverend Parker's sermons. Yet Trib never declares herself a voluntary permanent spinster; instead, it appears as if the circumstances for her (inevitable) marriage were somehow not right. This impression is reinforced by the touching relationship between her and John Sulie, a fatally wounded Virginia blacksmith who possesses all the attributes of true manhood. He never asks for the nurse's attention, but when told he is dying, she volunteers "the gentle tendency of a

woman's hands, the sympathetic magnetism of a woman's presence."
Seeing his silent tears of pain and loneliness,

"Straightaway my fear vanished, my heart opened wide and took
him in, as gathering the bent head in my arms, as freely as if he
had been a little child, I said, 'Let me help you bear it John.' "[80]

"Bashful and brave," he comes close to the childlike, yet fatherly
portrait Alcott drew of Frederick Bhaer in *Little Women*. A true man
will be tender-hearted as a woman, brave but not quite able to
manage life alone. He needs a motherly sort of woman to be his
partner and, as Jo says to Friedrich Bhaer, help share his burdens.

Franklin Sanborn submitted *Hospital Sketches* to the *Commonwealth*,
and the editions with these letters sold out immediately, prompting
two publishers, Redpath and Roberts Brothers, to offer contracts.[81]
Alcott chose Redpath. Scarcely pausing as the proofs and notices of
her book traveled back and forth from Boston to Concord, she also
sent "My Contraband" to the *Atlantic Monthly*. It was accepted, but
publication there paid better in prestige than in cash. The *Atlantic's*
checks were slow to arrive, and Alcott came to depend more on
Frank Leslie and his *Illustrated Newspaper*.

The publisher of "Pauline's Passion and Punishment" catered to a
public that enjoyed sensational gossip, reports of murder trials, and
lurid thrillers. He liked A. M. Barnard's work and offered the author
a regular sum of fifty dollars for a guaranteed monthly story.[82] And
so Alcott began a dual writing career. As Louisa May Alcott she
published such conventional domestic tales as "Cinderella," patriotic
sketches and stories of the Civil War, poems, and occasional children's fiction. As A. M. Barnard she supplied not only Frank Leslie
but the new Boston paper *Flag of Our Union* with thrillers.[83] Designed for family reading, *Flag* nevertheless included blood-and-
thunder tales of criminals, dope addicts, and fallen women. Its editor, James R. Elliott, tried to persuade A. M. Barnard to yield to
Louisa May Alcott's byline. But she was adamant and continued to
produce pieces under her assumed name. One of these stories,
"V. V., or Plots and Counterplots" was republished by Elliott in his
dime-novel series, but neither the three dollars per column she got

from the newspaper nor the sixty-five dollars she eventually received for the exciting *Behind a Mask* persuaded her to emerge from behind her own mask.

The first edition of *Hospital Sketches* ran to one thousand copies, bringing Alcott five cents a copy. She was hardly going to become rich on patriotic works, but she sensed that a respectable literary career depended upon keeping her more lurid creations under the name of an unknown male author.[84] A. M. Barnard's regular income was welcome, but his work revealed passions unacceptable in an Alcott.

Alcott wanted to travel to Port Royal on the Sea Islands of South Carolina, where an important experiment was taking place in the contraband community. The former slaves were producing valuable cotton for the Union and organizing themselves with the help of relief societies. Alcott had hopes of teaching them and sending letters home for another book. Sanborn warmly encouraged her: "Any publisher, this side of Baltimore, would be glad to get the book." She privately exulted that

> there is a sudden hoist for a meek and lowly scribbler, who was told to stick to her teaching and never had a literary friend to lend a helping hand. Fifteen years of hard grubbing may be coming to something after all; and I may yet pay all the debts, fix the house, send May to Italy, and keep the old folks cosey, as I've said I would so long, yet so hopelessly.[85]

Her long illness and recovery prevented Louisa Alcott from journeying south to serve the freed people.

It was difficult for the "scribbler" to reconcile her feelings of generous self-sacrifice with the resentment she felt at May's easier life. Her fictional characters began to display their author's ambivalence about good and bad fortune. On the one hand, she tried to accept hard times as character building for herself, and easier times as May's natural reward for a sunny disposition and an amiable talent. On the other, she enjoyed her self-sufficiency and the dependency of her family; she could find no other way to justify her writing. While constantly asserting that she was no good for anything but "peddling her poor stories," Alcott continued to read the

167

thing but "peddling her poor stories," Alcott continued to read the works of the great authors she admired, and took hours, sometimes days, to rework *Moods* and to plot out a new book, *Work*.[86]

Like many other women, she was discovering a new freedom through her work and was unsure of her right to say so. And also like others, she avoided the dangers of her own passion in a sexually unequal society by channeling her feelings into this work. In her lifetime, women emerged as writers, painters, and sculptors in unprecedented numbers. Alcott wrote about them. Still other women found outlets in the woman's rights movement, in teaching, and in relief work; these too she described in fiction. All her respectable heroines achieved a precarious balance between reason and desire through some form of self-sacrifice. Either they gave up their talents for home and family, or they remained single and developed their gifts for art, music, or self-denying activity.[87]

Only a single woman, Alcott felt, could take advantage of the opportunities newly won by women. But she was not a Margaret Fuller; she had a well-known family to judge her actions even as she provided for them. If her career as a respectable author depended upon her celibacy, however, it did not preclude gorgeously passionate heroines who dared the most outrageous acts in compensation for their betrayal or exploitation as women.

NINE

Passion and Punishment

"I'll not fail again if there is power in a woman's wit and
will! . . . Yes, the last scene shall be better than the first. Mon
dieu, how tired and hungry I am!"
                              Jean Muir in *Behind a Mask, 1866*

Several underlying motifs create striking links between Louisa
May Alcott's Civil War pieces and the acknowledged and pseudononymous Gothic thrillers she wrote for Frank Leslie's *Illustrated
Newspaper*, the *Flag of Our Union*, and the Ten Cent Novelette series.[1] Paternalism masks incest and exploitation in her stories about
slavery while patriarchy conceals incestuous passion and sexual exploitation in her thrillers. Alcott was now among the newly professional women writers, who celebrated women's capacity for self-
reliance and independence yet also warned readers to recognize and
temper their natural passions with moral sentiment. Unquestionably
the often lurid warnings against woman's misuse of her powerful wit
and will were also thrilling validation to female readers identifying
those forces within themselves. Hester Prynne in *The Scarlet Letter*,
as Elizabeth Hardwick notes, made a career out of her betrayal;
Alcott's heroines, however, seek revenge quite as often as they make
amends by living saintly lives after their sins.[2]

LITERARY POLITICS

Between 1863 and 1869 in particular Alcott's works are critically
situated in the dialectic of literature and biography. In these years
she surely mastered all the "generic variants"—as Nina Baym calls a
range of forms, available to women writers for women, with the
moral fable at one end of the scale the novel and the romance at the

169

other.[3] Alcott's New Year's Day journal entry for 1864 lists the ingredients of her writing career:

> earned by my *writing* alone *six-hundred dollars* since last January, . . . received from the *Commonwealth* $18 for a "Hospital Christmas." Wrote a fairy tale, "Fairy Pinafores." "Picket Duty" and other tales came out, first of Redpath's series of books for the "Camp Fires." Richardson sent again for a long story for the "Civil Service Magazine," tried for a war story, but couldn't make it go.[4]

A "lowly scribbler" still one year later, she nevertheless did her annual literary accounting with the air of a breezy professional: "Wrote a little on poor old 'Work' but being tired of novels, I soon dropped it and fell back on rubbishy tales, for they pay best, and I can't afford to starve on praise, when sensation stories are written in half the time and keep the family cosey. Earned $75. this month."[5]

Having begun her career behind a "little me" pseudonym, Flora Fairfield, between 1865 and 1867 Alcott adopted a new disguise, A. M. Barnard.[6] Pseudonymous and anonymous credits never really disguised Alcott from her own family and friends. Nor did she wish to be hidden from them, despite her own careful editing of diaries and letters. Later in life, she deliberately left intact her references to the sensation works with dates, remunerations, and publishers' names mildly disguised (as she did most names) with their initials. Madeline B. Stern and Leona Rostenberg, brilliant literary sleuths in our own time, gathered the clues and recovered many of Alcott's anonymous and pseudonymous thrillers.[7] To bring them out for the enjoyment and scrutiny of today's readers, Stern traced decades of pirated reprints, noting that "V. V.," for instance, "bound in blue wrappers, took its place in the literature of the dime novel and is today one of the rarest and most desirable of those ephemeral pamphlets thumbed to death in the nineteenth century, treasured in the twentieth."[8]

Therein lies a partial solution to the case of the disappearing sensationalist scribbler. She never really erased that part of her self—her pseudonymous literary reputation as a writer of sensation romances and dime novels vanished with the genre itself, leaving only the clues followed successfully by modern literary detectives. Alcott did not lose her passion, wit, or will in helping to create the All-American Girl. But the disappearance of dime novels and Gothic thrillers, in the reactionary "mauve decade" of literary politics, combined to sanitize the reputation of Louisa May Alcott, author of *Little Women*. The American Girl, emerging in the 1860s, reappears over the years as Jo March, Nancy Drew, and Katharine Hepburn. Strong, independent, long-legged and coltish, she has a passionate daredevil side, understandable only when we note that she also rises from the fallen woman in Alcott's pseudonymous, anonymous, and acknowledged thrillers.

There is one more literary explanation for Alcott's disguises to go along with the personal forces that impelled her to mask authorship. Alcott frequently stole from her own works—not an uncommon practice, but one which paid off better with a mixture of acknowledged and pseudonymous works. Three examples of self-pirating suffice to bridge the separation between pure literary strategy and deeply personal preoccupations. Alcott repeated scenes, themes, dialogue, and emblems because she wrote rapidly to earn money for her family and also because she struggled with a complex and recurring personal dilemma.

BLACK SPANISH LACE AND BLOND HAIR

"Pauline's Passion and Punishment," the tale that earned a one-hundred-dollar prize from Frank Leslie, features a Cuban heroine-villainess.[9] She appears as a blond version of Ottila, in a sunset-streaked room very similar to the opening scene in *Moods* (1865). Passionate and willful, Pauline Valery Laroche appears a striking costume: "A black lace scarf lay over her blond hair as Spanish women wear their veils." Then, in the form of a Ten Cent Novelette called "The Skeleton in the Closet" (1867), L. M. Alcott introduces Mathilde Arnheim, a lovely, drooping widow, coming slowly down the terraced steps of a European chateau, "a black lace scarf was thrown about her, one end drawn over her blond hair, as the Spanish women wear their veils."[10] Both heroines have lustrous dark eyes and blond hair, and each acquires a faithful love-slave in a boy/man who will dare anything for her sake.

In the pseudonymous tale, Pauline's passion for revenge is so boundless that it propels two innocents over a cliff to their death. Manuel Laroche and poor "spaniel like" Babie, Redmond's wife, go down clinging to one another. Pauline and Redmond remain alive, standing at the edge of the cliff; they are punished by surviving together. "Anonymous" also says, "beware of your wish—you may get it."

L. M. Alcott's Mathilde, on the other hand, gives up true love to dutifully care for an "idiot" husband who hides his genetic flaw from her when they are wed. Mathilde delicately pretends that she is a widow even when her husband is still alive and then she must, honorably, reject the friendship of an eighteen-year-old boy (a recovering invalid), who declares his love for her. But Mathilde's husband finally does die and, after being deceived once more by false friends, she gets her man in the end.

Allowed to win out because she has repeatedly forsaken revenge, Mathilde scarcely recognizes her youthful lover in the bronzed, bearded fellow who comes back to her, but his maturity and her patience, Alcott insinuates, ensure a happy ending. There is a deeper borrowing evident in this Patient Griselda theme. In "The Skeleton" the lady in the Spanish veil, Mathilde, reminds her young lover of the English poet's Lady of Shalott. The 1882 edition of *Moods*, revised as Alcott said "with experience," added this poem at the end of Sylvia's happy river trip. In "The Skeleton," Alcott again presents a young woman, tempted by the looking-glass reflection of reality, all that is conventionally available to her. Significantly both Sylvia (the second) and Mathilde escape the Lady of Shalott's sad fate.

Clearly Alcott played out the possibilities of love and marriage during this period. Her Civil War experience generated calamitous visions; her trip to Europe (1865–1866) generated a more optimistic view of woman's self-transforming powers. She was moving closer to her most famous plea in behalf of female adolescence as a trying-out period, necessary to win woman's equality in the largest sense. As literary scholar Angela Estes points out, "the thrillers offered Alcott a certain amount of freedom. What if the self-reliant, self-directed man attempting—at Emerson's suggestion—to become a new fulfilled American, a new 'Adam,' is a woman? In the thrillers, Alcott answers this question."[11]

The main difference between the acknowledged and masked fiction is that Alcott wrote under a disguise whenever she created silky villainesses as heroines. Her acknowledged heroines are passionate creatures too, but part of their acceptable self-transformation involves timely disciplining of their passions. Some remain single, feeling that their moody natures are a lifelong burden controlled only by constant self-awareness. Others pass through a stormy adolescent period, but with patience, loving homes, and trial flights into the larger world they become not passionless so much as able to control their dangerous impulses. In the anonymous or pseudonymous thrillers heroines often wake up too late, having drugged themselves with opium and powders; suicide then is their only escape.

Alcott's life experiences help to fully explain the progression of her fiction from "Little Genevieve" in 1856 to *Behind a Mask* ten years later.[12] Her disguise as A. M. Barnard helped Alcott move from exiling a fallen woman in "Genevieve" to installing the villainess, Jean Muir, as lady of the manor house. Between these two works, Faith Dane in "My Contraband" had an ex-slave assume her last name to fight, as she wanted to fight, in a black volunteer regiment. In the decade after the Civil War, however, fictional heroines, following real-life women, increasingly go out into the world to battle for themselves. When she went off to nurse in the Civil War, Alcott was one of many women who began that self-assertive movement. After that service she faced the problem of all returning veterans, the reconstruction of home.

In a very real sense, she was fighting for her own life when she entered the Union Hotel Hospital. Her sister Elizabeth was dead, Anna was married and expecting her first child—home was no longer a sisterhood. Alcott was thirty years old and, as she said, "the blood of the Mays is up."[13] She was not referring just to the Revolutionary spirit of her maternal grandfather because Bronson's ancestors also fought in the War of Independence. Alcott strongly identified with her mother's passionate nature and her constant battle to curb her will.

Alcott did portray Abba's constant struggle with her temper in *Little Women* but she also had to deal with Bronson who seemingly conquered his own passions effortlessly to achieve a famous serenity.

He also succumbed to deep depressions but they must have seemed, to his daughter, like the undeserved consequences of being too good for this world. Certainly Emerson alleged that his friend's only fault lay in living out what other philosophers merely preached. Alcott rarely identified with Bronson's struggles; her fears centered on her maternal inheritance of passionate feelings, pride, and stubborn will. "Pauline's Passion and Punishment" presents the first of many heroines distinguished by Alcott's own virtues and her often confessed faults. Supposing for a moment that she fell passionately in love, how could she protect herself against not only a possibly deceitful lover, but also her own passionate inclination to punish betrayal? How, moreover, could she hope to sustain the devoted self-sacrifice and serenity that her culture and her family prescribed for a married woman? Sylvia's father, in *Moods*, was no help at all in providing a safe shelter for trial flights from home. Sylvia asks him to protect her from suitors at the beginning of both editions of the novel; Alcott makes it clear that he cannot do so. Abba Alcott's father, however dignified and respectable, also failed to protect his daughter from a passionate but unsuitable marriage.

Alcott's Civil War nightmares must be considered once more, this time in the context of her self-scrutiny and the construction of her sensation stories. In the dreams she had married a stout, handsome Spaniard dressed in black velvet, with very soft hands, and a voice that was continually saying, "Lie still, my dear." She suspected that it was her mother's voice. Finding comfort in mother's presence, she also acknowledged that "there was blended an awful fear of the Spanish spouse who was always coming after me, appearing out of closets, in at windows, or threatening me dreadfully all night long."[4]

Alcott's nightmares remained with her for a long time; through them her literary emblems are visibly connected to their sources. Spanish lace and long blond hair reappear in four Alcott works—a novel, two romances, and an evil fairy tale. In Alcott's tales motherless daughters are repeatedly seduced by surrogate fathers entrusted with their care. The sins of mothers are visited upon their daughters. Bronson had confided to his *Journals*, "Two Devils, as yet, I am not quite divine enough to vanquish—the mother fiend and her daughter."[5]

LOVE AND DEATH IN THE OTHER AMERICAN NOVEL

"A Whisper in the Dark," Alcott's chilling Gothic romance, was first published in June 1863, a few months after her delirious nightmares.[16] Under the familiar cover of a standard formula—an orphan girl goes out into the world to test her wits and find a home—Alcott draws the reader slowly into a nightmare of maternal madness and patriarchal betrayal.

Seventeen years old, blond, and somewhat spoiled by a loving governess, Sybil tries flirting with her guardian uncle. He first gives her narcotic cigarettes and then shuts her up in a manor house prison when she refuses his proposal of marriage. Under the uncle's orders, a sinister alchemist-physician next tries to disinherit the girl by driving her mad. Sybil hears footsteps in the room above her chamber and a voice compulsively crooning a lullaby. Eventually she discovers that it is her own mother, driven mad years ago and locked in the attic. The madwoman warns Sybil to escape, writing, "Child! Woman! whatever you are, leave this accursed house while you have power to do it."[17]

A crazy experiment by the doctor results in blowing up Sybil's prison and she escapes. Fleeing the disaster, she encounters her cousin, Guy, who tells her the whole story of her uncle's vile betrayal of her mother years before. Alcott ties up the story by marrying Sybil off to the cousin who loves her and can be trusted to help her back to health and management of her fortune. The wicked uncle is really a stepuncle who receives his just end for persecuting what he has called "a mother-fiend and her daughter." Both the imaginary and the real terror of solitude are banished in a happy ending. The reader nonetheless remains troubled by this bizarre Gothic treatment of a little women theme. Sybil's uncle links mother and daughter together as fiends in a manner reminiscent of Bronson Alcott's anger at Louisa and Abba. The mad mother's warning to a "child! woman!" also resonates back to Abba's sense of imprisonment in domesticity.

Alcott, like her heroine, slowly recovered from her illness and her nightmares, though she was never entirely healthy again. Despite pain and fatigue, she fulfilled the roles of housekeeper, aunt, and writer. Unlike Sybil, she rejected marriage and therefore, within the confines of Alcott values, did not "deserve" a home of her own. Back and forth from Concord to Boston she went, renting a room in which to write, then returning to clean and sew for the family. Nevertheless she did say when Anna was married, "I'd rather be a free spinster and paddle my own canoe," acknowledging that the domestic tranquility her sister gained through marriage was not possible for someone of her temperament and ambition.[18]

Unquestionably there were single women households and "Boston marriages" (female couples) in her own time, but Alcott did not yet earn enough to support two households. Loving her parents, especially her mother, she could not abandon them nor quite reject Abba's model of self-sacrifice. The double message contained in "Whisper" is that the mad mother whispers "Escape, while there is still time," but mother and daughter still are bonded as one in sharing women's domestic responsibilities, part of woman's culture. Alcott's nightmares resonated in her fiction, making the repetition of Gothic conventions all the more compelling for her readers.

The following winter of 1865 the *Flag of Our Union* carried two more serials on the same theme, one by "A Well Known Author" and the other by A. M. Barnard. The first of these, "V. V. or, Plots and Counterplots," is a glittering story written against the fairy tale.[19]

Virginie, an actress, is unprincipled, vain, greedy, thrill seeking and heartless. Victor, her partner, as dark as Virginie is fair, loves her passionately but, it seems, chastely; he tatoos his initials, V. V., on her arm with a lovers' knot, while chasing away her numerous, dishonorable suitors. Before he can claim his prize, she is successfully wooed by a young Scottish nobleman, Allan Douglas. They marry secretly and just after consummating their union, Victor, not knowing that Allan is "husband, not lover," kills him in Virginie's bedroom.[20]

From then on Virginie and Victor travel around the globe, changing costumes, makeup, and names faster than the reader can follow. Virginie has a child from her one night of marriage, who ultimately dies. She is involved in love affairs, murder, and seduction dressed in a purple gown and Spanish black lace. Learning of her baby's death, she secretly drops poison from her opal ring into her glass of wine. For the first time in the romance, Virginie is "passive, brilliant and brave." Dying, her last words are "I have escaped." She finally has the "pale image of serenity if not the reality of healthy repose.[21]

The power of this tale lies in the author's ability to make readers admire and even hope that Virginie will somehow find safety without losing her pulsing vitality. The wicked fairy is both delicate and indomitable. Her disguises sparkle and her acting genius conveys a glowing intelligence and an exquisite taste. Her creator keeps insisting that Virginie is shallow, greedy, and materialistic but what emerges much more believably is a devastating portrait of a heartless, sentimental aristocracy that confuses romance and sentimentality with true love. Virginie escapes through suicide (which Sybil only contemplated). Both heroines prefer death to imprisonment; the good girl and the bad fairy have one thing in common, Alcott's own desire for independence.

"The Marble Woman or the Mysterious Model," with its household imprisonment and threat of incest, is perhaps the most frightening of Alcott's stories written under the name A. M. Barnard.[22]

Again the absence of a nurturing mother gives the heroine more freedom of action, but this tale, like "A Whisper in the Dark," hints that the sins of a mother are visited upon her daughter. The innocent heroine is Cecilia Bazil Stein, who under the care of a guardian— whom she calls "Master"—grows into beautiful young womanhood in virtual isolation from school, friends, or suitors except for the boy next door, Anthony.

Rejecting Anthony's proposal, she agrees to an affectionless marriage with her guardian. Driven to take opium, she almost renders herself the passive, "marble woman," acceptable to her sculptor husband, who had rejected her passion for him.

Alcott allows the "marble woman" no easy solution. Cecil gives up the drug and works still harder on self-control. She becomes romantically involved with an older man who, unknown to her, is her father. In the end the truth is revealed, her father dies, releasing Cecil to become a wife. Sharing the truth transforms her "master" into a companionate, loving husband.

A woman's power, Cecil's, destroys the marble statue and her warm desirability melts the sculptor into a humble supplicant. Alcott aimed a powerful blow at the patriarchal notion that a husband can and should assume a father's power over a young wife. For all its positive happy ending, however, the story presents a tempting, forbidden union, suggesting once again that domesticity comes dangerously close to incest. The family must provide a stable training ground for children and a conservative bastion against the tidal changes of mid-nineteenth-century America. At the same time such an insulated, private arrangement releases incestuous passions. As in the second edition of *Moods*, the author kills off a father to bless a daughter's marriage.

Cecil's power grows as her father's will ebbs, and as he says, "I may claim you at last, for I am dying. Let my heart speak; come to me, my little Cecil, for as God lives I am your father," Cecil's response is immediate. "In an instant she understood the attraction that led her to him owning the tender tie that bound them, and was gathered to the father's bosom, untroubled by a doubt or fear."[23]

The scene is one of the most powerful love duets ever written by Alcott. Once again Alcott fictionally reverses her own reality. Cecil rescues her father in the end of their story—Jo sells her hair to rescue Father in *Little Women*. Yet it was Bronson who traveled to Washington and rescued his daughter.

Alcott's diaries from the 1860s onward describe Bronson as "the old gentleman," a phrase she repeats in describing fictional elderly suitors.[24] Bronson, in turn, did not seem particularly anxious to validate Alcott's womanliness. Both parents increasingly accepted Alcott as "the son" of the household, committed to providing both comfort and prestige for the family.

By the end of the war Alcott's fiction provided her family with subsistence and small comforts, if not affluence. The war had drastically changed her status inside her family, confirming her decision to remain single. It also changed her place in society. Alcott was not the romantic heroine of a poem, but she had seen the larger world and chose to live in it, leaving Concord to Bronson and Abba. She would return to Orchard House for the next twenty years to serve the household when they needed her, but she wanted something more. To the Alcotts, her career was proof that she lacked an instinct for marriage and motherhood; without these, any overt sexuality was unthinkable. In the 1860s most feminists thought that genteel women could not pursue both careers and families. Many working women were forced to combine both, but their lives were scarcely to be envied. A career allowed little escape from domestic self-sacrifice. In July 1865 Alcott prepared for a working holiday. William Weld had asked her to accompany his ailing daughter, Anna, on a year's trip to Europe as a nurse and companion. Bronson let her go, but admitted in his journal that he would miss her "activity and her money, she having contributed largely of her means derived from writing to the payment of family debts and gladly will more as her ability shall allow. A serving visit will be of great profit to her and brings spoils for future literary labor."[25] Bronson, who had accepted the largesse of friends in providing a European trip when he needed relief, sanctimoniously approved that his daughter earn her own way with a "serving trip." He was so generous as to forgo her regular contribution to his living expenses and debts.

She certainly experienced a full year of self-sacrifice in Europe as the paid companion of Anna Weld. Living in Swiss pensions for Anna's health cures eliminated much of the sightseeing available to wealthier young women. But she found a romantic young companion, Ladislas Wisneiwski, an eighteen-year-old Polish refugee, during their stay at Vevey. She and Anna Weld listened to his exciting tales of fighting for Polish liberation and fleeing for his life, experiences that contrasted dramatically with months of fetching shawls and pushing Anna about in a wheelchair, a genteel servitude Alcott could scarcely bear. Yet she considered him a mere boy despite his heroism. She remembered his dark eyes, curly hair, and piano playing well enough, however, to use him as a model for Laurie in *Little Women*. When Alcott finally decided to leave Anna Weld after nearly a year abroad, she found a friendly guide around Paris in her Polish "boy." As Jo's rejected suitor and Amy's eventual husband, Laurie captivated *Little Women* readers.

In somewhat less than luxurious accommodations on the *Africa*, Alcott sailed back to America. In New York John Pratt met her at the dock and escorted her to Concord. During her absence the family had hired a housekeeper, but they dismissed her on learning of Alcott's return. So in addition to her family's open arms, magazine offers, and the debts for her English holiday, she was greeted by household chores. Moreover, Abba was feeling old, sick, and tired;

she needed costly medical attention and careful home nursing all that fall. Alcott fell into her old routine; she nursed Abba, wrote *Behind a Mask*, and even found time to act in Concord plays. When Abba felt strong enough to move about the house, Alcott noted in her diary that "all her fine hair was gone and face full of wrinkles, bowed back and every sign of age. Life had been so hard for her and she so brave, so glad to spend herself for others. Now we must live for her."[26] Despite spells of nursing at home, Alcott was fiercely determined to live alone and write in Boston. Only writing could take care of the accumulated bills and provide the housekeeping services that she frankly dreaded. Again and again she confided to her journal that she was ill, stifled, and depressed in Concord.

THE PLAY'S THE THING

Jean Muir, the heroine of *Behind a Mask, or a Woman's Power*, is a demonic creation, as frantic as Louisa Alcott herself must have been when she wrote the melodrama. Europe had been a candy-shop window against which her face hungrily pressed. Then, three months spent touring England's stately homes, meeting gentry who had the "friends, health and a little money," she craved, were her reward for what Abba called nine months of "hard work and solitary confinement."[27] Once home, in Concord, the desperation of thwarted independence and ambition combined to create Jean Muir, a twilight embodiment of a woman's power.[28]

The scene opens in the stately English country house of the Coventry family. The Coventry ensemble impatiently awaits a brief diversion, the expected arrival of Bella's new governess. Jean Muir, who appears as the governess, seems to be a Jane Eyre sort of person, small, black-robed, pale-faced, and colorless. Behind the selfless serving-girl's mask the real Jean Muir disguises herself. After she has been interviewed and ensconced in her room, she removes her disguise, revealing an older, scheming adventuress. A professional actress, her costume includes false teeth, fake hair, and rouge. Only her "mobile features" are natural, a consistent trait of both the little governess and the weary actress.

She conquers the hearts of the family including both sons, who come to blows over her. The younger learns her true identity and he buys a revealing packet of letters written by Muir to her only friend, another actress named Hortense. Jean Muir, in the meantime, manages a marriage with the Coventrys' uncle, Sir John, and she defiantly destroys all the evidence against her. Leaving with her new husband, she turns at the end of the last scene saying "in her penetrating voice, 'is not the last scene better than the first?' " Indeed it is. Alcott has created a fallen angel whose power overleaps that of Pauline, Virginie, and Cecil. All the heroines of Alcott's other thrillers possess some genuine "womanly" feelings. Pauline finally does love her husband even though her passion for revenge kills two people. Cecil is a tenderhearted creature who loves her mother, her guardian, and her father. Jean Muir alone says, "Bah, how I hate sentiment."[29]

Jean's seeming lack of all womanly feeling leads feminist scholar Judith Fetterley to conclude that the "radicalism of Alcott's *Behind a Mask* is precisely Muir's impersonation of a 'little woman.' " Women must put on the masks of "little womanhood" in order, Fetterley says, to survive in a society where "there is no honest way to make a living."[30] Jean Muir's letters do reveal that she arrived at the Coventry house desperately sure that this role is her last—she must play it for all she can, resolving to commit suicide rather than go back to the street. Embittered by the cruel treatment of poor working women like herself, Jean Muir aims to punish her tormentors and share whatever fortune she may gain with Hortense.

Jean will give Sir John precisely what he pays for. The only game in town is to marry for a living, and Alcott makes Jean "an honest woman" by turning social hypocrisy upside down. This is a hierarchical society, and the Coventry clan is silent in deference to Sir John's lordly erasing of history: "Come home, love," he says to Jean, and "forget all this."[31]

Muir, for all that she is rescued by Sir John, begins her own ascent earlier in the story. She has one important sentiment left—she feels genuine gratitude. Even after the younger son learns that she is an older divorced actress and gives her three-days' notice, he sends Jean more than a year's salary: "No word accompanied the gift, yet the generosity of it touched her, for Jean Muir had the relics of a once honest nature, and despite her falsehood could still admire nobleness and respect virtue. A tear of genuine shame dropped on the paper, and real gratitude filled her heart, as she thought that even if all else failed, she was not thrust out penniless into the world, which had no pity for poverty."[32]

Her tear signals the rise of the fallen woman. Alcott conquers sentimentality with sentiment, insisting that Muir deserves to survive and win at her last chance. Alcott's domestic fiction receives a powerful impulse from Jean Muir's triumph. Despite the Coventrys' knowing that Jean Muir is a divorced actress and, worse still, a confidence woman, they must suffer and be still about it. The Coventrys' own conventions insist that a lady is above reproach, and Jean Muir becomes Lady Coventry.

Jean Muir does not, however, stand alone in Alcott's imagination. There is a thin red thread running from Milly in "An Hour," to Ottila, Pauline, and Virginie, in their veils of Spanish lace, and then continuing on to Cecil, playing the marble woman. All of them, once we have met Jean Muir, appear self-transformed not only by the shred of fine sentiment kept alive inside bruised souls, but also by the glow of their righteous anger. They are fallen angels who can fully rise up only in a better world, one they paradoxically must make themselves. Rejecting Romantic individualism as the means to creating that world, Alcott went on to fashion a network of reform-minded heroines and heroes. Knowing whether her goal was ultimately to reform domesticity or to "expose the entire concept of family as a corrupt and dishonest institution," as Angela Estes suggests, depends upon understanding both Alcott's "gorgeous fancies," and her perspective on woman's rights.[33]

THE GOLDEN EGG

Children's fiction was a reliable source of income for women writers by mid-century, and Alcott received an attractive offer from *Merry's Museum*, a popular juvenile magazine. She would receive five hundred dollars a year for her editing skills and her contributions of stories, poems, and advice column.[34] In the earlier part of the nineteenth century children's fiction had been generally pious, dull, and curiously unspecific about the details of everyday life. But by the

1860s Bronson's romantic faith in the innocence of infants had become part of a popular sentimentalization of childhood. It helped improve the quality of juvenile fiction, at least in terms of rich detail and mildly adventurous plots. Even the Sunday School societies, which published their own tracts and stories for children, agreed that lively fiction was a positive moral aid to parents. Secular publishers developed a large market for juvenile literature, and they encouraged their authors to write in detail about children's dress, food, and games.[35] Most important, the children themselves were now the central figures in their stories; adults were only accessory characters. Louisa May Alcott became editor of *Merry's Museum* and A. M. Barnard disappeared under her new aliases, Aunt Wee and Cousin Tribulation. Those two worthies contributed stories, advice, and poems to the magazine.

By the time of the Civil War, childhood was accepted with equanimity as a stage in life, but youth or adolescence was increasingly regarded as a troubling period for both parents and their offspring. Adults feared precosity most of all, the tendency of young people to grow up too fast and make impetuous decisions that would affect their whole lives. Also, some social goals were contradictory. The family was expected to teach young people about the land of opportunity outside the cottage door, but it was also supposed to preserve innocence by protecting youth from reality. Reading material for older youth developed quickly as an aid for parents in coping with this unsettling period.

Thomas Niles, Roberts Brothers' literary representative, suggested that Alcott write a girls' book.[36] It was not an idle suggestion, because Niles wanted to tap the market for girls created by such popular writers of boys' fiction as Oliver Optic. The author's real name was William Taylor Adams, and like Alcott he was a member of a respectable Massachusetts family. In addition to boys' Great Western Series, Lake Shore Series, and Yacht Club Series, he had also produced a promising girls' story about Katy Redmond. His heroine was a self-reliant twelve-year-old whose exploits signaled a change in girls' fiction, a change that struck a responsive note in Alcott.[37]

She considered the possibility of writing a two-hundred-page girls' story for Roberts Brothers. She was thirty-five years old and a little bored with writing the idealized versions of her own and her sisters' childhood adventures. Still, she wrote them easily and the Alcotts needed the money she sent home from thrillers, children's stories, and poems. After her European trip she turned out a two-hundred-page adult novel, *A Modern Mephistopheles*, only to have it rejected for serialization in the *Flag of Our Nation*.[38] To keep up her apartment in Boston and the Alcott home in Concord, and to help May teach art in Boston and Concord, Alcott decided to try her talents at what paid best, a girls' book. She had earned the $1,000 she set as her goal in 1867, but now she needed spectacles to work and called herself "Minerva Moody." She wrote to Abba, "Keep all the money I send; pay up every bill; get comforts and enjoy yourselves." She also sent regards to Bronson as Plato and asked if her father didn't want any new socks or other clothes.[39]

Bronson urged Alcott to accept Niles's offer for a story, and he assumed that she would move back to Concord to write it. He was anxious to please Niles, who had agreed to publish parts of Bronson's diaries under the title, *Tablets*.[40] In May 1868 Alcott did move back to Concord, and in her old room at Orchard House, seated at the tiny desk her father had built years ago in front of her window, she began to write her girls' book.

She sent the first twelve chapters to Niles in June, and admitted to herself that "he thought it dull, so do I." On July 15 her diary notes, "Have finished Little Women and sent it off—412 pages. May is designing some pictures for it. Hope it will go . . . very tired, full of pain from overwork, and heart heavy about Marmee who is growing feeble." Roberts Brothers gave her the choice of a few hundred dollars as a flat fee, or a percentage of the sales and her own copyright. She took a chance on the copyright, and years later wrote gratefully, "an honest publisher and a lucky author, for the copyright made her fortune and the dull book was the first golden egg of the ugly duckling."[41]

Little Women made the case for an enlightened family life as the best means for raising a new woman and saving the Union. By setting her story in the Civil War years Alcott easily linked the cause of domestic reform to patriotism and abolition. Within a few years after its publication, the problem of uniting female and Negro rights split the feminist movement. Alcott herself insisted that the two were inseparable even if woman's suffrage withdrew for a moment in support of "the hour of the Negro."[42] She continued writing domestic dramas. These gradually expanded the egalitarian nuclear family of *Little Women* into personalized, public institutions to educate, support, and house Americans. Melodramatic heroines would henceforth appear as healthy outlets for the dramatic talent of All-American girls, saved from Jean Muir's tragedy by democratic social arrangements.

TEN
Writing Little Women

I don't understand it. What *can* there be in a simple little story
like that, to make people praise it so?
Jo March in *Little Women*, chapter 42

Little Women portrays fifteen years in the life of the March family.
As all Louisa Alcott's readers know, it is essentially the story of her
own family and its domestic adventures. Contemporary readers
could also recognize the author's friends and acquaintances. Perhaps
the novel's greatest strength lay in her comfortable assertion that
domesticity and feminism were not only compatible but essential to
one another.[1]

Beneath this conventional story, in which girls learn to sacrifice
and conquer faults on their way to becoming true women, flows a
subterranean river. Partly buried within the girls' everyday experiences runs a troubling current of sexual definition, an intrinsic part
of the woman problem in Alcott's time. Does achieving one's individual identity, for instance, mean nothing more than growing up to be
male or female? In the second chapter of *Little Women* the Laurence
boy enters the story as the March sisters' benefactor. Laurie, who
lives next door in his wealthy grandfather's mansion, becomes a fifth
sister in effect. Jo is his sponsor, and together Jo and Laurie become
the best-loved and most memorable characters in all of Alcott's fiction. Introducing an adolescent boy into a mid-nineteenth-century
all-female household was no small feat. Moreover, at any given moment (in the first part of *Little Women*), it is difficult to tell whether Jo
is a boy, Laurie is a girl, or vice versa, which is exactly the author's
intent.[2]

ROMANTICS AND RATIONALISTS

By mid-November 1868, Alcott had been working on the second half of *Little Women* for more than two weeks, completing a chapter a day.[3] She was pressed by devoted fans who wanted to know who the little women married. Alcott was determined not to marry Jo to Laurie to please anyone—"as if marriage were the only end and aim of a woman's life."[4] She was also tired of writing. For diversion she accompanied her father to a meeting of the Boston Radical Club to hear the Unitarian minister, John Weiss, read a "fine paper on Woman Suffrage," as she later recorded it. The "good talk afterward" pleased her as much as the paper did. She incorporated what some called the "rose colored view of the future" into *Little Women*.[5]

The essential point of Weiss's paper was that women and men should combine their talents in political as well as domestic arrangements. Emerson, who was in attendance, did not agree. Given to understand that most women did not like public life, he declared that "women of refinement and culture" would shrink from engaging in political reform. Ednah Cheney countered that refined men were as indifferent to political activism as refined women. Nothing would be accomplished toward the "purification of politics" until "refined intellectual men and women" worked for political reform together. Neither Emerson, who had once spoken in behalf of mechanics and farmers, nor Cheney, who represented the new, educated, and "refined" women reformers, had much faith in conventional political parties. There were others present, however, who wanted to create a reform coalition of laboring people, farmers, and reformist intellectuals.[6]

The contested terrain was nothing less than the reconstruction of American society. Behind the parlor exchange lay a major debate in Alcott's circle about the means and ends of such reform. Two perspectives represented overlapping generations of reformers. Alcott's generation—including Cheney, Frank Sanborn, William Torrey Harris, as well as Abigail May, Abigail May Alcott's younger cousin— had been inspired by the Romantic individualism of the older generation, who believed with Thomas Carlyle that great men make history.[7] The new historical perspective, which Alcott learned partly at the Radical Club lectures on the English historian Henry Buckle, was being widely disseminated through such books as John Lathrop Motley's *Rise of the Dutch Republic.*[8] Cheney recommended Motley's book to the Alcotts and urged them even more strongly to read his *Historic Progress and American Democracy.* Opposing the view that individuals make history, Motley placed individuals within history and under the constraint of a historical law that governs "all bodies political as inexorably as Kepler's law controls the motions of planets. The law is Progress: the result is Democracy."[9]

Buckle and Motley argued that human history displays the unfolding of "order, symmetry, and law."[10] Persons are only instruments of history, having little or no power to influence the course of events. The progress of events is the progress of impersonal ideas and tendencies working through human society. Only the steady application of existing laws, not the intervention of individual "will," would create a new rational order in the world.

The proponents of each perspective claimed that democracy was embodied in their viewpoint. The Romantic or Transcendental view of the "will" elevated the inner voice of each individual to a commanding position above the restricting laws and institutions of conventional society. Bronson Alcott, Emerson, Margaret Fuller, and Thoreau had all found the courage to be individuals and reformers in opposition to existing social mores. At the Radical Club Bronson still argued that "great men were always the prophets of an age to come; the world has to be educated up to them. Through the great minds, the revelations are made to the multitude."[11] Even in 1868 Bronson saw the conflict between this patriarchial conception of leadership and genuine democratic aspiration. He added Queen Elizabeth to his list of great figures, but insisted that she carried the scepter of female culture and beauty, without which there would have been no Raleigh or Shakespeare. Perhaps for the first time in a public discussion Elizabeth I was credited with exercising "spiritual influence, rather than naked power over her subjects."[12]

From the point of view of Louisa Alcott and Ednah Cheney among others, Buckle and Motley promised a different and grander democratic notion of history. The new rationalist progressives held that God "does not and cannot incarnate himself wholly in any one person, but must have all humanity for his organs. He works through the whole."³ The question was the reconciliation of personal will and responsibility, which none of the idealists wanted to discard, despite their enthusiasm for new theory of social law.

Thomas Wentworth Higginson, the famous abolitionist, was very much a feminist in this discussion. He invoked the great Transcendentalist himself, Emerson, to reconcile individualism with the new theory. Emerson "had shown how the leader was fed from all sources and all other times were constantly pressing upon him." As for himself, Higginson (who would later embrace an American variant of socialism) maintained that "the longer he lived, the more weight he attached to the general voice."⁴ William T. Potter, a liberal Unitarian and a member of the Radical Club, also extolled the virtues of the new historical perspective. The Civil War, he said, was most emphatically "a people's war," while Lincoln and Stanton, however great as individuals, were effective leaders because they represented the "courage, patriotism, and love of justice, in the heart of the nation."⁵

As for woman, she was the heart of the nation in this new view. The universal laws of symmetry and balance held as true for social as for personal relationships. Theodore Parker had said something similar years before, so it was appropriate that a meeting of the Radical Club should end with a reading from one of Parker's speeches. Parker's words seemed to unite everyone in the room. "Everywhere," he had declared,

in the family, the community, the Church and the State, we want the masculine and feminine element co-operating and conjoined. Woman is to correct man's taste, mend his morals, excite his affections, inspire his religious faculties. Man is to quicken her intellect, to help her will, translate her sentiments to ideas, and enact them into righteous laws. Man's moral action, at best, is only a sort of general human providence, aiming at the welfare of a part, and satisfied with achieving the "greatest good of the greatest number." Woman's moral action is more like a special human providence, acting without general rules, but caring for each particular case. We need both of these, the general and the special, to make a total human providence.

189

Granting men and women social equivalence, Parker had said, would redress the evils of history. Without it, "property must be theft, law the strength of selfish will, and Christianity what we see it is, the apology for every powerful wrong."[16]

After this inspiring conclusion, Alcott lunched with women friends and relaxed at the Women's Club. The next day, however, she was back at work, so inspired that she could scarcely stop to eat or sleep, going out only for her usual, solitary run. Her thirty-sixth birthday came and went, her single gift a copy of her father's new book, *Tablets*.[17] She had already satirized the Radical Club debates in the chapter entitled A Friend in *Little Women*. Jo and Friedrich Bhaer attend a fashionable "select symposium" in New York, in which debates about "speculative philosophy" and "universal laws of progress" are presented by the fictional philosophers, each riding his favorite "hobby."[18]

Despite the satire, the John Weiss lecture and discussion helped clarify Alcott's plan of action for Jo. Her heroine could not remain a child forever, even for so good a cause as liberty. The rationalist argument that society needed the harmonious blend of both male and female principles suited the author, who would not marry Jo to Laurie. Instead, Alcott created a situation in which Jo could share in supporting a home with a husband who could share in nurturing. The Radical Club discussions were only the culmination, after all, of domestic reforms which Alcott supported ever since the Syracuse Woman's Rights Congress of 1852. They included coeducation, household democracy, woman's right to individual development of her talents, work, and suffrage of course.[19]

Significantly, Alcott's first biographer was Ednah Littlehale Dow Cheney, who had sat with her and Bronson at the Radical Club debate. Cheney found it necessary to remind Alcott readers, only twenty-one years after the publication of *Little Women*, that there had once been another "newness": "the great question of the transcendental period was truth to the inward life instead of the outward law." She compared Jo March in *Little Women* to Sylvia Yule in *Moods* and observed that *Moods* fails because "the marriage question is not stated strongly, it does not reach down to this central principle." A "double relation" such as Sylvia's marriage to Moor could be endured only if the situation is "completed by fate, fate of character and overpowering circumstances."[20] In other words, Sylvia does not obey the laws of circumstance; she is in a "double relation" because she obeys only her romantic fancy. On the other hand, "stormy Jo," the creation most like Alcott herself, "is a real presence to us . . . whom we take to our hearts, in spite of her faults."[21] Alcott, like Jo, was saved from Sylvia's fate "by the discipline of family work and love." Jo did not marry the wrong man and she did demand respect of her individuality and hard work.

Cheney had difficulty because Alcott, who Cheney claimed was not much interested in love and marriage, presented an important treatment of marriage from the liberal feminist perspective. She was well aware that Alcott had written a tribute to spinsterhood shortly before writing *Little Women*. She wrote an advice column for the *New York Ledger* called "Happy Women,"[22] and Cheney observed that the professionals and artists Alcott portrayed were all "easily recognizable" as the sort of unmarried women Theodore Parker called a "glorious phalanx of old maids."[23] Alcott probably intended Jo's words to be taken seriously: she preferred to remain unmarried. Readers, however, did not want it that way. Alcott was saved from making a false romantic compromise by presenting a new kind of egalitarian marriage.

Cheney, like Frank Sanborn, was a family friend who knew both the models for Alcott's characters and the issues they dramatized. In fact, Alcott's journal entries for the year she wrote *Little Women* describe an expanding social life, full of new issues and friends. In 1868 she enjoyed more than Radical Club lectures with her friends. With her cousin Abigail May, she watched Fanny Kemble perform in *The Merchant of Venice*. Afterward they went to the home of Mary Parkman and dined with Fanny Kemble herself. Mary Parkman and Abigail May, both Republicans and part of the American Social Science Association, as recording secretary and executive board member respectively, invited Alcott to attend the New England Woman's Suffrage Association meetings. In its early years the Social Science Association had a strong feminist orientation; this was the work in part of Caroline Dall, a close friend of Abba, who had read Dall's book on women and work. Sanborn and William Torrey Harris were also leading Social Science members. They published numerous articles in its journals, and disseminated the rationalist views of Buckle along with their own more Romantic versions of Hegelian idealism. As she finished the last pages of *Little Women*, Alcott helped her father pack for his westward trip to visit Harris.[24]

In November 1868 she also joined the New England Woman's Suffrage Association. Formed by feminists, including her own family and friends, the association favored the Republican party as a vehicle for women's enfranchisement. As the widely recognized author of *Hospital Sketches* and *Little Women*, Alcott was an asset to the feminist cause. She attended the first organizational meeting of the association and listened to reformers debate the relative political importance of suffrage for blacks and women. Frederick Douglass, the famous black abolitionist and supporter of woman's rights, told the group: "Woman has a thousand ways by which she can attach herself to the ruling power of the land that we have not." He urged his audience to put the cause of black suffrage ahead of women's rights for the moment.[25]

Lucy Stone replied that the woman's cause was no less pressing than that of Negroes. But the political struggles of the previous year had convinced many that the coalition between woman's and Negro's rights was unproductive. In 1867 the national Equal Rights Association had been badly defeated trying to gain black and woman's rights to vote on the Kansas referendums. Republican lack of enthusiasm for the woman's rights cause had led to a shameful alliance between feminists and racist Democrats. Late in the campaign, some Republican men including Gerrit Smith and Henry Ward Beecher finally issued an "Appeal to the Voters of Kansas" that urged a vote for woman's rights. It was too late. When both referendums failed, the united front collapsed.

The New England association attempted to repair the coalition by making votes for women its ultimate goal while giving priority to black suffrage. Julia Ward Howe was elected the first president of the association; she made it clear that her right to vote could wait upon black male enfranchisement. In February 1869, when Alcott had just finished the second part of *Little Women*, Congress passed the Fifteenth Amendment to the Constitution of the United States. It ensured the right of citizens to vote regardless of "race, color, or previous condition of servitude." It ignored the rights of women, both black and white.[26]

Like many other radical abolitionists in the woman's movement, Alcott tried to believe that universal male suffrage would inevitably lead American men to accept women's political rights. The women worked state by state, hoping to secure the right to vote from state legislators. Alcott signed the "Appeal to Republican Women in Massachusetts." Lucy Stone wrote Sam May that the temperance reformers in the Massachusetts legislature would favor woman's rights, but they did not, voting twenty-two to nine against female suffrage.[27]

Although Alcott devoted much of her energies to the cause of woman's rights over the next twenty years, her domestic fiction constituted her most important feminist contribution. She made woman's rights integral to her stories, and above all to *Little Women*. And she remained convinced that woman's rights were linked to universal human reform efforts despite the betrayals of party politics.

Alcott was never actively involved in party politics again, although she campaigned locally in Concord for temperance. Having sent Bronson to visit the St. Louis Hegelians, and settled Abba at Anna's house, Alcott with her sister May left for the Bellevue Hotel in Boston, where she made the final corrections on *Little Women*. Owned and operated by Dio Lewis, principal of Boston's Normal Institute for Physical Education, the Bellevue Hotel was a haven for reformist women, who could exercise freely and learn the principles of preventive medicine. Living on the seventh floor, which Alcott called their "sky parlor," the "working sisters" had the advantages of steam baths, elevator service, and lobster salad luncheons.[28] An active life and healthy food accompanied coeducation, household democracy, and woman's suffrage in the liberal circle of fashion. In her notes for "Happy Women" Alcott wrote: "Liberty is a better husband than love to many of us."[29] With May for company and plenty of writing to do, she found herself exhausted and happy.

How did the woman who hated to "pack for home" and leave a quiet room of her own manage to write an exquisite tribute to American home life? She was often lonely, in ill health from the effects of too much medication and overwork, and she chose to remain unmarried. The answer lies in being close to the realization of her "dream of supporting the family and being perfectly independent."[30]

Alcott never questioned the value of domesticity; instead, she challenged the price ordinarily extracted from women like herself.

Anna and John Pratt on the other hand seemed ideally suited to marriage and home life; she portrayed them as Meg and John Brooke in *Little Women*. As a sort of private family joke, she memorialized the fact that John Pratt's family had been at Brook Farm by giving Anna's fictional husband the family name Brooke. The "old people," as she called Bronson and Abba, lived in the same Orchard House cottage as their fictional counterparts, Mr. and Mrs. March—all provided for by their daughter.[31] For her part, Alcott wanted to believe that a democratic household could evolve into a feminist society. In *Little Women*, she imagined that just such an evolution might begin with Plumfield, a nineteenth-century feminist utopia.

ELEVEN

Reading Little Women

I may be strong-minded, but no one can say I'm out of my
sphere now, for woman's special mission is supposed to be
drying tears and bearing burdens. I'm to carry my share, Friedrich, and help to earn the home. Make up your mind to that,
or I'll never go.

Jo March in *Little Women*, chapter 46

The title of Louisa May Alcott's most famous book is a commonplace nineteenth-century expression. In the opening chapter, Marmee reads a Christmas letter from her absent husband to his daughters, which tenderly admonishes them to "conquer themselves so
beautifully that when I come back to them I may be fonder and
prouder than ever of my little women."[1] This sentimental diminu-
tive is puzzling in an author who was concerned with enlarging,
rather than diminishing, woman's status. Such belittlement was part
of the woman problem, as Alcott knew. This title appears even more
puzzling when we consider that *Little Women* deals with the problems common to girls growing into womanhood.

Alcott had no intention of depreciating the struggles of young
women, so we must look elsewhere for explanations of the title. We
find one in the works of Charles Dickens, which Alcott read and
took with her to the Union Hotel during the Civil War. For several
decades Dickens had moved English and American readers to tears
with his tender depictions, imitated but never equaled, of childhood
woe. Dickens cared most deeply for the misery of exploited children—abused strangers in a venal adult world, but often remarkably
capable of fending for themselves. Dickensian girls are particularly
self-reliant, able to care for their siblings by the time they are "over
thirteen, sir," as the girl "Charlie" says to Mr. Jarndyce in *Bleak
House*. In this novel the term "little women" makes a prominent
appearance when Esther, ward of the generous, sweet-hearted Mr.

Jarndyce, is told by her guardian, "You have wrought changes in me, little woman," indicating that she has widened and deepened his sensibilities and hence his philanthropy.[2]

Esther saves many people during the course of the novel, including the girl Charlie whom she takes in and nurses through a bout of smallpox. Charlie herself had contracted the disease from Jo, another pathetic Dickensian orphan. Inevitably, Esther comes down with smallpox, which leaves her face scarred and sets her musing about the meaning of "little woman."

Although only twenty-one, Esther has been close to death and realizes now how short time is for "little women." No longer a child, yet not an adult, she finds life fleeting and precious. Dreadfully confused, she talks about the stages of her life, feeling herself at once "a child, an elder girl, and the little woman I had been so happy as." The problem, she thinks, is that the stages are not so distinct as she had once innocently supposed. Rather, they seem joined together and weighted down by similar "cares and difficulties," which are hard to reconcile or understand.[3]

When Louisa May Alcott employed the term "little women," she infused it with this Dickensian meaning. *Little Women* portrays just such a complex overlapping of stages from childhood to elder child, little woman to young woman, that appears in *Bleak House*. Like Esther, each of Alcott's heroines has a scarring experience that jars her into painful awareness of vanished childhood innocence and the inescapable woman problem.

Esther's role as part-time narrator in *Bleak House* is given to Jo in *Little Women*, but the resemblance between the two characters ends there. Jo comes close to bounding off the pages of her book; an American heroine, she has fits of exuberance alternating with moments of half-chastened humility. Unlike Esther, and very much like her creator, Jo writes a story that succeeds miraculously even though she "never knew how it happened." "Something," Jo declares, "got into that story that went straight to the hearts of those who read it." She put "humor and pathos into it," says saintly Mr. March, sure that his daughter had "no thought of fame or money in writing" her story.[4]

Louisa May Alcott of course, unlike Jo, produced the story of *Little Women* in record time for money. As she reviewed the first page proofs, she found that "it reads better than I expected; we really lived most of it and if it succeeds that will be the reason of it."[5] Five succeeding generations have laughed and cried over *Little Women*. Each generation may well have its own favorite incidents and lessons. And every generation's readers indisputably love Jo, who is never an orphan though she often feels like one in moving from girlhood to womanhood.

Alcott's acknowledged mentors in the writing of *Little Women* also include Susan B. Warner and Charlotte M. Yonge. Contemporary readers could not miss the significance of Jo sitting in the family's apple tree, crying over *The Wide Wide World*.[6] The March sisters, in fact, name their apple tree "Ellen-tree" after Ellen Montgomery, the orphaned heroine of that story. Amy and Jo put a saddle on a "nice, low branch," and use the tree as a hobby horse, not being fortunate enough to get a real pony as Ellen does in Warner's novel. Jo is also discovered eating apples and crying over *The Heir of Redclyffe* in the privacy of a garret inhabited only by her pet rat, Scrabble, who probably also witnessed Jo's reading of another Yonge novel, *The Daisy Chain*.[7] Yonge's heroine in the latter novel, like Ellen Montgomery in *The Wide Wide World*, is by nature a rebellious, moody girl. Ethel May is a "thin, lank, angular, sallow girl, just fifteen, trembling from head to foot with restrained eagerness as she tried to curb her tone into the requisite civility."[8]

Women's fiction in the nineteenth century has been characterized as following a formula in which the heroine, often orphaned, progresses through a series of lonely ordeals that prove her inherent worth and her ability to survive independently. She finds help along the way, usually in the form of an expanding female network. A heroine's ordeals prompt her perceptual transformation or change of heart; she grows considerably during the process.[9] In Alcott's time, *The Wide Wide World* was the most popular rendition of this women's fiction formula. Juvenile literature, in this categorization, merely simplifies women's fiction; young heroes and heroines grow up because circumstances force them out into a cruel and heartless world where they see the light and become the best they can be, converting others in the process.

Because it is juvenile literature, *Little Women* seems to some critics to represent a decline in the radical power of women's fiction.[10] The novel may also be considered a diminishment of women's capacity for independence precisely because Alcott's heroines are not orphans or widows but members of a particularly embracing family. And, since the Victorian middle-class family leaves women's work famously unpaid and undervalued, it hardly seems an environment conducive to empowering little women. Just as American heroines are portrayed provoking Civil War and ending slavery, they are seemingly remanded to a private sphere in *Little Women.* Historians of juvenile fiction consequently join with many historians of women's literature in placing *Little Women* at the top of a downward spiral.[11]

DOMESTIC REALISM

Romanticism provided two powerful impulses to the development of juvenile literature. Shaping our modern view of "human nature," the Romantic perspective insists that children are born as pure, unique wellsprings of creativity. Building upon this belief, children's vision of the world seems particularly honest and sincere. Placing children at the center of the action, Romantic juvenile fiction also encourages them to reveal adult hypocrisy. Sometimes, childhood ends with the pragmatic necessity of growing up to join the hypocrites. In sentimental novels, however, a pure child's ability to convert adults conversely restores grownups to the lost world of children's innocence.[12]

The golden age of children's literature in England produced a remarkable glow emanating from fairy rings and fictional children who stubbornly refused to grow up; as runaways, they poked sharply at both the bourgeois family and the deadening blights of industrial capitalism. Historians of childhood and juvenile literature understandably revel in analyses of *The Water Babies, Alice in Wonderland, Peter Rabbit, Peter Pan,* and *The Wind in the Willows;* all these works, like the women's fiction categorized by Nina Baym, provide significant social commentary and criticism. America, with the same Romantic heritage to inspire its juvenile genre, produced the *Little Women* series, followed by a host of imitators from *Rebecca of Sunnybrook Farm* to the Pollyanna books and the Bobbsey Twins series. *Little Women* does not betray the author's Romantic birthright, nor does it belittle women's fiction. Louisa May Alcott combines many conventions of the sentimental novel with crucial ingredients of Romantic children's fiction, creating a new form of which *Little Women* is a unique model. In it Alcott created the American Girl reflecting her myriad facets in the diverse personalities of Meg, Jo, Beth and Amy March. Alcott's work indisputably enlarges the myth of American womanhood by insisting that the home and the women's sphere cherish individuality and thus produce young adults who can make their way in the world while preserving a critical distance from its social arrangements. All the March sisters are engaged in a search for their adult selves and all—Jo most painfully and powerfully—fear that their unique human potential will be lost or destroyed in the process of growing up. Balancing their fears with castles in the air, the sisters also hope that their individuality will somehow be recognized and specially rewarded in the adult world.

Jo writes the first part of *Little Women* in the second half of the novel. As a story based on her own childhood, her narration signals a successfully completed adolescence. She has preserved the unique child within herself, disciplining her talent to create a work of art which is also a recipe for achieving an adult self. The trial or ordeals as well as the perception of a change of heart necessary to a heroine's progress in adult women's fiction are also present in *Little Women*. Alcott's added ingredient is the social arrangements defining the March family. A loving female creation, the March cottage is a nest from which the sisters fly out, testing themselves in the larger world. Marmee counsels and rules, but also lets her daughters go, one by one. *Little Women* significantly reassures young readers, who are generally younger than Amy March in the first part, that they will remain truly themselves in growing up. The March girls, after all, are easily recognizable in the persons of the March women. Readers need only the bit of "gossip" provided by the author to fill in what has transpired between the end of childhood and the beginning of young womanhood.

Adult women still reread *Little Women*, traveling backward to recover toys in the attic, precious objects that have been mislaid or put away over the years. The gap between an authentic self and a modern identification with functional social roles grows wider with each decade. As it widens adult readers return longingly to *Little Women* where the source of fragile individuality rests, Alcott argues, in the memories of those who knew us in childhood—in our families. The March sisters share the same parents and the same stable childhood environment yet each little woman has a unique self; the recognition of their differences and their bond is an important aspect in *Little Women*'s domestic realism. Jo, the self-proclaimed historian of the family, has custody of objects and memories connecting past to present in March history. And the family history reassures readers that each of them has a human value beyond the marketplace.

THEMES IN *LITTLE WOMEN*: DOMESTICITY

The novel develops three major themes: domesticity, work, and true love. All of them are interdependent and each is necessary to the achievement of a heroine's individual identity. The same motifs appear in *Little Men, Jo's Boys, Eight Cousins, Rose in Bloom*, and *An Old-Fashioned Girl*. None of these novels has been out of print since first published. Together they comprise a fictional record of liberal woman's rights ideology, process, and programs from 1867 through 1886 in America.

From the outset Alcott established the centrality of household democracy, underscoring the importance of "natural" cooperation and mutual self-sacrifice within family life. The March cottage shelters the sisters and their parents, all of whom love and depend upon one another. Even the family poverty, so reminiscent of Alcott's own, serves to reinforce democratic practice in the family. With the help of Hannah, who worked as a maid for Mrs. March in better days and now considers herself a member of the family, all the women work together to accomplish household chores, making the most of meager means by sharing everything.

The virtues of mutual self-sacrifice and domestic cooperation, however, must be proven to the March girls before they can recognize the importance of such virtues to their self-realization. Independent-minded and childishly selfish, the girls must learn how to shape their individualities in harmony with the interests of the family. In an important episode Alcott describes the tactics used by Mrs.

March to win her daughters to a higher social standard, which is in a sense to "conquer themselves."

After listening to Jo, Meg, Beth, and Amy pine for the "vacations" enjoyed by wealthier friends, Marmee agrees to release them from domestic duties for one week. She allows them to structure their time in any way they please. On the first morning, the neat inviting cottage is suddenly a different place, and after a day of small troubles, the girls are grumpy and ill-tempered. The experiment, however, is not over. Excessive attention to self-pleasure produces a scarcity of necessities, including food. Emulating the little red hen, Mrs. March decides that those who do not work shall not eat. She gives Hannah a holiday, and the maid leaves with these parting words: "Housekeeping ain't no joke." Unable to rely on the experience and counsel of Hannah and their mother, the girls produce a breakfast featuring boiled tea, very bitter, scorched omelette, and biscuits speckled with saleratus. Jo caters a luncheon for friends, forgetting that she can't make anything "fit to eat" except "gingerbread and molasses candy." So she sails off to purchase "a very young lobster, some very old asparagus, and two boxes of acid strawberries." She boils the asparagus for an hour until the heads are "cooked off" and the stalks "harder than ever." She undercooks the lobster and the potatoes, and sprinkles salt instead of sugar on the strawberries.

In the midst of this culinary chaos, Beth discovers that her canary, Pip, is dead from lack of water and food. Her sisters and the assembled guests, including Laurie, try to help, but to no avail. Amy proposes that they warm the bird in an oven to revive him. "Overcome with emotion and lobster," sickened by the death of her bird, Beth rebels. "He's been starved," she says of her bird, "and he shan't be baked, now he's dead . . . and I'll never have another bird . . . for I am too bad to own one."

Returning home to find her daughters miserable over their failures as homekeepers, Mrs. March easily persuades them to admit that "it is better to have a few duties, and live for others." This experiment, she says, was designed to show "what happens when everyone thinks only for herself. Now you know that in order to make a home comfortable and happy," everyone in it must contribute to the family welfare. Marmee has also proven to the girls that domestic work is real work, giving women a "sense of power and independence better than money or fashion." She has shown them that home life becomes a "beautiful success" only if work alternates with leisure, independence with cooperation and mutual concern.[13]

Although this episode deals almost exclusively with girls, Alcott integrated men into her vision of cooperative family life. Men too should benefit from and participate in this family experience, but only on the grounds that they respect the independence and equal authority of women within the home.

Accepting, even glorifying the importance of women's domestic work, Alcott emphasizes that men are homeless without women. Since the ability to create a home and sustain a family supercedes fame and money as evidence of success and civilization, it follows that women have already proved themselves in the world; thus their ability to extend their sphere is unquestioned in *Little Women*. Homeless men, despite wealth, wages, and worldly experience, are motherless children. Meg's suitor, John Brooke, is attracted to the March cottage in large part because he is a lonely young man who has recently lost his mother. Laurie is motherless, which excuses most of his faults, and Mr. Laurence, his grandfather, has no wife, daughter, or granddaughter. Mr. March alone has a proper home and knows his place in it, returning from the war to enlarge, but not supercede, Marmee's authority. He wholly accepts the female abundance around him, tending the flock of his tiny parish and leaving domestic arrangements to his womenfolk.

The question of whether men can be integrated into domestic life on democratic terms first appears in the relationship between young Laurie and the March sisters. Laurie starts out right. The offer of food is an excellent way to gain acceptance into an alien tribe. Meg, Jo, Beth, and Amy, having given up their Christmas breakfast for a starving German immigrant family, are happily surprised by a compensatory feast sent over by the Laurences. Mrs. March has encouraged her daughters to pack up their hot muffins, buckwheat cakes, bread, and cream early Christmas morning and deliver the meal to the hungry Hummels. After a full day spent giving gifts to Marmee and then performing a homemade opera for their friends, a fashionable supper of "ice cream—actually two dishes of it, pink and white—cake and fruit and distracting French bon-bons" is exactly what the unfashionable March girls crave. Three huge bouquets of hothouse flowers complete the Laurence boy's offerings. With the proper motive of rewarding their self-sacrifice, he is also courting them.[14]

Laurie and Jo reverse the gift giving and also their sexual personas when Jo visits her new friend on his home ground, the mansion next door.[15] She suggests a visit from girls, because her sex ordinarily is "quiet and likes to play nurse." Jo arrives and unpacks a maternal abundance of gifts, including her own womanly touch; she brushes the hearth, straightens books and bottles, and plumps Laurie's pillows. It is this shy confession that he has been watching them together, coupled with the "hungry, solitary look in his eyes," that turns Jo from boy to little woman to foster mother in a twinkling. Juvenile readers are warned away from any other interpretation of the unchaperoned visit by Alcott's firm assertion that Jo "had been so simply taught that there was no nonsense in her head, and at fifteen, she was as innocent and frank as any child."[16]

A boy's acceptance of motherly abundance encourages an innocent young girl to treat him as her sister or alternatively to make him, as Jo says, her "boy" or foster son. An adult romance emerging out of this familiar relationship is fraught with incestuous complications. The worst one, from Jo's viewpoint, is that such frozen domestic roles preclude female independence within marital union; democratic households cannot be incestuous.

Alcott advances ideas about the place of men in the family which emerged out of her domestic experiences with her parents, despite her belief in universal laws of progress and democracy. On the whole, she does not paint a compelling picture of marital equality in *Little Women*. Instead she presents the possibility of educating a new generation of little men and little women. In the second part of *Little Women* Alcott describes the married life of John and Meg Brooke. Theirs is not a modern egalitarian marriage. The single wage earner for his family, John provides a domestic servant but does not share domestic chores himself, except for disciplining his son in the evening. Meg is totally dependent upon his income for both household and personal expenses.

In a chapter called "On the Shelf," Meg's docility appears as her greatest virtue and her most serious domestic flaw. Docility is a fine quality in a daughter, even a sister, Alcott admits, but dangerous in a wife. Meg becomes dowdy and dependent, isolated in her little cottage with two small children.[17] Mrs. March shares her domestic secret with her daughter: a good marriage is based on mutuality of interests and responsibilities: "We each do our part alone in many things, but at home we work together, always."[18]

According to Alcott, the reform of domestic life required restoration of a mutuality that had vanished with the separation of home and work. Yet of all the domestic advice presented in *Little Women*, this lesson carries the least conviction. As we shall see, Alcott can offer model domesticity only in utopian settings where cooperative communities reappear in sexually democratic forms.

FLYING UP: LITTLE WOMEN GROW UP TO BE THEMSELVES

When Alcott finished writing part two of *Little Women*, she suggested "Wedding Marches" as a possible title. She changed it, however, to "Birds Leaving the Nest," or "Little Women Grow Up," because she did not wish to suggest that marriage should be the focal event for growing girls. Instead she argues that girls who take trial flights from secure homes will find their own paths to domestic happiness. They might choose an independent single life or some form of marital bonds that range from partial to complete "household democracy." For Alcott, sisterhood and marriage, though often contradictory, are equally valuable possibilities for women. Fully realized sisterhood becomes a model for marriage, not simply an alternative to it. Together, marriage and sisterhood guarantee that individual identity and domesticity will be harmonious.

Meg, the eldest and most docile daughter, does not attain Alcott's ideal womanhood. Democratic domesticity requires maturity, strength, and above all a secure identity that Meg lacks. Her identity consists of being Marmee's daughter and then John's wife. When Meg leaves home to work as a governess she accepts a three-year engagement period, dreaming that she will have much to learn while she waits. But John says, "You have only to wait; I am to do the work." Alcott accepts the limitations of temperament and circumstance in Meg, as she does in all her characters. In *Little Men*, however, Meg's widowhood grants her the circumstances to develop a stronger side of her character.

Fashion provides a counterpoint to woman's rights in *Little Women*. Jo's strong sense of self is established in part by her rejection of fashion, which she perceives as a sign of dependency and sexual stereotyping. Amy, on the other hand, struggles against her burden of vanity, which has its positive side in her "nice manners and refined way of speaking." Amy must learn that appearances can be deceiving, whereas Jo must learn that appearances do count in the larger world.

Jo's lack of vanity about clothes at first conceals her pride both in her writing talent and in her exclusive relationship to Laurie. Laurie enjoys Jo's vivid imagination; it gives color and vivacity to his own lonely childhood. Keeping Amy out of pleasurable excursions with Laurie is one of Jo's main "faults." Left at home once too often, Amy burns a collection of Jo's painstakingly written fairy tales as revenge. Furious, Jo leaves her behind again when she and Laurie go skating. Amy follows behind and is almost killed by falling through the thin ice. Penitent, Jo vows to curb her temper and cherish Amy. Jo realizes that she is not the only independent and talented member of the family; accepting that fact is part of her growing up.[19]

Her notion that she is "the man of the family" is a more serious problem in the story. In a strange way this too plays itself out around fashion. Jo has her first serious encounter with Laurie at a neighborhood dance, where she is uncomfortably dressed up. She finds her sartorial model in the opposite sex and decides she can grow up to be a splendid woman with neatly laced boots and clean linen. She does not want Laurie as a sweetheart; she wants to adopt both him and his air of freedom and elegant comfort.[20]

Amy's trials are rewarded when Aunt Carrol, hearing of her niece's delicate manners, talented fancy work, and Christian forbearance at the charity fair, rewards her with a trip to Europe as her companion. Poor Jo is left behind, too unfashionable and forthright to be patronized. On one occasion Jo tells Amy, "It's easier for me to risk my life for a person than to be pleasant to him when I don't feel like it." Amy replies that "women should learn to be agreeable, particularly poor ones; for they have no other way of repaying kindnesses they receive. If you'd remember that, and practice it, you'd be better liked than I am because there is more of you." It is precisely because Jo is indeed more substantial that the author grants Amy a free holiday in Europe and eventually a wealthy indulgent husband.[21]

Amy and Laurie grow up together in Europe. Both are fashionable, inclined to coquetry. Both have talent, Amy for painting and Laurie for music, but only enough to please friends in polite salons. Neither is put to the test of earning a living. Both are also inclined toward "illusion" in dressing themselves and appreciating each other's refined taste. Their growing up, however, does require a degree of honesty: they admit that "talent isn't genius and you can't make it so."

Despite the sniping and competition for parental love, social approval, and material rewards, Amy and Jo share one great loss that matures them both. The central tragedy of *Little Women* is Beth's death in the final part of the book.[22] Loving home the best, gentle Beth never wants to leave it; perhaps she would never have done so. She grows more fragile each year, and in her last months confides to Jo the feeling that she was never intended to live long. Her short speech is also her longest in the novel:

> "I'm not like the rest of you; I never made plans about what I'd do when I grew up; I never thought of being married, as you all did. I couldn't seem to imagine myself anything but stupid little Beth, trotting about at home, of no use anywhere but there. I never wanted to go away and the hard part now is the leaving you all. I'm not afraid, but it seems as if I should be homesick for you even in heaven."[23]

Jo's maturation is sealed by her grief over Beth's decline. The chapter entitled "Valley of the Shadow" sketches a household that revolves around Beth's room for one year. Everyone, including Beth, knows she is dying. Jo writes a long poem to her sister in which she acknowledges that true sisterhood is born in shared domestic experiences, and that such loving ties cannot be severed:

Henceforth, safe across the river,
I shall see forevermore
A beloved, household spirit
Waiting for me on the shore.
Hope and faith, born of my sorrow,
Guardian angels shall become,
And the sister gone before me
By their hands shall lead me home.[24]

Wasted away, suffering with "pathetic patience," Beth's death releases her parents and sisters to "thank God that Beth was well at
last." Beth's self-sacrifice is ultimately the greatest in the novel. She
gives up her life knowing that it has had only private, domestic
meaning. Only the March family knows and loves her sweet "household spirit."

Nobody mourns Beth more than Jo, her opposite temperament as
well as her partner in the bonds of sisterhood. Their commonality
lies in the simple fact that both of them value their sororal relationship above any other unions.

When Meg becomes engaged and Jo feels she is about to lose her
"best friend," Laurie declares that he will stand by Jo forever. But
Laurie turns out to be a boy, not Jo's sister after all. Jo rejects
Laurie's suit, which is her first grown-up act, and her trip to New
York to become a writer is her first flight into the world. Beth's
death, through which she escapes the awful problem of growing up,
triggers Jo's maturation. Jo's journey is the only fully complete one
in *Little Women* and it involves her learning to tell true love from
romantic fancy. She must do so in order to reproduce her lost sisterhood in a new, democratic domestic union.[25]

TRUE LOVE FOUND

The ability to distinguish true love from romantic fancy is one of
the prerequisites for a woman's growing up in *Little Women*. True
love involves mutual self-sacrifice and self-control and requires the
kind of man who can make the household the center of his life and
work. Romance, on the other hand, is inherently selfish, passionate,
and unequal.

Ultimately the surviving heroines are paired off in true love. Jo, however, proves closest to Alcott's ideal because she rejects Laurie Laurence. At one point she tells him that they are unsuited to one another because both have strong wills and quick tempers. Unpersuaded and unreasonable, the spoiled young man presses his suit, forcing her to tell him a harder truth: she does not love him as a woman loves a man, and never did, but feels simply motherly toward him.

Jo does not want to be an adoring adornment to a fashionable man's home. Nor will she give up her writing to satisfy Laurie, and his proposal reveals just how much "scribbling" really means to her. If merely saving her "pathetic family" from poverty were her only motivation, she might marry Laurie and enrich them all. She might even produce leisured, graceful literature under his patronage. But she won't be patronized and she won't concede. "I don't believe I shall ever marry," she declares. "I am happy as I am, and love my liberty too well to be in any hurry to give it up for any mortal man."[26] Possibly, Jo also recognizes passions in herself, however hard she struggles to keep them under control. She certainly experiences more than "moods"; she has genuine emotional depth and active fantasies, which she usually transforms into tragicomic family operas or melodramatic stories just as Alcott did.

In the nineteenth-century world of *Little Women*, there are only two alternatives following the relative sexual equality of childhood: romantic love or rational affection. With considerable regret Jo chooses the latter, because she must forgo forever the equality she once knew with Laurie, her exuberant companion in childhood. Jo's decision, as Alcott knew, presents the reader with a bitter pill, for nearly everyone wants Laurie to win Jo. Yet the author has her heroine firmly reject any "silliness" from the start. She enjoys being Laurie's chum, plays at being his mother, but is never tempted to be his domestic companion; once wed they will cease to be equals.

It is precisely because Alcott makes Laurie such an irresistible boy-man that the reader must take Jo's refusal seriously. The youthful sweet surrogate sister develops into a handsome, passionate suitor. Moreover, Jo is physically attracted to Laurie, and she frequently observes his handsome face, curly hair, and fine eyes. The reader as well as Jo feels the power of Laurie's sexuality and the power he tries to exert over her. Yet if he calls her "my girl," meaning his sweetheart, she calls him "my boy," meaning her son.

Jo's refusal is not prompted by love for a rival suitor. In New York she works as a governess to children in her boardinghouse and writes for the penny-dreadful newspapers. She soon encounters Friedrich Bhaer helping a serving maid. Bhaer's life, unlike Laurie's, is not the stuff of romance. Forty years old, "learned and good," he is domestic by nature and darns his own socks. He loves flowers and children and reads good literature. Moreover, he insists that Jo give up writing blood-and-thunder tales and learn to write good fiction. He gives her his own copy of Shakespeare as a Christmas present. "A regular German," Jo says,

> rather stout with brown hair tumbled all over his head, a bushy beard, good nose, the kindest eyes I ever saw, and a splendid big voice that does one's ears good, after our sharp, or slipshod American gabble. His clothes were rusty, his hands were large, and he hadn't a really handsome feature in his face, except his beautiful teeth; yet I liked him, for he had a fine head, his linen was very nice, and he looked like a gentleman, though two buttons were off his coat, and there was a patch on one shoe.[27]

Bhaer is a man Jo can love and marry without fear of inequality. A mature adult capable of raising his two orphaned nephews, he does not need Jo to mother him, although she is drawn to do so. Bhaer is more attracted to her youth and independent spirit. Nevertheless, he bestows his affection upon her by appreciating both her Old World "gemutlichkeit" and her American self-reliance. In a way he is Santa Claus, giving gifts despite his poverty to friends and servants alike. In one scene Bhaer buys oranges and figs for small children while holding a dilapidated blue umbrella aloft for Jo in the rain. Unlike Father March, who is a fragile invalid, Father Bhaer is a strapping, generous man.

There is no end to his domesticity or his capacity for cooperative self-sacrifice. Matching his paternal benevolence to Jo's maternal abundance, Bhaer does the shopping for both himself and Jo. As Alcott describes him, he "finished the marketing by buying several pounds of grapes, a pot of rosy daisies, and a pretty jar of honey, to be regarded in the light of a demijohn. Then, distorting his pockets with the knobby bundles, and giving her the flowers to hold, he put up the old umbrella and they travelled on again."[28] Contrast this fulgent account of a man who understands the "household spirit" with Laurie, who cannot even direct the maids to plump his pillows properly, or with John Brooke, who magisterially sends the meat and vegetables home to Meg (no knobby bundles in his pockets!).

Meanwhile, Laurie has returned from Europe with Amy, and they tell the story of their Swiss romance. Laurie has found a perfect mate in Amy, who will be very good at giving orders to their servants, having practiced in her imagination for years. Theirs will also be an equal marital partnership, though somewhat different from that of Jo and Fritz, and very different from the frugal conventions of Meg and John.

Jo, the last sister to leave home, might never have accepted Professor Bhaer's proposal were it not for Beth's death. Fritz has found a poem of Jo's expressing the deep love and devotion she feels for Meg, Amy, and Beth. We are "parted only for an hour, none lost," she writes, "one only gone before." Tenderly Bhaer declares: "I read that, and I think to myself, she has a sorrow, she is lonely, she would find comfort in true love. I haf a heart full for her."

Bhaer has all the qualities Bronson Alcott lacked: warmth, intimacy, and a tender capacity for expressing his affection—the feminine attributes Alcott admired and hoped men could acquire in a rational, feminist world. As Marmee says, he is "a dear man." He touches everyone, hugs and carries children about on his back. Bronson, despite all his genuine idealism and devotion to humanity, was emotionally reserved and distant. Fritz Bhaer loves material reality, is eminently approachable, and values all the things that Bronson Alcott rejects, such as good food, warm rooms, and appealing domestic disorder.

They decide to share life's burdens just as they shared the load of bundles on their shopping expedition. Jo hopes to fulfill "woman's special mission," which is "drying tears and bearing burdens," so that nobody will ever again call her unwomanly. She resolutely adds the feminist postscript: "I'm to carry my share, Friedrich, and help to earn the home. Make up your mind to that, or I'll never go."[29] The marriage contract they arrange is very different from that of Meg and John at the end of the first part of *Little Women*.

LOVE AND WORK

Having grown up with a working mother, each surviving March sister tailors her marital arrangements with work appropriate to her talent and temperament. At the opening of *Little Women* Marmee's arrival is anticipated in a manner generally reserved for welcoming working men: "The clock struck six; and, having swept up the hearth, Beth put a pair of slippers down to warm. . . . Meg stopped lecturing, and lit the lamp, Amy got out of the easy-chair without being asked, and Jo forgot how tired she was as she sat up to hold the slippers nearer to the blaze."[30]

Arriving home after a day of Civil War relief work, Mrs. March does not repair to the kitchen; instead her daughters fly round and serve tea, sharing the day's news, and generally demonstrating that a fully employed female household is commonplace, at least in the middle of a war.

Vanity, envy, selfishness, and pride are conquered by work in *Little Women*. Unlike the shallow, gossiping ladies of fashion in the novel, Marmee March is a true woman largely because she is a working woman; her employment is an extension of her motherly duties, the entire world is therefore her sphere. Marmee's management abilities and her self-discipline are examples to her daughters. She knows how to delegate work and does so from her entrance in the first scene to her last crisis management when Mr. March and Beth are ill.

Meg's marketable talents are those most commonly associated with a modern American wife. She is very pretty, with good taste and acting ability, and she develops her mother's managerial sense. Marriage to John provides Meg with a full-time job once she has children. Alcott does take marriage-as-work seriously, and Meg's growing household staff reflects myriad chores: child raising, domestic planning, nursing, shopping, accounting, and entertaining preclude any other career.

Impatient Jo has a harder time reconciling domestic duties, talent, and work. Starting off as a paid companion to her wealthy aunt, she gains access to a good library but cannot sharpen her literary skills in the scant "leisure" time gleaned from earning her bread and helping to bake it. She begins her writing career as an unpaid contributor to a cheap newspaper just as Alcott did. When the family can finally spare her domestic services, Jo goes off to New York and works full time as a governess, writing sensational stories at night. She has already noted that what the public considers a "first-rate story" is really the "usual labyrinth of love, mystery, and murder," in which "the passions have a holiday, and when the author's invention fails, a grand catastrophe clears the stage of one-half the dramatis personae, leaving the other half to exult over their downfall."[31] A good living is to be had writing such stories, and "Mrs. S.L.A.N.G. Northbury" is Alcott's version of E.D.E.N. Southworth, ebullient author of *The Hidden Hand, The Curse of Clifton, Ishmael,* and *Self-Raised.* Southworth wrote for *The New York Ledger* and also completed fifty novels.[32] As Northbury Jo imitates Southworth and wins a prize for what we know was "Pauline's Passion and Punishment." Scarcely bothering to hide behind her pseudonym, Alcott then credits Jo with writing "The Duke's Daughter," "A Phantom Hand," and "Curse of the Coventrys" (*Behind a Mask*). Work, while remunerative, is not yet a fulfillment of Jo's vocation. The sensation stories give Jo satisfaction because with the money she earns "she could supply her own wants, and need ask no one for a penny."

Having entered the market as a paid writer, Jo then rewrites her novel for a fourth time and submits it to three publishers. Finally she gets it accepted on condition that she cut it, and omit all the parts she particularly admired. In a family council, much like the one Alcott herself convened to discuss *Moods,* Jo's father advises her to maintain artistic integrity and wait for recognition. Mrs. March has faith in publishers and in critics' taste; she counsels following their advice. Jo admits that she really cannot judge the quality of her own work. Meg likes the novel as it is; Amy says to make "a good, popular book, and get as much money as you can." Achieving success, she says, an author can then afford such luxuries as "philosophical and metaphysical" characters.[33]

Jo's first novel suffers the same fate as Alcott's *Moods.* And, like Alcott, Jo also keeps on trying because the second part of *Little Women* makes clear that writing is her true vocation. Jo wants to do "something splendid," and after Beth's death, Alcott lifts her heroine up once more from the Slough of Despond; Jo takes up writing again "as a comfort." And, ignoring both market and immortality, she writes the "simple little story" that is *Little Women*.[34] It is this departure from the actual truth of writing *Little Women* which troubles modern feminist scholars. In reality, we know that *Little Women* was suggested by Alcott's publisher Thomas Niles and was written posthaste as a juvenile story for money. Alcott does not disguise the truth in her journals.[35]

One explanation for the discrepancy between the real writing of the novel and the fictional rendition is that Alcott's life is telescoped in *Little Women*. Louisa was thirty-five years old when she wrote the novel and Jo is ten years younger. Elizabeth Alcott had been dead for ten years before Louisa began *Little Women;* in the novel Beth's death occurs the same year that Jo takes up writing as a comfort. The difference between real and fictional time surely does not explain the difference between writing a solicited juvenile story and writing as comfort. Also Louisa May Alcott's journals show that she had no idea of the power in her *Little Women* serial as she wrote the first part. She was the hard-working editor of *Merry's Museum*, and she labored overtime as a writer of children's fairy tales and sensation thrillers for adults.[36]

Louisa Alcott was often the worst judge of her own writing. But there is more to her bewilderment over *Little Women's* reception. The novel *is* "something splendid" and Alcott searches, in the second part of the story, for the key to its success. She has Jo's father acknowledge it, "There's truth in it, Jo—that's the secret, humor and pathos make it alive, and you have found your style at last."[37] The real question is what prevented Alcott from developing *Little Women's* successors with the power and skill she demonstrated in the first history of the March family? Louisa May Alcott was a conscious student of good literature as well as a professional writer. Her ideal of a splendid work included *The Scarlet Letter*, *Faust*, *Jane Eyre*, the essays and poetry of Emerson and Whittier, and the works of Charles Dickens. She loved *Uncle Tom's Cabin* and frequently quoted from it: Stowe was, moreover, a commercial success and Alcott aspired to the same reward.

Louisa May Alcott found it almost impossible to include *Little Women* in the canon of good literature as she knew it. Contemptuous of an audience that loved "Mrs. S.L.A.N.G. Northbury," perfectly cognizant of the commercial basis for the growing genre of juvenile fiction, and brought up on Concord's canon of "splendid" works, it is no wonder that *Little Women*'s author was skeptical of her own achievement.

Professor Bhaer respects Jo's dedication to writing; his literary tastes accord with her own. Her real passion was expressed in writing, and marriage to impoverished, scholarly Bhaer makes Jo's writing career not only possible but necessary. Jo's castle in the air, the one she builds while still a little woman, consists of writing books, and "getting rich and famous." It is only at the end of *Little Women* that Jo, while on a sort of "maternity leave," admits to hoping that she may "write a *good* book yet."[38]

Unquestionably Alcott intends Jo to go on writing and to make good writing more important than being "rich and famous."[39] Jo's partner in this harvest time is Amy, her temperamental opposite but a kindred spirit in attempting serious work. Jo and Amy both wanted to be artists but Amy is more certain of her talents, as was May Alcott. Her "modest desire," as Alcott wrote of Amy, was to be the "best artist in the whole world." She works hard to this end but Louisa May Alcott does not yet know how to predict the outcome of her sister's aspirations. In Europe with "lazy Laurence," Amy says that "Rome took all the vanity out of me." She insists that talent isn't genius and she wants "to be great or nothing." Not wishing to be a "common-place dauber," she intends to polish up her other talents and "be an ornament to society, if I get the chance." Amy, bluntly, during one stage of growing up, intends to marry for a living if she can't be a great artist. Alcott cannot abandon her beloved sister and rival to such a fate however and Amy has a change of heart. She falls in love with Laurie and seems to be making matrimony her career, in an upper-class version of Meg and John's union.

Amy ultimately proves to be a complex heroine, who changes her perspective on life and work several times. Having married and borne a baby, she again revises her work plan:

"like Jo, I don't relinquish all my artistic hopes, or confine myself to helping others fulfill their dreams of beauty. I've begun to model a figure of baby, and Laurie says it is the best thing I've ever done. I think so myself, and mean to do it in marble, so that, whatever happens, I may at least keep the image of my little angel."⁴⁰

The marble image of Amy's fragile daughter, named after Beth, has an ambiguous meaning. It appears to make Amy's work merely a memorial keepsake. Amy's explicit alliance with Jo and her words about her work are clear indications that Alcott validates her own as well as her sister May's determined vocation. Neither of them will be confined simply to domestic self-sacrifice or ornamental status.

THE MODEL SOCIETY: A HARVEST OF RATIONALISM

Jo March and Friedrich Bhaer embark on more than a model marriage in the second part of *Little Women*. Together they set out to construct a model society which institutionalizes many of Jo's (and Louisa Alcott's) feminist ideals. Both Jo and Professor Bhaer are keenly interested in new ideas and reforms. In New York City, during Jo's trial flight away from home and from Laurie's unwelcome attentions, the new friends attend a symposium together where they participate in a wide-ranging discussion in which the "world was being picked to pieces and put together on new and according to the talkers, on infinitely better principles than before."

At first disturbed by the flirtations and by the disillusioning talk around her, Jo soon becomes enthralled by the debate. Speculative philosophy fascinates her, "though Kant and Hegel were unknown gods, the subjective and objective unintelligible terms." Less delighted by the discussion, Bhaer defends older beliefs, standing "his colors like a man." Not the intellectual equal of the philosophers in the room, he nevertheless insists upon speaking up because "his conscience would not let him be silent." It is that conscience that Jo so admires. "Character," she believes, "is a better possession than money, rank, intellect, or beauty and to feel that if greatness is what a wise man has defined it to be, 'truth, reverence, and good will,' then her friend Friedrich Bhaer was not only good but great."⁴¹

If Bronson moves through the second part of *Little Women* ideal-

READING LITTLE WOMEN

ized as Mr. Bhaer, he takes on a more "muffled" guise as Mr. March. Madeleine Stern observes that Bronson "would be atypical in a book on the American home . . . with his vegetarianism, his fads, and his reforms."[42] Hence Louisa divides him into two characters. The older Bronson surely resembles Mr. March, and in Friedrich we see the man he might have been with the aid of a rational, feminist reform movement. Bhaer's devotion to humanity—embodied in his acceptance of a "merry little quadroon" at Plumfield and also by his brave speech at the symposium—are direct homages to Bronson.

Alcott's modified view of her father paralleled the emergence of her conception of a model society. At the end of *Little Women*, she remakes her father's experiment at Fruitlands into her own fictional experiment at Plumfield. A fortunate inheritance from Jo's former employer, Aunt March, enables her to turn the suburban estate of Plumfield into a "good happy, homelike school" with herself as head-mistress and Friedrich Bhaer as headmaster. Laurie and Amy provide scholarships and Meg sends her son and daughter as model pupils, which ensures that the school will be coeducational from the start. Mr. and Mrs. March beam like benevolent household gods at the assembled, extended family as the book closes on Mrs. March's sixtieth birthday celebration.

As Jo watches John and Laurie playing cricket with the boys at Plumfield, she speaks to Amy in a "maternal way of all mankind." Jo, the tomboy, has attained the final stage of true womanhood; she has accepted maternal responsibility for the whole world. The conflict between feminist selfhood and domestic self-sacrifice has been resolved by expanding the home to include the world, making everyone equally responsible for human nurturance. If woman's rights are enlarged with her responsibilities, men's rights are also granted to them—but "nothing more," as Elizabeth Cady Stanton demanded in *The Revolution*.

Sororal bonds, Alcott argues, are forged between equals. A female family, therefore, is naturally democratic; while accepting conflict, like "birds in a nest," sisters must share household tasks, pool their incomes, and lend one another their personal treasures. The Marchs' household democracy is perfectly represented by Hannah's daily provision of hot turnovers, which warm Jo and Meg's hands on the way to work. Meg and Jo, even while they labor outside the home, have no special exemption from domestic chores in *Little Women*.[43]

Alcott made little attempt to conceal the parallels between her life and her fiction. The family name of March is a simple substitute for May. Unlike Fruitlands, however, with its disappointing poverty, Plumfield is a feminist utopia that promises an abundance of puddings, free fields to roam in, and festivals in apple-picking season. Having admitted the "female element" to full equality with the male, Plumfield's harvest will have "more wheat and fewer tares every year." Commemorating the the bittersweet fall of Fruitlands, Alcott tucks in a reference to Mr. March strolling about with Mr. Laurence enjoying "the gentle apple's winey juice." Since Alcott admitted that Mr. Laurence was modeled on Grandfather May, we can assume that the Mays would smile approvingly on Plumfield. And unlike Sam May, who withdrew family money from Fruitlands, the Laurence family provides scholarships to Plumfield. True love is not denied at the end of *Little Women*; it is linked, as Fritz Bhaer put it, "to the wish to share and enlarge that so happy home."[44]

Unquestionably *Little Women*'s message was powerfully transmitted not only to Alcott's readers but to her best imitators. Within three years of *Little Women*'s publication as a book, stories for young readers were advertised in *Our Young Folks* as "likely to find popularity in the large circles that read Miss Alcott's books." And, *The Boston Traveller* noted that *Little Women* "is a book that parents will be glad to have their sons and daughters read, but so interesting that they will be apt to insist on reading it through for themselves first." Elizabeth Stuart Phelps, Harriet Beecher Stowe, and Louisa May Alcott were advertised in the same pages of juvenile magazines. Their names lent prestige to the notices of *Oliver Optic*, *Farming for Boys*, and *History of My Pets*.[45]

Phelps's serialized story, "Our Little Women," exemplifies one version of Alcott's new form.[46] A prosperous widow and her two daughters, Hannah and Mary Alice, are tried and almost found wanting by the visit of their half-cousins. The relations are another widow and her daughter, Margaret and Lois McQuentin. Mrs. McQuentin is a paid housekeeper who comes to Boston seeking surgery for an incurable tumor. Her daughter arrives from her work in a Lynn shoe shop to nurse her mother. Hannah, the narrator, and Mary Alice are deeply embarrassed by their poor relations. Although Lois does not wear a "red feather and a purple veil" as expected, her gruff manner and her callused hands offend the genteel sisters. Their change of heart is occasioned by Mrs. McQuentin's pitiful suffering but also by Lois's gentle courage and innate sensitivity. She has, as her mother says, never had "a chance." Hannah takes a long time trying to understand the meaning of this remark. In fact the dying widow scarcely says anything else besides muttering, "little woman, little woman," as she strokes "Lois's short, thin hair."[47]

Lois goes back to working in the shoe shop after her mother's death; she must support herself and she is seeking some solace in hard work. Mary Alice gets engaged and Hannah is left particularly lonely and depressed, being in love with her sister's fiancé. Lois McQuentin then comes back to visit announcing that earning her own living is a necessity but she has sought and found a deeper meaning in work. Lois has lost her earlier incentive; both she and her mother were working and saving for a home of their own. Having "always had something to earn *for*," Lois plans to earn her way through school and become a doctor. Confronted with the years of required education, her lack of means, and the prejudices against women physicians, Lois coolly replies that she will live on "shoes" while studying. She is accustomed to hard work and will go into the shop on vacations and Saturdays too.[48]

Hannah remarks that Mrs. McQuentin used to call her daughter "little woman," and being a doctor seems so "strong minded, and that." Lois replies very much in the manner of Jo March:

And don't suppose that I know, and my mother knows, and you ought to know, that if it means *anything* to be a 'little woman',—I don't care whose,—it means to be the most, and the best, and the noblest, and the most needed thing that you can get or make the chance to be.[49]

TWELVE

Girl-Boys and Boy-Girls

"Never mind: I'm tired of dolls, and I guess I shall put them all
away and attend to my farm; I like it rather better than playing
house," said Mrs. G. unconsciously expressing the desire of
many older ladies, who cannot dispose of their families so easily
however.

Louisa May Alcott, *Little Men*, chapter 15

Louisa May Alcott wrote and published eight popular novels and
numerous short stories in the next twenty years; some critics feel
that success permanently imprisoned her in sentimental conventions.[1] The first history of the March family developed a new form,
however; its sequels are variants of that form, lively invitations to
social reform and raising a progressive generation of little women
and little men.[2]

Alcott's later heroines, unlike their contemporaries Tom Sawyer
and Huckleberry Finn, cannot run away from civilization to nature;
this fact underpins the sexual division of labor.[3] Little women must
cleanse and order the larger world in order to gain even half a day to
themselves, as Theodore Parker had predicted.[4] A New England
regionalist at heart, mistress of its vernacular, Alcott nevertheless
enlists the Marchs' democratic family in the national post–Civil War
reform movement. Her genuine feeling for people caught up in the
impersonal forces of a rapidly expanding society is evident. The
predicament of her characters is wholly believable and real even
when her solutions are utopian.

If men return to the natural world to gain liberty, women create
civilization to gain their freedom. Alcott gradually accepted "progress" as the only solution to the woman problem. A progressive
society must free women, she argued, because it needs their labor
and influence. She uneasily set aside the Romantic belief that great
men and women are the principal actors in history. Ordinary men

and women also make history, she asserts, because large, impersonal historical forces work through common people. The heroines of *An Old-Fashioned Girl, Little Men, Jo's Boys*, and *Shawl Straps* are talented women, Alcott's version of Emerson's exemplary social types.[5] But they are not Romantic rebels like Jo in *Little Women*, Sylvia in *Moods*, or Virginie in "V.V."

A NATURAL BRIDGE

An Old-Fashioned Girl, Shawl Straps, and *Little Men* form a natural bridge from the Romantic reform movement to a new progressive coalition for institutional change. *Little Women*'s success gave its author access to a popular audience, one receptive to proposals for social change presented within the familiar construct of domesticity. The idle rich and fashionable of both sexes, Alcott claimed, were responsible for hollowness of heart, and consequently for a mistrust between men and women. Her heroines increasingly criticized sentimentalism and argued for the creation of genuine trust by making themselves lovable examples of health and dress reform, woman's rights, and true love. Moreover, she presents these reforms as part of "old-fashioned" virtues.

Alcott argues for woman's rights as nothing less than the restoration of democracy. Making women useful and dignified citizens will restore domestic tranquility in the largest sense. Grandmother's tales in *An Old-Fashioned Girl* ignore patriarchal history and install in the minds of children a grand legacy of women's heroism in Revolutionary America. The novel's subsequent action frees women to organize around a single national standard of values. Polly Minton, the novel's active do-gooder, moves from girlhood to womanhood by leaving her family home and serving as missionary to the rich. The March sisters had essentially accomplished that old-fashioned task of course in *Little Women* but Polly also becomes part of a sisterhood in a boarding house—a foreshadowing of the settlement houses that spread throughout the United States between the 1880s and early twentieth century. Polly's supportive establishment is part of a genuine neighborhood; it gains the confidence of its poor inhabitants by sharing their troubles and informs the rich neighbors of the horrors outside townhouse doors.

Abba May Alcott had begun with giving advice to the poor on chastity, sobriety, and thrift before shifting her concern to the social causes of poverty. Her daughter now moved farther, and asserted that a certain causality underlaid the individual greed of employers, and social remedies lay beyond the capacity of the poor to achieve prosperity through self-restraint and diligent work. Although causes as well as remedies were outside the individual's domain, Alcott thought self-sufficiency could be restored by giving the less privileged an institutional helping hand—above all, some experience in cooperation and self-government. Voluntarism might be restored if a sense of community, similar to that of village life, could be instilled in a modern nation of strangers.

Reformers such as Alcott were aware that an integrated identity is forged within a political process; such a process could not be shaped, they thought, by an ignorant backward populace. In *Little Men, Jo's Boys*, and *Work*, Alcott spelled out the gentry's role in reconstructing urban society. As her focus shifted, the personal battle between an individual's sinful nature and God's redeeming grace gradually disappeared from her fiction even as it disappeared from the American reform perspective at large. The essence of modernity (however reluctantly and unevenly digested) lay in a symmetrical fit between individuality and social role. If men or women felt alienated from themselves in the performance of a given social role, they needed the warm approval of caring authorities and peers. At the same time, Alcott's own experience had taught her that inner struggle shaped courageous, creative people. Romantic characters are therefore present throughout her later fiction; they are all "gentled" or "tamed," however, much as (she herself noted) a wild colt is domesticated through love and dependence upon its captor.

AN OLD-FASHIONED GIRL

Little Women, Part Second, went on sale on April 14, 1869. In one month thirteen thousand copies were sold at one dollar and fifty cents for each illustrated volume.[6] That summer, as a reward for their labors, Louisa Alcott and her sister May vacationed in the Canadian summer home of their cousin, Octavius Brooks Frothingham. A New York City leader of the Free Religion movement and a close friend of the late Theodore Parker, he had contributed to the *Cincinnati Dial*, as had Conway, Sanborn, and Bronson Alcott.[7]

From the *Dial* Alcott was familiar with rational reform proposals and philosophies, and even had read a spirited review of Charles Darwin's *Origin of the Species*.[8] She already knew that Thoreau had read and liked Darwin's book.

Frothingham was a perfect host. Alcott relaxed in the company of sympathetic liberal reformers, drinking tea, playing croquet, and going for long drives about the countryside. The Alcott sisters traveled to Maine for another month, where Louisa learned that twenty-three thousand copies of *Little Women* had been sold. Her royalties amounted to ten cents on each volume; she was almost rich and certainly famous. By New Year's Day the thirty-seven-year-old author had a check from Roberts Brothers for $8,500.[9]

That late summer and fall in 1869 are a chapter in Louisa May Alcott's life that sympathetic biographers never tire of retelling. It seemed that her worries were finally over. Having paid off every penny of the Alcotts' old debts, she seized her chance to please *Little Women* fans clamoring for more stories. The result was *An Old-Fashioned Girl*. If it sold even nearly as well as its predecessor, she would earn the "competence" that brought independence. Yet Alcott was slightly mystified by her popularity, unsure to what extent her own character in the guise of Jo had created her success. Nor could she help recalling her readers' disappointment at Jo's refusal of Laurie. Quickly she revised the *Hospital Sketches* and *Camp and Fireside Stories*, which were reissued together by Roberts in one handsome volume. The tales of soldiers longing for home and kin would appeal, she reasoned, to readers of *Little Women*.[10]

Alcott settled Abba and Bronson in Anna's home for the winter, and rented rooms on Beacon Hill for herself and May. The circumstances for writing *An Old-Fashioned Girl* were certainly better than the cold, lonely, fourteen-hour days spend on *Little Women* and *Merry's Museum*. She also enjoyed May's circle of convivial artistic friends. Encouraged by the presence of sister and friends, she wrote her new novel as a reformer's critique of fashionable life. In its place she offered a program for domestic reform with an enlarged, more equal position for woman in society.

The freedom of May's circle contrasted sharply with Abba's state of mind, a constant reminder to Alcott of the contradiction between traditional domesticity and female independence. Abba was in fact ill, at times deeply depressed. A year earlier she had penned a notation that might pass for humor in one of her daughter's domestic dramas, but followed by a series of similar protests and longings, seems only pathetic. She wrote, "All alone! Alone! Alone! . . . I love all family employments but cooking—I think I should live on rice and apples if I lived alone—ha! I should have a cordial cup of tea once a day."[11] Alcott perceived that for her mother's generation of women domestic duties were eternal. Moreover, the strained relationship between the Alcott sisters and their parents could only be eased if she earned enough money for housekeeper services as well as full maintenance for herself and her parents.

Abba wanted to live with Anna, to be cared for by her eldest daughter as if she were Anna's child. She spoke of being proud of her daughters, happy that they enjoyed "a larger better woman-hood" than she had known. But she added that it would be hard to find "a freer life than my husband leads." This left Abba the only enslaved family member in her own eyes. Wistfully she hoped that "some arrangement be made for which May and Mr. Alcott can be cared for and leave me free."[12] In fact, she was no longer able to keep up with the housekeeping or the valet services attendant on preparing Bronson for his trips to the West.

Alcott's own independence would only follow that of her family. It all depended on her earnings.[13] The task was now complicated by constant illness. Her formerly strong constitution was now a memory; she was hoarse from a chronically sore throat probably worsened by heroic applications of caustic remedies. Constant neuralgia affected her facial muscles, and her joints were inflamed; one leg was lame. She did not yield to the pain, but kept on writing with her "left hand in a sling, one foot up, head aching and no voice." She added sarcastically, "Yet as the book is funny, people will say, 'didn't you enjoy doing it?' "[14]

A MISSIONARY TO THE RICH

Alcott called *An Old-Fashioned Girl* funny because the Shaw family's fashionable world is seen through Polly Milton's critical gaze. A "fresh faced little girl" of fourteen, graced with pretty brown curls and a "half-shy, half-merry look in her blue eyes," she is a country mouse come to the city to visit Fanny Shaw. Fanny is two years older than her friend, a spoiled, affected young lady fond of her own reflection in the mirror. Polly, dressed in blue merino, "stout boots, and short hair," stares at Fan's elaborately frizzed bangs, topped by a false chignon, and her suit with its big sash and panniers. Innocently she asks, "Don't you ever forget to lift your sash and fix those puffy things before you sit down?"[5]

Alcott quickly introduces the rest of the Shaws, and a bewildered Polly notes that all the Shaws need love, but not one knows how to give or receive it. Lacking a sensible Marmee, the Shaw children must nevertheless grow up through all the complex stages of adolescence and young adulthood identified in *Little Women*. Grandma Shaw can offer only the memory of a time when girls and boys were children until eighteen; then, having learned their chores at home, they left to create new homes for themselves. The narrative tension in *An Old-Fashioned Girl*, unlike that in *Little Women*, does not stem from the relationship between external hardship and internal self-discipline, at least at first. Polly observes that the Shaws have no material problems, but gradually she and the reader learn that rich, fashionable society has hard times of its own.

Without Polly, a motherly missionary for woman's rights in her "simple gray cloak and blue knitted mittens," the Shaws would continue without a chance of redemption. It takes eight years to complete Polly's mission. She visits the Shaws annually, setting a good example of growing up to be an independent woman capable of cooking, cleaning, dressmaking, and earning her own living by teaching music. She never gains much in the way of property, but she does rent a room of her own.[6] She furnishes it with a shining teakettle, a kitten, and a canary who dwell harmoniously together by the hearth. The novel does not, however, end with a happy, old-fashioned girl making her way in the world. Polly is proud that her wages are helping her family but she also envies wealthy girls going to and from theater parties in their warm carriages. Alcott develops the relationship between private warmth and public cold noting that "by the time the little teakettle had lost its brightness, Polly had decided that getting one's living was no joke, and many of her brilliant hopes had shared the fate of the little kettle . . . working for a living shuts a good many doors in one's face even in democratic America."[17]

At this turning point of the novel, Alcott introduces two remarkable, wholly different sewing circles, which illustrate the distance between women who work for a living and those who do not. Polly's landlady, Miss Mills, who is "old and homely, and good and happy," tells the story of little Jane, a seamstress unable to find work at a decent wage. Jane finally chooses suicide over prostitution, leaving a note for Miss Mills, her landlady. The truly independent woman has a home to share, and Miss Mills takes Jane in as her sister.[18] The unconditional sharing of home is, for Alcott, one of the most powerful links between individual identity and household democracy. Without loving cooperation, the author argues, an individual can literally disappear without a tear shed by anyone.

Miss Mills persuades Polly to join the cause of poor working women. The rich, she says, may not really be hard of heart, but they are ignorant and careless of the poor. They pay low wages and do not trouble to find out how much it costs working women to live. The solution is not philanthropy but fair wages. Through her landlady Polly then comes to know another set of working women, artists and writers. These women have another reason to help one another; they are "a little sisterhood of busy, independent girls, who each had a purpose to execute, a talent to develop, an ambition to achieve, and brought to the work patience, and perseverance, hope, and courage."[19]

In the name of their special vocations these women virtually eliminate both genteel housekeeping and domestic service. Alcott presents herself in the person of Kate King, a "shabby young woman" who has just written "a successful book by accident, and happened to be the fashion just then." The circle of independent women stage an impromptu picnic to which Kate contributes a "bag of oranges and several big, plummy buns," and Polly donates a pot of jam and cake because her friend Fan likes sweets. "Then coffee, milk, sardines, and nuts appear, the contribution of the other women," and the feast begins. Kate sets an example for the enjoyment of both female abundance and a kitchenless house by eating with "such a relish" that the others fall to, and following her directions "take the sardines by their little tails," and wipe their fingers on brown paper napkins, enjoying a meal which nobody cooked and nobody served.[20]

The specifically female friendship in the "little sisterhood" saves poor working girls and provides an alternative to marriage for women who have special vocations. A sculptor and an engraver live together and take care of one another in a nest quite different from the March family cottage. Alcott insists that they are friends who cannot be parted. Fanny remarks that sooner or later a male lover will part the two artists, but Polly vehemently disagrees and sees the two as dedicated to art and to each other.

Alcott offers independence to a transitional generation and the friendship of other dedicated women. The new woman may have a palette and a ballot box while also keeping the needle and the broom as symbols of her sex. Domesticity and working for a living, Alcott implies, are possible, even pleasurable, to free single women. Husband and child might unbalance the new woman still struggling for individual identity in a world that makes wives and mothers wholly responsible for a family's domestic life.

In all of Alcott's novels, a woman who accepts the love of a man thereupon owes her first allegiance to child rearing. This fact often makes spinsterhood the preferred status for a first generation of woman's rights "graduates." Just when the reader considers the new possibility of Polly's happiness as a useful spinster, however, her personal charity case, the Shaws, diverts her attention. Mr. Shaw loses all his money, having "gone under" as a result of relentless, impersonal forces of competition, Alcott intimates. The Shaws are thus thrust down into a world they scarcely knew except through Polly's stories.

She rescues them by helping them to help themselves. True love and Christian charity go hand-in-hand, and Polly's reward is young Tom Shaw, who has disciplined his energies toward earning a living for his family.

Offered the example of a band of independent women, Polly

draws back, however, suggesting that a man's hand is necessary to help the new woman along. Unlike Sylvia Yule, who takes a "masculine" voyage down river in *Moods*, or Jo who longs to soldier in the Civil War, Polly yearns only to dress up and go to the opera. She has neither nature nor war to provide a rite of passage into maturity. Almost impatiently it seems, Alcott tries to make marriage Polly's great adventure, with Tom Shaw, poor and unremarkable, part of her propaganda for rational feminist reform.

THE WOMAN WHO DID NOT DARE

Alcott offers a new reform strategy, one familiar to readers of the *Woman's Journal*, the weekly newspaper of the American Woman Suffrage Association. The AWSA was an integrated organization; it welcomed both black and white men and women. Louisa Alcott, along with the entire wing of the New England abolitionists, wrote for the *Woman's Journal* and regarded woman's suffrage as a key element in universal reform. The National Woman Suffrage Association was formed by Elizabeth Cady Stanton, Susan B. Anthony, and Ernestine Rose. Their organ, *The Revolution*, was devoted to securing the ballot to women of the nation on equal terms with men. Alcott's strategy, in all her fiction, agreed with the regulars of her old antislavery set. Women must make the cause of their sex important in their lives because women's participation in all areas of life is essential to universal reform. Those who accept dependency in marriage because they are infatuated or because they seek higher social status or economic security, are dangerous to themselves and to the rest of society; they help to perpetuate sexual injustice. Finally, every woman's duty, married or single, is to form associations with other like-minded reformers.

An Old-Fashioned Girl offers convinced reformers a strategic argument. Alcott uses a Colonial and Revolutionary dame, Madam Shaw, as a model for the stalwart independent woman, disdainful of vapors and lack of domestic skills. To the fashionable reader the author points out that business cycles may turn this year's belle into next year's sewing woman. She goes further, noting that fashionable young women commonly become engaged several times and calculate the "respective values" of their fiancés; they should know, she says, that men do the same. Every bride must face the tawdry fact that her husband has probably discussed the fortune of girls he preferred, but "could not afford to marry." Such a system is not calculated to make either partner very secure, and marriages based on such a material base will certainly break apart in economic crisis. Romance and sentimentality are just disguises for the "business" of courtship and marriage in the Shaws' set.

Polly offers her friends the alternative of her love for Tom. The most important quality in a man for Polly, is a warm generous heart, which she knows him to have. Like Jo and Friedrich Bhaer in *Little Women*, Polly and Tom are friends and partners in adversity.

As a semiprivate joke to reformist readers, Alcott entitles the chapter in which Polly and Fanny Shaw wait for marriage proposals "The Woman Who Did Not Dare." In 1869 Epes Sargent wrote a novel, *The Women Who Dared*, in which a woman artist proposed to her chosen mate and married him.[21] Polly is much too bashful to propose to Tom, so she waits. Finally, Alcott proves that perfect equality and true love may admit sentiment as a touching embellishment. Tom proposes to Polly; the sentiment introduced at the end is a rose Tom has been carrying from the birthday cake Polly baked him the previous year. Keeping it carefully in his pocketbook, he explains that this "bit of nonsense kept me economical, honest and hard at it, for I never opened my pocketbook that I didn't think of you." The author ends her book with "a matrimonial epidemic," intending to pair off "everybody I can lay my hands on."[22]

SPINSTERHOOD FOREVER: LES DAMES AMÉRICAINES

Having married off nearly everyone in *An Old-Fashioned Girl*, Alcott with her sister May and her friend Alice Bartlett—a triumphant trio of spinsters—escaped to Europe. They sailed March 31, 1870, on a French steamer bound for Brest and the start of their Grand Tour. Alcott's happiness abroad can best be understood through the sketches and stories she fashioned from letters and notes. It was partly her new-found financial security that prompted these remarkably open feminist pieces. Collected, they were published as *Shawl Straps*, a volume in Alcott's series *Aunt Jo's Scrap Bag*. Already a sure success, twelve thousand copies of *An Old-Fashioned Girl* were sold in advance, and the *Boston Transcript* on the day of her departure printed a sketch of Miss Alcott paying glowing tribute to her "genius for naturalness."

An Old-Fashioned Girl was announced as *Little Women* reached sales of forty-two thousand. It made Louisa Alcott America's best-paid author in 1870. And, if imitation is really the most sincere form of flattery, she should have been delighted with Martha Finley's imitation of her work in 1871. The author of *Elsie Dinsmore* rushed into print with a story called *An Old-Fashioned Boy*, published by William B. Evans of Philadelphia, and bound in the same style as Louisa Alcott's book. Accused of blatantly trading on Alcott's success and possibly trying to fool her fans into thinking that *An Old-Fashioned Boy* was hers, Evans replied that Miss Alcott did not have an exclusive right to the term old-fashioned. And, he imagined that Alcott's fans would also like Finley's book and appreciate having matched volumes![23]

Alcott detailed the itinerary of their tour in narrative sequence. They first visited France, then Italy, Switzerland, and finally England. Alice Bartlett spoke French fluently, and Italian and German well enough to interpret for her friends. There was no shortage of money, and Alcott—who described herself variously as Lavinia, Livy, the Raven, Granny, and the Old Lady—enjoyed spoiling her sister and pleasing herself with odd bargains. In her stories, May was Matilda and Alice Amanda, and each represented a type of American female independence. Together they proved that their countrywomen need not "wait for man;" as Lavinia advises,

Take your little store and invest it in something far better than Paris finery, Geneva jewelry, or Roman relics. Bring home empty trunks, if you will, but heads full of new and larger ideas, hearts richer in the sympathy that makes the whole world kin, hands readier to help in the great work God gives humanity, and souls elevated by the wonders of art and the diviner miracles of Nature.[24]

Alcott and her companions did not bring home empty trunks. We enjoy learning about what they purchase, pack, and unpack and what they see and what we see of them. Everywhere the travelers see peasant women keeping house, rearing children, knitting garments, tending shops, markets, gardens, and farm animals with ease and skill. Their labor, however, brought no more equal reward in Brittany than in America.

The Americans were perhaps most amazed at the contrast between the power and strength of older married women and the cloistered, childlike dependency of young unmarried girls. The European custom of arranged marriages, the elaborate property settlements between families, and the French bride in their pension being more interested in her trousseau than her fiancé both amused and horrified the American women. Europe seems to offer nothing better than a poor choice between unmarried seclusion and married woman's exploitation.

As they travel Alcott paints a comical but not demeaning picture of herself as an old maid who loves plain English beef and ale, angora cats, and cuddling by the fire to warm her aching bones. Various activities show that independent women can be frivolously feminine and boyishly active at the same time. They clamber up and down rocks, see the churches and castles, and spend one whole evening in France drinking mulled wine and manicuring their fingernails. Avoiding the Franco-Prussian war was a more serious matter, however, and they leave France to enjoy Switzerland and Italy.

Reaching London, the companions part company. Matilda remains to study art, as did May Alcott; Amanda returns home to her family; and Lavinia, like Alcott, goes back to Concord. Only two factors kept Louisa May Alcott from semipermanent residence abroad. The first was the discovery that increasing lameness and constant attacks of neuralgia were not just the effects of overwork and constant worry. Her Grand Tour was a completely delightful holiday, except for there being no real improvement in her health. Alcott had discovered in Brittany that her pains were due to mercury poisoning from the old calomel dosing. Her ill health linked her to Anna's husband, John, who also suffered from neuralgia and had been dosed with calomel. In Rome the two sisters had received news from Boston that John Pratt had died. He was only thirty-seven, and Alcott worried that her sister and her nephews would be without that secure competence she so desperately wanted for her whole family. She set to work immediately on a sequel to *Little Women*.

Little Men, a thoroughly American utopia, was written in Rome, interrupted only by the great flood when the River Tiber overflowed its banks three days after Christmas in 1870.[25] Alcott's incentive to write *Little Women* had come from the successful Oliver Optic series, and their simple moral: with integrity and hard work the individual triumphs over himself and social adversity.[26] The Oliver Optic stories firmly eschewed any notion of institutional changes in the face of poverty.

In *Little Men* Louisa May Alcott presents an institution so invitingly sugared and toasted that it warms the hearts of readers and coaxes them to accept democratic institutional responses to the problem of social inequality. Alcott maintained her belief that men and women could live together equitably and therefore harmoniously if they were trained to do so in their earliest years. Moreover, citizens accustomed in their youth to a prosperous equality, would help generate change in the larger society. A school for boys proved a socially acceptable device to promote the spirit of cooperation and democracy, but coeducation, especially in a boarding school, was another matter. Alcott solved this difficulty by gradually introducing three very different little girls to the fifteen assorted boys at Plumfield.

In *Little Women*, Alcott's special appeal was her ability to create fireside, family adventures. *Little Men*, however, is set at Plumfield, a boarding school. Having established the estate's origins in the March family, the author smoothly woos her readers to accept a model institution in lieu of the private family. Missionary work began and ended with one family in *An Old-Fashioned Girl*, but Alcott identified larger problems than even the best feminist family could solve. Chief among them was the increasing geographical and social distance between rich and poor. Rich citizens, never having worked, did not know the value of labor and stinted wages to the poor. The lower classes despaired, and in their distress became the "dangerous classes."

In the first scene of *Little Men*, a ragged, homeless Nat Blake arrives at Plumfield's suppertime. He is immediately greeted by Meg

Brooke's twins, Daisy and Demi, on the first floor of an old-fashioned hospitable house aswarm with boys. A delicious aroma tantalizes his "hungry little nose and stomach." To his left, just inside the hallway, a long supper table is laid with "great pitchers of new milk, piles of brown and white bread, and perfect stacks of the shiny gingerbread so dear to boyish souls. A flavor of toast was in the air, also suggestions of baked apples."[27] As Nat, an orphaned street musician, is welcomed and gradually won over by Plumfield's routine, the reader discovers along with him that this model farm school raises most of the food that appears in scene after scene of nutritious abundance. Unlike Fruitlands, this experiment has a resident experienced farmer who is in charge of the students' outside work and the tasks necessary to a profitable farm operation. It is never clear how much of Plumfield's income comes from tuition and how much from the farm and charitable contributions. We do learn that there are all sorts of pupils in residence.

The domesticity that nourishes them all is created by Jo Bhaer (in her roles as wife, mother, and aunt); Jo is ably assisted by at least three other women. The kitchen is presided over by Asia, a black cook whose dominion in her sphere is unchallenged. She is aided by Mary Ann, the maid, and by "Nursey," the pathetic Frau Hummel in *Little Women*. Mrs. Jo is famously uninterested in domestic chores, though she insists that the three female students learn simple cooking, laundry, and sewing. The coeducational experiment begins when Meg Brooke's twin, Daisy, is joined by Naughty Nan, or little Annie Harding. Nan, whose mother is dead, is a tomboy and a perfect foil for the naturally domestic Daisy. Mrs. Jo says forthrightly to Fritz, "You know we believe in bringing up little men and women together, and it is high time we acted up to our belief."[28] The third little girl, Bess, is really just a frequent visitor.

Bess, as faithful readers of *Little Women* will recall, is named after Beth March, and like Beth she is a fragile creature who almost perished from an unnamed ailment in her infancy. In *Little Men* she has become a gentle but all-powerful queen. Her beauty is armed by her firm ability to withdraw favor from those who indulge in rude screams and romps; she helps tame Nan. Bess occasionally evokes the sentimental dominion of little Eva in *Uncle Tom's Cabin*, but she does not die out of sheer goodness.

By the 1890s Bess has a successor in the famous "Little Colonel," a creation of Annie Fellows Johnston.[29] This incarnation of ideal beauty uses her feminity and infant innocence to socialize conflicting races and classes. Everyone wants her love and everyone knuckles under to the new standard she represents. Bess is a transitional heroine, more active than little Eva, but less powerful than the little colonel.

All the Plumfield children (except the visiting Bess) have garden plots and projects of their own to earn money, to acquire useful skills, and incidentally to learn that cooperation is both necessary and efficient in a model political economy. Most important, they all learn the advantages of helping one another, and gain wisdom from learning that different skills as well as temperaments are useful. Alcott makes it clear that differences in temperament and class, as well as sex, will greatly shape children's futures. But there is some hope, through the Plumfield regime, of greater equality of opportunity for the poor. Wealthier pupils learn to admire the good qualities of their poorer schoolmates, and by working rich boys and girls may learn the labor theory of value.

Alcott, like Mark Twain, presents a longed-for world of childhood in her most popular fiction. Unlike Twain's boys, however, Alcott's male characters are "little men," the functional partners of "little women." Neither boyhood nor girlhood in Alcott's novel represents the sacred liberty found in Twain's Mississippi odyssey. Plumfield has a small, tame stream with a playhouse refuge in the willow tree overhanging its banks; grownups and children climb up and share confidences with one another. In Twain's scheme of things neither girls nor white adults can really be trusted. Only boys and "niggers," both social outcasts, are existentially free.

Children's good feelings, Alcott maintains, should be evoked to socialize them. Nan is temperamentally no less wild and freedom loving than Dan in Little Men. The motherless daughter of a genteel family, she is nevertheless as easily tamed by loving discipline as Dan; she too is hungry for home. Nan is also bound to her friend Daisy because they are two girls in a boys' world. When separated, each falls victim to the domination of little men. Daisy's domesticity leaves her prey to exploitation by hungry, selfish little boys who devour her cooking and leave her with the messy remains of their feasts. Nan's determination to be one of the boys is thwarted by their primitive male bonding, and her life and limbs are endangered by mean-spirited dares to prove herself in reckless physical competition. The girls find safety, support, and maturation in sisterhood. Learning to value one another despite their differences, Alcott intimates that Daisy and Nan are models for the woman's movement. Girls, like boys, must learn that females are not all the same.

Plumfield has often been interpreted as Louisa Alcott's tribute to her father's Temple School. Certainly the Alcotts continued to hope that Bronson was a genius before his time (especially after Alcott's success with *Little Women*), and they were delighted with public pedagogical reforms that seemed to vindicate Temple School. Plumfield, however, goes far beyond such Temple School methods as peer-group pressure and Socratic dialogues to evoke children's natural purity. Self-control seemed to Alcott less and less the product of the independent human will; indeed, she joined many of her contemporaries in presenting human personality as largely the product of social interaction. The problem, she argues, is that the stable and organic social code that once shaped individual character no longer existed. Plumfield presents the old virtues (cooperation, hard work, patience, and thrift) as a means to loving acceptance by one's peers and betters.

In effect, the author of *Little Men* steals America's children. She removes them from their parents' unreliable care and makes their school the center of learning in the fullest sense. Intellectual and practical skills, peer-group approval, adult love, and authority are all included in one institution. Public schools were to take another forty years to attempt what Plumfield represents: an integrated social institution.

There is no conflict between the values espoused by Jo and Fritz and the true nature of their pupils. Resistance to the house parents' code of behavior is treated much like evidence of a physical disease; the adults offer love, warm soothing cough syrup, clean linen, and a reassuringly firm schedule of appealing daily activities. Social approval is Plumfield's household god, and it works because there are no alternative deities to venerate or propitiate.

It is sufficient, Alcott argues, to prepare children to be useful, self-supporting citizens who understand the need for corporate welfare. And so Daisy, Demi, and even Dan and Nat join forces to soften

Nan's bondage, but the children do not form a band of brigands and run away to the river. Instead, Daisy picnics her dolls on the lawn so Nan can watch the show, Demi reads a story aloud for her amusement, Nat plays her a tune, and Dan brings her a little tree toad as a sign of his sympathy. Grownups always maintain their authority in Alcott's fiction, in large measure by posing as children's best friends and companions. They accomplish this by recalling that they too were once children. Sarah Josepha Hale understood the source of Alcott's power over her juvenile fans quite well: "Miss Alcott has a faculty of entering into the lives and feelings of children that is conspicuously wanting in most writers who address them; and to this cause, to the consciousness among her readers that they are hearing about people like themselves instead of abstract qualities with names, the popularity of her book is due."[30] Plumfield, in short, is a kind of settlement house. It employs neighborhood people and offers shelter while allowing its clients to move in and out at various stages.

The extended March family is present but muted, usually offstage in this domestic drama, and even Fritz and Jo play minor roles. The children themselves take center stage. There is no real plot in *Little Men*, but the book holds reader interest because Plumfield seems "the nicest place in the world," and in such a place it seems there are no really bad people or serious misfortunes. Guardians of the uneducated masses are however a necessity in order to prevent dictatorship and the worship of false gods. The smaller children, closer to tribal life, enjoy scaring up an imaginary creature, called Kitty-Mouse, who threatens terrible punishments for disobedience to its commandments. Demi, who is the inventor and prophet of Kitty-Mouse, announces the event of "sacerryfice." The children build a big fire, and according to Demi, who has heard a garbled version of Uncle Fritz's lecture on Greek sacrifice, they must all burn their most cherished possessions. Rob throws his wooden toy village on the fire, Daisy gives up a new set of paper dolls, and Teddy, not knowing what is happening, comes along with his stuffed lamb and his favorite doll, Annabella. The entranced children watch the destruction of their toys, and when the wooden people of the toy village are burned, Teddy throws his lamb and then poor Annabella on the "funeral pyre." What ensues is a horrible lesson about giving up what one loves most to dictators. Annabella, being covered with kid, did not blaze, but did what was worse, she squirmed. First one leg curled up, then the other, in a very awful and lifelike manner; next she flung her arms over her head as if in great agony; her head itself turned on her shoulder, her glass eyes fell out and with one final writh of her whole body, she sank down a blackened mass on the ruins of the town.

Teddy ran screaming for "Marmar" as loud as he could. Lions, lambs, and the sacrifice of dear possessions resonate back to Fruitlands; they also testify to a fear of demagoguery among the "dangerous classes," who, like children, are prey to their primitive instincts. Most of the children's mistakes are harmless, real enough to provoke sympathy and calculated to teach the moral of the story. That moral, in direct contrast to the Oliver Optic books, is that cooperative, democratic institutions prove Aunt Jo's belief: "If men and women would only trust, understand and help one another, as my children do, what a capital place the world would be."[31]

Jo's father urges her to keep on with Plumfield because the world will see a utopian possibility "by the success of your small experiment." In the last scene of the book, Jo replies that she is not so ambitious as that. She wants simply to give the children a home and teach them things that will make their life less hard in the outside world. Father and Mother Bhaer are a successful, miraculously unconflicted example of reform domesticity. They address each other as Jo and Fritz, but have no roles outside of Mother and Father in the novel. If they have a more private life, the reader never learns of it, and perhaps does not care, because the Bhaers seem so united and fulfilled as overseers of Plumsfield. There is a gentle refuge in social roles, Alcott intimates to her readers.

TRUST, UNDERSTAND, AND HELP ONE ANOTHER

Adult and juvenile readers depended upon periodicals for a regular supply of Aunt Jo's stories. A particularly witty example of Alcott's ability to blend politics, humor, and suspense for adults

and children appeared in a *Heart and Home* serial for the month of
May 1872.[32] "Cupid and Chow-Chow" are names given to, respectively, a small "girl-boy" in velvet clothes and blond curls, whom
his Mamma calls Cupid, and his cousin Chow-Chow, a "boy-girl"
in brown linen frock, dusty boots, and a head of wild black hair,
pinned up with a red bow. This unlikely pair play out a suspense-
ful courtship and, not incidentally, work out the current politics of
"Elective Franchise." Chow-Chow, named after a sweet and sour
pickle relish, is frenetic, domineering, an unlikable caricature of her
mother, Aunt Susan. Stamping her foot, imitating a harangue she
has obviously overheard many times, Chow-Chow screeches: "This
is our platform: Free speech, free love, free everything; and Woman's Puckerage for ever."[33] Alcott's point is serious, however, reflecting her own commitment to the New England Woman Suffrage Association and to the *Woman's Journal* position within the
woman's rights disputes.

Cupid is a tender-hearted, domestic little fellow, a trifle timid and
vain but possessed, nonetheless, of the right stuff from Alcott's perspective. He genuinely wants to win his cousin's love and is willing
to "cure" all his faults to be worthy of her. He takes her criticism
seriously and brings the shears to Chow-Chow; she delightedly
"snipped and slashed," leaving his "dandy-prat" curls on the floor. It
is just the beginning of her reign and Cupid's trials; Chow-Chow's
"Love of power grew by what it fed on." She teases animals and tests
Cupid until she accidentally smashes his fingers in a hay-cutting
machine. The injury is serious and a long period of doctor's visits,
painful probes, applications of caustic, and bandages ensues. Cupid
bears it all bravely and refuses to blame Chow-Chow for his misery.
She, in turn, waits upon her cousin tenderly, nurses him, and in the
process, has a genuine change of heart, agreeing to Cupid's heart's
desire: playing house together on an old swan island in the pond.

The story is not over with this conversion: even loving and admir-
ing Cupid, Chow-Chow, it seems, cannot live out her best feelings.
She will not marry a poor boy, and, finally playing house, she insists
on replicating what is obviously her parents' unhappy marriage.
Cupid must go off to work and when he comes home and wants to
spend the evening companionably in front of the fire with Chow-
Chow, she insists on his going off to his club to smoke while she trots

off to a "Woman's Puckerage" meeting. Cupid is perfectly happy to go to the lecture with her, but Chow-Chow replies, "No, you can't! Papa *never* goes; he says they are all gabble and nonsense, and Mamma says his club is all smoke and slang, and they *never* go together."

At last we are at the heart of the matter, Aunt Susan and Uncle George, along with Mrs. Ellen and Cupid's Papa, have been watching the children's play, seeing themselves in a new way, and speculating on the outcome. Cupid's parents are pleased that he becomes a "trump" instead of a "dandy-prat," and Chow-Chow's parents have a change of heart in watching their daughter's conversion. Her father puts his arm around Aunt Susan and she resolves to make their house a home. In the final adventure, Chow-Chow brings a secretary down on her head by climbing up its open drawers to effect a platform for "Woman's Puckerage." Cupid scrambles under the falling marble top and saves his beloved cousin. The parents quickly rescue both children but not before Chow-Chow resolves never to play "that nasty old puckerage any more," and her mama replies, "Nor I either, *in that way*." The little girl curiously inquires whether her mother has hurt herself too, and Aunt Susan replies, "I am afraid I did."

The outcome of this tale is a wiser understanding of woman's rights all around. Mr. George wants his daughter to be sure her platform is all right before she tries again, "else it will let you down when you least expect it, and damage your best friends as well as yourself." Mrs. Ellen admits "there is some sense" in woman's rights and that the "real and true will come to pass when we women learn how far to go, and how to fit ourselves for the new duties by doing the old ones well." Cupid's father thinks "happy womanly women" will "have the most influence after all," and he is glad to lend a hand toward also giving the "bitter, sour discontented ones" "their rights in all things." Cupid and Chow-Chow's romance is therefore sealed by sharing a pie, " 'zactly in halves," because, "Mamma says that's the right thing to do always."[34]

Aunt Susan, Chow-Chow's mother, is a thinly disguised Susan B. Anthony, who often criticized women with husbands and children who did not make the "cause" their primary effort.[35] Alcott wholeheartedly joined the efforts of Lucy Stone, Julia Ward Howe, Thomas Wentworth Higginson, and their allies on the *Woman's Journal* in working for "woman suffrage and all other reforms."[36] Knowing about family duties firsthand, she wrote to Lucy Stone in 1873 that she was so busy at that moment, "proving woman's right to labor," that she had no time to "help prove woman's right to vote." Alcott could and would not betray her mother's lifelong labors in behalf of family and reform of all kinds, Abba Alcott who, at seventy-three, was "determined to go to the polls before I die, even if my three daughters have to carry me."[37] Then Alcott was firmly convinced that woman's rights were part and parcel of general reform; she had remained true to the bonds between abolitionists and suffragists and she continued to believe in "the good time coming."[38]

Little Men was published in England while Alcott was still there in 1871. When her ship docked in Boston harbor, she found that the American publication date coincided with her homecoming that same year. Fifty thousand books sold out in advance. That June was pleasant, despite Abba's being so enfeebled that Alcott vowed never to go far away from her again. That summer Samuel J. May died. At thirty-nine she determined to put off any more holidays, taking her turn at family responsibilities until May came home. Her earnings bought a steam furnace for the Concord house. By December, May was in charge at home and Louisa could enjoy Boston and the Radical Club again.

Alcott's letters and notes became a series of European travel sketches, but she never ventured on the lecture circuit as did Mark Twain after publishing *Innocents Abroad* in 1869. Also unlike Twain, Alcott accepted both Old World "romance" and the value of aristocratic ancestors—especially if one views Quincys, Sewalls, and Mays as America's only aristocracy. Yet she perceived the impressive housewives of Brittany and France as a whole as kin to our lusty, hardworking foremothers. American women could recover their former industry and get paid for it this time, she argued.

By 1872, aware that neither literary success nor secure earnings brought a diminution of her domestic responsibilities, Alcott wrote in her journal:

Work is my salvation. . . . Got out the old manuscript of Success and called it Work! Fired up the engine and plunged into a vortex with many doubts about getting out. Can't work slowly; the thing possesses me, and I must obey till its done.[39]

Her most autobiographical novel, *Work*, written for adult readers, was Alcott's attempt to mediate between classes and so to provide a domestic and civil union, with justice for all. Independence and a home remained her cry on behalf of American women. *Diana and Persis*, together with *Jo's Boys*, completed her analysis of the proper means to that end.

THIRTEEN

To Earn a Home

It is not always want, insanity, or sin that drives women to desperate deaths; often it is a dreadful loneliness of heart, a hunger for home and friends, worse than starvation, a bitter sense of wrong in being denied the tender ties, the pleasant duties, the sweet regards that can make the humblest life happy; a rebellious protest against God, who, when they cry for bread, seems to offer them a stone.

Louisa May Alcott, *Work*, chapter 7

Despite literary and financial success, Louisa Alcott never created a permanent domestic environment of her own. As a single women, the "tender ties" of home and friends remained elusive. It was not until 1880, when her niece came to live with her, that the fifty-two-year-old author wrote, "I do mean to set up my own establishment in Boston," and added: "Now I have an excuse for a home of my own, and as the other artistic and literary spinsters have a house, I'm going to try the plan, for a winter at least."[1]

Alcott's hunger for home and her fierce desire for independence were part of a larger social issue she examined in her adult fiction. In *Work* she argues that expanded education, training, and jobs for women would give the next generation of women what had been denied hers; such changes, however, would come about through the hard work of reformist associations and sustained mutual sacrifice. Alcott portrayed the experiences of working women as powerfully as she lived them, faltering only in her earnest depiction of social mediators between "the helpers and the helped." In a valiant effort to bridge the growing chasms among races, classes, and generations, she wrote of her proposed alliance as if it were an imminent reality.

In a brief romance about herself and May, then, she sketched the lives of two artists who choose different paths to fulfill their need for creative work and domestic ties. One chooses spinsterhood and friendship; the other tries egalitarian marriage, motherhood, and an expanded family circle. An individual might be lucky enough to find personal solutions to a social problem, she argued. At the same time, she knew that the woman problem could be solved only through institutional changes in society.

SUCCESS AND WORK

The Christian Union asked Louisa for a serial story in November 1872. Having just spent a good deal of money on clothes and a trunk for Bronson, who left on another Western trip "all neat and comfortable," she was delighted to oblige the editors in return for a payment of three thousand dollars. The serial was *Work: A Story of Experience.*[2]

Writing short tales for useful sums, the great Boston fire, and visits from Anna and her boys interrupted the manuscript's completion. In letters to her mother from her "writing room" in Boston, Alcott also admitted that she had "transcendental days" in which the Radical Club claimed her attendance with its "funny mixture of rabbis, and weedy old ladies, the 'oversoul' and oysters." She was keeping a separate account for the "family income" and living off the money earned by her "little tales."[3]

By January she managed to get back to marathon writing sessions on *Work*. A month later her diary recorded family obligations that could not be bought, it seemed, for money:

Anna very ill with pneumonia; home to nurse, Father telegraphed to come home, as we thought her dying. She gave me her boys, but the dear saint got well and kept the lads for herself. Thank God! Back to work with what wits nursing left me. Had Johnny for a week to keep all quiet at home. . . . Finished *Work*—twenty chapters. Not what it should be—too many interruptions. Should like to do one book in peace and see if it wouldn't be good.[4]

Alcott quoted Thomas Carlyle on the title page of her new novel: "An endless significance lies in work; in idleness alone is there perpetual despair." The dedication, "To My Mother, Whose Life has been a long labor of love," is certainly appropriate, as *Work* argues powerfully for female independence and cooperative domesticity.[5] Alcott's earlier books reasoned that young women were incapable of effective child care if they were excluded from education and employment in the larger society. The principles of loving service, compassion, and sisterhood, however, were increasingly threatened by the same marketplace that provided women's sole source of independent income. Alcott struggled to resolve this contradiction. Her first task was to find a satisfactory definition of the status and role of women. Once again she looked to Theodore Parker for confirmation of what he called "The Public Function of Women."[5]

Moncure Conway recalled that during Parker's last illness the Alumni Association of the Harvard Divinity School refused to pray for his restoration to health and work. Parker's denial of divine miracles and his radical political stand in behalf of working people, women, and slaves cost him the support of conservative Unitarians.[6] While in Italy Alcott had visited Parker's grave with memorial flowers, but her best tribute to him was the character Reverend Power in *Work*. As she told Ednah Cheney, "Christie's adventures are many of them my own; Mr. Power is Mr. Parker."[7]

Christie Devon, the heroine of *Work*, is an orphan and thus freed from the obligations that customarily befall the daughter of a farm household. She uses the language of the Seneca Falls Convention to claim her rights ("There's going to be new Declaration of Independence") and emphasizes "her speech by energetic demonstration in the bread trough, kneading dough as if it were her destiny, and she was shaping it to suit herself."[8]

Christie's experience so far has been entirely rural and domestic; all her skills have been learned either at a village school or at home. She leaves the farm knowing that "work was always to be found in the city," and perceives the wage system as the means to independence. She finds a room in a boardinghouse and begins hunting for a job, free for the first time from the endless round of tasks that define domesticity and dependency. Christie soon learns that the skills of general housewifery are not wanted by employers; unable to call herself a professional cook or nursemaid, she goes into service as the lowliest maid-of-all-work, just as Louisa Alcott did.

When her first employer refuses to call Christie by her own name, she learns the anonymity of wage earners firsthand. Her employer is pleased that, unlike the Irish servant girls previously employed (all called "Jane"), Christie does not object to working with a black cook. It is the cook who gives Christie a lesson in humility, kindness, and patience. Hepsey knows that slavery is more degrading than any sort of paid work.

Domesticity produces a consciousness of work not only as "craft," but also as a process quite apart from wages and hours. Consequently, many servant "girls" preferred factory work to the long hours and endless tasks set by household employers. Lucy Maynard Salmon, in discussing the "social disadvantages of domestic service," found the lack of "home privileges" to be a serious source of distress to female servants. "Board and lodging do not constitute a home, and the domestic can never be a part of the family whose external life she shares."[9] As one girl reported, "One must remember that there is a difference between a house, a place of shelter, and a home, a place where all our affections are centered."[10]

Domesticity was quite different from domestic service, and the substitution of a wage for affection and interdependence made the one a house to clean and the other a home to live in. This consciousness of work as distinct from job was to cause some confusion in Alcott's heroine. In her first twenty-four hours of service Christie learns that she is expected to do tasks with the devotion of a family member but without any rewards of a family relationship.

Christie's first job does not last long. Her employers, a family of upwardly mobile social climbers worse than the Shaws in *An Old-Fashioned Girl*, exploit and then fire her in the first chapters of *Work*. Christie, on her own once again, remains linked however to Hepsey by friendship and a new commitment to abolition and racial integration. Hepsey's loyalty to her enslaved family, whom she hopes to free with her wages, had its real counterpart in many black families.

Hepsey is the first link in a chain of sisterhood forged by Christie Devon, who discovers (as did her creator) that jobs are better than chattel slavery but do not bring full independence. Female friendship in her boardinghouse subsequently gives Christie the opportunity to try a stage career. Alas, sexual familiarities are commonplace and rivalries among actresses prevented real companionship, and so Christie leaves acting. Warned that stage experience is an impediment to "genteel" employment, she refrains from mentioning it and secures an appointment as governess to a wealthy family.

The bachelor brother of her employer, Philip Fletcher, is a wealthy snobbish invalid; he proposes to Christie, despite having learned that she was formerly an actress. Lonely and tired, she is tempted to "marry for a living."[11] Fortunately, realizing that marriage to Fletcher can only mean subordination and dependency, she rejects his proposal after a conversation about *Jane Eyre*, which she has been reading. Her suitor suggests that a man's faults can be cured by the love of a good woman, such as herself. Christie replies, "If he has wasted his life he must take the consequences, and be content with pity and indifference, instead of respect and love. Many good women do 'lend a hand,' as you say, and it is quite Christian and amiable I've no doubt; but I cannot think it is a fair bargain."[12] Later in the novel Fletcher goes to war and becomes a more worthwhile suitor as a result of his adversity training. Christie still refuses him because she does not love him.

All the jobs Christie finds in the first half of *Work* are ill paying and humiliating. Her female employers are not true women; as the husbands and fathers participate in the competitive marketplace, their wives and daughters maneuver in the social world of fashion to augment their husbands' chances for success. They never extend hands in friendship to those who serve them. Theodore Parker had remarked that it was not work that crushed the spirit of the laboring people, but rather

> the tacit confession on the part of the employer, that he has wronged and subjugated the person who serves him; for when these same actions are performed by the mother for her child, or the son for his father, they are done for love and not money, they are counted not as low but rather ennobling.[13]

The turning point in the novel is Christie's employment as a seamstress in a factorylike workroom. She holds herself aloof from the other factory "hands," but is attracted to Rachel, a quiet romantic looking girl. Clearly of fallen gentry hired for her "superior taste," Rachel is Christie's first friend of her own age and sensibilities, a true heart's companion. The respectable workshop owner, Mrs. King, is dependent upon her forewoman, Miss Cotton, who discovers that Rachel is a fallen woman. Readers could hardly miss the irony of "King Cotton," an infamous phrase with double meaning for abolitionists. Cotton was indeed the king of American crops in the antebellum period, and as the country's leading export commodity, it led Northern factory and workshop owners to ignore the cruelty of slavery in the name of profits. Mrs. King fears losing Miss Cotton and so, although the owner knows better, she fires Rachel in order to validate the hypocritical sensibilities of Miss Cotton. Christie herself does not immediately protest or resign when Rachel is dismissed. It takes Alcott's heroine a few hours to recover her true feeling for Rachel. At first, Christie has a conventional response; she feels personally betrayed by the discovery of Rachel's hidden past.

The importance of Rachel and Christie's friendship cannot be overemphasized. The power of female friendship in *Work* redeems a fallen woman, as it does in Harriet Beecher Stowe's novel, *We and Our Neighbors*, published in 1875. Rachel's plight, like that of Stowe's heroine, points to the inadequacy of conventional charity institutions. Her dismissal from work is the beginning of Christie's search for a religious faith more liberal than conventional Christianity, a faith that can link her to others and change a society that promises opportunity and delivers oppression.

Christie leaves her job as a sign in protest and solidarity with Rachel, but soon finds herself alone, ill, reduced to piecework, and close to suicide. But Rachel appears and sends Christie to stay with Cynthie Wilkins, a humble laundress with a shiftless husband and a brood of small children. A new alliance and a new agenda for reform emerge from the domestic haven of Cynthie's humble cottage. Mrs. Wilkins is a laundress who advertises her services with a sign, "Cynthie Wilkins, Clear Starcher," and her vision of the world is as clear as her starching: social change will come about through a new Christian union in which Christ washes whitest of all. Her chaplain and the head of this new union is the Reverend Power, who as Cynthie says, "starts the dirt and gits the stains out, and leaves 'em ready for other folks to finish off."[4]

Reverend Power sends Christie to David Sterling for a job. Sterling, the owner of a greenhouse, is Alcott's idealized portrait of

Henry David Thoreau. It is through friendship and growing recognition of their common interest in equality and reform that Christie and David fall in love. They marry during the Civil War, David leaves to fight and Christie becomes a nurse. After only a few months together, most of them spent visiting on the battlefield, David is killed. Christie survives the loss only because she finds hope in bearing his child.[15]

Her daughter, Pansy, becomes the focus of her energetic plans for a new generation of women. Instead of retiring on her widow's pension, Christie runs a cooperative greenhouse with her mother-in-law, Pansy, and Rachel. Together the old and the young women work and share their profits equally. And we learn of the causes Christie supports—"the freed people . . . wounded soldiers, destitute children, ill-paid women, young people struggling for independence, homes, hospitals, schools, churches, and God's charity all over the world."[16] Christie has formed a "loving league" with Hepsey, Reverend Power, Cynthie Wilkins, and the rest of her family and friends; they are a band of dedicated reformers. A new field of labor opens for the heroine of *Work* when, at the age of forty, she joins an association of working women. She notices the widening gap between middle-class reformers and working people.

Alcott's *Work* is based upon the realities of everyday life for working women and also upon the powerful moral sentiment of the second book of *The Pilgrim's Progress*. Christie, by the end of *Work*, has achieved a cooperative household, a loving band of reform sisters and brothers, and the dignified independence of widowhood. Her unsuitable suitor, Mr. Fletcher, having redeemed himself through service in the Civil War, is now Colonel Fletcher. Christie "was a woman who could change a lover into a friend, and keep him all her life." Fletcher's friendship is demonstrated through the gift of a beautiful painting depicting Mr. Greatheart leading the fugitives from the City of Destruction, a painting in which the characters of *Work* see themselves portrayed.

The most striking change in Alcott's version of the story is that the hero is not Christian, husband of Christiana, but rather Mr. Greatheart, a knight and friend of both pilgrims in Bunyan's epic. David Sterling's mother recognizes her son in the figure of Mr. Greatheart. David Sterling, like Mr. Greatheart, is the heroine's more experienced partner. He takes her part of the way toward the Celestial City and then he leaves, confident that she can lead her companions toward the Promised Land. Christie's is definitively a woman's lot, and she travels with Rachel, who is drawn after Mercy in *The Pilgrim's Progress*. In that book Christiana hires young Mercy to accompany her and the children on their pilgrimage and her concept of Christian sisterhood triumphs. "I will hire thee, and thou shalt go along with me as my servant. Yet we will have all things in common betwith thee and me."[17]

A woman's rights polemic, *Work* is also Alcott's strongest portrayal of women's lives. Christie moves through a period of adolescent struggle in which she demands her individual rights as a daughter of the American Revolution, and then learns she is only one of "that large class of women, who moderately endowed with talents, earnest and true-hearted, are driven by necessity, temperament, or principle out into the world to find support, happiness and homes for themselves."[18] By herself she cannot find work, happiness, or home. Her progress throughout the novel depends upon mutuality, cooperation, and loving league with others.

Christie finds true womanhood in association with all the social classes Alcott wants to unite in a search for democratic harmony. Middle-class women can aid their working sisters by using their social status and influence to find education, jobs, and homes for the less privileged. The problem, Alcott insists, is a lack of communication between those who have much to give and those who desperately need help to get started. The creation of institutions to provide that help is proper work for the veterans of the first fight for emancipation. Christie's greenhouse and cooperative household are further examples of Alcott's settlement-house proposals.

Alcott distributed the money earned from the sales of *Work* according to her sense of family and social responsibility. One thousand dollars went to May to help her study art in Europe. Another part went into the "Alcott sinking fund," as she called the family investments, and some money went as a "thank offering" to "the silent poor to which we belonged for so many years—needy, but respectable and forgotten because too proud to beg."[19]

The publication of *Work* had two additional results. The first was a new housekeeper. Alcott was curious "how she came to us," and discovered that "she had taught and sewed, was tired, and wanted something else; decided to try for a housekeeper's place, but happened to read *Work*, and thought she'd do as Christie did—take anything that came."[20] The second outcome of *Work* was a small but disquieting stream of criticism. *The Lakeside Monthly* condemned the book "as an immoderate apotheosis of Madam Work pointing out to the author that slavery had been abolished and with it the necessity of cant on the subject of Negro rights."[21]

The reviewer at *Harper's* argued that Alcott's name and reputation would carry the book, and not the book itself. Ignoring *Moods* the writer called *Work* "Miss Alcott's first real novel." As a "serious didactic essay on the subject of woman's work," it came dangerously close to "preaching in the guise of story telling." The reviewer was quite right in recognizing the defects of *Work* as fiction; it was a forthright report on laboring women.[22]

In 1869, at a meeting between working and middle-class women of Massachusetts, a Miss Phelps has stood up and spoken about working women in much the same language later used by Christie Devon in *Work:*

"We do not think the men of Massachusetts know how the women live. We do not think if they did they would allow such a state of things to exist. Some of us who signed the petition have had to work for less than twenty-five cents a day, and we know that many others have had to do the same. . . . Do you not think that they feel the difference between their condition and that of rich, well dressed ladies who pass them? If they did not they would be less than human. . . . Only help us to earn a home that we can attach ourselves to, that will make us feel that we have a country. It has been said that we can go anywhere and be at home. Women cannot. It is because they have no homes. They have a husband's or a father's home, but none of their own. . . . I am often met with the objection that these women can go to California or Nevada. But our mothers live here. We know not these distant places. . . . Girls love independence, girls love society, just as much as men do. A woman must have some intellectual society or she goes down. I am no speechmaker—only a worker."[23]

Alcott knew enough about adversity to write powerfully about woman's wrongs as a social question. But her most puzzling problem remained the contradictions between private domestic life and woman's individuality. For herself there was no longer a personal question. Forty years' experience with the difficulties of supporting a family while gaining a modicum of independence led her to cry out, "Spinsterhood forever." But she also knew the familiar loneliness for "tender ties" and "pleasant duties" performed by and for loved ones. She came close to proposing a social answer to this problem when she created a happy community of dedicated spinsters in *An Old-Fashioned Girl*, the model school run by family members and open to homeless waifs in *Little Men*, and a cooperative household and business in *Work*.

For the most part, however, she presented the problem as a simple alternative: a woman must choose either a single life dedicated to truth, art, and humanity at the cost of those "pleasant duties" and "sweet regards," or marriage to a man who supports woman's rights and accepts her work, maternity, and wifehood as compatible vocations. In 1879 she wrote an unfinished romance about Diana and Persis, two artist friends who try different paths to domesticity and feminism.[24]

Alcott is the Diana of her unfinished story, and her sister May is Persis. May's daring try for independence, love, and maternity leads us to ask to what extent the order of the children's birth and the fluctuating family circumstances of the Alcotts affected the lives they chose to lead. Abba Alcott dreamt that women would be bankers, teachers, judges, writers, artists, and doctors by the year 1900, and Alcott depicted them in training at Laurence University. But these hopes were clearly incompatible with the subordination of self to husband and children. Could girls brought up to value self-sacrifice learn to cherish individual identity and demand freedom from household drudgery with no regrets? May was able to do so, while Alcott and her mother watched her with pleasure perhaps tinged with envy.

After finishing *Work* Alcott gave up her room in Boston and moved back to Concord to take up family chores. She sent May to

Europe, expecting her to return eventually, or if fortune favored them both, to visit her there. Although thirty-three, May's letters home seem written by a young girl, and she describes her housekeeping arrangements as if she were playing house.

May's copies of Turner won John Ruskin's praise in London. She was learning to turn out "pot boilers," as her sister called her own quick novels and May's art copies. In 1874, when May returned once more to help at home, Alcott's health seemed much worse. Rheumatism and blinding neuralgic headaches made writing and caring for the family too heavy a burden. But in the spring of 1876 she agreed to send May back to Europe: "She cannot find the help she needs here and is happy and busy in her own world over there. God be with her, she has done her distasteful duty faithfully and deserves a reward."[25]

May never returned to Concord. She established herself in Paris, living close to several other woman artists. She described working in an all-woman studio with nude models and criticism of students' work by leading painters. She wrote a guidebook for American artists abroad, and carefully listed those male artists who took female students. Her vivid letters describe a comfortable, supportive group of young female artists who shared breakfasts, Thanksgiving dinners far from home, and encouraged one another's ambitions.

Abba's health was failing as she faithfully copied her "good child's" letters into her journal. Meanwhile, her youngest daughter made plans to stay in Europe. She reassured the family that she would make occasional summer visits home "if you want me very much." The tug of war with silken cord between Concord and Paris continued for a year. Abba wrote, "I think she has realized what a sacrifice to me it has been to have her gone so far, and has conscientiously tried to gratify me and her sisters by these frequent and interesting accounts of her progress in Art." May's still life won a red ribbon at the Paris Salon, and Bronson sent her a congratultory note in red ink. At the same time he mentioned Alcott's book (*A Modern Mephistopheles*) in the forthcoming No Name Series.[26] Alcott had directed Thomas Niles to send May a copy.

Abba's insistence upon the primacy of obligations within the family did not deter her from taking strong public positions on woman's rights in her last years. Concord's centennial celebration led her to pen a fiery declaration demanding "no taxation without representation;" she addressed it specifically to women in their status as "wives, mothers, daughters, and sisters." The signatories include not only Abba herself, Louisa, and Anna, but also Lidian Emerson, Sophia Hawthorne, and eighty-seven other "Female Taxpayers of Concord."[27] Pasted beneath this declaration in Abba's journal is a handbill for the National Woman Suffrage Association with the names of William Lloyd Garrison, Julia Ward Howe, Elizabeth Blackwell, Lucy Stone, and Amos Bronson Alcott.

On her seventy-seventh birthday Abba Alcott penned her last words, a notation of "the coming of May's letter full of pleasant news."[28] Abba died a few days later.

May wrote repeatedly of her remorse at being so far away when her mother died, but she did not return. Instead she praised her sister and encouraged her to

> be grateful enough that *you* have been the one who could make dear Marmee, and Papa too, so comfortable and happy these last years by your generosity and devotion, for money has done what affection alone could never do, unromantic as it sounds to say so, and you have delighted in making us all happy in our own way tho' much of your own life and health has been sacrificed in doing it, and this I feel more perhaps than anybody.[29]

May went on with her work. "If mine can't be a happy domestic life . . . perhaps the Good God meant me for great things in other ways. . . . Perhaps this sacrifice I have freely chosen to make in losing one year of Marmee's life may make me work better."[30] In this fashion May manages to argue that the duties of work force her to sacrifice her responsibilities at home. One month later May had a new admirer in Ernest Nieriker, a handsome Swiss businessman, fourteen years younger than herself. Four months after Abba's death she married him.

Undoubtedly May was emotionally vulnerable in the months following her mother's death. But if one accepts the conviction in May's letters, she married Nieriker because she loved him. He fully encouraged her to keep working as a serious artist, and his family joined him in urging her to continue her career.

May wrote repeated invitations for Alcott to stay with them in Paris. Her sister would have loved to come, but May was pregnant in 1879, and Alcott feared that the household would have two women to care for if she went to visit the Nierikers. By some strange irony she recovered, while May died a few weeks after giving birth to Louisa May Nieriker. May had noted in her diary that her sister is "at the Bellevue writing her Art story in which some of my adventures will appear."[31]

The uncompleted romance of Diana and Persis is only four chapters long. In the first chapter we meet two female artists, Diana, a sculptor, and Persis, a painter. Both are orphans; they are also dear friends who encourage each other's work and share small pleasures. Resolved to study in Paris, Persis leaves Diana for a year, hoping for a rendezvous there to continue their life and work together. Fearing that the younger Persis, already a collector of male hearts, will find a lover abroad, Diana exacts a promise of fidelity. Persis says, "I will keep myself like a vestal virgin and keep the vow I make to my chosen goddess Diana."[32]

The second chapter provides descriptions of the artistic life led by young American women studying in Paris, which are almost direct copies of May's letters to her family. Persis's letters urge Diana to join her quickly. Diana is, however, hard at work, "no nun in her cell ever led a more austere and secluded life than this fine creature intent upon her self-appointed task."[33]

The course of the story then changes abruptly. In the next chapter it is evident that a long period of time has passed in which Persis marries and has a daughter. Diana longs to go and see her but restrains herself with "a certain proud yet sad conviction that she was no longer first and dearest" in her friend's heart. Then the impulse to be with her friend, and the curiosity to see the new domestic arrangement overtakes her and Diana goes to Paris.

She finds her friend seated in a small apartment and is welcomed by August, for whom Diana represents independence and the time to work at her art with few distractions.[34] Diana has already noted that the delightful apartment's studio is the only dusty room, with dried paint upon Persis's palette. The friends quickly restore their relationship, however, with August discreetly leaving them hours together to sketch and paint. The scene closes in a tantalizing fashion; August and Diana discuss art and politics with August insisting that a woman's life can be as full and free as a man's. Diana is clearly impressed with the marriage but hers is not the narrative voice. Louisa Alcott stands aside, allowing Diana to wonder "if she could be happy with a musical husband in a home like this," while Persis is "undecided between fish and cutlets," for the next day's dinner.[35]

In the final chapter of the unfinished romance, Diana is in Italy, thinking of Persis and imagining her "happy in the nest that filled so fast the mother bird had little time for friendship." Working hard, succeeding at her sculpture, but somewhat lonely, she meets little Nino. He is motherless and his father is a famous sculptor, an expatriate American named Antony Stafford. The widower admires Diana's work, particularly her statue of a mother and child: "I am glad a woman did that . . . because it is so strong. There is a virile force in this, accuracy as well as passion—in short—genius."[36] Diana notes that few men would say that to a woman, and the author adds, "The masculine fibre in her nature demanded recognition as it does in all strong natures and, having won it, she could permit the softer side of her character to assert itself without forming the accusation of weakness which she hated like a man."[36]

The story ends with the hint that Stafford and Diana may be "comrades." Stafford, impressed by Diana's strength and patient tenderness, is eager to help her. When he leaves her studio she is working on the arched head of a boy to which she adds a pair of winged shoulders, calling it Puck. But clearly Diana has chosen a single life.

THE WHITE MARMOREAN FLOCK

A larger history remains hidden behind this obviously personal story of the Alcott sisters. May had written a grateful description of the brave women artists who lived and studied abroad before her generation. Alcott in turn entitled one chapter of her story "Puck," a tribute to May's work and to Harriet Hosmer's sculpture of the same name. Years before, in one of her "stage struck" periods, she admired the great actress Charlotte Cushman. A visitor to the Alcott's home, Cushman was also a member of the Radical Club, and sent letters to the club when world-wide engagements kept her from regular attendance.[37] Cushman befriended Harriet Hosmer, the New England sculptress, and urged her to come to Rome. Hosmer had created the famous marble figure; copied many times, it also served as the motif for Hawthorne's novel, *The Marble Faun*.

How many levels of meaning attend Alcott's brief romance we shall never know. She knew about the Roman circle, of which Hosmer was a part,[38] and she debated the choice between companionship within the egalitarian marriage and spinsterhood with the tender ties of friendship. Given the circumstances of her own life and the relative ease of May's new opportunities, financial security, and status as the youngest of the family, one easily understands that Alcott might depend upon sisterhood and mistrust marriage a great deal more than May.

The years between 1846 and 1880 recorded a small but significant rise in the percentage of American women who never married. Louisa's birth cohort included about 6.5 percent of women who remained spinsters throughout their lives. By the immediate postwar period, girls born between 1866 and 1870 might have a 9.6 percent chance of remaining spinsters. The small rise remained a demographic fact until the late 1890s, when the upward curve reversed itself and dropped to a new low of 4.8 percent for the group born between 1921 and 1930.[39]

Historians have been hard pressed to explain this rise of spinsterhood in the late nineteenth century, but they have generally agreed with Daniel Scott Smith that "the numerically tiny majority who remained single had far larger historical significance than their numbers would suggest." Smith does not find the rise surprising in view of the "tides of the woman's movement."[40] Alcott's works and life experience enlarge the dimensions of such an observation. Certainly there were new educational and vocational opportunities for women and, as Alcott repeatedly noted and publicized, the opportunities were best seized by spinsters. Perhaps more important was the problem of reconciling domestic responsibilities, conventionally borne by women, with the desire for individual identity and achievement. A sense of self was highly prized by Romantic reformers; it was not abandoned in the shift to a more rationalist perspective.

May Alcott tried to solve the problem of marriage and female individuality by marrying later than most women, and by marrying an enlightened Swiss gentleman of means. She was outspoken in blaming her mother's lifelong problems on Bronson's stubborn if comfortable ignorance of the economic facts of everyday life. He took domestic comforts for granted when he had them, and praised his own simplicity of taste when times were hard. Alcott, however, agreed with May and her mother that financial independence made the woman problem easier to bear; she devoted most of her life to securing a "competence," thereby maximizing the choices available to her sisters, nephews, and niece. But this personal solution did not satisfy Alcott as a prescription for society. She went on to write *Jo's Boys*, developing Plumfield into Laurence University, a feminist utopia graced with cooperative housekeeping and coeducation. Dress and health reforms shared center stage with Greek, chemistry, and philosophy in her educational curriculum.

Moreover, Alcott argued that for many "the social influence was the better part of the training they received." Middle-class and genteel taste in dress, manners, and social and political values assured a single standard without violating the principle of individuality, at least in Alcott's view. She assumed that the greatest inequalities were the lack of opportunity to acquire refinement and taste, and the lack of independent means to dignify the humblest home with "a good picture or two hung on the walls," books, and flowers.

She presented a two-fold plan for reform. First, hungry young women could find the means to earn a decent living once they acquired a college education equal to that of young men. Women's success at academic studies would prove their fitness to hold jobs and occupy professions hitherto reserved to males. Second, "especial care was taken to fit them to play their parts worthily in the great republic which offered them wider opportunities and more serious duties."[41] They would become practical missionaries of the "social influence" acquired at college. If they could earn a decent living and acquire refined tastes and congenial friends, these young women would possess the essential requirements for freely choosing between egalitarian marriage or spinsterhood. Alcott's fictional plan was identical to that developed by the American Woman Suffrage Association.

FOURTEEN
The Social Influence

"The female population exceeds the male, you know, especially in New England, which accounts for the high state of culture we are in, perhaps," answered John.

"It is a merciful provision, my dears, for it takes three or four women to get each man into, through and out of the world. You are costly creatures, boys, and it is well that mothers, sisters, wives, and daughters love their duty and do it so well, or you would perish off the face of the earth," said Mrs. Jo solemnly.

Louisa May Alcott, *Jo's Boys*, chapter 1

The 1870s and 1880s witnessed a fresh challenge to woman's rights in the name of science. The notion of woman's limited mental ability, supposedly the evolutionary price for her specialized reproductive capacity, was a serious obstacle to women pressing for social equality. Alcott impatiently took up this challenge in the pages of *Eight Cousins, Rose in Bloom*, and *Jo's Boys*. Women's minds, she insisted, had every bit as much curiosity as men's; female anatomy, however biologically suited for procreation, presented no impediment to serious mental work.

Louisa May Alcott in 1873 wrote to Maria S. Porter defiantly asserting woman's right to the largest sphere:

In future let woman do whatever she can do; let men place no more impediments in the way; above all things let's have fair play—Let simple justice be done, say I. Let us hear no more of "women's sphere" either from our wise (?) legislators beneath the gilded dome, or from our clergymen in their pulpits. . . . Let woman find out her own limitations, and if, as is so confidently asserted, nature has defined her sphere, she will be guided accordingly—but in heaven's name give her a chance! . . . Then, and not until then, shall we be able to say what woman can do or what she cannot do, and coming generations will know and be able to define more clearly what is a "women's sphere" than these benighted men who now try to do it.[1]

Motives for the renewed differentiation between the sexes were complex, but clear enough to Alcott and her liberal contemporaries. Women were working outside their homes in ever greater numbers, and they were often played against men in the labor market. Middle-class women, both conservative and liberal, were uniting in serious campaigns to reform public life and public policy in the name of family welfare. Each new role played by women seemed to spur their sex on to greater demands for education, suffrage, and even equal pay for equal work.

Consequently, Dr. Edward Clarke, a popular science lecturer, drew the boundary line between sexes on Alcott's home ground, speaking at the New England Woman's Club of Boston in 1872.[2] He cited Darwin and Spencer, arguing that it was not so much that one sex was superior, but that the sexes were widely different. His arguments were elaborated in his book, *Sex in Education: Or a Fair Chance for the Girls.*[3] Men, he claimed, had evolved with a higher metabolic rate than women and a greater tendency to vary; hence they grew progressively stronger and more intelligent than women over time.[4] Because of their biological specificity (and consequently diminished capacity for variance) women were dependent upon men for protection. Motherhood therefore granted women a gentle immunity from the struggle of natural selection, but that same immunity also rendered women biologically unfit for the mental efforts that stimulated and developed man.

YOURS FOR REFORM OF ALL KINDS

Feminists replied to Clarke in the *Woman's Journal*, and Julia Ward Howe assembled a brilliant array of essays under the title *Sex and Education: A Reply to Dr. Clarke's "Sex in Education."*[5] Louisa May Alcott began her own refutation of Clarke's theses with the novel *Eight Cousins.* She wrote the first chapters on a farm in Conway, Massachusetts, during a summer holiday in 1874. Anna and her sons had accompanied her, and Alcott drew heavily on the boys' adventures as well as her own childhood recollections. At first she seems intent on creating another version of *Little Men* for *St. Nicholas*, the most successful and prestigious magazine for children in late nineteenth-century America.[6] But unlike *Little Men* the new serial focused on one particular heroine. Attacking the presumption of woman's innate fragility, it demonstrates that mental and physical strength are products of environment and education.

Rose Campbell, the sheltered rich orphan in Alcott's tale, joins an array of strong-minded girls depicted in *St. Nicholas* from the 1870s through the early twentieth century. The editor of this magazine, Mary Mapes Dodge, set a remarkable standard for young people's literature. She published the fiction of Rebecca Harding Davis, Sarah Orne Jewett, Helen Hunt Jackson, and Helen Stuart Campbell among others, as well as impressive nonfiction works. *Eight Cousins* appeared for twelve months in 1874 and 1875 among with reports of the Agassiz Club's naturalist projects and accounts of children's temperance union meetings.[7] These offerings were aimed directly at a middle-class audience, and though the tone was uniformly patriotic and genteel, the pervading message was that character is environmentally rather than biologically formed. This conviction enabled Alcott to claim woman's rights as a benefit for both the health of girls and the social welfare of America.

Rose arrives at the refined home of her Aunt Peace and Aunt Plenty, who cosset and spoil her. Her seven male Campbell cousins assume that Rose is delicate, which indeed she is at the start of the book.[8] Part of Rose's education involves learning (through the orphan maid Phoebe) how the other half lives. Her schooling also includes learning to cook and sew, because her remarkable Uncle Alec, a physician and her guardian, believes that all men and women should be self-reliant.

Doctor Alec Campbell must battle his fashionable sisters-in-law and his own spinster sisters to provide a sensible wardrobe and a healthy diet for his niece. He wins out and, with the aid of plenty of outdoor exercise, Rose's character, intelligence, and physical strength bloom harmoniously during the year-long educational experiment.

Phoebe the maid does not need lessons in domestic science, nor is her life lacking in physical exertion. But Rose finds that her "maid, friend, teacher" needs to learn to read and write. Realizing that her well-stocked library and her leisure for reading are unusual privileges, she sets out to share her knowledge and supplies with Phoebe. Finally Uncle Alec agrees to send Phoebe to school.

Rose continues to go on monthly sojourns to her cousins' homes as a missionary, where her efforts not only benefit them but help to improve her own character and physical health. Alcott's message is clear: true womanhood involves setting a civilized example to rude male savages; in turn, such cares strengthen and improve little women. Rose announces that she has learned what girls are made for—"to take care of boys."

ROSE IN BLOOM

Even in Concord Alcott found that "young American gentlemen, as well as farmers and mill hands," did a great deal of drinking. She expected it, she said, "among the Irish," but such dissolution among native-born Yankee men testified to the need for a wider social influence on the part of reformers. At Franklin and Louisa Sanborn's home she met regularly with Julia Ward Howe and William Torrey Harris, and at least once partook of tea with Walt Whitman.[9] Her network of intergenerational reformers stretched from Whitman, with his professed love of cold water baths and plain carpenter's dress, to the Woman's Congress at Syracuse, New York, where Julia Ward Howe led the "Battle Hymn of the Republic," and even to elegant New York City drawing rooms, where an international coterie of free religionists, actresses, writers, and charity organizers met regularly.

Between the publication of *Eight Cousins* and *Rose in Bloom*, Louisa Alcott learned the full range of this reformers' network. At Vassar College she listed her duties: "talk with four hundred girls, write in stacks of albums and schoolbooks, and kiss every one who asks me." Vassar students even formed a Little Women Club.[10] Their teacher, the astronomer Maria Mitchell, refused to give grades; she acknowledged her ties to Emerson and the Transcendental Circle: "You cannot mark a human mind because there is no intellectual unit."[11] Vice-president of the American Social Science Association, mature both intellectually and emotionally, Mitchell embodied Alcott's ideal of true womanhood.

In 1875, Mitchell offered an opening prayer from the platform of the Women's Congress at Syracuse.[12] Alcott, who hated making speeches, attended this conference and signed numerous autographs while listening carefully to the discussion of woman's issues. Temperance, coeducation, domestic science, suffrage, and the wrongs of poorly paid working women were represented and eloquently described. *Rose in Bloom* and *Jo's Boys* put these issues before a sympathetic middle-class audience.

Later she visited New York City, where she found the contrasts between rich and poor described at the woman's congress all too visible. Dressed in silks, she attended the opera and the theater, and found herself the honored guest of Sorosis, the most advanced and liberal women's club in the city. At one reception she found herself sharing guest-of-honor status 'with the young poet Oscar Wilde. Twenty-seven years old, he had just won the Newdigate Prize for English verse. Alcott met socially prominent people at the Frothinghams' and the Bottas', and also sampled the water cure and spartan diet of the Bath Hotel in lower New York. Thanksgiving Day found her sharing a carriage ride with her friend Sallie Holley, teacher and missionary to freedmen and women.[13]

On Christmas Day during the same trip to New York, Louisa visited the Tombs, a well-known home for newsboys, and Randalls Island Hospital. She helped give out toys and sweets to poor babies "born of want and sin" who suffered "every sort of deformity, disease, and pain."[14] The vivid contrast between fashionable drawing rooms and Randalls Island became the focus for *Rose in Bloom*. Alcott has her heroine, Rose Campbell, take up the causes of poor children, ill-paid working women, and temperance. Having been finished abroad on a grand tour with her Uncle Alec and Phoebe, Rose returns to exercise sweet influence on her seven male cousins. Stretched to its limits in this novel, the domestic sphere of influence collapses and Rose loses the sentimental power she held as a young girl. Her exemplary purity cannot save her Prince Charming— Charlie, the most dashing of the cousins—from the lures of alcohol and her self-denying philanthropy merely sets a sweet example.

Rose feels her own helplessness and is especially envious of Phoebe and her cousin Mac, the novel's most active, self-fulfilling characters. Rose's envy of talented busy people is the problem without a solution in this novel. Too properly educated in woman's rights and wrongs, Rose cannot be satisfied with a fashionable life. She determines to make philanthropy her career. She finances a home for distressed gentlewoman and does volunteer work in a hospital for orphans and poor children. Her good works prove tiresome and discouraging, however, her tenants complain, "things were neglected, waterpipes froze and burst, drains got out of order, yards were in a mess, rents behindhand."[15] Worst of all the adult recipients of Rose's charity are not grateful, and Uncle Alec has to remind his niece that a good conscience and not gratitude is her proper reward.

Alcott makes no secret of the limitations on a lady's good works. The death of the alcoholic Charlie, whom she deeply loved, does not provide a moral turning point for Rose. Instead it reenforces her powerlessness and her isolation. Rose's only real contact with the larger world is her briefly mentioned union with other reform-minded benevolent women.

The temperance message is very strong in *Rose in Bloom*. Louisa Alcott's own background included her father's enjoyment of New England hard cider, and the author herself admitted she liked a glass of champagne at fashionable New York suppers. Her temperance advocacy is nonetheless genuine; it was immoderate indulgence by members of their own class that led many liberal, sophisticated reformers to support temperance. A founder of the Concord Women's Temperance Society, Alcott linked that cause to woman's suffrage.[16]

Conservative church women, previously aloof to woman's rights activities, often became public activists in the Women's Crusade, the temperance organization which soon became the Women's Christian Temperance Union. Frances Willard, subsequently president of the WCTU, regarded alcohol as the single most important issue in persuading women of the helplessness of their sex to defend self and family. If women were dependent upon men as a natural consequence of biology, they were also helpless before the ruin visited upon them by intemperate men. Historian Barbara Epstein concludes further that "in the context of discussing men's drinking, it was possible for women to talk about their own isolation and loneliness." Moreover, "women could hardly object to their husbands' involvement in their work, since women's livelihood depended on it, but they could object to their husbands' socializing with other men in their free time. The saloon thus became a symbol for the larger issues of the exclusion of women and children from men's lives.[17]

Rose must come to terms with her own lack of talent and ambition. Ultimately she receives an orphaned baby girl from her cousin Mac who has rescued the child from abuse and neglect. Rose adopts the child, naming her Dulcinea, and a few months of kindness, food, and fresh air restore the little girl.

The point Alcott makes with this incident is that woman's rights and motherhood go hand in hand; Dr. Edward Clarke's books, ironically, help feminists to unite the two. Frances Willard in the 1870s, for example, argued that women needed suffrage in order to protect their homes from demon liquor.[18] Certainly there was opposition within the woman's temperance movement itself to Willard's firm linkage of woman's suffrage and temperance, but she and her allies persevered in making the connection. In 1879 Willard was elected president of the WCTU and remained in that office until her death. Alcott, who was committed somewhat contradictorily to both woman's special virtue and woman's natural rights, corresponded with President Willard.[19]

Rose must marry because a spinster heroine might prove Clarke's charge that education and full-time public service made women unfit for motherhood. Mac is determined to make her love him, and Rose, impressed with Mac's ability to do and get anything he wants, does. Rose accepts Mac's proposal because marrying him will give her something to do and a measure of emotional security. Rose blooms in the last rays of sentimental power; she must be content with having inspired a good man to become better.

Rose in Bloom led Roberts Brothers' list of juvenile sales for the centennial year, 1876. After all, it had a good love story, the publisher said, "the best she had done since *Little Women*." Its preoccupations with social problems annoyed some readers as was the case with *Eight Cousins*.[20]

Rose admittedly has no special talents; she does possess inherited money, which Alcott darkly intimates could only leave her prey to unscrupulous fortune hunters in the absence of a watchful, temperate mate and philanthropic endowments. Rose will have affectionate security if not the joys of a large family and household production. Genuine vocations are reserved to spinsters, a real choice that is offered in *Jo's Boys*. Alcott's fictional couples are companionable, if not passionate, and they reflect the demographic transformation in her own lifetime. The March women's progeny are limited to three children for Meg, two for Jo, and only one for Amy. *Jo's Boys* offers the full range of demographic changes nonetheless; each of the March women lives out a genuinely representative mid-nineteenth-century woman's life cycle.[21]

A SOCIAL WHOLE

Louisa May Alcott took seven years to finish the last of the March family chronicles, working on *Jo's Boys* only fitfully. She described herself as "the "tired historian on the March family" in the last chapter. From 1875 through 1885 her success brought a flood of invitations to appear at reform meetings, women's colleges, prisons, and refuges. Family responsibilities scarcely diminished either, although her stream of fiction assured the Alcotts of a comfortable living. Louisa and her sister Anna shared the care of Bronson, Anna's two sons, and Louisa May Nieriker, May's daughter. It seemed for a few years that Miss Alcott could be everywhere at once. Despite recurring lameness, severe headaches, and digestive problems, she was enjoying her hard-won success.

Bronson Alcott, Frank Sanborn, and Wiliam Torrey Harris, with the aid of Julia Ward Howe and Elizabeth Peabody among others, organized and taught the Concord School of Philosophy for several successive summers. When they proposed that Alcott write a biography of her father, she gently told Sanborn that he himself was better equipped to write the biography. Sanborn's lectures on the new social science, along with Julia Ward Howe's courses on the ancient and modern views of women, touched on Alcott's new concerns.[22] Bronson was now popularly known as the grandfather of the little women because his past eccentricities had been forgiven in the new national enthusiasm for institutional reforms. Unquestionably Bronson enjoyed his daughter's success and, even more, they both took pleasure in his later career as an educational ambassador to the West where he included Alcott family anecdotes in his lectures.

William Torrey Harris thoroughly reconstructed Bronson Alcott and his philosophy for the new order. Once, Harris claimed, Bronson had "broken himself against the old order of things." Like John Brown, Garrison, and Theodore Parker, Bronson Alcott had been a heroic moral censor, braving the disapproval of the mobs. Harris argued, on the basis of long conversations with his mentor, that the founder of Fruitlands had been converted by his family after the failure of that experiment; his later career was marked by "a growing compromise with things as they are." Now Bronson was sympathetic with the "spirit of progress, which is more or less outspoken belief in evolution."[23] Clinging to his idealism, Bronson Alcott saw evolution as the spiritual development of all mankind, accompanied by great material advancement.

Newly converted to the industrial age, Bronson Alcott now saw socialism, in all its forms, as a reversion to more primitive types of human development. History, he claimed, witnessed a steady upward march from the family (the most natural social unit) to village, feudal manor, and finally to the highest stage of civilization, "free industrial competition, free suffrage and representative government."[24] Mechanical inventions were helping man to recover his lapsed omnipotence in nature; relieved of earning his bread by the sweat of his brow, man could at last achieve spiritual perfection. Moreover this glorious promise was now close to democratic realization. Wealth, Bronson assumed, was now more diffused, "capitalists holding kings and presidents in check while playing the better game of civilization." Criminals were being cured as well as punished and "all things are undergoing reform and reconstruction . . . laying broad and deep the foundations of new institutions."[25] Such institutions, which Louisa Alcott described in *Work* and *Jo's Boys*, included prisons, shelters, churches, schools, and hospitals. She signed herself "Yours for reform of all kinds" in letters to the *Woman's Journal* and wondered, "why discuss the unknowable till our poor are fed and the wicked saved."[26]

Alcott could not have repeated the simple landscape of *Little Women* in her last March story, and did not try. She knew that the "walking city" of Jo's girlhood was gone, taken over by the street-car.[27] The direct personal charity she depicted earlier was also impossible. Large numbers of Irish and German Catholic immigrants had changed the image and cultural life of northeastern cities. Many genteel residents were frightened by the possibilities of engulfment in the immigrant tide; after all, there was a decline in the native-born birth rate, a proportionately higher immigrant fertility rate, and a doubling of American divorce rates between 1870 and 1890.

The leaders of American reconstruction still believed, along with the Alcotts, that a "social whole" in which "each helps all and all help each" was possible. They conceived of society as one physical organism, not unlike the human body, with each class and sex interdependent in its functions. Individuality would be respected; as William Torrey Harris interpreted Bronson Alcott, "Respect for the self activity of others is necessary, or else the individual ego will collide with all other egos, and they will make common cause against him, and thus return on him his own negative deeds."[28] The individual "will" was now socially related; indeed, only social activity could preserve one's reason. Institutions were necessary not only to educate children and immigrants and to reform criminals, but also to readjust those individuals gone mad through social isolation or denial of organic symmetry and interdependence.

Education was now women's work.[29] The old faith in an individual's ability to earn a living and rise to a better class had to be restored, Alcott felt, and taught to poor people, immigrants, freedmen, and women. All these classes were suspicious of gentry. Mutual mistrust, in turn, prevented orderly progress through economic and geographic expansion. "True relations with each other" were needed, and Alcott insisted that working people were eager for light, "ready to be led if some one would only show a possible way."[30] The Civil War experience demonstrated that it was possible to organize vast numbers of citizens; Alcott's own group had mobilized a million and a half men and vast supplies in behalf of the Union. After the war, her set prospered along with the new middle class. The new educators, including many of the old "radicals" such as Bronson Alcott and his daughter, believed in economic expansion and social influence as progressive partners.

The expansion of territory and industry on a national scale was linked to the expansion of reform institutions in both Alcott's life and fiction, particularly in her later novels. Samuel Sewall, Abba's cousin, chose to invest Louisa's earnings in railroad stocks and other "sure" securities after the war.[31] In view of the vast expansion of track from 35,000 miles at the start of the war to 70,000 by 1875 and 166,700 miles fifteen years later, Sewall was not risking Alcott's savings by his choice of investments.[32] In retrospect, however, these investments embody contradictions that seem to have escaped the reformers. Alcott, for instance, was genuinely and deeply sympathetic with the plight of American Indians forced off their lands; she enthusiastically endorsed Helen Hunt's novel, *Ramona*, a romantic indictment of settlers and governments for stealing Indian homelands.[33] *Jo's Boys* takes up the plight of Montana tribes, yet manages to present Western lands as the just spoils of manifest destiny, a white man's paradise of cheap land and social mobility.

The railroads brought white settlements West and, helped by the Homestead Act of 1862, railroads and settlers drove the Indian tribes out. Western farmers subsequently depended upon railroads as carriers of grain and beef to market. By the end of Alcott's life, railroads were locked in bitter conflict with small farmers and shippers who could not compete in markets dominated by monopolistic and unequal freight charges. In the decade following *An Old-Fashioned Girl* and *Jo's Boys*, populists began to demand regulation of railroad charges and an end to corporate control of markets.[34]

Alcott's ideal in the last twenty years of her life was to make bourgeois entrepreneurship a genuine possibility for all Americans. At the same time she was critical of money making and cities full of "temptations with nothing to do but waste time, money and health." Her notion of the safeguards against individual corruption were still "good principles, refined tastes, and a wise mother."[35] Some people were lucky enough to be born with all three; for the others she was willing to provide both public and private institutions to act in loco parentis.

THE BRAVE AND THE STRONG: *JO'S BOYS*

The tamers of the West, healers of the sick, and missionaries to the poor are being trained and sent forth from Laurence University.

There the March women with their husbands and children live and work together again, ten years after the last chapter of *Little Women*. Three houses—Plumfield (still inhabited by Fritz, Jo, and their children), Parnassus (a new mansion inhabited by Amy, Laurie, and Bess), and the Dovecote (a replica of Meg and John's cottage)—stand on the grounds of Aunt March's old estate. Endowed by Mr. Laurence's will, the school has become a university in *Jo's Boys*.

In *Little Men* Mr. March suggested that a small family experiment could serve as a model for society. By 1886, after firmly rejecting both the family and the utopian colony as practical agents for solving social problems, Alcott created a college community with Fritz Bhaer as president, Mr. March as chaplain, and Jo as surrogate mother and home missionary.

The young institution had not yet made its rules as fixed as the laws of the Medes and Persians, and believed so heartily in the right of all sex, colors, creeds, and ranks to education, that there was room for everyone who knocked, and a welcome to the shabby youths from up country, the eager girls from the West, the awkward freedman or woman from the South, or the well born student whose poverty made this college a possibility when other doors were barred. There was still prejudice, ridicule, neglect in high places, and the prophecies of failure to contend with, but the Faculty was composed of cheerful, hopeful men and women who had seen greater reforms spring from smaller roots and after stormy seasons blossom beautifully, to add prosperity and honor to the nation.[36]

Many reformers argued that only a coeducational environment would produce household democracies, and a virtuous republic. And not surprisingly, coeducation was decried by Alcott's reviewers. One critic came directly to the point: "The book is apparently intended to champion co-education, the uninterrupted acquaintance of boys and girls in their everyday life and a good comrade sort of marriage." He reminded the American public that marriage was not supposed to be based on either equality or romantic love, but on a "dignified and holy relation which brings sweetness and self-sacrifice to a woman's life."[37]

The dangers of Alcott's scheme were evident to another reviewer, who foresaw that young women might demand more than a passive role in family decision making, not to mention in society at large. Girls should be taught to respect and obey their future husbands, not to argue or challenge their supremacy:

> We would add that while co-education needs no advocate at this day, it might be possible to look for a co-educational institution where the ordinary rules of good breeding are as little observed as among these students of "Laurence College." In our opinion, no respectable boy would stand some of the abuse which several of these boys receive from their high spirited girl friends.[38]

What the reviewer saw as "abuse" the author saw as healthy signs of the new woman.

LONG-HAIRED MEN AND SHORT-HAIRED WOMEN

Nan Harding is just the sort of "spirited girl friend" Alcott presents as the model for a new woman. Nan represents what Alcott called "a third class of ambitious girls." They were a mixed group. Some "hardly knew what they wanted, but were hungry for whatever could fit them to face the world and earn a living, being driven by necessity, the urgency of some half conscious talent, or the restlessness of strong young natures to break away from the narrow life which no longer satisfied."[39]

Plumfield's coeducational experiment in *Little Men* sowed the seeds for the adult women's challenge to male dominance at Laurence University, the setting of *Jo's Boys*. In *Jo's Boys* Nan is a physician and "the pride of the community." She is also Alcott's ideal American Girl—handsome, "with a fresh color, clear eye, quick smile, and the self-poised look young women with a purpose always have."[40] She easily outwalks her old suitor Tommy Bangs, and leaves him behind in their medical studies as well.

The coeds who flock to the weekly sewing circle are given a new woman's education in just such possibilities. In a chapter called "Among the Maids," a happy sisterhood passes on domestic skills and reform literature along with genteel hints on health, dress, and deportment. Alcott seemed, at last, to have harmonized her personal and political perspective. Her new generation of girls notes that "old maids aren't sneered at half as much as they used to be, since some of them have grown famous and proved that woman isn't half but a whole being and can stand alone."⁴¹ Nevertheless, traditional family life still offered the only "tender ties" allowable in conventional society. Work, social life, and ultimately security were shaped by the sexual division of labor. Coeducation challenged that division, and by implication it then challenged the right of one social unit, the conjugal family, to stand as the only basis for social harmony and progress.

Jo's Boys's challenge to the conjugal family as the only home for a woman is clear. Educated spinsters can now do useful work in the largest sphere and make homes for themselves. Elizabeth Keyser, a modern literary scholar, is correct however in seeing through the novel's smooth resolution of sexual conflicts: "The real conflict," she argues, in March novels, "is never between love and self-sacrificing duty but instead, between love and self-sacrificing duty on the one hand, and self-fulfillment through vocation on the other."⁴² Nan's example is simple: she is thankful that her profession will enable her to be both independent and happy. She is not tempted by man or woman to passionate, personal involvement. Cool, skillful, she trembles only at the thought of injuries or illness beyond her professional expertise. Jo, however, in this last March novel, is strangely conflicted about her own past decisions and about settling the personal lives of her boys and girls.

Talking about the "superfluous" single women in New England, Jo jokes with the Plumfield set about how many women it takes to care for one man. And then, in the same scene, she wonders if she has missed her true vocation, musing about the possibilities of spinsterhood for herself. It is only a fleeting thought sandwiched in between expressing pride in Nan's useful spinsterhood and darning a large ragged blue sock, the emblem of her own maternal cares. Ted hugs his mother, effectively smothering her treacherous yearning for freedom. Then when Emil offers to take Aunt Jo to sea, as his mate, sailing round the world on the adventures she always longed to have, Jo admits that marriage and motherhood have not tamed her spirit.

Despite her matronly disguises, Jo's famous distaste for cooking, fine clothes, and the chores of entertaining guests has not changed a bit since *Little Women* and *Little Men*. And she continues to act in plays and to write. There are two plays authored and produced by Jo in *Jo's Boys*. The first production, "Owlsdark Marbles," satirizes the gods and goddesses of Parnassus. Jo depicts herself as a marble statue. "Mrs. Juno" is roasted by her husband, who alludes to her domestic ill-temper, jealousy, sharp tongue, and inclination to bossiness. He does praise her warm heart and peace-making inclinations as well. Jo, after the performance, resolves to curb her temper and her critical tongue—familiar resolutions to readers of Alcott's novels.

The second play in the novel is a domestic drama about a country widow and her wayward children. Meg March Brooke, the widow, turns out to be the star. Playwright-producer Jo insists, "I'm tired of love-sick girls and runaway wives. We'll prove that there's romance in old women also."[42] Historian Karen Halttunen wisely observes that in *Jo's Boys* "Louisa May Alcott was suggesting that domestic drama might prove the instrument for bringing true domesticity to the entire nation."[43] Alcott's theatricals present her own conflicts as well and what she perceives to be the social boundaries of desire.

Jo March Bhaer writes for a living in this novel, calling herself a "literary nursery-maid who provides moral pap for the young," in comparison with Emerson and Whittier, whose time is worth more than money. Jo's chief problem as a famous writer is avoiding enthusiastic fans who confuse the author with her heroine. Still more disturbing, Jo no longer hopes to write a really "good" book. Harassed by deadlines for her money-making serials, she dreams of escape trips around the world in company with her boys.

Dan Keane, the boy whose origins are largely unknown, presents the most compelling dilemma of the novel. Danger is surely an intrinsic quality of romantic love and Dan is a passionate, dangerous hero in search of transcendance. Constantly described as hungry, searching, questing for something, after his prison experience, he is "ready to learn and that's something."[44] Alcott frees him to die fighting to save Montana Indians. In the romantic tradition, Dan, despite any real flaws save his passion for justice and his love of a marble statue, is best exiled beyond the frontiers of ordered, passion-less society. There is no heroine to match him in *Jo's Boys*. Jo herself is safe, matronly—all she can do is mother her bad boy and accept his exile and death.

VIRTUOUS ANCESTORS

Laurence College makes spinsterhood a viable choice, and it pro-vokes women to demand egalitarian marriage, making *Jo's Boys* very interesting for its time. Even more important, despite its acceptance of a single standard of middle-class morality and taste, the book presents women who are willing to criticize free enterprise as the means of life. No longer hostages to fortune, women want men to free themselves too.

Meg Brooke, the most dependent and "housewifely" little woman (she moved to Laurence University after being widowed), objects to her son choosing bookkeeping as his profession. In *Little Men* John Brooke died revered by all who knew him for being conscientious and above reproach in all things. His widow wants something better for her son, demanding social mobility and some restoration of entre-preneurial opportunities.

Louisa May Alcott never resolves contradictions between Roman-tic individuality and the standardized shaping and control of "all sex, colors, creeds and ranks" inherent in rational feminist reform ef-forts.[45] If society was truly one social organism, she imagined that it resembled her friends in the "regular anti-slavery set." After all, a "long line of virtuous ancestors," as she called them, were everyone's "founding fathers" by right of acculturation. The opportunity to acquire that culture and its values was a right she championed for all Americans.

Great fortunes in the hands of old families are a mainstay of Laurence University. Theodore Laurence, having outgrown his vul-gar college-boy pranks, now dedicates himself to helping worthy, impoverished students. They all want to dress like the Laurences and appreciate art and music just as their patrons do. Amy and Meg, in particular, provide advice on making over coeds' bright green or pink silk gowns with demure muslin over-layers, trimming them with suitable fresh flowers. When Laurie says to Jo, "Come and have a dish of tea, old dear, and see what the young folks are about," the contemporary reader of *Jo's Boys* is reassured that progress and reform are in capable hands.[46]

Nevertheless, Jo does not relinquish her old belief in the sanctity and privacy of each individual soul. Her system of "conscience books" is put aside once the little men and women have grown up, but she still chooses private moments to have missionary chats with each errant young student. In a conversation with one coed, she admits to preferring Charlotte Brontë over George Eliot because "the brain is there" in Eliot, but the "heart is left out."[47] The key to her preference is more fully expressed in the novel she wrote in 1877, *A Modern Mephistopheles*, wherein a self-sacrificing heroine reasserts the romantic message of *The Scarlet Letter*. The unpardonable sin is still a "want of love and reverence for the human soul, which makes a man pry into its mysterious depths, not with a hope or purpose of making it better, but from a cold philosophical curiosity."[48]

The possibility of separating intellect from feeling is Alcott's only problem with the new social sciences, one she solves by placing Jo Bhaer among the maids at Laurence. Jo's notion of household democracy expands with utter self-confidence into social housekeeping. Theodore Parker's vision is fully realized at Plumfield, but it is not technology which frees the little women. Jo's earnings buy security for the whole family, and together with the Laurence endowment, help create a cooperative domesticity involving all three houses.

The story ends happily enough, with the various children growing up well. Young Nat eventually becomes a modest success and thereby wins Daisy, the most exemplary homebody in all of American fiction; it seems obvious that he will never stray far from Meg Brooke's careful monitoring. Unhappy unions in Alcott's fiction usually result from an attempt to unite a woman with a suitor of lesser social standing. A young woman might marry upward, as Phoebe did in *Eight Cousins* and *Rose in Bloom*, but only after her character was proven by hard work. Moreover, Alcott's socially mobile young women are miraculously adopted by the families they marry into before romance blooms—characters of lesser origins must become fictive kin before wedlock. Old-fashioned girls with genteel backgrounds may marry monied men with little problem. It is precisely

their lack of wealth and fashionable lifestyle that fits these
gentlewomen for the task of domestic reform.

PROFITS AND PLEASURES

Charity, even when profered by the most genteel, tenderhearted
philanthropists, was not enough for the "deserving" poor in Alcott's
later fiction. She tentatively explored the social conditions for self-
reliance in a diverse, industrial society. "Mountain Laurel and Maidenhair," a story included in *A Garland for Girls* (1888), typically blends
Transcendental themes with a social science analysis of society.[49]
The plot centers around a developing friendship between two girls.
Emily, the dainty daughter of wealthy city-folk, is "tuckered out
doing nothing," while Becky Moore, a sturdy "red-haired freckle-
faced" country girl, has boundless energy despite a full workload of
farm and family chores. Emily is taken in by Becky's mother to continue her lifelong recuperation from leisure. The two girls discover a
mutual interest in literature as Emily develops a hunger for farm food
in the fresh country air.

Alcott invokes the natural environment itself as a teacher for Emily, and she soon ventures out into the fresh air. The Moore family is
busy at chores, including a market garden, chickens, butter-making,
strawberry picking and the cooking of meals for five paying guests.
Gradually Emily discovers that her friend not only reads and recites
poetry, but writes it too, in between cooking, weaving carpets, and
teaching in the local school.

Discovering one of Becky's poems, "Mountain Laurel," Emily
fancies a brilliant and well-paid career for her friend and herself, but
it is another summer visitor, a wealthy and practical widow who was
once a country girl herself, who presents a way for the Moores to
keep their farm. Unlike "Eli's Education," this story argues that a
widow and her daughters can be self-supporting.

There are some interesting turns to Emersonian theories of nature
and democracy in this late nineteenth-century story. The mountain
laurel is a sturdy flower, like Becky herself, but the delicate maidenhair fern will not grow as luxuriantly in the wild as it does in Emily's
greenhouse. Becky has transplanted the ferns, from "nooks on the

274

mountain hidden under the taller ferns and in sly corners." The laurel, however, will not thrive in a greenhouse, and Becky warns Emily to leave the bushes alone and enjoy them in the country.

The female reformers in the story believe that the laws of progress derive from empirical relationships in the real world. These women are not planting a new Eden based on self-culture and denial of material abundance. On the contrary, one young woman strengthens another with mouth-watering meals, and a female-headed family stays together by shipping strawberries and asparagus to market on the railroad.

All the heroines in *A Garland for Girls* are like the "May flowers," Alcott writes, who "being Boston girls, of course got up a club for mental improvement and, as they were all descendents of the Pilgrim Fathers, they called it the May Flower Club."[50] The less well-to-do young women work for a living at teaching, sewing, even fishmongering. Becky Moore, however, the most advanced of these new little women, remains a happy spinster, helping out at home until the younger children are able to manage the farm. Then she turns to teaching in which there was both profit and pleasure.

DOMESTICITY AND FEMINISM

Only one young man in Alcott's later fiction actually cooks, overturning the domestic hierarchy of *Little Women* and *Little Men*. "Letty's Tramp" is really a foundry watchman and a poor orphaned sewing girl finds a friend in him.[51] Joe offers her shelter from a storm, a pallet by his fire, hot coffee, and a sandwich. The author knows that a working girl needs the stimulant that only overexcites a lady of leisure in *Eight Cousins*. Joe cooks Letty's supper and shares his breakfast with her next morning and then he finds work for her after learning that the putting-out system pays Letty only six cents for each shirt she sews. Deciding to reject the products of sweat labor, he orders a bale of red flannel and stakes Letty to a small shirtmaking business, the finished products to be sold to his fellow foundrymen. Jo and Letty marry eventually but we never learn if he continues to make coffee and sandwiches.

Alcott steadily moves from identifying the woman problem

through all the strategic solutions offered in her time. *Moods* presented a large class of women identified as a "sad sisterhood," forced by unfortunate circumstances into the world. *Work* expanded on their trials and sufferings in a hostile world. *Little Women*, in turn, gave domestic reformers an opportunity to demonstrate the possibilities for women in democratic households. Alcott later reached toward enlarged institutions to reproduce the March family's mutual sacrifice. *Little Men* began a coeducational experiment in cooperative democracy. Then, in the uncompleted *Diana and Persis*, Alcott expresses her suspicion that a private domestic solution to the woman problem is not possible. Even at Laurence University, in *Jo's Boys*, the true union of domesticity and feminism is incomplete. Jo herself is free to write and supervise community morality, but her domestic freedom depends upon the excellent money she earns; her husband, moreover, never challenges her household authority. Even earning a living and having an agreeable, almost invisible spouse is not enough; Jo's liberty also depends upon domestic help from various sources, including her own paid household staff.

The March sisters and their progeny at Laurence University never really yield control of their lives to anyone. It is not even clear that children of the March family attend classes there. The college really exists for those who lack family, wealth, or social influence to place them comfortably in the world. The March sons and daughters find their way in that world through a network of family and friends, with only vague references to college educations. Laurence, then, is a vehicle for presenting the feminist demand for coeducation in a pleasing, comfortable way. It is also Alcott's means of reassuring her public about new reformist institutions. Like *Little Women*, *Little Men*, and *An Old-Fashioned Girl*, the final March novel tries to make social change seem like old, familiar history.

Little Women has a timeless resonance which reflects Alcott's grasp of her historical framework in the 1860s. The novel's ideas do not intrude themselves upon the reader because the author is wholly in control of the implications of her imaginative structure. Sexual equality is the salvation of marriage and the family; democratic relationships make happy endings. This is the unifying imaginative frame of *Little Women* which then expands into *Little Men* and bravely attempts to work itself out as historical law in *Jo's Boys*.

The last effort fails, but Alcott is in good company. The progressive social imagination embodied in the utopian works of Twain, Howells, and Gilman (only a few years after *Jo's Boys*) accepted human nature as constant, but posited history as advancing toward ideal freedom. The inherent contradictions of this position troubled all utopian writers, perhaps Alcott most of all. She made her choice after the Civil War in favor of the progressive framework, but its concepts never fully live in the fictional worlds she created. Also, despite her romantic belief in conflict as the source of creativity, she feared the radical implications of conflict after the war.

It was not enthusiasm that frightened her. Alcott was on the side of Anne Hutchinson and Hester Prynne; it was time to realize the brave new relationship between the sexes prophesied in *The Scarlet Letter*. By the 1880s, that new relationship was as contradictory in her own work as it was in the woman's rights movement itself. She insisted on the full human status of her heroines while also claiming that women must play a major role in society because of their capacity of nurturance. Daisy exercised that gift traditionally by caring for her extended family, while Nan demonstrated her womanly nature by becoming a woman's physician and healing the members of her own sex. Both heroines, of course, deserve suffrage, and therefore the right-minded heroes in *Jo's Boys* support their claim.

Sexual segregation permitted Harvard's President Charles W. Eliot to claim that "the world knows next to nothing about the natural mental capacities of the female sex."[52] Alcott therefore insisted that coeducation was the best method of teaching one sex about the capacities of the other. Having made a strong case for woman's natural rights, Alcott then admits a fear that girls, overly protected in youth, might lack the aggressiveness necessary in traditionally masculine territory. She recognized the intellectual and physical skills alone were not enough, and notes in *Rose in Bloom* that "we do our duty better by the boys . . . the poor little women are seldom provided with any armor worth having; and, sooner or later, they are sure to need it, for every one must fight her own battle, and only the brave and strong can win."[53]

In order to reform society, women must have some means of maintaining their own sense of idealism and mutual sacrifice in a coeducational world. The March sisters therefore re-create the old sewing circle, passing on the little women's spirit of egalitarian domesticity to a new generation of coeds who might otherwise succomb totally to male values, and consequently reject the domestic habits that link them to ordinary women outside the university community. Women, Alcott arges, will not remake the world by becoming just like men. Both sexes are united in the old familiar way at the close of *Jo's Boys* when Nat plays the street melody he gave them the first night he came to Plumfield. All of the others remember it and join in singing about a longing for home and family. Alcott's longing for the good old days unconsciously reenforces the patriarchy she is vigorously scouring away in *Jo's Boys*.

ANCESTORS AND IMMIGRANTS

Next to civil war, the conflict Alcott and her friends feared most was brewing in the struggles of immigrants, freedmen, women, industrial workers, and angry small farmers. These groups constituted growing numbers that would become a majority in the United States. True, progressivism at its most rigorous argues that "The Law is Progress: The Result Democracy."[54] But for Alcott a popular victory was cause for celebration only when the victors were familiar native stock whose leaders were of unquestioned good breeding and reputation, such as her friends.

When late nineteenth-century American society expanded beyond the communal myth of the March cottage, Louisa Alcott shifted her perspective uneasily. The primacy of biology over culture, an idea which had never really been defeated by antebellum reformers, made a strong comeback in reaction to the woman's rights movement. Combatting this resurgence strengthened Alcott's conviction that no inherent differences existed between races and ethnic groups either. If environment actually shaped human behavior, then she and her set were more determined than ever to provide a single national culture fashioned in their own image. They generally assumed that their own dominance was the result of social laws beyond individual control, thereby absolving themselves from responsibility for institutionalizing poverty, racial and sexual discrimination, and the virtual annihilation of American Indian tribal life. Much of the injustice seemed a regrettable by-product of progress; ultimately there would be abundance for all. They counted upon social influence to blend Americans within a balanced society. In *Jo's Boys*, for instance, Alcott tries to accept the social structure around her as given.

She never questioned its historical origins. Believing that her beloved band of reformers had fought for progress, she found it hard to question their achievement. Indeed, there had been great changes: the emancipation of slaves was the greatest of all victories. Alcott deliberately used the old antislavery language in 1885, telling Lucy Stone, "After a fifty year acquaintance with the noble men and women of the anti-slavery cause, the sight of the glorious end to their faithful work, I should be a traitor to all I most love, honor and desire to imitate, if I did not covet a place among those who are giving their lives to the emancipation of the white slaves of America."[55]

Although they defend social stability, Alcott's last works also attempt to persuade readers to accept and advance social change. That there were contradictions between democratic ideals and social reality, Alcott never denied. She had lived through a period of extraordinary social ferment. Like many of her circle, including Harris, Sanborn, Cheney, Abba May, and Julia Ward Howe, she was less fearful of destroying the individual than she was of civil war. In any case, molding society into line with the values already held by her set seemed more or less the natural working out of Providence—with a little help from the "best people." Alcott never forgot the examples of Henry David Thoreau, Frank Sanborn, and John Brown. Once she had fiercely supported the effort to arm slaves against their masters, knowing that ownership of human beings is the worst example of property rights. Similarly, she thought that good people would refuse to accept the degradation and exploitation of their fellow human beings after emancipation.

Social roles now seemed to have some intrinsic merit. In Alcott's earlier fiction, stepping out of a role allowed her heroines to see society more truly—as Jo does when she stomps around in unlaced boots uttering rather mild boyish slang. But Jo's role-swapping did not change society. In *Jo's Boys*, her namesake Josie does not need to pretend at being a boy. A modern girl, never outside her role, she plays tennis in comfortable clothes, swims and dives like a porpoise, and insists on acting as a profession, not as a mere vent for pent-up feelings. Women's social role had indeed changed between 1868 and 1885, and the "great changes" are evident in the hope Alcott holds out to a generation of coeds at Laurence University.

From a nineteenth-century woman's rights perspective, women needed a social structure to replace the code of laissez-faire individualism. They could not desert that culture and light out to the territories as does Dan (the closest hero to Huck Finn in Alcott's work). Alcott, moreover, does not set her utopia backward, as Twain does in *A Connecticut Yankee in King Arthur's Court* (1889), or forward as Bellamy does in *Looking Backward* (1888). If her society at Laurence University somewhat resembles that in Charlotte Perkins Gilman's *Herland* (1915), Alcott does not remove men from utopia to achieve social harmony and rational planning.

Jo's Boys is set in Alcott's last historical moment. It chronicles the gains made in her lifetime, but gathers them up into one great cornucopia at Plumfield. There her readers may observe the scattered gains already integrated into a social system. Young men and women have a free, open relationship with one another. They eat healthily, exercise, and work hard in anticipation of happy useful lives. Their education and talent is dedicated to social welfare. Only indolent, dull sons of wealth loll at Harvard with no important plans for the future; Alcott intimates that they will be superfluous in the new order.

There are moments of nostalgia in *Jo's Boys*, but they are for former days of adversity. Moreover, the poor young people at Laurence acquiesce too easily to advice about patience, hard work, and dressmaking. Alcott has not lost her feeling for youth—Dan's plight is evocative of brave John Sulie in *Hospital Sketches*—but somehow the new little women seem a tame group. It is as if life lies outside the gates of utopia. The ragged children who wander in and out of stories in *St. Nicholas* and the collected tales of *Aunt Jo's Scrap Bag*, for example, have the warm spark of Alcott's earliest heroes and heroines. Her later men and women have benefited greatly from the earlier band's efforts and they do care about the ragged children and working men and women. Alcott never quite saw the world she imagined in *Jo's Boys* and she could not portray it as reality. To the end, a "cry for bread and hunger for home" was the woman problem as she knew it.

EPILOGUE

On September 19, 1880, Louisa Alcott welcomed her niece and namesake Louisa May Nieriker to Boston. "Miss Alcott's baby" filled the last years of her life with the everyday pleasures and trials of motherhood. It was a new world for her, one in which she told stories, kissed hurts, and escaped occasionally to the Bellevue, where she maintained her traditional, separate "writing room." Maternal feelings now linked Alcott comfortably to women friends—she wrote to Betsey William, "My poppet is a picture of health, vigor and delightful naughtiness."[56]

Alcott's financial success enabled her family to rent a succession of comfortable mansions in Boston and to keep up Anna's "Thoreau House" as their stable Concord home. Louisa adopted John Pratt so Anna's elder son could file for royalties from her fiction after she died. She made a will, precise enough to satisfy the most conservative May spirit. Her own ill health and a terrible awareness of the Concord circle's passing led her to these precautions. Emerson died in 1882, and then Wendell Phillips too was gone. With Frank Sanborn, Alcott edited a new edition of Theodore Parker's prayers as a memorial to the old antislavery set.[57]

In the fall the Alcotts sold Orchard House to William Torrey Harris; it seemed right to pass on reform headquarters to one of Bronson's disciples. Then Bronson was paralyzed by a stroke. Rushing back to Concord, Alcott joined Anna and a team of nurses and doctors in caring for him. He recovered, and although never fully his old self, he could nevertheless sit through sessions of his Concord School of Philosophy on warm summer afternoons.[58] Alcott migrated back and forth between Concord and a summer cottage at Nonquitt, New York, or Boston.[59]

Alcott did not much care for her status as a public figure, but she loved to hear that "the books go well" because the doctors insisted she limit her writing to two hours a day. Her fears of financial distress alternated with periods in which she accepted her increasing fragility. Finally she retreated to a nursing home owned by Dr. Rhoda Lawrence, her friend and a homeopathic physician. Dr. Lawrence supervised a diet of milk, rest, and regular massage. For a while, even after a twenty-five-pound weight loss, it seemed that she might be cured. She went on a final holiday with Dr. Lawrence to New Hampshire, where the mountains looked down over the old experiment at Fruitlands. But her list of symptoms, painfully recorded in a red-leather diary, were irreversible.[60]

Alcott was apparently a lingering casualty of the Civil War. Calomel, mercurous chloride, is not normally expelled from the body. Unless taken with saline laxatives, it accumulates through successive doses. The doctors who used calomel to treat typhoid in Alcott's lifetime often seemed indifferent whether or not the drug was administered with a laxative. Her symptoms, which included weakness, fatigue, loss of appetite, weight loss, sore throats, tremors, and lameness all point to slowly incapacitating mercury poisoning.[61]

On March 1, 1888, she drove in a carriage to see Bronson, who was seriously ill at the family's rented house on Louisburg Square. It was cold, and Louisa was carefully wrapped in a fur cloak. Bronson could only murmur, "I am going up, come with me." Hurrying back to her own sickbed, the daughter he called "duty's faithful child" left off her warm wrap. Chilled, weakened, and grieving, she sank into a fever. On March 6, two days after her father's death, Louisa May Alcott died in her sleep at the age of fifty-six.[62]

In 1889 Roberts Brothers brought out a posthumous volume containing two early Alcott romances, *A Modern Mephistopheles* and *A Whisper in the Dark*. Both are treatments of romantic sexual conflict; each heroine resists possession of her soul by a more dominant masculine will. In the "modern" version of Faust, an innocent girl, Gladys, marries a handsome young poet who owes his fame and fortune to a wealthy diabolic genius, Helwyze. Unknown to Gladys, her husband's poetry is really written by Helwyze, who has arranged her marriage to Felix Canaris, the young poet, only because he wants them both under his roof where he can enjoy Gladys's fresh beauty. She almost succumbs to the evil man after he tricks her into taking hashish one night, but her true love for Felix (the young poet) is strong enough to prevent seduction. In the end her unhappy husband confesses his awful debt to Helwyze, and is freed at the cost of Gladys's life. She dies in childbirth, escaping both men.

Madeleine Stern has suggested that success prevented Louisa Alcott from writing any more of the passionate tales exemplified by *A Whisper in the Dark*. Sybil's voice, never acknowledged as Alcott's own in her lifetime, nevertheless reverberates across the years. Under the gold-leaf title of a posthumous edition of the story, the "Author of *Little Women*" admits that "over all these years, serenely prosperous, still hangs over me the shadow of the past, still rises that dead image of my mother, still echoes that spectral whisper in the dark."[63]

Notes

BIBLIOGRAPHICAL NOTE

Significant use has been made of the following manuscript collections:

Houghton Library, Harvard University
   Abigail May Alcott, Fragments of an Autobiography: these include incomplete diaries of Abba May Alcott with original entries and entries copied by Louisa May Alcott for use in a projected biography of her mother. Both sets of entries were to be destroyed after LMA's death according to her written instructions. Fortunately for scholars her instructions were not carried out.

   Alcott Family Papers
   Alcott-Pratt Collection
   Amos Bronson Alcott, Autobiographical Collections
   Amos Bronson Alcott, Autobiographical Index
   Amos Bronson Alcott, Manuscript Journal
   Emerson Papers
   Louisa May Alcott, Letters and Papers
   Memoir of Abigail May Alcott, Notes and Materials left by Amos Bronson Alcott, 1878
Olin Library, Cornell University
   Samuel J. May Papers
Boston Public Library
   Alcott Collection
   Samuel May Papers
Concord Free Public Library, Concord, Mass.
   Alcott Papers
   Franklin Sanborn Papers

Onondaga Historical Society, Syracuse, N.Y.
   Samuel J. May Papers

ABBREVIATIONS

ABA   Amos Bronson Alcott
AFP   Alcott Family Papers
AMA   Abigail May Alcott
APC   Alcott-Pratt Collection
FA   Fragments of an Autobiography, in Alcott Collection, Houghton
      Library, Harvard University
HL   Houghton Library, Harvard University
LMA   Louisa May Alcott

INTRODUCTION

1. Margaret Fuller, *Memoirs; Memoirs of Margaret Fuller Ossoli*, ed. R. W. Emerson, W. H. Channing, and J. F. Clarke (Boston, 1884), 1:297.

2. Ibid., p. 237. See also Bell Gale Chevigny, *The Woman and the Myth: Margaret Fuller's Life and Writings* (New York, 1976).

3. Ednah Cheney, ed., *Louisa May Alcott: Life, Letters and Journals* (Boston, 1928), p. 39.

4. See Madeleine B. Stern, *Louisa May Alcott* (London and New York, 1957), p. 288.

5. ABA, "Observations on the Spiritual Nurture of My Children" and "Researches on Childhood," APC.

6. Sarah J. Hale's review is quoted as an advertisement in the endpiece for Louisa May Alcott novels after *Little Women*, in the Roberts Bros. series.

7. A complete bibliography of Alcott's works is available in Madeleine B. Stern, ed., *Louisa's Wonder Book* (Mount Pleasant, Mich., 1975), and a number of Alcott's works are reprinted in Elaine Showalter, ed., *Alternative Alcott* (New Brunswick, N.J.: 1987).

8. Nina Auerbach, *Woman and the Demon: The Life of a Victorian Myth* (Cambridge and London, 1982), p. 15.

9. Cheney, ed., *Alcott*, pp. 228–229.

10. Thomas Beer, *The Mauve Decade* (New York, 1926), pp. 17–24, 25. Beer describes the lawyer Joseph Choate, turning on a witness with the cry, "Good God, Madame! Did you think that your husband was one of Miss Alcott's boys?"

11. Ibid., p. 25. See also T. Jackson Lears, *No Place of Grace* (New York, 1982), for an excellent discussion of ambiguous "modernity."

12. LMA, "Transcendental Wild Oats," *The Independent* 25, no. 1307 (Dec. 18, 1873).

13. LMA, *Hospital Sketches and Camp and Fireside Stories* (Boston, 1863). Clover Hooper Adams (Mrs. Henry Adams) was inspired to work for the Sanitary Commission by reading *Hospital Sketches*. See Eugenia Kaledin, *The Education of Mrs. Henry Adams* (Philadelphia, 1981).

14. Cheney, ed., *Alcott*, pp. 223–234.

15. LMA, *Work: A Story of Experience* (Boston, 1873; rpt. New York, 1977), chap. 7.

CHAPTER 1: SOMETHING TO LOVE AND LIVE FOR

1. LMA, *Little Women* (Boston, 1868, 1869), chap. 1, "Playing Pilgrims." References to *Little Women* are cited by chapter numbers and titles which remain consistent in all editions.

2. The May family's history is documented in several sources, including Madeleine B. Stern, *Louisa May Alcott* (London and New York, 1957); Madelon Bedell, *The Alcotts: Biography of a Family* (New York, 1980); Thomas Joseph May, *A Memorial Study, Samuel Joseph May* (Boston, 1898); Catherine Covert Stepanek, "Saint before His Time: Samuel J. May and American Educational Reform," Master's thesis, Syracuse University, 1967.

3. Direct references to Bronson Alcott's ancestry and early life are largely drawn from Odell Shepard, *Pedlar's Progress: The Life of Bronson Alcott* (Boston, 1937); Odell Shepard, ed., *The Journals of Bronson Alcott* (Boston, 1938); and Richard Herrnstadt, ed., *The Letters of Amos Bronson Alcott* (Ames, Iowa, 1969); and Frederick C. Dahlstrand, *Amos Bronson Alcott: An Intellectual Biography* (London and Toronto, 1982). Dahlstrand's biography provides the clearest portrait of Bronson Alcott's early passion for democracy and dissent.

4. Odell Shepard notes that Bronson found his cousin Riley Alcox's copy of John Bunyan's *The Pilgrim's Progress*, the Dublin edition of 1802, and that he read it many times, "memorizing large parts of it and acting it out in some rude dramatic form of his own division" (*Pedlar's Progress*, pp. 34, 36).

5. Ibid., pp. 62–63.

6. Bedell, *The Alcotts*, p. 15.

7. Clara Endicott Sears, *Bronson Alcott's Fruitlands* (Boston, 1915), p. 84.

8. LMA, "Eli's Education," *St. Nicholas* 11, no. 5 (Mar. 1884); rpt. in LMA, *Spinning Wheel Stories* (Boston, 1931).

9. Herrnstadt, ed., *Letters*, p. 26. The same story is discussed in Bedell,

The Alcotts, pp. 8–9, with a somewhat different understanding of Bronson's relationship to his mother.

10. Herrnstadt, ed., *Letters*, p. 26.

11. *Alcott Memoirs of Dr. Frederick L. H. Willis* (Boston, 1915); William Leach, *True Love and Perfect Union* (New York, 1980), p. 216.

12. Stepanek, "Saint," p. 399.

13. *Boston Recorder*, May 11, 1827, clipping of an article on ABA, at HL.

14. Samuel May, *Common School Journal* (Boston, 1839), 2:220.

15. See Samuel J. May, "The Importance of Our Common Schools," *Lectures Delivered before the American Literature Institute of Instruction at Pittsfield, August 15, 16, 17, 1843* (Boston, 1844), p. 231; Samuel J. May, "Address Delivered by the Rev. S. J. May at the Opening of a New and Highly Improved District Schoolhouse in Hanover, Mass., June 20, 1839," *Common School Journal*, 2:14; Samuel J. May, "Capital Punishment: Six Reasons Why It Should Be Abolished," *New York Tribune*, July 25, 1851. See also William Andrus Alcott (Bronson's cousin), ed., *Juvenile Rambler* (1831, 1832), probably the first magazine for children published in the United States. William was much better known as a public educator than his cousin.

16. See Bedell, *The Alcotts*, pp. 3, 4.

17. Ibid.; AMA's Diary, Aug. 5, 1828, FA.

18. Rose Hawthorne Lathrop, *Memories of Hawthorne* (Boston, 1897), p. 16; Bedell, *The Alcotts*, p. 15.

19. ABA's Manuscript Journal, Sept. 21, 1828, HL.

20. Ibid., Apr. 9, 1830.

21. Stepanek, "Saint," p. 11.

22. Ibid., p. 9.

23. Ibid., p. 31.

24. Ibid., pp. 69–70.

25. AMA, "Autobiographical Sketch," FA.

26. Samuel May to Abigail May, July 21, 1828, AFP.

27. Abigail May to Amos Bronson Alcott, June 10, 1829, AFP.

28. AMA's Diary, FA.

29. William A. Alcott, *The Young Wife or Duties of Women in the Marriage Relation* (Boston, 1827; rpt. New York, 1972), p. 37.

30. ABA's Manuscript Journal, July 28, 1828, HL.

31. AMA's Diary, Aug. 1828, from notes and materials left by ABA for the Memoir of Abigail May Alcott, HL.

32. Abigail May to Samuel J. May, Aug. 1828, AFP.

33. Joseph May to Abigail May, July 6, 1829, AFP.

34. ABA's Manuscript Journal, Oct. 15, 1828, HL. The two most recent

biographers of the Alcotts disagree on the nature of Abigail and Bronson's courtship. Martha Saxton, in *Louisa May* (New York, 1977), calls Bronson a narcissist and concludes that this journal entry typifies his inability to feel deeply for any other human being except as a reflection of his own idealized self-image. She finds Abigail May to be the personification of Victorian female hysteria. Madelon Bedell, on the other hand, is more sympathetic to the young couple. Setting their courtship in the context of their nineteenth-century lives and appreciating the differences in their backgrounds and temperaments, she finds Bronson to be shy, inhibited, but still a loving man. Abigail's mercurial moments are perceived as partly the expression of a passionate nature and partly a sensitive response to family traumas and difficult stages in her own life cycle (Bedell, *The Alcotts*). Alcott scholars tend to side with one or another of the family, which is difficult to avoid considering the intensity of the family's relationships and its self-conscious preservation of face. Still, Bronson Alcott's view of himself as an "original" seems to have infected many biographers—with the exception of Saxton, who ignores his impoverished state and the desire to be accepted by such gentlefolk as the Mays which helped form Bronson's self-image. His need to present himself as one of nature's noblemen was reinforced by the expectations of genteel reformers who hoped to find just such examples of modest virtue among the common people. Very few acquaintances, among them Father Hecker and Rose Hawthorne Lathrop, caught the subtle mixture of Bronson Alcott's "insinuating" ways and his genuine passion to "be good."

35. Abigail May to ABA, June 10, 1829, AFP.

CHAPTER 2: MODEL CHILDREN

1. A. J. Graves, *Women in America* (New York, 1843), p. xv, discussed in Mary P. Ryan, "The Empire of the Mother: American Writings on Women and the Family, 1830–1860," *Women and History* 1, no. 2–3 (Spring 1983).

2. Several excellent studies exist on the changing aspects of domestic prescription and practice. Among them are Linda Kerber, "The Republican Mother: Women and the Enlightenment—An American Perspective," *American Quarterly* 28, no. 2 (Summer 1976): 187–205; Anne Kuhn, *The Mother's Role in Childhood Education* (New Haven, 1947); Ann Douglas, *The Feminization of American Culture* (New York, 1972); Kathyn Sklar, *Catharine Beecher: A Study in Domesticity* (New Haven, 1973).

3. ABA, *Observations on the Principles and Methods of Infant Instruction* (Boston 1830); rpt. in Walter Harding, ed., *Essays on Education* (Gainesville, Fla., 1960).

4. Madelon Bedell, *The Alcotts: Biography of a Family* (New York, 1980), p. 54. Bedell thinks the printing may have been paid for by either Alcott himself or Robert Vaux.

5. The best discussion of Alcott's unpublished "Observations on the Spiritual Nurture of My Children," is in Charles Strickland, "A Transcendentalist Father: The Child Rearing Practices of Bronson Alcott," *Perspectives in American History* 3 (1969): 5–71. The quotations cited here are from Strickland's article. Strickland's second, longer version appears in *History of Childhood Quarterly: The Journal of Psychohistory* 1, no. 1 (Summer 1973). The complete manuscript of "Observations on the Spiritual Nurture of My Children" can be consulted at HL, bound in one volume with Alcott's "Researches on Childhood." See also Charles Strickland, *Victorian Domesticity: Families in the Life and Art of Louisa May Alcott* (University, Alabama, 1985).

6. Samuel J. May's library included these works. May lent them to Henry Barnard, and both men lectured publicly on Pestalozzian theory. Catherine Covert Stepanek, "Saint before His Time: Samuel J. May and American Educational Reform," Master's thesis, Syracuse University, 1967, pp. 86–87. Social historians of education who find commonality in the reformers' theories include Lawrence A. Cremin, *The Transformation of the School* (New York, 1961); Freeman Butts and Lawrence A. Cremin, *History of Education in American Culture* (New York, 1953); and E. P. Cubberly, *Public Education in the United States* (Boston, 1919).

7. ABA, "Pestalozzi's Principles and Methods of Instuction," *American Journal of Education* 4 (Mar–Apr. 1829): 97–107.

8. M. H. Abrams, *The Mirror and the Lamp: Romantic Theory and the Critical Tradition* (New York, 1953), p. 69.

9. This struggle is detailed in Butts and Cremin, *History of Education*, in Cubberly, *Public Education*, and in Cremin, *The Transformation of the School*. Recent revisionist treatments of the struggle include an excellent analysis by Michael Katz, *The Irony of Early School Reform* (New York, 1968); and Michael Katz, ed., *Social Issues in American Education* (New York, 1974).

10. Bedell, *The Alcotts*, p. 54.

11. Strickland, "Transcendentalist Father," p. 6.

12. Lydia Maria Child, *The Mother's Book* (Boston, 1831).

13. ABA, "Observations on Spiritual Nurture," p. 27; cited in Strickland, "Transcendentalist Father," p. 6.

14. AMA to Samuel J. May, Mar. 27, 1831, AFP.

15. ABA, "Observations on Spiritual Nurture," cited in Strickland, "Transcendentalist Father," p. 76.

16. Ryan, "The Empire of the Mother." Ryan emphasizes Godey's popularity; it was read by 150,000 people in 1860.

17. ABA, "Observations on Spiritual Nurture," cited in Strickland, "Transcendentalist Father," p. 10.

18. Ibid., pp. 45–46; see also Child, *The Mother's Book*. I stress the similarities between Child's regimen and Bronson and Abigail Alcott's descriptions because their diaries seem very radical only when compared to more conservative advisors, such as the Rev. John C. Abbott in *The Mother at Home* (see Strickland, "Transcendentalist Father," p. 18). In fact, the general stream of advice in the 1830s and 1840s was becoming very liberal, or at least more inclined toward the emotional persuasion of children. Like Strickland, I agree with Lewis Mumford that a "major legacy of transcendentalism was the belief that childhood could be happy" (Strickland, "Transcendentalist Father," p. 12). But the believers in happy childhood included many nontranscendentalists.

19. ABA, "Observations on Spiritual Nurture," pp. 45–46, cited in Strickland, "Transcendentalist Father," p. 22.

20. LMA, *Little Women* (Boston, 1868, 1869), chap. 38, "On the Shelf." References to *Little Women* are cited by chapter numbers and titles which remain consistent in all editions.

21. ABA to Col. Joseph May, Nov. 1832, HL. Bedell notes (from Bronson's "Observations on the Spiritual Nurture") that Louisa's life "began in struggle." Her mother's milk did not come in until five days after she was born (Bedell thinks that she almost starved to death). Moreover, she was not washed until she was a week old; during this time she remained soiled with meconium, a situation Bronson thought life threatening. On the other hand, Bronson also wrote to his mother that the baby was "a very fine, fat little creature" (Bedell, *The Alcotts*, p. 63).

22. AMA to Samuel J. May, Feb. 20, 1837, AFP.

23. Ibid. Bronson Alcott did observe "detail" about Louisa's character during her infancy. He remarked on her "boldness and amplitude" and her luxuriant nature, and called her "fit for the scuffle of things"; he also noted her "will" later on (ABA, "Observations on Spiritual Nurture, pp. 73–74). I agree with Bedell that "all we know of Louisa's later life and career, of the invincible, spirited woman of power, talent and drive, confirms this analysis of her character made by her father in the first year of her life" (Bedell, *The Alcotts*, p. 66). Bronson granted to baby Louisa some of Abba's obvious sensuality. Both Alcotts thought that Louisa resembled her mother physically and emotionally. See AMA to Joseph May, March 11, 1833, AFP.

24. Martha Saxton in *Louisa May* (New York, 1977) and Bedell agree that

this was a "separation." Bronson wrote that "subtle ties of friendship . . . are worn away by constant familiarity" (Bedell, *The Alcotts*, p. 69). See my discussion below of Louisa May Alcott's treatment of such problems in Chapter 11, "Reading *Little Women.*"

25. Bedell, *The Alcotts*, p. 69.

26. Ibid.

27. Actually, the figures for Abigail Alcott's cohort are probably higher. Uhlenberg offers a 35 percent rate of infant mortality in Louisa and Anna's cohort—that is, these born in the 1830s. See Peter R. Uhlenberg, "A Study of Cohort Life Cycles: Cohorts of Native Born Massachusetts Women, 1830–1920," *Population Studies* 23, pt. 3 (Nov. 1969): 407–420. He also reports that the 1867 Massachusetts Vital Registration Report attributed about 10 percent of female deaths to childbearing.

28. Odell Shepard, *Pedlar's Progress: The Life of Bronson Alcott* (Boston, 1937).

29. ABA's Manuscript Journal, Oct. 10, 1834, HL; see also Strickland, "Transcendentalist Father," pp. 45–55, and Strickland, *Victorian Domesticity.*

30. LMA, *Little Men: Life at Plumfield with Jo's Boys* (Boston, 1871), chap. 3, "Sunday." References to *Little Men* are cited by chapter numbers and titles which remain consistent in all editions.

31. Strickland, "Transcendentalist Father," pp. 45–55.

32. ABA, "Observations on Spiritual Nurture" and "Researches on Childhood," as cited in Strickland, "Transcendentalist Father," pp. 59–60.

33. See Elizabeth Peabody, *Record of a School: Exemplifying the General Principles of Spiritual Culture* (Boston, 1836).

34. ABA, "Observations on Spiritual Nurture," as cited in Strickland, "Transcendentalist Father," pp. 59–60.

35. Ibid.

35. Ednah Cheney, ed., *Louisa May Alcott: Life, Letters and Journals* (Boston, 1928), p. 18.

37. Ibid.

38. Madeleine B. Stern, *Louisa May Alcott* (London and New York, 1957), pp. 11–12.

39. ABA, ed., *Conversations with Children on the Gospel* (Boston, 1837). Feminists in the 1870s and later made a strong case for sex education of children. See William Leach, *True Love and Perfect Union* (New York, 1980), pt. 1.

40. William Alcott, *The Physiology of Marriage* (Boston, 1855). See also Sylvester Graham, *Lectures on Chastity* (Glasgow, 1834). Graham assumed that marital intimacy reduced the dangers of romantic passion, in part be-

cause it removed the mystery of sexual act. Sexual excess, he found, was more the result of overstimulated imagination than instinctual drives. A vegetarian, bland diet also helped to insure that "intercourse is very seldom." Bronson became a lifelong vegetarian in this period, but Abigail harbored a dangerous taste for meat and occasionally fed it to the children until severe poverty forced her to discontinue the practice.

41. Saxton, *Louisa May*, p. 102.

42. Stern, *Louisa May Alcott*, p. 13.

43. During the Alcotts' separation in Germantown and Philadelphia, Bronson wrote that "sacrifices must be made to the spirit of the age . . . my family must feel the evil of this to some degree, but this should not deter me from striving to effect what has been attempted in conception of duty and right" (ABA's Manuscript Journal, Mar. 27, 1834, HL). For a more detailed analysis of this phenomenon see Douglas, *Feminization*.

CHAPTER 3: ARMIES OF REFORM

1. Martha Saxton, *Louisa May* (New York, 1977), p. 102.

2. Ralph Waldo Emerson, "Self Reliance" (1840), *Selections from Ralph Waldo Emerson*, ed. Stephen E. Whicher (Boston, 1960), p. 147.

3. Odell Shepard, *Pedlar's Progress: The Life of Bronson Alcott* (Boston, 1937), p. 268. I have relied on numerous general and specific treatments of American reform, including John L. Thomas, "Romantic Reform in America, 1815–1865," *American Quarterly* 17, no. 2 (Winter 1965): 565–581; Henry Steele Commager, *The Era of Reform* (Princeton, 1960); Clifford A. Griffin, *Their Brothers' Keepers: Moral Stewardship in the United States 1800–1865* (New Brunswick, N.J., 1960); Frank Thistlethwaite, *The Anglo-American Connection in the Early Nineteenth Century* (Philadelphia, 1959); Alice Felt Tyler, *Freedom's Ferment: Phases of American Social History to 1860* (Minneapolis, 1944); Robert Brenner, *From the Depths: The Discovery of Poverty in the United States* (New York, 1964); David Rothman, *The Discovery of the Asylum: Social Order and Disorder in the New Republic* (Boston, 1971); Elizabeth Cady Stanton, Susan B. Anthony, Matilda Joslyn Gage, eds., *History of Woman Suffrage*, vols. 1–3 (Rochester, 1881–1902); Mark Holloway, *Heavens on Earth: Utopian Communities in America, 1680–1880* (New York, 1951); Louis J. Kern, *An Ordered Love: Sex Roles and Sexuality in Victorian Utopias* (Chapel Hill, 1981); Russel Nye, *Society and Culture in America, 1830–1860* (New York, 1974); and Martin Duberman, ed., *The Antislavery Vanguard: New Essays on the Abolitionists* (Princeton, 1965).

4. Mary Wollstonecraft, *A Vindication of the Rights of Woman*, ed. Carol H. Poston (New York, 1967), p. 108.

5. Madelon Bedell has provided a moving account of Abba Alcott's

pregnancies and childbirth experiences, documented from the May and Alcott family papers; see Madelon Bedell, *The Alcotts: Biography of a Family* (New York, 1980), chap. 9.

6. The standard work is by Octavius Brooks Frothingham, *Transcendentalism in New England* (New York, 1876). It is not completely unbiased, as Frothingham was deeply involved in the movement and also related to Abigail May Alcott. A new, exciting interpretation of Emerson, Alcott, and Thoreau is found in Taylor Stoehr, *Nay-Saying in Concord: Emerson, Alcott and Thoreau* (Hamden, Conn., 1979). For an analysis of Transcendentalism as a genuine social movement see Anne C. Rose, *Transcendentalism as a Social Movement, 1830–1850* (New Haven, 1981).

7. Rose, *Transcendentalism*. Rose does not, however, include Thoreau as an active reformer.

8. See F. O. Matthiessen, *The American Renaissance* (New York, 1941).

9. This popular phrase has endured since John Louis O'Sullivan first coined it in the early nineteenth century as a Democratic party slogan.

10. Shepard, *Pedlar's Progress*, p. 279.

11. Ralph Waldo Emerson, "The American Scholar" (oration delivered before the Phi Beta Kappa Society, Cambridge, Mass., Aug. 31, 1837), in *Collected Works of Ralph Waldo Emerson*, ed. Alfred Ferguson (Boston, 1971), 1:70.

12. Ibid., p. 52.

13. Ralph Waldo Emerson, "Nature," in *Collected Works*, 1:8.

14. Ibid., pp. 13, 14.

15. Ednah Cheney, ed., *Louisa May Alcott: Life, Letters and Journals* (Boston, 1928), p. 20.

16. Ibid., pp. 13, 14.

17. Shepard, *Pedlar's Progress*, pp. 233–245.

18. Ibid., p. 268.

19. Ibid.

20. Ralph Waldo Emerson, "Man the Reformer" (a lecture read before the Mechanics Apprentices' Library Association at the Masonic Temple, Boston, Jan. 25, 1841), in *Collected Works*, vol. 1.

21. ABA to LMA, June 21, 1840, Orchard House reproduction (Concord, 1974). Original letter in AFP.

22. Shepard, *Pedlar's Progress*, p. 267.

23. The controversies surrounding Colonel May's will are considerable. Saxton sets the amount received as $3,000 to each heir (*Louisa May*, p. 122). Madelon Bedell estimates the total amount of the estate at $15,000 with about $2,000 going to Abigail Alcott (Bedell, *The Alcotts*, p. 376). The original will, the executor's inventory, and the subsequent accounting in

probate court fully enumerates the assets and debts of Colonel May, and also the costs of legal services charged to the estate in court actions surrounding disbursements. The will itself is registered #32792, Suffolk County Court. The executors' final accounts are totaled as of Jan. 15, 1844, when the money was released from probate. The first inventory is dated Boston, Apr. 5, 1841. The entire matter is of some consequence in fully understanding not only the Alcotts' relationship to the Sewall and May families, but also the subsequent events surrounding the involvement of the Alcotts, the Mays, and Charles Lane in the Fruitlands experiment at Harvard. See my analysis in Chapter 4, "Transcendental Wild Oats."

24. Will of Col. Joseph May (executors' inventory).

25. Ibid.

26. Joseph May to AMA, Oct. 1, 1834, from notes and materials left by ABA for a Memoir of Abigail May Alcott, HL; also cited in Bedell, *The Alcotts*, p. 136.

27. AMA to Joseph May, Oct. 6, 1834, from notes and materials left by ABA for a Memoir of Abigail May Alcott, HL; also cited in Bedell, *The Alcotts*, p. 136.

28. AMA's Diary, Feb. 1841, from notes and materials left by ABA for a Memoir of Abigail May Alcott, HL.

29. Stanton et al., *A History of Woman Suffrage*, vol. 1.

30. Bedell, *The Alcotts*, p. 167.

31. Shepard, *Pedlar's Progress*, p. 300.

32. Saxton, *Louisa May*, p. 128.

33. Cheney, ed., *Alcott*, pp. 15–16.

34. The best account of Bronson's English visit is Bedell, *The Alcotts*, chap. 12. Shepard also writes a detailed description of Bronson's contact with the English reformers (*Pedlar's Progress*, pp. 303–342).

35. Shepard, *Pedlar's Progress*, p. 318.

36. Ibid., p. 195.

37. Bedell, *The Alcotts*, p. 195.

38. Ralph Waldo Emerson, "Lectures on the Times: Introductory Lecture," in *Collected Works*, 1:175–176.

39. Stoehr, *Nay-Saying*, p. 34.

40. AMA Diary, Sept. 1842, FA.

CHAPTER 4: TRANSCENDENTAL WILD OATS

1. Odell Shepard, *Pedlar's Progress: The Life of Bronson Alcott* (Boston, 1937), p. 352.

2. Ibid. Lane also informed Junius Alcott that "we are learning to hold

our peace, and to keep our hands from each other's bodies—the ill effects of which we see upon the little baby." Both Saxton and Bedell suspect that this line indicates the extremity of Lane's predilection for celibacy; see Martha Saxton, *Louisa May* (New York, 1977); and Madelon Bedell, *The Alcotts: Biography of a Family* (New York, 1980). He may also have been referring to the prohibition against both verbal abuse and chastisement of children in the cottage.

3. Charles Lane to William Oldham, Nov. 30, 1842, in Clara Endicott Sears, *Bronson Alcott's Fruitlands* (Boston, 1915), pp. 12−13.

4. AMA's Diary, Dec. 24, 1842, FA.

5. Ibid., Jan. 30, 1843.

6. Nina Baym, *Women's Fiction: A Guide to Novels by and about Women in America, 1820−1870* (Ithaca, N.Y., 1978), p. 257.

7. Sears, *Fruitlands*, pp. 12−13.

8. Shepard, *Pedlar's Progress*, p. 307.

9. Charles Lane to William Oldham, in Sears, *Fruitlands*, p. 18.

10. Charles Lane to Junius Alcott, Mar. 7, 1843, in ibid., p. 11.

11. Charles Lane to William Oldham, May 31, 1843, in ibid., p. 14.

12. Ibid., p. 15.

13. Ibid.

14. Ibid.

15. Samuel J. May to Ralph Waldo Emerson, Jan. 13, 1844, Emerson Papers, HL. Catherine Covert of Syracuse University provided this note from Samuel J. May.

16. Lester G. Wells, *The Skaneateles Communal Experiment, 1843−1846* (Syracuse, 1953).

17. Charles Lane to William Oldham, June 28, in Sears, *Fruitlands*, p. 28.

18. Anna Alcott's Diary at Fruitlands, June 1843, in ibid., p. 86.

19. Sears, *Fruitlands*, p. 36.

20. Ibid. p. 37.

21. Ibid., p. 209.

22. Anna Alcott's Diary at Fruitlands, June 6, 1843, and June 13, 1843, in ibid., 87, 92.

23. Ibid., July 20, 1843, p. 101.

24. Ibid., Sept. 6, 1843, p. 103.

25. LMA's Diary at Fruitlands, Sept. 14, 1843, in ibid., p. 107. "I ran in the wind and played be a horse, and had a lovely time in the woods with Anna and Lizzie. We were fairies, and made gowns and paper wings. I 'flied' the highest of all."

26. Ibid.

27. Ibid., Sept, 24, 1843, and Oct. 12, 1843, pp. 108−109.

28. Ibid., Oct. 12, 1843, p. 109.
29. Sears, *Fruitlands*, p. 108.
30. Annie M. L. Clark, *The Alcotts in Harvard* (Lancaster, Mass., 1902). There are four stanzas to the poem; the second reads:

> Oh why these tears
> And these idle fears
> For what may come to-morrow?
> The birds find food
> From God so good,
> And the flowers know no sorrow.

31. Sears, *Fruitlands*, p. 108.
32. Ibid., p. 109.
33. Ibid.
34. Isaac Hecker at Brook Farm, July 7, 1843, cited in ibid., p. 76. Hecker's complete diary at Fruitlands can be found in the Hecker Papers, at the Paulist Archives, New York City.
35. Ibid., p. 84.
36. Isaac Hecker at Fruitlands, July 17, 1843, cited in ibid., p. 79.
37. Ibid., July 21, 1843, in ibid., p. 81.
38. Sears, *Fruitlands*, p. 84.
39. Ibid., p. 125.
40. Sears, *Fruitlands*, p. 113. Lydia Maria Child's husband went to hear Alcott and Lane in a discussion with W. H. Channing. After listening to them he reported to her "Why, after I heard them talk a few minutes, I'll be cursed if I knew whether I had any mind at all."
41. Samuel J. May, Lexington, Mass., Jan. 13, 1844, copy forwarded to Ralph Waldo Emerson, Emerson Papers, HL.
42. Charles Lane to William Oldham, Nov. 26, 1843, in Sears, *Fruitlands*, p. 123.
43. ABA and Charles Lane to A. Brooke of Oakland, Ohio, in ibid., pp. 40–52; pub. under the title, "The Consociate Family Life," in *The Herald of Freedom*, Sept. 8, 1843; copy at HL.
44. Ibid.
45. Ibid. For a detailed account of the relationship between fertility patterns and women's interest in the Shakers, see D'Ann Campbell, "Women's Life in Utopia: The Shaker Experiment in Sexual Equality Reappraised, 1810–1860," *New England Quarterly* 2, no. 1 (Mar. 1978): 23–27. Louis J. Kern is quite right that Shaker theology found woman unclean and the separation of the sexes made her "a highly ambiguous entity; at once foundation stone of the new Order; harlot and saint" (*An Ordered Love: Sex Roles and Sexuality in Victorian Utopias* [Chapel Hill, 1981], p. 86).

46. Charles Lane to William Oldham, 1843, in Sears, *Fruitlands*, p. 8.

47. Ibid., pp. 40-52; rpt. in LMA, "Transcendental Wild Oats," *The Independent* 25, no. 130 (Dec. 18, 1873).

48. Taylor Stoehr, *Nay-Saying in Concord: Emerson, Alcott and Thoreau* (Hamden, Conn., 1979), p. 85.

49. Sears, *Fruitlands*, p. 143.

50. Emerson visited Lane in England at Ham in 1848. Lane had a school of sixteen children and married the matron, Hannah Bond, "who had lived at Owen's Community at Harmony Hall." Writing to Thoreau, Emerson said that Lane was "full of friendliness and hospitality" (Sears, *Fruitlands*, p. 134).

51. Richard Herrnstadt, ed., *The Letters of Amos Bronson Alcott* (Ames, Iowa, 1969), p. 656.

52. ABA's Manuscript Journal, in ibid., p. 84.

53. Stoehr, *Nay-Saying*, p. 85.

54. AMA's Diary, Aug. 26, 1843, FA.

55. Ibid.

56. LMA, "Transcendental Wild Oats" rpt. in *Silver Pitchers* (Boston, 1908), pp. 95-120. References in this chapter are to the *Silver Pitchers* rpt.

57. Alcott and Lane, "The Consociate Family Life," in Sears, *Fruitlands*, pp. 40-52.

58. Alcott, "Transcendental Wild Oats," p. 100.

59. Alcott and Lane, "The Consociate Family Life," in Sears, *Fruitlands*, pp. 40-52.

60. LMA, "Transcendental Wild Oats," p. 100.

61. LMA, *Little Men: Life at Plumfield with Jo's Boys* (Boston, 1871), chap. 1, "Nat." References to *Little Men* are cited by chapter numbers and titles which remain consistent in all editions. Nat Blake, an orphaned street musician, thinks he has found heaven when Aunt Jo and Nursey wrap him in a warm flannel nightgown, tuck him in a clean bed, and then administer draughts of "warm soothy stuff."

62. LMA, "Transcendental Wild Oats," p. 100.

CHAPTER 5: THE TRIALS OF LIFE BEGIN

1. Annie M. L. Clark, *The Alcotts in Harvard* (Lancaster, Mass., 1902), p. 31.

2. Ibid., p. 34.

3. Ibid., p. 37.

4. Suffolk County Probate Court, AMA, Petition addressed to Hon. Willard Phillips, Judge of Probate, County of Suffolk, Mass., May 20, 1844.

NOTES TO PAGES 79–84

5. Suffolk County, Mass., Probate Court, Samuel E. Sewall for himself and Samuel J. May, Aug. 13, 1844.

6. Samuel J. May to Ralph Waldo Emerson, Dec. 22, 1844, Emerson Papers, HL.

7. Ibid., Jan. 13, 1844.

8. Ibid.

9. Ibid.

10. Clark, *The Alcotts*, p. 42.

11. Ibid.

12. Ibid.

13. Carroll Smith-Rosenberg, "Sex as Symbol in Victorian Purity: An Ethnohistorical Analysis of Jacksonian America," *American Journal of Sociology* 84, suppl. (1978): S212–S247.

14. William Alcott, *The Physiology of Marriage* (Boston, 1855), p. 12; cited in Smith-Rosenberg, "Sex as Symbol."

15. Carroll Smith-Rosenberg, "Beauty, the Beast and the Militant Woman: A Study in the Sex Roles and Social Stress in Jacksonian America," *American Quarterly* 23 (Winter 1971): 562–584.

16. Madeline B. Stern, ed., *Behind a Mask: The Unknown Thrillers of Louisa May Alcott* (New York, 1975); and *Plots and Counterplots: More Unknown Thrillers of Louisa May Alcott* (New York, 1976). Stern's interesting analysis of the separation of domesticity from sexuality is similarly stated and expanded in Nancy F. Cott, "Passionlessness: An Interpretation of Victorian Sexual Ideology, 1790–1850," *Signs: Journal of Women in Culture and Society* 4, no. 2 (Winter 1978): 219–236. She notes; "Both women's participation in the creation of Victorian sexual standards and the place of passionlessness in the vanguard of feminist thought deserve more recognition. The serviceability of passionlessness to women in gaining social and familial power should be acknowledged as a primary reason that the ideology was quickly and widely accepted" (p. 235). By the mid-nineteenth century liberal feminists did not reject passion so much as they wanted to "rationalize" it. Coeducation, household democracy, and equal pay for equal work would remove the dangers of sexual passion, preserving healthy sexual relations and "true love."

17. Madelon Bedell, *The Alcotts: Biography of a Family* (New York, 1980), pp. 241–246.

18. Ibid. William Leach in *True Love and Perfect Union: The Feminist Reform of Sex and Society* (New York, 1980) provides the most complete and sympathetic account linking domestic reform, feminist social theory, and sexuality in mid-ninteenth-century America.

19. Clara Gowing, *The Alcotts as I Knew Them* (Boston, 1909), pp. 11, 9.

20. Ednah Cheney, ed., *Louisa May Alcott: Life, Letters and Journals* (Boston, 1928), p. 34.

21. Ibid.

22. Dr. Frederick L. H. Willis, *Alcott Memoirs* (Boston, 1915), p. 35. Gowing presents a similar description: Louisa was "tall and slim . . . the fleetest runner in school, and could walk, run and climb like a boy" (*The Alcotts*, p. 6.)

23. Willis, *Alcott Memoirs*, p. 44.

24. Ibid.

25. Ibid.

26. Cheney, ed., *Alcott*, p. 36.

27. Harriot K. Hunt, *Glances and Glimpses or Fifty Years Social, Including Twenty Years Professional Life* (Boston, 1855), p. 52. See also Eleanor Wolf Thompson, *Education for Ladies, 1830–1860* (Binghamton, N.Y., 1947), who presents a detailed account of the popular literature and its treatment of the "woman question," particularly education for young ladies in this period. H. W. Bellows's column on female education gives a plea for women's rights which clearly links abolitionism and feminism (*National Anti-Slavery Standard* 2, no. 47 [Apr. 28, 1842]: 188). Thomas Wentworth Higginson, another friend of the Alcotts, elaborated on the theme "no sex in mind," in the *Atlantic Monthly* 3, no. 16 (Feb. 1859). Louisa May Alcott was a contributor to the *Atlantic Monthly* in the 1860s and later read Thomas Wentworth Higginson, *Atlantic Essays* (Boston, 1871). Also of note are Catharine Beecher, *A Treatise on Domestic Economy* (Boston, 1841); Catharine Beecher and Harriet Beecher Stowe, *The American Woman's Home* (Boston, 1869), and Mrs. Sigourney, "The Comparative Intellect of the Sexes," *Ladies Magazine* 3, no. 6 (June 1830): 241–245. None of these writers is so radical as Hunt in linking coeducation, exercise, and work for women. All, however, argue in favor of "healthy" exercise and education for girls.

28. Hunt learned the practice of homeopathy from an English husband-and-wife team of physicians who treated her sister in 1833. A schoolteacher at the time, Harriot Hunt went to live with the two doctors Mott, conducted their business correspondence, and at the age of twenty-eight brought her mother and sister to live with them. The two Hunt sisters began nursing and then physician's training with their hosts.

29. Hunt, *Glances and Glimpses*, p. 217.

30. Cheney, ed., *Alcott*, p. 36.

31. Ibid., pp. 44–45.

32. Richard Libeau, *Young Man Thoreau* (New York, 1975). An excellent comparison of Emerson's, Alcott's, and Thoreau's views on nature, commu-

nity, labor, property, and family is Taylor Stoehr, *Nay-Saying in Concord: Emerson, Alcott, and Thoreau* (Hamden, Conn., 1979). Bedell and Stern agree on the significance of Thoreau's life to Louisa May Alcott (Bedell, *The Alcotts* and Madeleine B. Stern, *Louisa May Alcott* [London and New York, 1957]).

33. Libeau, *Young Man Thoreau.*

34. Margaret Fuller, "On Lidian Emerson, Sept. 2, 1842," quoted in Bell Gale Chevigny, *The Woman and the Myth: Margaret Fuller's Life and Writings* (New York, 1976), p. 128.

35. Ibid.

36. Ibid.

37. Bedell offers a full and engaging description of Louisa May and Anna Alcott's "home-made theatricals" (*The Alcotts*, pp. 252–253). Stern quotes generously from the plays, describes costumes and scenery, and weaves together the young Alcotts' role playing of Dickens's novels with their own original theatricals (*Louisa May Alcott*, pp. 53–55). Anna Alcott eventually edited Louisa's dramas and wrote an introduction to them, according to Cheney, ed., *Alcott.* See also Karen Halttunen, "The Domestic Drama of Louisa May Alcott," *Feminist Studies* 10, no. 2 (Summer 1984): 233–254.

38. Cheney, ed., *Alcott*, pp. 44–45.

39. Gowing, *The Alcotts*, pp. 17–20.

40. Ibid.

41. Bedell, *The Alcotts*, p. 269.

42. Ibid., pp. 270–271.

43. Ibid. Bedell mentions that Abba's "first venture into independence had been a failure, but she did not consider herself defeated." But Abba Alcott wished for a genuinely romantic union with her husband, something approaching interdependency. Waterford was a success in that it gave her the courage to "administer" in Boston. The separation from her daughters also stimulated her awareness of their need for a supervised "trying out" period. Alcott later divided the *Little Women* volumes into "Birds in the Nest" and "Birds Leave the Nest," attesting to the need for adolescent girls' "trial flights."

44. Ibid., p. 272.

45. Chevigny, *The Woman and the Myth*, p. 369.

46. Daniel Walker Howe, "American Victorianism as a Culture," *American Quarterly* 27 (Dec. 1975): 507–532.

47. Ibid., p. 515.

48. I am grateful to Susan Reverby for pointing out Eric Schneider's fine Ph.D. dissertation, "In the Web of Class: Youth, Class and Culture in

Boston, 1840–1940," Boston University, 1980. I have followed his guide to novels about Boston's pauperism and poverty in the 1840s and agree with his analysis of the significance of these works. They were cheap and widely available, but I have no direct evidence that Louisa May Alcott read them. Nevertheless, her descriptions of similar scenes in *Little Men: Life at Plumfield with Jo's Boys* (Boston, 1871) and *Work: A Story of Experience* (Boston, 1873) are striking. Schneider also identifies the term "dangerous classes," which was used frequently by reformers, journalists, and missionaries by the 1840s. Alcott's descriptions are closely modeled on her reading of the novels of Charles Dickens.

49. Bedell, *The Alcotts*, p. 272.

50. Schneider, "In the Web of Class," p. 20.

51. LMA, *Work*.

52. Bedell, *The Alcotts*, p. 274.

53. Joseph Tuckerman, *On the Elevation of the Poor: A Selection from His Reports as Minister-at-Large in Boston* (Boston, 1874; rpt. New York, 1971).

54. Ibid., pp. 121–122.

55. Catherine Covert Stepanek, "Saint before His Time: Samuel J. May and American Educational Reform," Master's thesis, Syracuse University, 1964, p. 110.

56. Ibid., p. 126.

57. Samuel J. May to Andrew Dickson White, Sept. 20, 1857, Samuel J. May Papers, Olin Library, Cornell University.

58. Schneider, "In the Web of Class," pp. 198–257. See also Barbara Brenzel, "Lancaster Industrial School for Girls: A Social Portrait of a Nineteenth Century Reform School for Girls," *Feminist Studies* 3 (Fall 1975): 40–54.

59. AMA's Diary, 1849, FA.

60. Ibid., Apr. 4, 1850. See also, AMA, "To the Ladies of the South Friendly Society" (Apr. 1830), in AMA, "Fragments of Reports while Visitor to the Poor," 1849, 1850, 1851, 1852, HL.

61. Bedell, *The Alcotts*, pp. 272–285.

62. *Proceedings of the Women's Rights Convention, Held at Syracuse, Sept. 8, 9, 10, 1852, Including the Worcester Call for the Syracuse Convention* (Syracuse, 1852).

63. Bedell, *The Alcotts*, p. 285.

64. Margaret Fuller, *Woman in the Nineteenth Century and Other Kindred Papers by Margaret Fuller Ossoli*, ed. Arthur Buckminster Fuller (Boston, 1855); cited in Alice Rossi, ed., *The Feminist Papers* (New York, 1973), p. 158.

CHAPTER 6: OUTWARD BOUND

1. Ednah Cheney, ed., *Louisa May Alcott: Life, Letters and Journals* (Boston, 1928), pp. 72–73.
2. Ibid., p. 47.
3. Ibid., p. 48.
4. Ibid.
5. LMA, *Work: A Story of Experience* (Boston, 1873), chap. 2.
6. AMA, Aug. 14, 1850, from notes and materials left by ABA for a Memoir of Abigail May Alcott, HL; cited in Madelon Bedell, *The Alcotts: Biography of a Family* (New York, 1980), p. 282.
7. Cheney, ed., *Alcott*, pp. 48, 49.
8. Ibid., p. 49. Louisa refers to a poem called "My Little Kingdom," written at the age of fourteen. The poem details self-control as the only power worth having.
9. Ibid.
10. Ibid. See Madeleine B. Stern, "Louisa Alcott, Trouper," *New England Quarterly* 26, no. 2 (June 1943):192–193.
11. Cheney, ed., *Alcott*, p. 52.
12. Bedell notes that Richardson attended Bronson Alcott's "Conversations" (*The Alcotts*, p. 318). Louisa May Alcott's own recollection of her service is "How I Went Out to Service: A Story," *The Independent* 26 (June 4, 1874).
13. LMA, "How I Went Out to Service."
14. Cheney, ed., *Alcott*, p. 52.
15. Ibid.
16. Ibid.
17. Bedell, *The Alcotts*, p. 284.
18. LMA, "The Rival Painters: A Face of Rome," *Olive Branch* 17 (Sept. 1851).
19. Cheney, ed., *Alcott*, pp. 53–54.
20. Ibid., p. 56.
21. Ibid., p. 55 (Feb. 1854, Pickney Street, Boston).
22. Ibid., p. 57.
23. Ibid., p. 58.
24. Ibid., p. 63 (Apr. 1855).
25. Ibid. (Jan. 1855).
26. Ibid.
27. Ibid. (added notation: "L.M.A. 1886")
28. Ibid.

29. LMA, *Flower Fables* (Boston, 1855).

30. Cheney, ed., *Alcott*, p. 65 (June 1855, Walpole, N.H.).

31. Ibid., p. 66.

32. Stern, "Louisa Alcott, Trouper," p. 196.

33. Karen Halttunen, *Confidence Men and Painted Women: A Study of Middle-Class Culture in America, 1830–1870* (New Haven and London, 1982). See especially chapter 6, "Disguises, Masks, and Parlor Theatricals: The Decline of Sentimental Culture in the 1850s." Halttunen's rich and complex discussion details the use of the theater as signifying ritual in the mid-Victorian period.

34. Stern, "Louisa Alcott, Trouper," p. 185.

35. Cheney, ed., *Alcott*, p. 100 (Aug. 1860).

36. Ibid., p. 68 (Oct. 1856).

37. Ibid.

38. Ibid., p. 78.

39. Odell Shepard, ed., *The Journals of Bronson Alcott* (Boston, 1938), pp. 303–305; Odell Shepard, *Pedlar's Progress: The Life of Bronson Alcott* (Boston, 1937), pp. 467–468.

40. Cheney, ed., *Alcott*, p. 78.

41. Ibid.

42. Ibid., p. 80. Louisa did say she would "forgive" John Pratt for taking Anna away if "he makes her happy."

43. Ibid., p. 81 (Oct. 1858).

44. Ibid., pp. 81, 82.

45. Ibid., p. 82. "I feel as if I could write better now,—more truly of things I have felt and therefore *know*. I hope I shall yet do my great book, for that seems to be my work, and I'm growing up to it" (Nov. 1858).

46. Ibid. She added, "but I think it is only the lesson one must learn as it comes, and I am glad to know it."

47. Ibid., p. 84. In 1859 Parker was in Italy, where he died; Alcott called him "my beloved minister and friend," adding, "to him and R.W.E. [Emerson] I owe much of my education. May I be a worthy pupil of such men!"

48. LMA, "Little Genevieve," *Saturday Evening Gazette* (Boston), Quarto Series (Mar. 29, 1856).

49. LMA, "The Sisters' Trial," *Saturday Evening Gazette* (Boston), Quarto Series (Jan. 26, 1856).

50. LMA, "The Lady and the Woman," *Saturday Evening Gazette* (Boston), Quarto Series (Oct. 4, 1856).

51. Cheney, ed., *Alcott*, p. 82.

52. LMA, "The Lady and the Woman."

53. Cheney, ed., *Alcott*, p. 102.

54. Louisa May Alcott, *Hospital Sketches and Camp and Fireside Stories* (Boston, 1863); see also Cheney, ed., *Alcott*, p. 103.

55. A. K. Loring to LMA, Sept. 1, 1864, cited in Madeleine B. Stern, *Louisa May Alcott* (London and New York, 1957), p. 383 (courtesy of the late Carroll A. Wilson).

56. Hannah Bewick, "Introduction to *Moods*," unpub. manuscript (courtesy of John A. Bewick). I am grateful to Barbara Solomon and Daniel Aaron of Harvard University for introducing me to Hannah Bewick's work, research cut short by her untimely death.

CHAPTER 7: *MOODS*

1. Henry James, "Miss Alcott's *Moods*," *North American Review* 101 (July 1865): 276; rpt. in Henry James, *Notes and Reviews* (New York, 1968), pp. 49–58.

2. LMA, *Moods* (Boston, 1882), preface. The first published version of *Moods* (Boston, 1865) is available on microfilm, Wright American Fiction, vol. 2, 1851–1865, no. 32, reel A5. Subsequent references in this chapter are to the 1882 edition; differences with the 1865 edition are noted.

3. Jane Tompkins, *Sensational Designs: The Cultural Work of American Fiction, 1790–1860* (New York, 1985), chap. 6.

4. *Harper's Weekly*, January 21, 1865, p. 35; *Reader* 5, April 15, 1865, p. 422–423. Excerpts reprinted in Madeleine B. Stern, *Critical Essays on Louisa May Alcott* (Boston, 1984), pp. 66–67.

5. A representative sample of women writers usually called sentimental, including both liberals and evangelicals, can be found in Lucy M. Freibert and Barbara A. White, eds., *Hidden Hands: An Anthology of American Women Writers, 1790–1870* (New Brunswick, N.J., 1985). The collection also includes critical essays by Jane Tompkins, "The Other American Renaissance," Nina Baym, "Woman's Fiction," and Ann Douglas Wood, "The 'Scribbling Women' and Fanny Fern: Why Women Wrote."

6. Tompkins, *Sensational Designs*, chap. 5, "Sentimental Power: Uncle Tom's Cabin and the Politics of Literary History," pp. 122–146.

7. *Proceedings of the Woman's Rights Convention, Held at Syracuse, September 8, 9, 10, 1852, including the Worcester Call for the Syracuse Convention* (Syracuse, 1852). There Samuel J. May listened to W. H. Channing, Harriot Hunt, and Ernestine Rose link egalitarian marriage and divorce as woman's rights. Reverend May in 1845 preached on "The Enfranchisement of Woman," saying "the family is the most important institution on earth." Where mar-

riages are prompted by "sordid, mercenary, or sensual motives," only "sorrow and sin" can flow (Samuel J. May Papers, Olin Library, Cornell University).

8. *Proceedings.*

9. Ibid.

10. Ibid.

11. Nina Auerbach, *Woman and the Demon: The Life of a Victorian Myth* (Cambridge and London, 1982), p. 185.

12. LMA, *Moods*, preface.

13. Alcott read both novels several times. She and her mother read Mrs. Gaskell's biography of Brontë (Elizabeth Gaskell, *The Life of Charlotte Brontë* [London, 1857; New York, 1873]). Abba noted, "Mrs. Gaskell has told the history of this interesting family well. Their struggle reminds me of my own dear girls" (AMA's Diary, May 1869, FA).

14. Charlotte Brontë, *Jane Eyre* (London, 1847), chap. 12.

15. LMA, *Moods*, p. 69.

16. Henry David Thoreau, *A Week on the Concord and Merrimack Rivers* (New York, 1849). See also George Whicher, *Walden Revisited* (Chicago, 1945), and Henry David Thoreau, *Poems of Nature* (Boston, 1895).

17. Henry James, "Miss Alcott's *Moods*," rpt. in James, *Notes and Reviews*, p. 49.

18. Harriet Martineau; cited in Gaskell, *The Life of Charlotte Brontë*, p. 420.

19. LMA, *Moods*, p. 84.

20. Ibid., p. 103.

21. Ibid., p. 125.

23. Ibid., p. 131.

23. Eliza Buckminster Lee, *Life of Jean Paul Richter* (Boston, 1864).

24. LMA, *Moods*, p. 248.

25. Karen Halttunen, *Confidence Men and Painted Women: A Study of Middle-Class Culture in America, 1830–1870* (New Haven and London, 1982), pp. 184–185. Hulttunen's work brilliantly delineates the importance of sincerity in the heyday of sentimental Victorian culture. and she argues that once "boundlessness" yields to firm middle-class economic, social, and cultural boundaries after 1850, American Victorians take conventional forms of etiquette as a convenient substitute for transparent displays of sincere feeling. Eventually it is simply assumed that, as she puts it, "the right people would always behave in the right way" (p. 188).

26. Nathaniel Hawthorne, "Warwick Castle," *Atlantic Monthly* 10 (July–Dec. 1862). The same year the *Atlantic Monthly* also featured Emerson,

Thoreau, and Elizabeth Peabody. Such was Louisa May Alcott's reformist inheritance and her early circle of friends.

27. LMA, *Moods*, p. 146.

28. Ibid., p. 147.

29. Ibid., p. 155.

30. Auerbach, *Woman and the Demon*, p. 157.

31. Ibid., p. 46.

32. Gaskell, *The Life of Charlotte Brontë*, p. 420.

33. LMA, *Moods*, p. 322.

34. Ibid., p. 30.

35. Hannah Bewick, "Introduction to *Moods*," unpub. manuscript (courtesy of John A. Bewick).

36. LMA, *Moods*, p. 236.

37. Ibid., pp. 234, 245.

38. William R. Taylor and Christopher Lasch, "Two Kindred Spirits: Sorority and Family in New England, 1839–1845," *New England Quarterly* 36 (Mar. 1963): 154.

39. LMA, *Moods*, p. 322. The sad sisterhood unites the old maid, the fallen woman, and the wife.

40. Ibid., p. 311.

41. Ibid., p. 250.

42. LMA, "My Contraband or The Brothers," *Atlantic Montly* 12, no. 73 (Nov. 1863):584–590; rpt. in LMA, *Hospital Sketches and Camp and Fireside Stories* (Boston, 1869).

43. Ibid., p. 584. This, I think, confirms Auerbach's iconography.

44. Ibid.

45. Faith Dane's cottage is very similar to Mrs. Vawse's mountaintop refuge in Susan Warner's *Wide, Wide World* (New York, 1850). Jane Tompkins astutely points out that "though deprivation is ostensibly the defining feature of this woman's existence—she has no money, no property, no relatives—her house is warm and comfortable, her surroundings are pleasant, she works at odd jobs to earn money when she needs it, and she obviously enjoys the company of her friends" (*Sensational Designs*, p. 167). The question of whether the sentimental novelists were radical or conservative, she argues, is a false question. The real problem, as she puts it, is understanding and appreciating their work (p. 220).

46. LMA, *Moods*, 1865 ed., p. 81.

47. In chapter 1 of the 1865 edition of *Moods*, Adam Warwick specifically repudiates Ottila for her lack of "moral sentiment that makes all gifts and graces subservient to the virtues that render womanhood a thing to honor as

NOTES TO PAGES 136–141

well as love." He will lose his own self-respect if he stays with her, but he is tempted. "He drew her to him, kissed the red mouth . . . a long sigh of desire and regret broke from him" and he broke away (p. 20).

48. LMA, *Moods*, 1865 ed., p. 216; 1882 ed., p. 272.

49. LMA, *Moods*, 1865 ed., p. 204; 1882 ed., p. 258.

50. LMA, *Moods*, 1882 ed., preface.

51. Auerbach, *Woman and the Demon*, p. 153.

52. Ibid., p. 155.

53. LMA, *Moods*, p. 242.

54. Ednah Cheney, ed., *Louisa May Alcott: Life, Letters and Journals* (Boston, 1928), pp. 95–98.

55. LMA, *Moods*, p. 239.

56. LMA, *Jo's Boys* (Boston, 1886). The spinster heroine is Nan Harding.

57. LMA, *Moods*, p. 323. The author also notes in the same chapter that Sylvia's older sister Prue "both rejoiced at and rebelled against" the newly tender relationship between Sylvia and Mr. Yule. Prue, in fact, marries a widower with nine children because she is "of no further use at home."

58. LMA to Thomas Niles, Feb. 12, 1881; cited in Cheney, ed., *Alcott*, p. 341.

59. LMA, *Moods*, preface.

60. LMA, *A Modern Mephistopheles and a Whisper in the Dark* (Boston, 1889).

61. LMA, *Moods*, pp. 252, 253.

62. See William Leach, *True Love and Perfect Union: The Feminist Reform of Sex and Society* (New York, 1980), esp. chap. 6, and Antoinette Brown Blackwell, *The Island Neighbors: A Novel of American Life* (New York, 1871). Blackwell claims that men and women must go forward together or else risk personal and social disunion. Lillie Devereux Blake, *Fettered for Life: Or Lord and Master* (New York, 1874), posed suicide as the alternative to divorce when married women are denied equality. See also Eliza B. Duffey, *The Relation of the Sexes* (New York, 1874). Alcott recommends Duffey to college girls in *Jo's Boys* so they will start out as equals to men.

63. Alcott's knowledge of the mainstream woman's rights position dates back to the *Proceedings of the Woman's Rights Convention*.

64. A. K. Loring to LMA; quoted in Madeleine B. Stern, *Louisa May Alcott* (London, and New York, 1957), p. 383. Loring was also the publisher of Horatio Alger's *Ragged Dick*, (Boston, 1867), which came out one year before LMA's *Little Women*. For an interesting comparison of the two works, see Thomas H. Pauly, "Ragged Dick and Little Women: Idealized Homes and Unwanted Marriages," *Journal of Popular Culture* 9 (Winter 1975): 503–592. Excerpt reprinted in Stern, ed., *Critical Essays*, pp. 120–125.

308

65. LMA, *Moods*, 1882 ed., p. 301.
66. Evangeline St. Clare is "little Eva" in Harriet Beecher Stowe, *Uncle Tom's Cabin*; Ellen Montgomery is the heroine of Susan Warner's *Wide, Wide World*.

CHAPTER 8: THE BATTLE CRY OF FREEDOM

1. Bessie Z. Jones, "Introduction to Louisa May Alcott," in LMA, *Hospital Sketches and Camp and Fireside Stories* (Cambridge, Mass., 1960), p. 17.
2. See Ednah Cheney, ed., *Louisa May Alcott: Life, Letters and Journals* (Boston, 1928), p. 115.
3. Cheney, ed., *Alcott*, p. 130.
4. As William Leach notes, the *Index*, a journal run by Free Religion advocates, was next door to the *Woman's Journal* on Tremont Place in Boston. Leach details the relationship among feminists, positivists, and adherents of Free Religion. Octavius Frothingham was Louisa Alcott's cousin and frequent host. Alcott mentioned enjoying the company of Julia Ward Howe, Caroline Dall, and Jane Croly. In the 1860s, 1870s, and 1880s Alcott's fiction shifted from romanticism toward a rational realism that closely followed the bricolage structure of American positivism. Free Religion and universal laws of progress seemed as familiar as the *Index* and the *Woman's Journal* to Alcott. See William Leach, *True Love and Perfect Union: The Feminist Reform of Sex and Society* (New York, 1980).
   In *Little Women* (Boston, 1868, 1869), Louisa May Alcott spoke of Jo March as belonging to "the church of one" and in *Jo's Boys* (Boston, 1886), she recommended the standard rational feminist polemics of the postwar period in the chapter "Among the Maids." References to *Little Women* and *Jo's Boys* are cited by chapter numbers and titles which remain consistent in all editions.
5. Cheney, ed., *Alcott*, p. 130.
6. Madeleine B. Stern, "Louisa Alcott, Trouper," *New England Quarterly* 26, no. 2 (June 1943): 183.
7. In April 1860, Alcott wrote in her journal that "Sanborn was nearly kidnapped for being a friend of John Brown; but his sister and A. W. rescued him when he was hand-cuffed, and the scamps drove off" (Cheney, ed., *Alcott*, p. 98).
8. Thomas Wentworth Higginson, *Cheerful Yesterdays* (Boston, 1898), p. 142. Higginson also related Bronson Alcott's heroism during the attempt to rescue Anthony Burns, a fugitive slave, in 1854. Strangely, Alcott never fictionalized her father's lonely march up the steps of Faneuil Hall to confront the armed federal marshals charged with returning Burns to slavery.

9. LMA, "With a Rose That Bloomed on the Day of John Brown's Martyrdom," *The Liberator* 30 (Jan. 20, 1860).

10. Cheney, ed., *Alcott*, p. 106.

11. This circle of friends all acknowledged their debt to Transcendentalism and then joined forces in the Concord School of Philosophy and the American Social Science Association in the 1880s. At some stage of their lives, all were also Unitarians. Their dedication to woman's rights raises the importance of liberal religion and rationalism to feminism in nineteenth-century America.

12. See Thomas Haskell, *The Emergence of Professional Social Science, The ASSA, and the Crisis of Authority* (Urbana, Ill., 1977), and Franklin Sanborn, "The Work of Social Science in the United States," *Journal of Social Science* 6 (July 1874).

13. Cheney, ed., *Alcott*, pp. 133–134.

14. Ibid., p. 120.

15. LMA, "My Contraband; or, the Brothers," first called "The Brothers," *Atlantic Monthly* 12, no. 73 (Nov. 1863): 584–590; rpt. in *Hospital Sketches and Camp and Fireside Stories* (Boston, 1869).

16. LMA, "M. L.," *Commonwealth* 1, nos. 21, 22, 23, 24, 25 (Jan. 24, 31, Feb. 7, 14, 22, 1863); rpt. in *Journal of Negro History* 14, no. 4 (Oct. 1929). "Hospital Sketches," *Commonwealth* 1, nos. 38, 39, 41, 43 (May 22, 29, June 12, 26, 1863); rpt. as *Hospital Sketches* (Boston, 1863). "An Hour," *Commonwealth* 3, nos. 13, 14 (Nov. 26, Dec. 3, 1864); rpt. in *Hospital Sketches and Camp and Fireside Stories*.

17. Edward Channing, *A History of the United States*, vol. 5 (New York, 1921), p. 148.

18. Lorenzo Dow Turner, *Anti-Slavery Sentiment in American Literature prior to 1865* (Port Washington, N.Y., 1929), pp. 33–34.

19. Ibid. Turner divides antislavery literature in America into five periods: 1641–1808, 1808–1831, 1831–1850, 1850–1861, 1861–1865.

20. In 1852, the year *Uncle Tom's Cabin* appeared as a book, George Aiken dramatized it for G. C. Howard, the manager of the Museum in Troy, N.Y. It had six acts and followed the novel closely. Turner notes nine other contemporary versions (p. 74).

21. Harriet Beecher Stowe, *Dred: A Tale of the Great Dismal Swamp* (Boston, 1856), and *The Minister's Wooing* (New York, 1859).

22. Jane Tompkins, *Sensational Designs: The Cultural Work of American Fiction, 1790–1860* (New York, 1985), p. 125.

23. Ibid., p. 134.

24. Ibid., pp. 141, 142. Tompkins's treatment of Rachel Halliday's kitchen as the setting of "the redeemed form of the last supper" is a forceful

evocation of "the earthly family." Women's power, in sentimental novels, will provide abundance through loving cooperation. Alcott's vision, like Stowe's, is "politically subversive." See Tompkins, *Sensational Designs*, chap. 5, "Sentimental Power."

25. Ann Douglas, "Mysteries of Louisa May Alcott," *New York Review of Books* 25 (Sept. 18, 1978), pp. 60–63; rpt. in Madeleine B. Stern, *Critical Essays on Louisa May Alcott* (Boston, 1984), pp. 231–240. Douglas was writing about Alcott before another "American Renaissance" transformed our reading of sentimental literature. Her superb pioneer work on women writers has put us all in her debt.

26. This quote from *Bettine*, one of Louisa May Alcott's favorite books, appeared in an essay by her mother's close friend, Lydia Maria Child, "Ole Bull," reprinted in John S. Hart, *The Female Prose Writers of America* (Philadelphia, 1852), pp. 118–122.

27. LMA, *Moods* (Boston, 1865 and 1882 eds.), chap. 19, "What Next."

28. Romans 2:14. My emphasis.

29. LMA, "M. L.," chap. 1.

30. Ibid., chap. 4.

31. Ibid.

32. Ibid. Paul and Claudia are specifically described at the end as being "like the pilgrims in that fable never old." They leave the shores of "Vanity Fair," go through the "Valley of Humiliation," and climb up to the "Celestial City."

33. LMA, "A Modern Cinderella; or, the Little Old Shoe," *Atlantic Monthly* 6 (Oct. 1860).

34. See LMA, "Thoreau's Flute," *Atlantic Monthly* 22, no. 73 (Nov. 1863); rpt. in Cheney, ed., *Alcott*, chap. 5.

35. Cheney, ed., *Alcott*, p. 104. While she worked, "stories simmered in the brain." Like Jo in *Little Women*, Alcott confided woes to a ragbag in the attic. John Brown's daughters were boarding with the Alcotts in the spring of 1861, making her writing time even more precarious.

36. L. P. Brockett and Mary C. Vaughan, *Woman's Work in the Civil War: A Record* (Boston, 1867). See especially the introduction by Henry W. Bellows, president, U.S. Sanitary Commission.

37. Ibid., p. 79.

38. Ibid., p. 56. Bellows, in the introduction, claimed that these American women were "the products and representatives of a new social era, and a new political development."

39. Cheney, ed., *Alcott*, p. 115 (Dec. 1862).

40. Ibid. (Union Hotel Hospital, Georgetown, D.C., Jan. 1863).

41. Alcott's views on this subject follow those of Harriot Hunt, Elizabeth

Cady Stanton, and Julia Ward Howe, among others. Her description of John Sulie, a fatally wounded Virginia blacksmith, expresses the feminist ideal of true manhood: "Under his plain speech and unpolished manner I seem to see a noble character, a heart as warm and tender as a woman's, a nature fresh and frank as any child's" (Cheney, ed., *Alcott*, pp. 116, 117). See also LMA, *Hospital Sketches and Camp and Fireside Stories*, p. 51.

42. LMA, "Hospital Sketches."

43. Cheney, ed., *Alcott*, pp. 117, 118.

44. Ibid., pp. 118, 117.

45. Ibid., p. 118.

46. LMA, *Hospital Sketches and Camp and Fireside Stories*, p. 75.

47. Ibid., p. 76.

48. Ibid., p. 76, 77.

49. See J. G. Randall and David Donald, *The Civil War and Reconstruction* (Boston, 1961), pp. 224–225, 399, 461.

50. Cheney, ed., *Alcott*, p. 119 (Jan. 21, 1864).

51. The Alcott's friend Moncure Conway did not publish his monumental two-volume work on demonology until 1879. He had however authored a tract for the Ladies Religious Publication Society entitled *The Natural History of the Devil* (Albany, 1859). Conway's interest in science and in Free Religion was sparked by his determination to rid the world of unchecked passion and the force of superstition. Conway and Bronson Alcott took the reality of the devil seriously in the 1850s. According to his biographer, Mary Elizabeth Burtis, eventually Conway maintained that "Orthodoxy was now pleading for charity at the hands of rationalism"; see *Moncure Conway* (New Brunswick, N.J., 1952), p. 163.

52. Nancy F. Cott, "Passionlessness: An Interpretation of Victorian Sexual Ideology, 1790–1850," *Signs: Journal of Women in Culture and Society* 4, no. 2 (Winter 1978): 219–236.

53. Rebecca Harding Davis, "Paul Blecker," *Atlantic Monthly* (June–July 1863), quoted in Cott, "Passionlessness," p. 236. Alcott met Rebecca Harding (Davis) in May 1862 at a Boston party given by Annie Fields. Alcott's journal records that Harding was a "handsome, fresh, quiet woman, who says she never had any troubles, though she writes about woes. I told her I had lots of troubles; so I write jolly tales; and we wondered why we each did so" (Cheney, ed., *Alcott*, p. 107).

54. LMA, "My Contraband."

55. Tompkins, *Sensational Designs*, p. 104.

56. "An Hour" was reprinted in *Camp and Fireside Stories*. See Daniel Aaron, *The Unwritten War* (New York, 1973). This superb analysis of Ameri-

can writers and the Civil War mentions only two women writers, Mrs. Chesnut and Emily Dickinson.

57. Turner argues that "M. L.," for instance, "might just as well have appeared during any other period of the anti-slavery movement," while the literature of the later Civil War period was "intended primarily to be an inspiration to the Union Army, in the success of which the authors of them saw the end of slavery" (*Anti-Slavery Sentiment*, p. 111) Although Turner never mentions "An Hour" or "My Contraband," both stories belong in the later antislavery category.

58. LMA, "An Hour," rpt. in *Camp and Fireside Stories*, p. 346.

59. Ibid., p. 377.

60. For critical discussion of this story, see Jan Cohen, "The Negro Character in Northern Magazine Fiction of the 1860s," rpt. in Stern, ed., *Critical Essays on Louisa May Alcott*, p. 31. A more historical treatment of Alcott's Civil War pieces and her approach to racial questions is Abigail Ann Hamblen, "Louisa May Alcott and the Racial Question," *University Review* 37 (1971): 307–313. Once again, Alcott readers are indebted to Madeleine Stern who has gathered these articles and a wide variety of reviews into the *Critical Essays*.

61. Willie Lee Rose, *Rehearsal for Reconstruction* (New York, 1964).

62. Although the terms Deist, Transcendentalist, and Unitarian are used here almost interchangeably in describing Louisa May Alcott, the reader should note that Unitarians often regarded Transcendentalists as part of the "lunatic fringe," that some Transcendentalists, like Emerson himself, rebelled against the "cold rationalism of Unitarians," and that Alcott's grandfather May, a Unitarian, was hardly a Deist. She described herself variously as a birth-right Unitarian, a Transcendental product, and a Deist.

63. Tompkins, *Sensational Designs*, p. 128.

64. Ibid., p. 130.

65. Alcott, *Hospital Sketches*, p. 76.

66. Tompkins, *Sensational Designs*, chap. 5, "Sentimental Power." Jane Tompkins does not deal with Alcott, and she is quite precise about sentimental power as evangelical. I therefore take certain liberties in claiming such force for Alcott's liberal Christian works.

67. Douglas, "Mysteries of Louisa May Alcott."

68. See LMA, *Hospital Sketches*, chap. 2, "Model Children."

69. This theme is especially true in *Little Women, An Old-Fashioned Girl, Rose in Bloom*, and *Eight Cousins; or the Aunt-Hill*.

70. LMA, "Thoreau's Flute."

71. Cheney, ed., *Alcott*, p. 122.

72. Ibid., p. 123. "Sanborn asked me to do what Conway suggested before he left for Europe; viz., to arrange my letters in a printable shape, and put them in the 'Commonwealth.' "

73. Leach, *True Love*, p. 122.

74. See Madeleine Stern, ed., *Behind a Mask: The Unknown Thrillers of Louisa May Alcott* (New York, 1975). Stern traces the publication history of these pseudonymous tales and presents "Behind a Mask," "Pauline's Passion and Punishment," "The Mysterious Key," and "The Abbot's Ghost" in their original forms. The companion volume, *Plots and Counterplots: More Unknown Thrillers of Louisa May Alcott* (New York, 1976), includes "V. V.," "A Marble Woman," "The Skeleton in the Closet," "A Whisper in the Dark," and "Perilous Play." Stern's volumes are invaluable, a brilliant piece of literary detective work.

75. Stern, ed., *Behind a Mask*, "Pauline's Passion and Punishment."

76. See Cheney, ed., *Alcott*, pp. 115–119.

77. Brockett and Vaughan, *Woman's Work in the Civil War*, p. 71.

78. LMA, *Hospital Sketches*, p. 7.

79. Theodore Parker, sermon, "The Public Function of Woman"; rpt. in Theodore Parker, *Sins and Safeguards of Society* (Boston, 1907), pp. 178–206.

80. LMA, *Hospital Sketches*, p. 62.

81. Cheney, ed., *Alcott*, p. 24.

82. Ibid., p. 126.

83. See Stern, ed., *Plots and Counterplots*.

84. Stern, ed., *Behind a Mask*.

85. Cheney, ed., *Alcott*, p. 126.

86. Ibid., p. 131.

87. This choice is made abundantly clear in *An Old-Fashioned Girl* (Boston, 1870) and *Little Women*. In both novels the ideal feminist goal is mutual sacrifice in friendship, true love, or marriage.

CHAPTER 9: PASSION AND PUNISHMENT

1. Madeleine B. Stern has laid out the titles, first publication, and reprint history of the unknown thrillers of Louisa May Alcott in *Plots and Counterplots: More Unknown Thrillers of Louisa May Alcott* (New York, 1976), pp. 316–319. As Edith Birkhead reminds us, the "sentimental, the scandalous, the mysterious and the horrid," were all one complex genre in the mid-nineteenth century. See Birkhead, *The Tale of Terror: A Study of the Gothic Romance* (London, 1921).

2. Elizabeth Hardwick, *Seduction and Betrayal: Women and Literature* (New York, 1974).

3. Nina Baym, *Woman's Fiction, A Guide to Novels by and about Women in America, 1820–1870* (Ithaca, N.Y. 1978), chap. 2.

4. Ednah Cheney, ed., *Louisa May Alcott: Life, Letters and Journals* (Boston, 1928), p. 156.

5. Ibid., p. 165.

6. The term "little me pseudonyms" is coined by Elaine Showalter in reference to such American women authors as Fanny Fern, Grace Greenwood, and Fanny Forester, who adopted these "nominal bouquets" to hide energy, "powerful economic motives, and keen professional skills." See Showalter, "Toward a Feminist Poetics," in Elaine Showalter, ed., *The New Feminist Criticism: Essays on Women, Literature, and Theory* (New York, 1985).

7. See Madeleine B. Stern, ed., *Behind a Mask: The Unknown Thrillers of Louisa May Alcott* (New York, 1975) and *Plots and Counterplots;* Leona Rostenberg, "Some Anonymous and Pseudonymous Thrillers of Louisa M. Alcott," *Papers of the Bibliographical Society of America* 37, no. 2 (1943).

8. Stern, ed., *Plots and Counterplots*, p. 22.

9. Anon., "Pauline's Passion and Punishment," *Frank Leslie's Illustrated Newspaper* 15, nos. 379, 380 (Jan. 3, 10, 1863); rpt. in Stern, ed., *Behind a Mask*.

10. L. M. Alcott, "The Skeleton in the Closet," *Ten Cent Novelette*, no. 49 (Boston, 1867); rpt in Stern, ed., *Plots and Counterplots*. Stern points out that the contrast between Saxon and Spaniard was a common emblem for Bronson Alcott's scheme of spirituality (idea) versus flesh (material). Black lace was also a prop in Alcott family theatricals.

11. Angela Estes points out the similarities between "The Skeleton in the Closet" and Alcott's last thriller, "Perilous Play," first published in *Frank Leslie's Chimney Corner* 8, no. 194 (Feb. 13, 1869). See Angela Estes, "An Aptitude for Bird: Louisa May Alcott's Women and Emerson's Self-Reliant Men," Ph.D. diss., Univ. of Oregon, 1985.

12. LMA, "Little Genevieve," *Saturday Evening Gazette*, Quarto Series, no. 13 (March 29, 1856); A. M. Barnard, "Behind a Mask; or, A Woman's Power," *Flag of Our Union* 21, nos. 41, 42, 43, 44 (Oct. 13, 20, 27, Nov. 3, 1866); rpt. in Stern, ed., *Behind a Mask*.

13. Cheney, ed., *Alcott*, p. 132.

14. Ibid., pp. 146–147.

15. ABA, *Journals*, ed. Odell Shepard (Boston, 1938), p. 173 (Mar. 16, 1846).

16. Anon., "A Whisper in the Dark," *Frank Leslie's Illustrated Newspaper*

16, nos. 401, 402 (June 6, 13, 1863); rpt. in *A Modern Mephistopheles and A Whisper in the Dark* (Boston, 1889).

17. Ibid. See also Mrs. Anne Radcliffe, *Sicilian Romance* (1790), and Horace Walpole, *The Castle of Otranto* (1764).

18. Cheney, ed., *Alcott*, p. 122 (June 1860). See also Edith Birkhead, *The Tale of Terror: A Study of Gothic Romance* (London, 1921).

19. A Well Known Author, "V. V.; or, Plots and Counterplots," *Flag of Our Union* 20, nos. 5, 6, 7, 8 (Feb. 4, 11, 18, 25, 1865); rpt. in Stern, ed., *Plots and Counterplots*.

20. Ibid. There is something of Friedrich Schiller's *Der Geisterseher* here in the dancer-acrobat-juggler, but more likely Alcott had read Mrs. Radcliffe's *Mysteries of Udolpho* (1794) again.

21. "V. V.," in Stern, ed., *Plots and Counterplots*, p. 129.

22. A. M. Barnard, "The Marble Woman or the Mysterious Model," *Flag of Our Union*, 22, nos. 20, 21, 22, 23 (May 20, 27, June 3, 10, 1865) rpt. in Stern, ed., *Behind a Mask*.

23. Ibid., p. 227.

24. In *Behind a Mask*, Sir John refers to himself as "the old gentleman" and as "father" when flirting with Jean Muir.

25. ABA's Manuscript Journal, July 5, 1865, HL.

26. Cheney, ed., *Alcott*, p. 51.

27. Ibid., p. 185 (Aug. 1866).

28. Alcott's melodrama has been performed as a play by the Hangar Theatre Company in Ithaca, N.Y., in an adaptation by Michael Carton, directed by Robert Moss. This version fell naturally into scenes, sets, action, and dialogue. See also Karen Halttunen, "The Domestic Drama of Louisa May Alcott," *Feminist Studies* 10, no. 2 (Summer 1984): 233–253.

29. A. M. Barnard, "Behind a Mask"; rpt. in Stern, ed., *Behind a Mask*, p. 99. Muir writes this in a letter to her friend Hortense, also mentioning a dream in which she was "playing Lady Tartuffe—as I am." Alcott had seen Molière's play in Nice in February 1866 (see Cheney, ed., *Alcott*, p. 181).

30. Judith Fetterley, "Impersonating 'Little Women': The Radicalism of Alcott's *Behind a Mask*," *Women's Studies* 10 (1983): 1–14. Fetterley's reading of *Behind a Mask* is bold and illuminating. I differ only in the pessimistic view she offers of *Little Women*. Alcott was not, I think, imprisoned behind a mask of femininity after *Behind a Mask*. Jean Muir's triumph, I agree, signals a brave turn in Alcott's fiction; environment becomes more determinant in shaping character but characters, particularly women, march out to change environments.

31. A. M. Barnard, "Behind a Mask," p. 104.

32. Ibid., p. 93.

33. For a radical feminist reading of Alcott's thrillers and their commonality with her children's fiction see Angela Estes, "An Aptitude for Bird."

34. Cheney, ed., *Alcott*, p. 152.

35. See Jane Benardette and Phyllis Moe, eds., *Companions of Our Youth: Stories of Women for Young People's Magazines, 1865–1900* (New York, 1980); Joy Marsella, *The Promise of Destiny: Children and Women in the Short Stories of Louisa May Alcott* (New Haven, 1983).

36. Cheney, ed., *Alcott*, p. 152.

37. Unfortunately, Adams's adult heroines were not allowed the freedom granted his twelve-year-old girls.

38. *A Modern Mephistopheles* eventually did rather well in the No Name Series (Boston, 1877).

39. Cheney, ed., *Alcott*, pp. 154, 155.

40. Ibid., p. 163.

41. Ibid., pp. 163, 164.

42. See Ellen Carol DuBois, *Feminism and Suffrage* (Ithaca, N.Y., 1978), chap. 6, for a full description of this problem.

CHAPTER 10: WRITING *LITTLE WOMEN*

1. I avoid the term "domestic feminism" here, because as used by Daniel Scott Smith it refers specifically to woman's growing power within the household. Smith links the "radical decline in nineteenth-century marital fertility to the increasing power of woman *within* the family" (his emphasis). See Daniel Scott Smith, "Family Limitation, Sexual Control, and Domestic Feminism in Victorian America," in *Clio's Consciousness Raised*, ed. Mary Hartman and Lois W. Banner (New York, 1974), pp. 119–136. Smith's use of "domestic feminism" does not relate to the links between a woman's power within the family and her extension of that power into the public sphere.

Egalitarian marriage, I argue, was at the heart of liberal American feminism in the nineteenth century. This chapter explores the centrality of feminists' wish for individuality and democratic domestic life.

2. Alcott's readers wanted Jo to marry Laurie; she was flooded with letters after Part One of *Little Women* appeared. Although Alcott depicted Laurie as a rich, handsome "Heathcliff" (or romantic hero), Alcott tried to domesticate him just as she tried to make Jo's boyishness acceptable. Her main characters are not androgynous, but their individuality does not reside in specifically sexual stereotypes either. Manhood and womanhood are a combination of physical resources and socialization.

3. Ednah Cheney, ed., *Louisa May Alcott: Life, Letters and Journals* (Bos-

ton, 1928), pp. 162–167. Alcott began writing Part One in May 1868. By June she sent twelve chapters to Thomas Niles at Roberts Brothers. Her journal for November 1, 1868, records, "Began the second part of 'Little Women.' I can do a chapter a day, and in a month I mean to be done" (p. 165).

4. Ibid., p. 165.

5. Ibid. (Nov. 16, 1868). The next day she recorded finishing the thirteenth chapter of *Little Women*.

6. "Women," the record of a lecture and discussion at the Radical Club appears in Mrs. John T. Sargent, ed., *Sketches and Reminiscences of the Radical Club of Chestnut Street, Boston* (Boston, 1880). Coalitionists present and speaking included Ednah Cheney, Thomas Wentworth Higginson, Bronson Alcott, Charles Everett, Ralph Waldo Emerson.

7. Alcott read Carlyle; Bronson's visit with Carlyle is described above in Chapter 3.

8. "Buckle and Carlyle," a paper delivered by W. J. Potter at the Radical Club, is summarized in Sargent, ed., *Sketches*, pp. 251–258. Cheney specifically mentions Motley's book in the discussion following Potter's lecture. That evening Bronson Alcott was still arguing that the world "has to be educated up" to accept the ideas of great "prophets." Higginson, Cyrus Bartol, and Cheney, together with Potter, carried the evening (p. 256).

9. John Lathrop Motley, *Historic Progress and American Democracy* (New York, 1869), p. 6, and *The Rise of the Dutch Republic* (New York, 1855). Motley's point is clear in volume 3 of *The Rise of the Dutch Republic*, published after *Little Women*; he is writing about a homogeneous "folk"; their rise is inexorable and they can trust one another to fulfill historical contracts. For an excellent discussion of the Bancroft-Motley approach as "whig," "progressive," "idealist," "liberal," or "Germanic," see Harry B. Henderson III, *Versions of the Past: The Historical Imagination in American Fiction* (New York, 1974), chap. 2.

10. Henderson, *Versions*, p. 23.

11. Bronson Alcott, quoted in "Buckle and Carlyle," in Sargent, ed., *Sketches*, p. 257.

12. "Woman," in Sargent, ed., *Sketches*, p. 43.

13. "Buckle and Carlyle," in ibid., p. 255.

14. Ibid., p. 257.

15. Ibid., p. 253.

16. See Theodore Parker's statement, read aloud at the end of the Radical Club discussion on "Woman," in Sargent, ed., *Sketches*, p. 45.

17. Cheney, ed., *Alcott*, p. 165.

18. LMA, *Little Women* (Boston, 1868, 1869), chap. 33, "Jo's Journal." References to *Little Women* are cited by chapter numbers and titles which remain consistent in all editions.

19. The Radical Club debates probably did not convert Louisa Alcott to liberal rationalism. Rather, they reflected a general shift in liberal reform ideology within Alcott's set. She, in turn, presents this shift in *Little Women* and in all her later fiction.

20. Cheney, ed., *Alcott*, p. 96.

21. Ibid, p. 95.

22. Louisa May Alcott, "Happy Women," *The New York Ledger* 24, no. 7 (Apr. 11, 1868). She wrote the article in a very lonely, hardworking period, planning it as she ate a "dilapidated" squash pie, and writing it with the one-hundred-dollar bill before her, noting that "liberty is a better husband than love to many of us" (Cheney, ed., *Alcott*, p. 162).

23. Cheney, ed., *Alcott*, p. 153.

24. Ibid., pp. 152–167. Alcott mentions the Radical Club, the Woman's Club, Emerson, Kate Field, Abba May, Fanny Kemble, among others, during the period she was writing *Little Women*.

25. See Ellen Carol DuBois, *Feminism and Suffrage* (Ithaca, N.Y., 1978), pp. 166–167.

26. Ibid., chap. 6. There is a tendency to view Howe and Stone among others as "conservative" feminists because they placed black male suffrage ahead of woman suffrage at this moment. Stanton and Anthony are then viewed as more radical on woman's rights. I would argue that Alcott's position—allied with Stone, Julia Ward Howe, Antoinette Blackwell, and Douglass—was not a betrayal of woman's rights, but a strategic attempt to preserve the liberal reform coalition.

27. Ibid., p. 169.

28. Louisa May Alcott claimed that the Bellevue Hotel was a bit too sociable for her taste; May, however, enjoyed it thoroughly. See William Leach, *True Love and Perfect Union: The Feminist Reform of Sex and Society* (New York, 1980), p. 315, for the links between Dio Lewis's hygienic school, the American Social Science Association, and friends and family of Louisa May Alcott, such as Abigail May and Caroline Dall.

29. Cheney, ed., *Alcott*, p. 162.

30. Ibid., p. 163.

31. Ibid., p. 164. Domestic chores remained a problem for the Alcott women. "No girl," Alcott wrote, tersely summarizing the servant problem in the Concord household. Admitting that "we don't like the kitchen department, and our tastes and gifts lie in other directions," Alcott knew she

had to earn enough to provide domestic help for Abba, May, Anna, and herself.

CHAPTER 11: READING *LITTLE WOMEN*

1. LMA, *Little Women* (Boston, 1868, 1869), chap. 1, "Playing Pilgrims." References to *Little Women* are cited by chapter numbers and titles which remain consistent in all editions.

2. Charles Dickens, *Bleak House*, 2 vols. (London, 1854). The first reference is in chapter 8. Mr. Jarndyce tried out several versions of "good little woman."

3. Esther's relationship to Charlie, whom she nurses through smallpox, is crucial to understanding Alcott's version of domestic democracy. Charlie is a servant and Esther is a lady; nevertheless, housekeeping duties and mutual nurturance unite them. Esther, "attached to life again" after her near-fatal illness, for she too got smallpox, recalls "the pleasant afternoon when I was raised in bed with pillows for the first time, to enjoy tea-drinking with Charlie!" Charlie has taken over Esther's housewifely tasks (2:15). The same relationship occurs between Phoebe and Rose in *Eight Cousins* and *Rose in Bloom*.

4. LMA, *Little Women*, chap. 42, "All Alone."

5. Ednah Cheney, ed., *Louisa May Alcott: Life, Letters and Journals* (Boston, 1928), p. 164.

6. Susan B. Warner [Elizabeth Wetherell], *The Wide, Wide World* (New York, 1852).

7. Charlotte M. Yonge, *The Heir of Redclyffe* (New York and London, 1853); *The Daisy Chain* (New York and London, 1856).

8. Humphrey Carpenter notes the resemblance between Ethel May and Jo March in his witty study, *Secret Gardens: A Study of the Golden Age of Chidren's Literature* (New York, 1985), pp. 86–102.

9. Nina Baym identifies this "overplot" of nineteenth-century women's fiction in *Women's Fiction: A Guide to Novels by and about Women in America, 1820–1870* (Ithaca, N.Y., 1978). She names several other characteristics of the typical woman's novel: a heroine and a villainess are paired; the heroine's childhood is miserable and only her mother's memory comforts her; heroines often acquire surrogate families; husbands are not as important to heroines as fathers, guardians, and brothers; women's faith is removed from a patriarchal setting. *The Wide, Wide World* does not conform to all of Baym's characteristics, but it is generally representative of her model.

10. See Baym, *Women's Fiction*, pp. 296–299. Judith Fetterley in "*Little Women*: Alcott's Civil War," *Feminist Studies* 5, no. 2 (Summer 1979):369–

393, argues for an "over reading" and a "subliminal" reading of Alcott's work, claiming that the rage expressed in *Behind a Mask* is repressed but still evident in *Little Women*. For a representative selection of *Little Women* analyses see Madeleine B. Stern, ed., *Critical Essays on Louisa May Alcott* (Boston, 1984).

11. See Carpenter, *Secret Gardens*, pp. 86–102, and the following other historians and writers who recognize *Little Women* as a positive contribution to juvenile literature: Joy A. Marsella, *The Promise of Destiny: Children and Women in the Short Stories of Louisa May Alcott* (Westport, Conn., 1983); Anne Scott MacLeod, *A Moral Tale: Children's Fiction and American Culture, 1820–1860* (Hamden, Conn., 1975); R. Gordon Kelley, *Mother Was a Lady: Self and Society in Selected American Children's Periodicals, 1865–1890* (Westport, Conn., 1974).

12. See Carpenter, *Secret Gardens;* Martin Green, "The Charm of Peter Pan," in *Children's Literature* 9 (New Haven and London, 1981): 19–27; Elizabeth Cripps, "Alice and the Reviewers," *Children's Literature* 11 (New Haven and London, 1983): 32–48.

13. LMA, *Little Women*, chap. 11. "Experiments." Nina Auerbach understands the "primacy of the female family" in the novel "both as moral-emotional magnet and as work of art"; see *Communities of Women* (Cambridge, Mass., 1978), pp. 56, 73. She argues, however, that Alcott's female family is a closed circle. Domestic democracy, I think, provides a launching pad for the "little" women's flight into the larger world.

14. LMA, *Little Women*, chap. 20, "Confidential."

15. Ibid., chap. 5, "Being Neighborly." Auerbach (in *Communities of Women*) writes with sensitivity about the role of Laurie in *Little Women*. Laurie needs the March family's harmony, but in order to gain entrance to the feminist household he must acquire some feminist virtues. A balanced domesticity, Alcott maintains, also depends upon the girls' acquisition of "masculine" courage, independence, and comfortable elegance. Elizabeth Lennox Keyser brilliantly observes that Jo's rescue of Laurie from the "enchanted palace" is a "reversal of the Sleeping Beauty tale; see "Alcott's Portraits of the Artist as Little Woman," *International Journal of Women's Studies* 5, no. 5 (1978): 445–459.

16. LMA, *Little Women*, chap. 5, "Being Neighborly." Anne Hollander notes that "fellowship, insisted on by Jo, appears here as an American ideal for governing the conduct between sexes"; see her "Reflections on *Little Women*," in *Children's Literature* 9:28–39.

17. LMA, *Little Women*, chap. 38, "On the Shelf." Meg has already made the case for true love, telling rich Aunt March, "I shall marry whom I please, and you can leave your money to anyone you like."

18. Ibid. See Patricia Spacks in *The Female Imagination* (New York, 1972), pp. 125–28. She argues that there is "no doubt about which sex really does things" in *Little Women*. According to Spacks, it is men who do things in the novel; hence female readers "yearned somehow to be boy and girl simultaneously" (p. 120). For a view closer to my own see Carolyn Heilbrun, *Reinventing Womanhood* (New York, 1979), p. 191.

19. LMA, *Little Women*, chap. 8, "Jo Meets Apollyon." Elizabeth Keyser views this incident quite differently, arguing that Amy is Jo's repressed greedy, childish self ("Alcott's Portraits," p. 450).

20. LMA, *Little Women*, chap. 3, "The Laurence Boy."

21. Ibid., chap. 29, "Calls."

22. Beth's death is not the sentimental artifact so brilliantly discussed by Ann Douglas in "The Meaning of Little Eva"; see *The Feminization of American Culture* (New York, 1972), chap. 1, Elizabeth Keyser argues that Beth's death relegates Jo to her younger sister's role of childish dependency ("Alcott's Portraits," p. 454).

23. LMA, *Little Women*, chap. 36, "Beth's Secret."

24. Ibid., chap. 42, "All Alone."

25. Ibid., chap. 24, "Gossip." Douglas (*The Feminization of American Culture*) finds Little Eva's death merely decorative in *Uncle Tom's Cabin*. Jane Tompkins argues for a different reading of this death in *Sensational Designs: The Cultural Work of American Fiction, 1790–1860* (New York, 1985), chap. 6. Beth March's death is closer, I think, to Tompkins's method of analysis. Jo is deeply affected and she is "all alone" as Alcott notes, a situation that occasions her change of heart and her reevaluation of Professor Bhaer's meaning in her life.

26. LMA, *Little Women*, chap. 35, "Heartache." Fetterley ("*Little Women*: Alcott's Civil War") sees Jo March's refusal as part of her internal battle between passivity and sexual rage.

27. LMA, *Little Women*, chap. 33, "Jo's Journal." Professor Bhaer has a younger, handsomer fictional counterpart in August Bopp, a twenty-three-year-old German immigrant gym teacher in Alcott's "King of Clubs and the Queen of Hearts," *Camp and Fireside Stories* (1869), pp. 99–142. His heavy German accent and his sincere romanticism appeal to Dolly, an all-American girl in his gym class. He is working to bring his little niece to America and he calls Dolly his "heart's dearest" or "mein liebchen"

28. LMA, *Little Women*, chap. 46, "Under the Umbrella."

29. Ibid.

30. Ibid., chap. 1, "Playing Pilgrims."

31. Ibid., chap. 27, "Literary Lessons."

32. See Baym, *Women's Fiction*, pp. 110–139.

33. LMA, *Little Women*, chap. 27, "Literary Lessons."

34. Ibid., chap. 42, "All Alone."

35. Cheney, ed., *Alcott*, p. 199 (June, July, August, 1868). In 1876 she appended, "Too much work for one young woman. No wonder she broke down."

36. Ibid. Having sent off 402 pages of *Little Women*, Alcott wrote, "Hope it will go, for I shall probably get nothing for *Morning Glories*. Very tired, head full of pain from overwork, and heart heavy about Marmee, who is growing feeble."

37. LMA, *Little Women*, chap. 42, "All Alone."

38. Ibid., chap. 47, "Harvest Time."

39. See Fetterley, "*Little Women:* Alcott's Civil War"; Keyser, "Alcott's Portraits"; Eugenia Kaledin, "Louisa May Alcott: Success and the Sorrow of Self-Denial," *Women's Studies* 5 (1978): 251–263.

40. LMA, *Little Women*, chap. 47, "Harvest Time." Anne Hollander's provocative reading of *Little Women* points to the complex character of Amy March and its development. See "Reflections on *Little Women*" in *Children's Literature* 9:28–39.

41. LMA, *Little Women*, chap. 34, "A Friend."

42. Stern, *Louisa May Alcott*, p. 176.

43. LMA, *Little Women*, chap. 1, "Playing Pilgrims."

44. Ibid., chap. 47, "Harvest Time."

45. "Our Young Folks Advertizer," in *Our Young Folks*, no. 95 (Nov. 1872).

46. Elizabeth Stuart Phelps, "Our Little Woman," serialized in *Our Young Folks*, pts. 1, 2, no. 95 (Nov. 1872): 654–662; pts. 3, 4, no. 96 (Dec. 1872): 727–737.

47. Ibid., pt. 2, pp. 728, 729.

48. Ibid., pt. 4, p. 734.

49. Ibid., pt. 4, p. 736.

CHAPTER 12: GIRL-BOYS AND BOY-GIRLS

1. See Nina Baym, *Women's Fiction: A Guide to Novels by and about Women in America, 1820–1870* (Ithaca, N.Y., 1978), and Judith Fetterley, "*Little Women:* Alcott's Civil War," *Feminist Studies* 5, no. 2 (Summer 1979): 369–393; Elizabeth Lennox Keyser, "Alcott's Portraits of the Artist as Little Woman," *International Journal of Women's Studies* 5, no. 5 (1978): 445–459, and Eugenia Kaledin, "Louisa May Alcott: Success and the Sorrow of Self-Denial," *Women's Studies* 5 (1978):251–263. I agree with Madeleine B. Stern, the foremost scholar of Louisa May Alcott's life and works, who takes

a more positive and subtle view, emphasizing Alcott's link to the *Woman's Journal*, the New England Woman Suffrage Association and the "causes of Humanity" (Stern, "Louisa Alcott's Feminist Letters," in *Studies in the American Renaissance* ed. Joel Myerson [Boston, 1978], p. 437.

2. See Ann Douglas, *The Feminization of American Culture* (New York, 1972); Douglas includes Alcott in the sentimental rather than the Romantic tradition of nineteenth-century authors. Alcott is sentimental in the sense of Jane Tompkins's use of "sentimental power" in *Sensational Designs* (New York, 1985).

3. Mark Twain's *Tom Sawyer* was published in 1876, *Huckleberry Finn* in 1885.

4. Theodore Parker, sermon, "The Public Function of Woman"; rpt. in Theodore Parker, *Sins and Safeguards of Society* (Boston, 1907), pp. 178–206.

5. Harry B. Henderson III, in *Versions of the Past: The Historical Imagination in American Fiction* (New York, 1974), provides an excellent discussion of holistic and progressive strains intertwined in the heroic models of American historical fiction.

6. Madeleine B. Stern, *Louisa May Alcott* (London, New York, 1957), chap. 10. See also Raymond L. Kilgour, *Messrs. Roberts Brothers Publishers* (Ann Arbor, Mich., 1952).

7. Moncure Daniel Conway, *The Autobiography of Moncure Daniel Conway*, 2 vols. (Boston, 1904). For details on the *Dial*, see 1:10.

8. Ibid., 1: chaps. 19 and 20, for discussions of the Alcott circle and Darwin. For Thoreau's reading of Darwin, see John W. Clarkson, Jr., "Mentions of Emerson and Thoreau in the Letters of Franklin Benjamin Sanborn," *Studies in the American Renaissance*, p. 403. See also Rosalind Rosenberg, *Beyond Separate Spheres: Intellectual Roots of Modern Feminism* (New Haven, 1881), and Antoinette Brown Blackwell, *The Sexes throughout Nature* (New York, 1875).

9. Stern, *Louisa May Alcott*, chap. 10. See also Kilgour, *Mssrs. Roberts Brothers*, pts. 2 and 3.

10. Stern, *Louisa May Alcott*, chap. 10. In 1872 Abba Alcott noted in her diary that her daughter had achieved "literary and practical power securing a maintenance for herself and family having well invested several thousand before the age of forty." AMA's Memoir, Apr. 20, 1872, HL.

11. AMA's Memoir, Mar. 2, 1868, HL.

12. Ibid., Sept. 1867.

13. Ednah Cheney, ed., *Louisa May Alcott: Life, Letters and Journals* (Boston, 1928), p. 159.

14. Ibid., p. 173.

15. Louisa May Alcott, *An Old-Fashioned Girl* (Boston, 1870), chap. 1, pp.

4, 9. All references to the text of *An Old-Fashioned Girl* are cited by chapter number, chapter name, and page numbers. Chapter numbers remain consistent in all published editions.

16. Ibid., chap. 8, "Six Years Afterward," p. 159. Polly takes the radical step of renting a room of her own, in the second half of the novel, "Six Years Afterward." Alcott's point is obvious: Polly is no longer visiting her rich friends; she is now a working woman.

17. Ibid., chap. 9, "Lessons," p. 164.

18. Ibid., pp. 173-175.

19. Ibid., chap. 13, "The Sunny Side," p. 255.

20. Ibid., p. 261.

21. Sargent was famous as the editor of the *New York Mirror* and the *Boston Transcript;* he turned to spiritualism in his later years and his last book was *The Scientific Basis of Spiritualism* (Boston, 1880). A year after Louisa May Alcott's *Little Women*, Roberts Brothers published Epes Sargent's *Woman Who Dared*, a wild "domestic narrative poem, in blank verse." See Kilgour, *Messrs. Roberts Bothers*, pp. 76-78.

22. LMA, *An Old-Fashioned Girl*, chap. 19, "Tom's Success," p. 371.

23. Kilgour, *Messrs. Roberts Brothers*, p. 103.

24. LMA, *Aunt Jo's Scrap Bag* and *Shawl Straps* (Boston, 1872), p. 225.

25. Cheney, ed., *Alcott*, p. 213. See also Stern, *Louisa May Alcott*, chap. 11.

26. See, for example, William Taylor Adams [Oliver Optic], *Try Again, or The Trials and Triumph of Harry West* (New York, 1857), and *The Way of the World* (Boston, 1867).

27. LMA, *Little Men: Life at Plumfield with Jo's Boys* (Boston, 1871), chap. 1, "Nat." References to *Little Men* are cited by chapter and page numbers. Chapter numbers remain consistent in all published editions.

28. Ibid., chap. 7, "Naughty Nan," p. 105. Mrs. Aunt Jo's belief in coeducation seems very close to Harriet Martineau's letter to the 1851 Woman's Rights Convention at Worcester, Mass. Printed in *The Liberator*, Nov. 21, 1851, Alcott may well have read it. Martineau was reading Auguste Comte at the time and she argued for "one true method in the treatment of either sex, of any color, and under any circumstances—to ascertain what are the powers of that being, to cultivate them to the utmost, and then to see what action they will find for themselves."

29. LMA, *Little Men*, chap. 12, "Huckleberries," pp. 205-209. See also Annie Fellows Johnston, *The Little Colonel* (New York, 1896).

30. Sarah Josepha Hale, quoted in Roberts Bros. advertisement for Louisa May Alcott's Writing, 1888.

31. LMA, *Little Men*, chap. 21, "Thanksgiving," p. 348.

32. LMA, "Cupid and Chow-Chow," *Hearth and Home* 4, nos. 20 and 21

(May 18 and 25, 1872); rpt. in *Aunt Jo's Scrap Bag* 3 (Boston, 1873): 5–40. Subsequent page references are from this edition.

33. LMA, "Cupid and Chow-Chow," p. 9.

34. Ibid., p. 39.

35. See Ellen Carol DuBois, *Feminism and Suffrage* (Ithaca, N.Y., 1978), offers an excellent overview of Stanton and Anthony. Alcott certainly did not find fault with Anthony on grounds of her spinsterhood.

36. LMA to the American Woman Suffrage Association from Concord, Mass., Oct. 1885; rpt. in Stern, "Louisa Alcott's Feminist Letters," in *Studies in the American Renaissance*, p. 449.

37. LMA to Lucy Stone, from Concord, Mass., Oct. 1, 1873, cited in Elizabeth Cady Stanton et al., *History of Woman's Suffrage* 2 (Rochester, 1881–1902), 831–832. As Madeleine Stern notes, this letter was read at the second session of the Woman's Suffrage Convention, Brooklyn, N.Y.; see "Louisa Alcott's Feminist Letters," pp. 437–438.

38. LMA to Lucy Stone, from Boston, Oct. 6, 1874; rpt. in Stern, "Louisa Alcott's Feminist Letters," p. 438. Eugenia Kaledin insists that "Cupid and Chow-Chow" is a painful story of Alcott's self-denial. She argues that "we are forced to conclude again that the promise of money forced her to compromise her [woman's rights] principles." I doubt it. Alcott is undeniably poking fun at "Aunt Susan"; her story, however, is genuinely witty and reflects the Alcott, Julia Ward Howe, Lucy Stone position on many issues. See Kaledin, "Louisa May Alcott," pp. 256–257.

39. Cheney, ed., *Alcott*, p. 267.

CHAPTER 13: TO EARN A HOME

1. Ednah Cheney, ed., *Louisa May Alcott: Life, Letters and Journals* (Boston, 1928), p. 222.

2. Ibid. The series appeared as LMA, "Work, Or Christie's Experiment," *The Christian Union* 6–7 (Dec. 18, 25, 1872; Jan. 1, 8, 15, 22, 29; Feb. 5, 12, 19, 26; Mar. 5, 12, 19, 26; Apr. 2, 9, 16, 23, 30; May 7, 14, 21, 28; and June 4, 11, 18, 1873); published as *Work: A Story of Experience* (Boston, 1873; rpt. New York, 1977).

3. Cheney, ed., *Alcott*, p. 225.

4. Ibid., p. 224.

5. Theodore Parker, sermon, "The Public Function of Women;" rpt. in Theodore Parker, *Sins and Safeguards of Society* (Boston, 1907), pp. 178–206. For a contrast to Parker's and Alcott's definition of true womanhood, see

Barbara Welter, "The Cult of True Womanhood, 1820–1860," *American Quarterly* 18 (Summer 1966): 151–175.

6. Moncure Daniel Conway, *The Autobiography of Moncure Daniel Conway*, 2 vols. (Boston, 1904), 1:295–297.

7. Cheney, ed. *Alcott*, p. 220. See also LMA, *Aunt Jo's Scrap Bag* and *Shawl Straps* (Boston, 1872), chap. 5.

8. LMA, *Work*, chap. 1, p. 2.

9. Lucy Maynard Salmon, *Domestic Service* (New York, 1911), pp. 148, 141. Fay Dudden, *Serving Women* (New York, 1983), offers a recent exploration of domestic servants in nineteenth-century America.

10. Salmon, *Domestic Service*, p. 150. Jean Fagin Yellin forcefully agrees that *Work* should be read as a feminist essay; she also credits Alcott for her "seemingly effortless use of the American vernacular." Yellin, however, finds that *Work* lacks an exposé of class differences among women. Jean Fagin Yellin, "From Success to Experience: Louisa May Alcott's *Work*," *Massachusetts Review* (Fall 1980):533.

11. "Marryin' for a livin' " is dismissed with contempt by Cynthie Wilkins in chap. 14, p. 327.

12. Ibid., chap. 4, p. 81.

13. Parker, "Public Function," p. 180.

14. LMA, *Work*, chap. 9, p. 204. Cynthie Wilkins uses the imagery of her trade as a laundress. Her satire is sharp, evocative of Carlyle's *Sartor Resartus*, and echoes from Jonathan Swift's *Tale of the Tub*. Cynthie discovers "how often does the Body appropriate what was meant for the cloth only" (Thomas Carlyle, *Sartor Resartus* [London, 1896], p. 218). Alcott read Carlyle and Swift's *Tale of the Tub*; she also wrote a poem about herself as laundress ("Labor: A Song from the Suds," AFP).

15. Alcott here (*Work*, chap. 19, p. 413) provides a prose version of her memorial poem, "Thoreau's Flute." David Sterling's flute, hung beside the window, is stirred by the wind, carrying a "supernatural" melody to his widow.

16. Ibid., chap. 19, p. 422.

17. John Bunyan, *The Pilgrim's Progress* (Westwood, N.J., 1986), Part the Second, p. 216.

18. LMA, *Moods* (Boston, 1882), p. 322.

19. Cheney, ed., *Alcott*, p. 224.

20. Ibid., p. 225.

21. Review of LMA's *Work* in the *Lakeside Monthly*, copy in APC.

22. Review of LMA's *Work* in *Harper's New Monthly Magazine* 47 (Sept. 1873): 614–615.

23. Miss Phelps, "Address to Working Women," quoted in Rosalyn Baxandall, Linda Gordon, and Susan Reverby, eds., *America's Working Women: A Documentary History, 1600 to the Present* (New York, 1976). Susan Reverby kindly brought this document to my attention.

24. LMA, *Diana and Persis*, ed. Sarah Elbert (New York, 1978). Original untitled manuscript is listed as "a holograph in Alcott's hand on light blue paper," APC.

25. Caroline Ticknor, *May Alcott; A Memoir* (Boston, 1928), p. 20.

26. Ibid., p. 127. See Raymond L. Kilgour, *Messrs. Roberts Brothers, Publishers* (Ann Arbor, Mich., 1952), for details of the "No Name" series.

27. AMA, May 1, 1875 (date of copy), APC. See also *Woman's Journal* 6 (May 1, 1875).

28. Ticknor, *May Alcott*, p. 248.

29. Ibid., p. 248.

30. Ibid., p. 255.

31. Madeleine B. Stern, *Louisa May Alcott* (London and New York, 1957), p. 275. I am grateful to Jean Stump, art historian at the University of Kansas, for the direct reference to May Alcott's diary entry, Jan. 28, 1879.

32. LMA, *Diana and Persis*, p. 56. In the spring of 1879, Alcott, missing her sister May, wrote, "No golden-haired, glue-gowned Diana ever appears now; she sits happily sewing baby clothes in Paris" (Cheney, ed., *Alcott*, p. 319).

33. LMA, *Diana and Persis*, p. 64.

34. Ibid., p. 122. I am grateful to Elaine Showalter, Leslie Mitchner, and Elizabeth Keyser for demonstrating to me that chapters 3 and 4 in *Diana and Persis* ought to be reversed in the published version. Clearly Diana does visit Persis in Paris before embarking on her own work in Italy.

35. Ibid., p. 130.

36. Ibid., pp. 103, 104.

37. Cushman's letters to the Radical Club appear at the end of Mrs. John T. Sargent, ed., *Sketches and Reminiscences of the Radical Club of Chestnut Street, Boston* (Boston, 1880). Louisa wrote to her Aunt Louisa Bond on Sept. 17, 1860, "Saturday we had J. G. Whittier, Charlotte Cushman, Miss Stebbins the sculptress, and Mr. Stuart, conductor of the underground railroad of this charming free country" (Cheney, ed., *Alcott*, p. 92).

38. The complete story of "white marmorean flock" (Henry James's description of this group of American women artists living in Rome) remains to be told. Nevertheless, Joseph Leach's *Bright Particular Star: The Life and Times of Chalotte Cushman* (New Haven and London, 1970), is an excellent study. See also Margaret Farrand Thorp, *The Literary Sculptors* (Chapel Hill, 1965); Henry James, *The William Wetmore Story*, 2 vols. (Edinburgh and

London, 1903); Cornelia Curred, *Harriet Hosmer: Letters and Memories* (New York, 1912); and Nathaniel Hawthorne, *The Marble Faun* (Boston, 1860).

39. Daniel Scott Smith, "Family Limitation, Sexual Control, and Domestic Feminism in Victorian America," in *Clio's Consciousness Raised*, ed. Mary Hartman and Lois W. Banner (New York, 1974), p. 121.

40. Ibid., p. 120.

41. LMA, *Jo's Boys* (Boston, 1886), chap. 1, "Ten Years Later," p. 23.

CHAPTER 14: THE SOCIAL INFLUENCE

1. Maria S. Porter, *Recollections of Louisa May Alcott, John Greenleaf Whittier, Robert Browning* (Boston, 1893), pp. 14–16.

2. The *Woman's Journal* reported Dr. Clarke's speech in its Dec. 21, 1872 issue. Julia Ward Howe, an editor, then followed with several months' coverage of the ensuing debates.

3. Edward Clarke, *Sex in Education: or A Fair Chance for the Girls* (Boston, 1873).

4. Charles Darwin, *The Descent of Man and Selection in Relation to Sex*, 2 vols. (London, 1871). For the popular depiction of the Darwinian controversy, see issues of *Popular Science Monthly* from the mid-1870s through the 1880s. The social significance of woman's biological specialization is discussed in Charles Rosenberg, *No Other Gods: On Science and American Social Thought* (Baltimore, 1976).

5. Julia Ward Howe, ed., *Sex and Education: A Reply to Dr. Clarke's "Sex in Education"* (Cambridge, Mass., 1874). See also Anna C. Brackett, *The Education of American Girls* (New York, 1874) and Eliza B. Duffey, *No Sex in Education: or An Equal Chance for both Girls and Boys* (Philadelphia, 1874). The latter two books are recommended in LMA, *Jo's Boys* (Boston, 1886), chap. 17, "Among the Maids."

6. Madeleine B. Stern, *Louisa May Alcott* (London and New York, 1957), pp. 236–245. For an excellent description of *St. Nicholas* and the importance of juvenile magazines, see Jane Bernardette and Phyllis Moe, *Companions of Our Youth: Stories by Women for Young People's Magazines, 1865–1900* (New York, 1980).

7. Stern, *Louisa May Alcott*. Louisa May Alcott continued to publish in juvenile magazines until the end of her career. Letters to Mary Mapes Dodge, in particular, appear throughout Ednah Cheney, ed., *Louisa May Alcott: Life, Letters and Journals* (Boston, 1928), chap. 11.

8. LMA, *Eight Cousins; or The Aunt-Hill* (Boston, 1890), chap. 2, "The Clan," p. 18.

9. Stern, *Louisa May Alcott*, p. 295. In 1862 Frank Sanborn married his cousin, Louisa Augusta Leavitt, after the death of his first wife, Ariana Walker. Ariana, a close friend of Ednah Dow Cheney, was consumptive, dying eight days after her wedding in 1854. Frank and Louisa Sanborn had three sons. Louisa May Alcott maintained close ties with the Sanborns, and included a poem by one of the Sanborn boys in *Under the Lilacs*.

10. Cheney, ed., *Alcott*, chap. 10 (Feb. 1875).

11. Helen Wright, "Biographical Sketch of Maria Mitchell," in *Notable American Women*, ed. E. James (Cambridge, Mass., 1971), 2:555.

12. Ibid. See also Cheney, ed., *Alcott*, chap. 10 (Sept. and Oct. 1875).

13. See Stern, *Louisa May Alcott*, pp. 297-298, and Cheney, ed., *Alcott*, chap. 10. Anna Charlotte Lynch Botta was a notable hostess, admired by Emerson among others, who called her home, "the house of expanding doors." Botta also contributed poetry to *The Democratic Review* and wrote *A Handbook of Universal Literature* in 1860. She taught for a time at the Brooklyn Academy of Women.

14. LMA to Alcott Family, Dec. 25, 1875, in Cheney, ed., *Alcott*, pp. 235-239.

15. LMA, *Rose in Bloom* (Boston, 1876); page references are to 1934 ed. (Boston, 1934), p. 256.

16. Cheney, ed. *Alcott*, p. 284.

17. Barbara Leslie Epstein, *The Politics of Domesticity: Women, Evangelism and Temperance in Nineteenth Century America* (New Haven, 1981), p. 106.

18. See Epstein, *Politics of Domesticity*, and Ruth Bordin, *Woman and Temperance: The Quest for Power and Liberty, 1873-1900* (Philadelphia, 1981).

19. Cheney, ed., *Alcott*, p. 283.

20. Raymond L. Kilgour, *Messrs. Roberts Brothers, Publishers* (Ann Arbor, Mich., 1952), p. 160.

21. For discussions about the drop during Alcott's lifetime of the mean number of children born to a hypothetical woman from 6.21 to 3.87, see Peter Uhlenberg, "Changing Configurations of the Life Course," in *Transitions: The Family and the Life Course in Historical Perspective*, ed. Tamara K. Hareven (New York, 1978); Robert V. Wells, "Family History and Demographic Transition," *Journal of Social History* (Fall 1975):1-19; and Linda Gordon, *Woman's Body, Woman's Right: A Social History of Birth Control Movement and America Society since 1830* (New York, 1978).

22. See Franklin Sanborn, *Recollections of Seventy Years*, 2 (Boston, 1909); Franklin Sanborn and William Torrey Harris, *A. Bronson Alcott: His Life and Philosophy*, 2 (New York, 1893); and Florence Whiting Brown, "Alcott and The Concord School of Philosophy," a paper read at the Concord Antiquarian Society, May 28, 1923; privately printed, Aug. 1926.

23. Sanborn and Harris, *A. Bronson Alcott*, 2:622, 627, 643. Harris praises Bronson Alcott as representative of Anglo-Saxon Protestants. His character, Harris said, was "the ideal of a strong, serious-minded, independent manhood, unswerved by personal interest, thoroughly patriotic and devoted to the public interest."

24. Ibid., p. 626.

25. Ibid., p. 645. Harris contrasts Broson's postwar *Tablets* (Boston, 1868) with his earlier works.

26. Cheney, ed., *Alcott*, p. 288. See also Stern, *Louisa May Alcott*, chap. 15.

27. Sam B. Warner, Jr., *Streetcar Suburbs: The Process of Growth in Boston, 1870–1900* (Boston, 1962).

28. Sanborn and Harris, *A. Bronson Alcott*, 2:655.

29. Maria Vinovskis and Richard M. Bernard, "Beyond Catharine Beecher: Female Education in the Antebellum Period," *Signs: Journal of Women in Culture and Society* 3 (Summer 1978): 860–886; and Sarah Elbert, "The Changing Education of American Women," *Current History* 70, no. 416 (May 1976): 220–224. "In Massachusetts, by 1860, women comprised 77.8 percent of all public school teachers and this only presaged the feminization of teaching in the twentieth century" (Elbert, p. 223). Thus, the feminization of teaching clearly preceded any large-scale feminist assault on higher education.

30. LMA, *Work: A Story of Experience* (Boston, 1873), chap. 20, p. 427.

31. Cheney, ed., *Alcott*, p. 172. In 1869 Alcott began to record the sums given to Samuel E. Sewall to invest for the Alcott family. One year later she mentions $10,000 invested. By 1872 she admitted that the family was "independent." By March 1877, she was able to give Anna Alcott Pratt four thousand dollars from the returns on Vermont and Eastern Railroad securities toward the purchase of Thoreau House.

32. See Peter N. Carroll and David W. Noble, *The Restless Centuries*, 2d ed. (New York, 1979), chap. 20.

33. Alcott wrote, "The H.H. Book [*Ramona*] is a noble record of the great wrongs of her chosen people, and ought to waken up the sinners to repentence and justice before it is too late. It recalls the old slavery days, only these victims are red instead of black. It will be a disgrace if H.H. gave her work and pity all in vain" (LMA to T. Niles, Sept. 18, 1885, in Cheney, ed., *Alcott*, p. 301). On the relationship among western expansion, Indian history, and farm agitation, see Robert Bartlett, *The New Country: A Social History of the American Frontier* (New York, 1974); Dee Brown, *Bury My Heart at Wounded Knee* (New York, 1971); and Helen Hunt Jackson, *A Century of Dishonor* (Boston, 1881).

34. An excellent discussion of this struggle is Charles M. Dollar et al., *America: Changing Times* (New York, 1979), pp. 574–577.

35. LMA, *Jo's Boys* (Boston, 1886), chap. 1, "Ten Years Later," p. 23.

36. Ibid., chap. 17, "Among the Maids," p. 222.

37. Review marked "Jo's Boys and How They turned Out," copy at HL.

38. Ibid.

39. LMA, *Jo's Boys*, chap. 17, "Among the Maids," p. 222.

40. LMA, *Jo's Boys* (Boston, 1953), p. 7.

41. Ibid., chap. 17, "Among the Maids," p. 224.

42. Elizabeth Keyser, "Women and Girls in Louisa May Alcott's *Jo's Boys*," *International Journal of Women's Studies* 6, no. 5 (1979): 457–471.

43. See Karen Halttunen, "The Domestic Drama of Louisa May Alcott," *Feminist Studies* 10, no. 2 (Summer 1984): 233–254.

44. LMA, *Jo's Boys*, chap. 20, "Life for Life," p. 328.

45. Ibid., chap. 17, "Among the Maids." p. 222.

46. Ibid., chap. 2, "Parnassus," p. 31.

47. Ibid., chap. 17, "Among the Maids," pp. 228–229.

48. LMA, *A Modern Mephistopheles and A Whisper in the Dark* (Boston, 1889), chap. 15.

49. LMA, "Mountain Laurel and Maidenhair," in *A Garland for Girls* (Boston, 1888), pp. 221–258.

50. LMA, "May Flowers," in *A Garland for Girls*, pp. 1–42. See Barbara Miller Solomon, *Ancestors and Immigrants: A Changing New England Tradition* (Chicago, 1956), for the full significance of Alcott's reassertion of "Pilgrim Fathers."

51. Louisa May Alcott, "Letty's Tramp," *The Independent* 27, no. 1412 (Dec. 23, 1875); rpt. in *The Women's Journal* 3, no. 5 (Jan. 29, 1876).

52. Quoted in Hugh Hawkins, *Between Harvard and America: The Educational Leadership of Charles W. Eliot* (New York, 1972), p. 198.

53. LMA, *Rose in Bloom* (1876), chap. 1, "Coming Home," p. 9.

54. John Lathrop Motley, *Historic Progress and American Democracy* (New York, 1869), p. 6.

55. LMA letter to *Woman's Journal* 14 (Jan. 20, 1883).

56. Cheney, ed., *Alcott*, pp. 282, 279.

57. LMA, Preface to *Prayers by Theodore Parker* (Boston, 1882).

58. Florence Whiting Brown ("Alcott and the Concord School") recalls Bronson Alcott's last sessons and "the days of the long-haired men and the short-haired women who sojourned" in Concord.

59. Ibid. The Nonquitt Cottage had no kitchen; a nearby hotel served meals. Alcott reported "Restful days in my little house, which is cool and

quiet, and without the curse of a kitchen to spoil it" (Cheney, ed., *Alcott*, p. 245).

60. Cheney, ed., *Alcott*, p. 306.

61. Edward John Waring states that "calomel exercises a powerful beneficial influence in the treatment of typhus and typhoid fever" (Edward John Waring, *A Manual of Practical Therapeutics* [London, 1854] p. 46). Calomel is mercurious chloride salt. I am indebted to Sander Kelman for information concerning the nineteenth-century use of calomel and also the modern research on inorganic and organic mercury poisoning (minamata disease).

62. Stern, *Louisa May Alcott*, p. 340.

63. LMA, *A Whisper in the Dark*, p. 337.

Index

abolitionism. *See* slavery

Abrams, M. H., 23

Adams, William Taylor (pseud. Oliver Optic), 183; message of, 231, 236, 317n37

adolescence: and female sexuality, 80–82, 300n27; fiction and, 183–184, 195–199; male, 81, 87; women's right to, 86–87, 121, 123–126, 130–132, 172

Alcott, Abigail May (Abba) (mother): death of, 252; domestic difficulties, 29–31, 38–39, 41, 48–50, 52, 57–59, 64–70, 105, 320n31; as domestic reformer, xiv, 28–29, 58, 68, 72–74, 79, 92–93, 250, 251; ill health of, 184, 223, 239, 251, 323n36; inheritance, 48–50; as mother, 21, 25–26, 45, 52, 55, 93, 101; in reform movements, 37, 47, 94–95, 97, 239, 251–252; in social work, 92, 94–95, 97–98, 102, 221; as wife, 49–50, 52, 54, 55, 57–58, 72, 76, 105, 292n24, 301n43. *See also* May, Abigail

Alcott, Anna Bronson (later Anna Pratt) (sister), 66, 67, 102–103, 108; adolescence of, 85–86; childhood of, 24–30, 34, 64–65; court-

ship of, 110, 112; employment, 93, 105. *See also* Pratt, Anna

Alcott, (Amos) Bronson (father): character of, 3–5, 6–7, 9, 24, 30, 55, 60, 66, 174, 289n34, 310n8, 331n23; child development studies, 24–30, 38, 291n18; courtship and marriage of, 14–20; death of, 282; early years, 2–6; as educational reformer, 7–9, 22–25, 31–35, 37–38, 234, 264; failure to support family, 29–31, 38–39, 41, 46, 48–50, 62, 67–68, 70, 80, 102, 105, 151; idealism of, 8, 36, 37, 46, 60, 61, 62, 93, 256, 265, 293n43; ill health of, 51, 99, 102, 281; in LMA's works, 5–6, 73–74, 127–128, 138–139, 140, 215–216; philosophy of childhood, xiv, 21, 25, 27, 32–33, 38, 162; and reform of society, xiii–xiv, 9, 37, 47–48, 54, 68–72, 74–76, 145, 188, 265, 318n8; as teacher, 7, 9, 34, 264; trip to England, 51–54; trips to West, 105, 111, 192, 223, 265; views on family, 68–72, 76, 174; writings of, 23, 24–25, 56, 68. *See also* Alcott, Louisa May; Alcott family; communality; Fruitlands

335

143, 151–152, 266; in LMA's
writings, 143, 146, 159–161, 184,
222; meaning of, 158–159, 186;
role in LMA's life, 116, 151, 152,
172, 173, 174, 178, 282; Washington during, 153, 155; women's
work during, 151–152
Clarke, Dr. Edward, *Sex in Education*, 258; feminist replies to,
258–259, 263
Commonwealth, LMA's publications
in, 146, 154, 163, 166
communality, 37, 41; and the
Alcotts, 57, 62; Bronson's dreams
of, 43–44, 47, 54; experiments
in, 46–47, 51, 59–60, 63, 68–69;
and the family, 68–70, 76. *See
also* Alcott House; Brook Farm;
Fruitlands; Oneida Community;
Shakers
Concord circle, 43, 88, 89, 122,
127, 279, 281
Concord School of Philosophy,
264, 281; participants in, 310n11
Conway, Moncure, 163, 243,
312n51; support for LMA, 163
Cushman, Charlotte, 254–255

Dall, Caroline, 191, 309n4, 319n28
Davis, Rebecca Harding, 158, 259,
312n53
Dickens, Charles, 90; influence on
LMA, 128, 301n37, 302n48
—*Bleak House*, 195–196, 320n2
Dix, Dorothea, 40, 152, 156, 165
Dodge, Mary Mapes, 259
domestic feminism: Abba Alcott's
views of, 17–18, 28–29, 57–58,
68, 72–73, 86, 93, 96, 98; and
household democracy, 200, 204,
216, 273, 276, 278, 320n3,

321n13; in LMA's writings, xvii–
xviii, 45, 73–76, 100, 106, 108,
127, 161, 186, 200–204, 207,
210, 216–217, 226, 232, 236,
243, 275–276; meaning of, xiii,
xvi–xvii, 248, 317n1
domestic service, 95, 244; Abba
Alcott's work concerning, 95,
102; exploitation in, 103–104,
244; LMA in, 101, 103–104, 179;
in LMA's fiction, 95, 243–244
Douglas, Ann, 148, 162, 311n25,
322nn22, 25, 324n2
Douglass, Frederick, 192, 319n26

education: coeducation, 96, 216,
231, 268–269, 270, 277–278,
325n28; new views of, 10, 266;
reform of, 10, 22–24, 25, 96,
256, 292n39; for women, 257,
269, 300n27; as women's work,
266, 331n29
Elliott, James R., 166
Emerson, Ellen, 90, 106
Emerson, Ralph Waldo, 146–147;
as family friend, 39, 43, 44, 51,
60, 70–72, 79–80, 88, 93, 104,
174, 281; influence on LMA, 44,
46, 100, 113, 134, 274; as LMA's
idol, 88, 90–91, 304n47; as reformer, 44–45, 54; and Romantic
reform, xvii, 186, 189, 279; views
on utopian reformers, 32, 54–55
—"Nature," 44–45
Epstein, Barbara, 262–263
Estes, Angela, 172
Everett, Abraham, 63

feminism, LMA's views of, xiv–xv,
xvii–xviii, 44–45, 90, 115–116,
119, 123–124, 135, 138, 141–

Thoreau, Henry David: and the Alcotts, 41, 88; death of, 150–151; influence on LMA, 89, 150, 151, 301n32; in LMA's fiction, 88, 124, 247; as LMA's idol, 88, 151

Thoreau, John, 41, 88

Tompkins, Jane, 118, 147, 307n45, 313n66, 322n25

Transcendental Club, 53; members of, 42–43

Transcendentalism: adherents, 3, 32, 45, 310n11; description, 32; fears of, 37; influence, 119, 260; philosophy of, 42, 44–45, 53, 88, 90, 140, 188; view of childhood, 291n18; and women, 89–90, 92, 119, 189

Tuckerman, Joseph, 95, 96

Twain, Mark: as actor and lecturer, 239; depiction of childhood, 233; as utopian writer, 277, 280

—*Huckleberry Finn*, xvi, 219, 280

Union Hotel Hospital, 152, 153–155, 195

Vaux, Robert, 22, 29

Warner, Susan B., 119
—*The Wide, Wide World*, 197, 307n45, 321n9

Weiss, John, 187, 190

Wilde, Oscar, 261

Willard, Frances, xix, 262, 263

Willis, Llewellyn, 85, 89, 90

Wollstonecraft, Mary, 40–41

woman problem, 1; and domesticity, xvii–xviii, xix, 38–39, 67–68, 190, 239; and fictional working women, 190, 211–214, 241,

243–247, 248, 249, 264; and financial independence, 50, 250, 256; legal status, 50–51; property rights, 50–51, 79, 80; and work, 38, 95, 98, 226, 230, 239, 241, 243, 245, 247–249, 276. *See also* domestic feminism; feminism; woman's rights

Woman's Journal, 227, 237, 258, 329n2; letters to, 265

woman's rights: and black rights, 184–185, 192, 319n26; conventions, xv, 99, 119–120, 190, 260, 261, 325n28, 326n37; in LMA's fiction, xv, 103, 114, 124, 141, 185, 193, 219–220, 234, 237–239, 257–258; movement for, 37, 96, 117, 220, 248, 259, 277, 310n11; need for, 141, 165, 189–190, 257, 258; and suffrage, 187, 191–193, 227, 237, 263, 319n26; and temperance, 193, 262–263

women: theme of fallen, 83, 137, 141, 171, 181, 246; as writers, 89, 119, 197, 212, 259, 267, 313n56, 315n6; writings for, xv, 82, 147–148, 169–170, 197–198, 320n9. *See also* feminism; sisterhood, theme of; spinsterhood; woman problem; woman's rights

Women's Christian Temperance Union, 262, 264

Women's Club, 190

Wordsworth, William, 21, 23, 24, 34

Wright, Frances, 15

Wright, Henry G., 53–56; defection of, 59–60

Yellin, Jean, 327n10

Yonge, Charlotte M., 197